GOD AND CREATION

God and Creation

An Ecumenical Symposium

Edited by David B. Burrell
and Bernard McGinn

UNIVERSITY OF NOTRE DAME PRESS
NOTRE DAME, INDIANA

Manufactured in the United States of America

Library of Congress Cataloging-in-Publication Data

God and creation : an ecumenical symposium / edited by David B. Burrell, Bernard McGinn.
p. cm.
Papers presented at the Ecumenical Symposium in Comparative Religious Thought, held at the University of Notre Dame and the University of Chicago, April 26–28, 1987.
ISBN 0-268-01020-X
1. Creation—Comparative studies—Congresses. 2. God—Comparative studies—Congresses. I. Burrell, David B. II. McGinn, Bernard, 1937– . III. Ecumenical Symposium in Comparative Religious Thought (1987 : University of Notre Dame and University of Chicago)
BL226.G6 1990
291.2'4—dc20 89-40382

Dedicated to the Memory of

FAZLUR RAHMAN

Scholar

Colleague

Friend

Contents

Preface ix

Contributors xi

PART I: SPECULATIVE ELABORATIONS OF THE SCRIPTURAL WITNESS

"In the Beginning God Created": A Philosophical Midrash • *Seymour Feldman* 3

Creation or Emanation: Two Paradigms of Reason • *David B. Burrell* 27

Ibn Sina's Theory of the God-World Relationship • *Fazlur Rahman* 38

PART II: PHILOSOPHICAL DEVELOPMENTS AND DIVERGENT THEOLOGIES

A. Background

Theism and Divine Production in Ancient Realist Theology • *John Peter Kenney* 57

Response, *Paul A. Dietrich* 81

B. Judaism

Three Meanings of the Idea of Creation • *Lenn Evan Goodman* 85

Response, *Josef Stern* 114

Creation and Time in Maimonides and Gersonides • *Tamar Rudavsky* 122

Response, *Barry S. Kogan* 147

Creation: What Difference Does It Make? • *David R. Blumenthal* 154
Response, *Jonathan W. Malino* 173

C. Christianity

Creation and Christian Understanding • *Robert Sokolowski* 179
Response, *David Tracy* 193

Do Christian Platonists Really Believe in Creation? • *Bernard McGinn* 197
Response, *Zachary Hayes* 220

Creation, Being, and Nonbeing • *Langdon Gilkey* 226
Response, *Charles Kannengiesser* 242

D. Islam

Creation in Time in Islamic Thought with Special Reference to al-Ghazālī • *Eric L. Ormsby* 246
Response, *Paul A. Hardy* 265

Fakhr al-Dīn al-Rāzī on God as al-Khāliq • *Jane Dammen McAuliffe* 276
Response, *Muhsin Mahdi* 297

Transcendence and Distinction: Metaphoric Process in Isma'ili Muslim Thought • *Azim Nanji* 304
Response, *Seyyed Hossein Nasr* 316

Name Index 323

Preface

In the Fall of 1985, we were privileged to participate in the second of the symposia that the Dumbarton Oaks Center in Washington organized under the title of "Mysticism and Philosophy." Much of the intellectual challenge of this meeting came from its ecumenical character—Jewish, Christian, and Muslim scholars engaging in serious conversation on issues of great import for their beliefs and practices.

Both of us had recently been working in different aspects of the meaning of creation in the three monotheistic faiths. As we reflected on the stimulus of the Washington meeting late one night—with an inspiration which may have owed something to the *Symposium*—we conceived of the idea of a similar ecumenical gathering to focus on the issue of God and creation in Judaism, Christianity, and Islam.

The final results of this late-night inspiration are to be found within. The purpose of this Preface is to thank, if only insufficiently, all those who made possible the transition from inspiration to realization.

"God and Creation: An Ecumenical Symposium in Comparative Religious Thought" was held at the University of Notre Dame and the University of Chicago April 26–28, 1987. Without the hospitality and support of these institutions this volume would never have seen the light of day. At Notre Dame, both the Department of Theology and the Center for the Philosophy of Religion made generous contributions toward the project. At the University of Chicago, the Institute for the Advanced Study of Religion of the Divinity School gave equally generous support. On both campuses, interested faculty and students were helpful in a wide variety of ways—we hope that they will all forgive us for so summary a mention of such invaluable assistance.

God *and* creation are no small issues—our group felt compelled to rest after only three days, rather than six! It will be up to our readers to judge whatever adequacy we have brought to such challenging topics. However successful we may or may not have been in the sight of others, we think it fair to say that all those who attended the actual symposium found it a profitable experience. The emphasis was on discussion and fruitful interchange. Only the three initial papers ("Speculative Elaborations of the Scriptural Witness") were given as public lectures; these, and the ten papers prepared for discussion within the group (those listed under "Philosophical Developments and Divergent Theologies") were all distributed before the meetings so that they could be read and digested before our intense three days of comment and discussion. The respondents to the ten "Development" papers made major contributions to the ongoing collaboration. What was most gratifying to us was not only the honest and critical nature of the interchange of ideas, but also the spirit that informed the group during our days together. This is why our greatest thanks are to our contributors. If this volume can reflect, if only in part, the excitement of our ecumenical interchange during those days, we think that it will find a receptive audience.

During the planning of the symposium, we were assisted in many valuable ways by our colleague and friend, Fazlur Rahman, who functioned as the third member for the planning committee for the event. Professor Rahman's contributions to the actual symposium, through his important paper, his valuable interventions, but perhaps most of all through the warm encouragement of his presence, were important factors in the success of our conversations.

As this volume was being prepared for publication, we received notice of Fazlur Rahman's death. His passing is a loss to a much larger world than that of our symposium, but we would like to add our voice to the many others that lament his loss by dedicating this volume to his memory.

Bernard McGinn
David Burrell

Contributors

DAVID R. BLUMENTHAL holds the Jay and Leslie Cohen Chair of Judaic Studies at Emory University.

DAVID B. BURRELL C.S.C., is Professor in the Departments of Theology and Philosophy at the University of Notre Dame.

PAUL A. DIETRICH is Associate Professor in the Department of Religious Studies at the University of Montana.

SEYMOUR FELDMAN is Professor in the Department of Philosophy and Dean of Arts and Sciences at Rutgers University.

LANGDON GILKEY is the Shailer Matthews Professor at the Divinity School of the University of Chicago.

LENN EVAN GOODMAN is Professor in the Department of Philosophy at the University of Hawaii, Honolulu.

PAUL A. HARDY is a Ph.D. candidate in the Oriental Institute of the University of Chicago.

ZACHARY HAYES is Professor of Theology at the Catholic Theological Union in Chicago.

CHARLES KANNENGIESSER is the Huisking Professor of Theology at the University of Notre Dame.

JOHN PETER KENNEY is Associate Professor in the Department of Religion at Reed College.

BARRY S. KOGAN is Associate Professor at the Hebrew Union College–Jewish Institute of Religion in Cincinnati.

JANE DAMMEN MCAULIFFE is Assistant Professor of the History of Religions and Islamic Studies at the Candler School of Theology of Emory University.

BERNARD MCGINN is Professor of Historical Theology and the History of Christianity at the Divinity School of the University of Chicago.

MUHSIN MAHDI is the Jewett Professor of Arabic in the Department of Near Eastern Languages and Civilizations at Harvard University.

JONATHAN W. MALINO is Assistant Professor of Philosophy at Guilford College.

AZIM NANJI is Professor of Islamic Studies at the University of Florida, Gainesville.

SEYYED HOSSEIN NASR is the University Professor of Islamic Studies at the George Washington University in Washington, D.C.

ERIC L. ORMSBY is Professor of Islamics and Director of Libraries at McGill University in Montreal, Canada.

FAZLUR RAHMAN was the Harold Swift Distinguished Service Professor in the Oriental Institute of the University of Chicago.

TAMAR RUDAVSKY is Associate Professor of Philosophy at the Ohio State University.

ROBERT SOKOLOWSKI is Professor of Philosophy at the Catholic University of America in Washington, D.C.

JOSEF STERN is Associate Professor of Philosophy at the University of Chicago.

DAVID TRACY is the Greeley Distinguished Service Professor at the Divinity School of the University of Chicago.

PART I

Speculative Elaborations of the Scriptural Witness

Jews, Christians, and Muslims share a belief in the free creation of the universe by a God who needed nothing of the sort to be divine. That is a startling affirmation, and one which stood in direct confrontation with a Hellenic world of thought. For the presumption of the Greeks had been that the universe offered the everlasting context for being and thought about what is. To be sure, Aristotle had argued that the unity of the cosmos demanded a first principle to account for the activity therein. Moreover, those who followed him developed a way of thinking which connected Plato's image of the *good* as source of being and intelligibility with Aristotle's assertion that the unmoved first principle moves by "being desired." The result, notably in Plotinus (205–70 C.E.), was a first principle which became the source of all that is: the One. From this One, or "First," as the Islamic philosopher al-Farabi would call it, emanates all that is, on the model of theorems from an initial set of axioms. So it appeared convenient for Jews, Christians, and, somewhat later, Muslims to think of God's creating all things as their emanating from the one God. Indeed, much of the drama of the confrontation between these religious perspectives and Hellenic (or Neoplatonic) thought, and indeed some of the drama of our symposium, comes from trying to determine how appropriate such an emanation scheme can be to formulate what Jews, Christians, and Muslims believe about creation.

The controversy smoldered for many centuries, only to erupt full-blown in what we call the medieval period.[1] Yet the early reflections of Philo (20 B.C.E.–50 C.E.) set the stage for a philosophical encounter with the Bible, and the sixth-century work of John Philoponus (also in Alexandria) entered directly into the conflict between a creation which initiated the universe with time and a necessary emanation from the One which would have no beginning. The first three essays in this book set the stage for what follows by highlighting dimensions of this controversy characteristic of Jewish, Christian, and Muslim philosophical reflection. They are not intended to be exhaustive, but rather to offer soundings of the preoccupations peculiar to each religious tradition as it sought to employ the resources of philosophy to elaborate its faith. Seymour Feldman displays some of the philosophical exegetical styles which developed in Jewish thought following the inspiration of Philo. David Burrell shows how Thomas Aquinas might be regarded as responding to al-Ghazālī's critique of emanation by offering an alternative paradigm for the activity of creating: that of productive reason. Fazlur Rahman moves us effectively beyond the received account of the views of Ibn Sina (Avicenna) regarding the relation of the universe to its origin in God. After these overviews, we shall consider each tradition in turn.

NOTE

1. Excellent sources for this discussion are Richard Sorabji, *Time, Creation and the Continuum* (Ithaca, N.Y.: Cornell University Press, 1984), and Herbert Davidson, *Proofs for Eternity, Creation and the Existence of God in Medieval Islamic and Jewish Philosophy* (Oxford: Oxford University Press, 1987).

"In the Beginning God Created": A Philosophical Midrash

Seymour Feldman

I

It is a basic principle of Judaism that "the gates of interpretation are open."[1] Or, to use a different metaphor, Scripture is porous. My purpose in this paper is to illustrate this general thesis by focusing upon a specific set of passages in Genesis 1—"the story of creation"—and by using a particular genre of Jewish biblical exegesis—the philosophical mode. This exegetical style deserves special attention, if only because of its venerable provenance. Philosophical readings of the Bible appear quite early; in fact, as written documents they antedate even the earliest rabbinic *midrashim.* So even if we are to adopt, at least in this context, the egalitarian rule that all styles of interpretation are valid, nevertheless, the philosophical genre should be regarded as *primus inter pares* by virtue of its age.[2]

In claiming the antiquity for this style I was of course alluding to the exegetical works of a person who has also been characterized as "the first Jewish philosopher"—Philo of Alexandria.[3] Most of Philo's writings are in fact *midrashim* on various parts of the Pentateuch. The Philonic exegetical style was to become extremely important, especially in Christianity, for the early Greek Church Fathers were familiar with Philo's books and absorbed some of his ideas and much of his style.[4] Although Philo had no direct impact upon Jewish biblical exegesis, the basic principles of his method were to reappear in the Jewish exegetical tradition in the Middle Ages, and in their unacknowledged "renaissance" became, if not orthodox, at least widespread.[5] Two particular Philonic postulates are especially relevant: (1) the Bible is a multilevel text, whose more profound stratum of meaning is "below" the surface—the "symbolical," or "allegorical," meaning; and (2) this more profound dimension to Scripture is to be understood and explicated through philosophy.[6] The Bible is then a *philosophical* book, at least to those who know how to read it properly.

These methodological assumptions were taken up by some of the medieval exegetes, most notably Maimonides, whose philosophical *magnum opus* should be more properly classified and understood as a book in biblical exegesis *more philosophico*. As he makes clear in the preface to the *More Nevuchim*—"The Guide of the Perplexed"—his purpose is to explicate certain biblical words, passages, and chapters whose linguistic properties have perplexing philosophical implications. Like Philo, Maimonides assumes that the biblical text is "porous," that it is open to diverse interpretations, of which some are more acceptable than others. He further assumes that *the* most authoritative kind of interpretation is the philosophical; indeed, philosophy for Maimonides is *the* key, or legend, to the biblical code, for it makes clear the frequent unclear messages found in the text, which are sometimes altogether opaque, occasionally cryptic, and often ambiguous.

Among the more difficult sections of this particular code is its very opening. Just think of a book whose first chapter allows for divergent readings, of which some are the direct contradictories or contraries of others! This is certainly the case with "the account of creation." Already in Philo's time the cosmological debate was not only old but still alive, with the Stoic and Epicurean philosophers adding their voices to the chorus of cosmological doctrines, already loudly reverberating from the presence of Plato and Aristotle. Philo specifically records that some philosophers even *denied* that the universe was created. Of course, this was Aristotle, who claimed that the world is eternal.[7] Maimonides too, eleven centuries later, reports that the debate was still raging and expresses even more alarm at its implications for the Jewish religion. For Philo an eternal world is a world devoid of divine providence; for Maimonides it is a world devoid of miracles.[8] Both thinkers thought it necessary to resist and combat these implications and the premise from which they are derived. My exegetical story, however, will take Philo and

Maimonides only as points of departure, whose methodological postulates showed the way for subsequent philosophical-minded exegetes. I shall assume these rules and apply them to several later thinkers who, like Philo and Maimonides, read the Bible philosophically and who saw in Genesis 1 a story containing important philosophical-cosmological teachings.[9]

II

A close reading of the opening verses of Genesis 1 often stimulates the reader to ask, "What about the waters?" We are told about the creation of the heavens, the earth, the light, the firmament; but *when* and *how* did God create the waters? Of course, no answer is forthcoming, at least from Genesis 1. If anything, the account there suggests that the waters are with God all along. After all, it says right at the beginning, "And the spirit of God hovered over the deep" (Gen. 1:2). Moreover, the creation of the firmament is described as taking place in the waters. To someone familiar with Plato's *Timaeus* these remarks can easily suggest that like Plato's *demiurgos,* the God of the Bible makes the universe in or out of some primordial thing.[10] Ever since Aristotle, Plato's cosmological matrix has been dubbed "the primordial formless matter,"[11] and throughout this paper I shall continue to speak of Plato's theory in these terms. It seems then that Plato and Moses agree in depicting the initial cosmological act as involving a divine cause and a material receptacle in or from which the physical world has its origin. This convergence of Greek and Jewish cosmological myth making has its literary exemplar in the Hellenistic-Jewish apocryphal book *The Wisdom of Solomon,* wherein the God of the Bible is described as fashioning the world out of a primeval formless stuff.[12]

Although by the early Middle Ages this Platonic cosmological model was eclipsed by the theory of creation *ex nihilo,* a doctrine that was to become authoritative in Christianity and Islam and virtually so in Judaism,[13] Plato's myth was not completely forgotten. Both Jehudah Halevi and Maimonides suggested that the Platonic model was an acceptable reading of Genesis 1, albeit not the traditional belief.[14] Why and how the doctrine of creation *ex nihilo* came to overshadow the view of *The Wisdom of Solomon* is a story that still needs to be written. But in the Middle Ages there was at least one important Jewish philosopher who was still asking our initial question, "When were the waters created?" Not finding any answer in Scripture he came to the conclusion that they were not created at all. Indeed, he became convinced on purely philosophical grounds that the traditional doctrine of creation *ex nihilo* was false—in fact, absurd. Not afraid to go against tradition in these matters he wrote a large philosophical work in which he defended the thesis that God created the world out of an eternal formless matter, or in biblical terms, out of the primeval waters. This cosmological theory was then read into the Bible as *the* meaning of Genesis 1. This philosopher was Levi ben Gershom, or Gersonides (1288–1344). Since Gersonides' cosmology has received recent scholarly attention,[15] I wish I could speak of another Jewish proponent of this model; but no one else in the Jewish tradition defends this doctrine with so much vigor and in so much detail as Gersonides.

Although he reverentially confesses that it was the Torah itself that suggested this hypothesis to him,[16] as is his habit with many of his own philosophical theses, Gersonides' rejection of *ex nihilo* creation is primarily based upon the philosophical-scientific principle that nature abhors a vacuum. Assuming Aristotle's disproof of the possibility of a vacuum in or outside of the physical universe,[17] Gersonides believed that the hypothesis of *ex nihilo* creation implied such a vacuum, and thus is false. Let us imagine the following situation. We have an empty box into which we put a baseball. Prior to our insertion of the ball into the box there was nothing in the box but air; however, the box is a receptacle and can "receive," or contain, objects up to a certain size and volume. After we have placed the ball in the box, the box is still in part empty, and the ball is surrounded by empty space, or air. Now creation *ex nihilo* is akin to our putting the ball into that box in the following way. Before God created the world, there was, *ex hypothesi,* nothing; then there was something, the world. It is as if God "put" a large ball into empty space. Now, according to Aristotle, the void, or vacuum, is a place in which there is no body but which could be occupied by a body. So, in creating the world, God filled up, so to speak, one region of empty space, the void, with a finitely large body, the universe. Thus, a void existed *ante mundum.* Moreover, it still exists *post creationem,* since our finite universe is still surrounded by empty space *ad infinitum.* Accordingly, the doctrine of creation *ex nihilo* is incompatible with Aristotelian science.[18]

This argument is strengthened if we introduce another principle that is reminiscent of Leibniz's Principle of Sufficient Reason. Again, let's go back to our baseball. In putting the ball into, say, the middle of the box, we were in a sense arbitrary: we could have put it into one of the corners; or, for that matter, we could have put it *anywhere.* Now, this arbitrariness doesn't bother us, since we know that sometimes we mortal creatures do act arbitrarily. But God, for many medieval Aristotelians, as well as for Leibniz, is not arbitrary. Indeed, God always acts for a sufficient reason. So why did God put the universe *where* He did? He could have put it anywhere! If the void is a homogeneous expanse of empty space, perhaps even infinite, then the world could have been made *anywhere throughout* this infinite expanse. Since no sufficient reason can be given why it would occupy any particular place, it wouldn't occupy any such place but would fill the whole domain of space, and hence be infinite.[19] But for Aristotle the universe is only finitely large.[20] Again, *ex nihilo* creation has been shown to be incompatible with Aristotelian physics.

Having already demonstrated on independent grounds that the universe was created, and now having shown that *ex nihilo* creation is incompatible with physical reality, Gersonides has no alternative but to adopt the Platonic model of creation out of matter. This is quite evident, not only in his philosophical masterpiece, *The Wars of the Lord,* but in his *Commentary on Genesis* as well. I shall focus upon the latter work in this essay.

At the outset he lays down two postulates which serve to define some of the key terms in the opening verses of Genesis 1. The first postulate concerns the opening phrase, "In the beginning". It states that the apparent temporal order of the six days of creation is not to be construed literally. Following a rabbinic tradition, which Maimonides also adopted, Gersonides claims that the whole universe was created *altogether,* albeit according to a definite order; but he interprets this order nontemporally.[21] Aristotle had already distinguished several senses of the concept of priority, of which one is the substantival, whereby one thing is prior to another insofar as one is substance, whereas the other is accident. Aristotle also calls this priority by nature.[22] Gersonides characterizes this kind of priority as also one of causal priority. Accordingly, X can be prior to Y insofar as X is the cause of Y, yet both X and Y can be simultaneous; the posteriority of Y is based upon the fact that it *depends upon* X in some important way. Thus, for Gersonides, even though the heavens and the earth were all created at the same moment, the heavens are causally and naturally prior to the earth, since by means of the former the latter derives its sustenance and motion.

Gersonides' second postulate concerns the primeval waters, which he identifies with the primordial formless matter. Right at the beginning of his *Torah Commentary* he states that the waters spoken of in Genesis 1 are the very stuff out of which God made the universe; indeed, this primeval liquid can still be observed, he states, flowing between the heavenly spheres. Now, when it is said in Genesis 1:2, "And the earth was unformed and void and darkness was on the face of the deep, and the spirit of God hovered over the face of the waters," the three terms 'void' (*bohu*), 'deep' (*tehom*), and 'waters' (*mayyim*) all refer to one and the same entity, the primeval waters. It is out of this stuff that God made the world. The Hebrew term *bohu,* 'the void', is especially important here. Gersonides interprets it in Platonic fashion as the receptacle, or matrix, in and out of which the world is made; literally, the term means "in it it is." Speaking Aristotelian, Gersonides also calls it the primary matter (*ḥomer rishon*), which in Aristotelian physics can receive many forms. But unlike Aristotle's notion of prime matter, Gersonides' primary matter *actually* exists without any definite form. This is why he likes to refer to it by the complex expression, "the matter that doesn't keep its shape."[23]

With these key terms defined by these two postulates, Gersonides proceeds to explain the other expressions in the opening verses of the first day. This approach leads him to make several significant departures from a long tradition that construed "the heavens and the earth," "the spirit of God," and "the darkness" as referring severally to the natural elements, as interpreted in Aristotelian, Stoic, or Platonic physics. Thus, unlike Saadia Gaon, who interpreted the term 'the heavens and earth' of Genesis 1:1 as referring to the elemental fire and earth,[24] Gersonides construes this expression as denoting the world as a whole, encompassing all its various elements and compounds. In fact, he doesn't believe that the heavens were created first, even in a causal, atemporal sense. In the causal, but not temporal, series of created things, *light* is the first creature. But the light in verse 3 of Genesis 1 is not the visible light produced by the sun and stars, but represents the realm of the Separate Intellects, or the angels.[25] For, although the heavenly bodies are causally prior to the earthly bodies, and thus are created on the second day, whereas the terrestrial things are created subsequently, the Separate Intellects are the movers of the heavenly bodies, and thus are causally prior to them. Accordingly, they are created on the first day. Here Gersonides departs from rabbinic tradition, wherein the creation of the angels is usually assigned to the second day.[26] For him the creation of the heavenly bodies is assigned to the second day, wherein the Scripture speaks of the creation of the firmament, which he takes as a general term referring to the various heavenly bodies.

Let us now apply this "legend" to the biblical code of Genesis 1:1–3. Gersonides understands these verses as follows: In the beginning of the creative act whereby God brought into existence the entire universe—including the heavenly and earthly domains and all that is contained therein—there was nothing besides God except the formless, shapeless waters, from which the corporeal world, both celestial and terrestrial, came forth. For His first creation God created the world of the Separate Intellects, that is, the unmoved movers of the heavenly bodies, which in the Bible are referred to in general as "light" and in particular as "angels." This whole creative act was instantaneous, the "days of creation" symbolizing only the atemporal causal relationships amongst the various levels of creatures. Moreover, the primeval light, or the intelligible world, is not created from the primeval waters, as is the corporeal world, but is created from God Himself; for God is the First Separable Intellect, *Nous Haplōs*.[27] Thus, verse 2, which for Gersonides describes the primeval waters, or primordial matter, is really a long parenthetical remark, indicating to the reader the characteristic state of this "matter that doesn't keep its shape." This matter can be compared also to darkness: just as darkness is the privation or absence of light, so this matter lacks form or shape. The first divine creature, light, is therefore a counterforce to the primary formless matter; it is the world of form, structure, and clarity, whereas the world of pure matter is chaotic, random, and obscure.[28]

With the Separate Intellects at one extreme of the ontological ladder and the primary formless matter on the other, God now creates the heavenly bodies. This creative act is described in the Bible as "the second day of creation," the day on which God made the "firmament" (*ha-raqiᶜah*). The heavenly bodies are made out of portions of the formless matter. They are "formed" not by the information of forms in matter, as is the case with the formation of earthly bodies, but by having the Separate Intellects as their separate forms, or movers. This difference is signaled by the fact that the creation of the latter precedes the creation of the firmament, or heavenly bodies, as taking place in or between the upper and lower waters, that is, the formless matter. Thus, some of this shapeless stuff is made into the celestial realm having the Separate Intellects as their formal principles, whereas other parts of it are manufactured into the "lower matter," the world of the corporeal compounds, whose forms are the elemental forms, or contraries. In this manner the fundamental Aristotelian "two-sphere" model wherein the heavenly and terrestrial domains are sharply differentiated is preserved. The former, where the forms are the Separate Intellects, is the world of actuality and permanence; the latter, where the forms are the changing contrary elements, is the world of potentiality and destruction. It is for this reason that the rabbis have said, Gersonides reminds us, that the phrase "and it was good" is *not* stated in connection with the second day. For on this day the corporeal world was created, and it is this world where we find imperfection and evil.[29]

III

Gersonides' Platonic reading of Genesis 1 was certainly nontraditional. But in his own time a rival cosmological model was slowly insinuating itself into Jewish philosophical circles that was not only not traditional but even heterodox. From the early thirteenth century to at least the end of the fourteenth century there was a group of Jewish thinkers who actually believed that Genesis 1 was compatible with the philosophical thesis that the *world is eternal.* Not only this: some of these philosophers had the temerity to claim that this thesis is the real meaning of Maimonides' *Guide of the Perplexed* and that the "exoteric" teaching of creation in the *Guide* was only a subterfuge hiding Maimonides' real "secret of creation." This reading of both Genesis 1 and the *Guide of the Perplexed* was suggested by the first translator of the *Guide* into Hebrew, Samuel ibn Tibbon,[30] and Joseph ibn Kaspi and Moses Narboni, the two most important philosophical commentators on the *Guide.*[31] Independently of these writers it was advocated also by Isaac Albalag, a Jewish philosopher who lived during the latter half of the thirteenth century, most likely in northern Spain.[32] Now whatever the differences these various thinkers exhibit, it is clear that they were all influenced deeply by the philosophy of the Muslim philosopher ibn Rushd, or Averroes. This is most evident in the case of creation. In this essay I shall examine one member of this group, perhaps the most radical and pronounced Averroist, who is quite explicit about the philosophical truth of the doctrine of eternal creation—Isaac Albalag. Albalag is especially interesting because he is committed to a "double truth theory," according to which the truth that philosophy teaches about creation is incompatible with the truth that religious tradition has taught.[33] However, it is his intention to show that on this particular issue, the incompatibility is not inherent in Scripture, that it is more a question of different interpretations of Scripture than an irreconcilable conflict. As the rabbis themselves have taught, "The Torah has seventy faces."[34] I now turn to that face which says to us that the universe which God *created* is *eternal.*

Albalag's most extensive discussion of this thesis occurs in chapter 30 of his book *Tiqqun ha-Deᶜot,* which is a translation of and critical commentary upon Al-Ghazali's philosophical encyclopedia, *The Intentions of the Philosophers,* which is essentially a compendium of the philosophical doctrines of Ibn Sina.[35] But before Albalag attempts to read into Genesis 1 his cosmology, he prefaces his commentary with a philosophical argument in behalf of this cosmology. In this respect he employs the same method adopted by Gersonides: first give the philosophical arguments for the position, and then read this position into the scriptural text.

As Philo had already emphasized at the very beginning of this debate, the notion of creation is essentially linked to the thesis of divine activity. Thus, the idea of *agency* is crucial. Albalag begins his discussion of creation with a philosophical analysis of the term 'agent' (*poᶜel*). Like Maimonides he makes no significant distinction between the terms 'cause' (*ᶜila*) and 'agent' (*poᶜel*).[36] Clearly, the term 'cause' is in this context Aristotle's efficient cause, the agent that is the source of change, the agent that *brings about* some effect.[37]

Now in all cases of efficient causation, a causal process is embedded in a series of further causal processes, constituting the causal chain, which may be continuous or discrete. Although these chains are often quite complex and long, nevertheless they ultimately terminate in a First Cause who is the "remote cause" of all causal processes. This First Efficient Cause is the "remote agent" of all events.[38] We have here of course the famous proof for God's existence, suggested initially by Aristotle and advocated explicitly by Avicenna, Averroes, Maimonides, Aquinas, and Scotus.[39] So far Albalag has merely reproduced a medieval commonplace. But what is significant is the corollary that Albalag now proceeds to draw from this proof, a consequence that neither Maimonides (at least the exoteric one) nor Aquinas was prepared to make or accept. Like his mentor Averroes, Albalag now argues that this First Efficient Cause *eternally produces* the universe.[40]

Albalag's argument involves two additional premises: (1) the First Cause is eternal; and (2) an eternal agent is eternally active. The first is also a medieval truism and needs no further comment; the second premise was also a common medieval notion *in some sense.* The trouble is that the phrase "eternally active" is ambiguous, and it was construed differently by various thinkers. For Averroes and Albalag an eternally active First Cause continuously produces an eternal product; otherwise, such an agent wouldn't be eternally active. What sense is there in the idea of an eternally active but nonproductive agent? This eternal product is therefore *continuously generated* by its agent. The term Albalag uses here is instructive: *ḥidush,* which corresponds to the Arabic *ḥadath.* The usual English translation for these terms is "creation." Accordingly, for Albalag the universe is continuously being created (*mitḥadesh tamid*) by its continuously creating cause (*meḥadesh tamid*). This generating process is, however, eternal. This is, Albalag asserts, the doctrine of creation according to the philosophers, for whom the doctrine of eternity of the world is no more than the thesis of eternal creation (*ḥidush nitzḥi*).[41]

With this philosophical preamble established Albalag is now ready to proceed to the exegesis of Genesis 1. For him, as well as for some of his predecessors, the most important yet most vexing word in this story is the first. Indeed, even from a purely grammatical perspective this word is difficult. Its morphology suggests that it is the first word of a genitive construction, and thus the opening phrase should be rendered as: "In the beginning of ______." But no noun phrase follows; only the verb 'created'. Moreover, how are we to construe the term 'beginning'? Does it have its usual temporal connotations, which had occasioned several well-known philosophical difficulties, already noted by Maimonides and Gersonides?

Albalag's analysis of this opening phrase attempts to clear up these and other difficulties. The term *bereshit* connotes, he claims, an atemporal causal principle that God uses in continuously creating the world—wisdom. Fully aware that this interpretation is a venerable one, Albalag cites Prov. 8:22ff., the Jerusalem Targum to Genesis 1:1, and several rabbinic dicta. If he knew Greek, he would have been able to cite in addition *The Wisdom of Solomon* and Philo. All of these earlier texts construe the divine creative act in Platonic terms: God creates the world in the same way as a sculptor makes the statue, that is, according to a plan. In these earlier sources wisdom is hypostatized: in Proverbs it is a person; in Philo it is the *kosmos noētos;* in the rabbis it is the Torah. Yet in all of these texts there is the common notion that the creation of the world is according to a definite blueprint, one that embodies the highest perfection. This plan functions as the atemporal cause, or principle, of the physical universe. By means of this exegesis Albalag is able to combine his philosophical commitment to the Aristotelian-Plotinian thesis of the eternity of the world with his adherence to the religious tradition of Judaism that emphasizes the priority of Torah and its unique role in God's creative activity. Albalag states explicitly and boldly that his interpretation "derives the philosophical theory of eternal creation from the Torah and the words of the Rabbis."[42] Indeed, for Albalag the theory of eternal creation, which the Torah *properly interpreted* teaches, is the "perfect (*shalēm*) cosmological doctrine," whereas the theory of temporal creation, which the *vulgus* believe, is the "faulty" (*garuʿa*) doctrine.[43]

Given Albalag's stronger commitment to Aristotle and Averroes, it is not surprising that his exegesis of some of the other crucial phrases in the opening verses of Genesis also differs from Gersonides' interpretations. For example, Albalag is more traditional in his exegesis of the problematic *tohu va-bohu,* "the unformed abyss." For, although like Gersonides he sees these terms as referring to the

Aristotelian principles of matter and form, he assigns these Hebrew terms differently and defines the notion of matter in a more "orthodox" Aristotelian manner. *Tohu* is for him the prime matter of Aristotle, so utterly potential that it has no reality of its own; it is real only when it takes on a particular form. Moreover, this term is the original word from which the term *tehom,* "the primeval deep," is derived. And when it is said that darkness was on the surface of the deep, the term *ḥoshekh,* "darkness," connotes the absolute *privative* nature of prime matter; for darkness is the absence, or privation, of light. As Aristotle emphasized, matter is privation in so far as it has no definite form but can become form.[44] Accordingly, the biblical phrase—"And darkness was on the surface of the deep"—should be translated as: "And complete privation is the property of prime matter."[45]

By interpreting the term *tohu* in this way Albalag not only expresses a different conception of prime matter but also shows, somewhat paradoxically, closer affinity with rabbinic tradition. For in the classic passage in the Babylonian Talmud Hagigah 12a where the primordial *tohu* and *bohu* are discussed by the rabbis, the term *tohu* is described as a line that circumscribes the physical universe and is the source of darkness. Albalag explains this dictum as follows: just as a line is not really something that exists in its own right but is potentially present in a body, so is prime matter not anything real in itself. Albalag confirms his interpretation by citing several biblical passages in which the term *tohu* signifies the properties of emptiness, incompleteness, or imperfection.[46] On the other hand, the rabbis identified the primeval *bohu* with "polished stones sunken in the deep from which the waters originated." To Albalag the fact that the term 'stones' is plural expresses the plurality of the elemental forms. Thus, by assigning *tohu* to prime matter and *bohu* to elemental forms, which reverses Gersonides' procedure, Albalag understands Genesis 1:2 as a description of the nature of the terrestrial domain, which has as its general principles primary matter (*tohu*) and elementary forms (*bohu*). Unlike Gersonides' matter that doesn't keep its shape, Albalag's primary matter is a conceptual abstraction; it, like the darkness, has no reality of its own. It is, to use a modern locution, a theoretical construct, a term of art that has a meaning only within a specific physical theory. Gersonides' primordial matter, however, still exists in its pristine state of formlessness scattered throughout certain regions of the heavenly domain. If he is right, perhaps one day a cosmonaut will bring back some of it for us to touch and hold.

Having interpreted the primeval waters and darkness in this Aristotelian manner, Albalag now turns to the original light of the first day of creation. If the waters and darkness refer to prime matter, the principle of privation—indeed, nonbeing—then light, the opposite of darkness, must refer to being. For Albalag light represents reality (*metziut*), or being. Most appropriately this is the first object of God's creation. Indeed, the terms 'day' and 'morning', as well as their opposites 'night' and 'evening', that occur at each chapter of the story of creation express the contrariety between being and privation. On each "day" of creation a new form of created being is displayed. But in Aristotelian physics privation, or nonbeing, is also a principle of nature, and so it too must be included in the story of creation. Accordingly, each occurrence of the words 'night' and 'evening' in the *hexaemeron* refers to the presence of privation in the natural processes of corruption and generation. Note, Albalag insists, how Scripture places evening before morning; for the generation of one natural substance proceeds out of the corruption of another substance—after the evening comes the morning, after darkness comes light. In this sense, form, or true reality, is posterior to nonbeing, even for Aristotle; for out of privation comes the generation of a form in prime matter.[47] Herein lies the true meaning of creation *ex nihilo*. Thus, whereas for Gersonides the primordial light denotes the world of the Separate Intellects, or angels, which are created out of God Himself, for Albalag this primordial light designates the whole of created reality, which is created *ex nihilo* in the sense of its being subject to the natural law of privation.[48] On the "first day of creation" God brought forth the whole domain of natural being, the world of corruption and generation. The next five days describe separately a distinct type of generated being: the heavenly bodies, the dry land and waters, plants, animals, and finally human beings. But keep in mind, Albalag reminds us, that this sequence is *not* a temporal order. The term 'day' does not signify here a temporal unit, no matter how long; rather, it connotes a distinct kind of created being, which, although included in the creation of light, or existence, is given specific mention as a separate stage in the creative act.

Finally, a comment upon the creative act itself. At least since Saadia, Jewish exegetes were sensitive to the undesirable connotations of the phrase "And God said." After all, does God really *speak?* Accordingly, in his Arabic translation of the Torah Saadia translated these phrases in Genesis 1 as "And God willed." Maimonides accepted his explanation of this phrase.[49] Albalag rejects this interpretation. Like his mentor Averroes, he has some difficulty with the notion of God as a voluntary agent. Voluntary agents act usually because they need, that is, lack, something. Clearly this cannot be said of God, even in a loose sense. Accordingly, Albalag doesn't even accept Maimonides' somewhat tolerant allowance of this translation of "And God said" as "And God willed." God is for Albalag neither a voluntary agent nor a natural agent, but an agent *sui generis:* one who acts from choice, and thus is unlike a natural agent, yet does not act out of need. The creative act is neither one of speech nor of volition, but of thought. God creates by thinking: His eternal thinking generates the Separate Intellects, whose thinking in turn generates the separate spheres, whose motions generate the terrestrial substances.[50] Here Plotinus is joined with Aristotle to produce a theory and a reading of Genesis 1 that is closer to the spirit of the *Enneads* and *Metaphysics* Book 12 than to the letter of the Bible.

IV

The last chapter in this exegetical story takes place at the end of medieval Jewish philosophy. The main character in this last act was a person who took upon himself the role of defending the main tenets of the Jewish religion against its critics, especially the philosophers. Although trained in philosophy and having written several philosophical treatises in his early career, Don Isaac Abravanel came to regret his youthful speculative forays and devoted the remainder of his literary career to biblical exegesis. In his mode of exegesis the main concern is to defend the literalness and integrity of the biblical text *against* its philosophical interpreters, who in Abravanel's eyes have introduced foreign fire into the inner sanctuary. This is especially true, he claims, in the very first chapter of the Torah, where too much philosophy has covered up what is to Abravanel a relatively simple yet basic truth, that God created the whole universe, including matter, *ex nihilo.* This is for Abravanel *the* point of the story of creation, *the* fundamental dogma of Judaism, if Judaism has any dogmas at all.

Now it would be quite natural for someone to ask, why take Abravanel as a representative and defender of creation *ex nihilo,* since he enters the drama quite late in the story? As I have indicated earlier in this essay, creation *ex nihilo* was already by the tenth century regarded by some as the cosmological dogma in Judaism. My choice of Abravanel as the defender of the creation *ex nihilo* model is based upon the fact that living as he did at the end of the Middle Ages he was in a good position to survey the whole history of the problem and thus was able to respond to the various alternative cosmological readings of Genesis 1. His books are virtual encyclopedias of the preceding literature, which is copiously cited and criticized. Since Abravanel is most concerned to refute Gersonides, whom he often refers to as his personal opponent (*baᶜal rivi*), and all defenders of the view that the world is eternal, no matter how this thesis is interpreted, Abravanel is an especially important figure in our exegetical story. Since Abravanel's treatment of creation is quite detailed, I shall focus only upon his defense of creation *ex nihilo*—interpreted as the creation of a finitely enduring universe both *a parte ante* and *a parte post* out of no antecedently existing material substratum. In defending this thesis Abravanel first shows that this theory *is* logically possible; then he attempts to argue for its truth by demonstrating the falsity of the Platonic model.

Most people find the notion of *ex nihilo* creation absurd, Abravanel begins, because they are too wedded to an empiricist outlook that limits their metaphysical imagination. To be sure, virtually every case of a natural generation and artistic creation is such that some matter is involved. But whoever said that the creation of the world is either natural or artistic? Indeed, Gersonides himself often distinguishes between total generation (*havayah kelallit*) and partial generation (*havayah peraṭit*).[51] So why didn't he apply this distinction to differentiate between the unique creative act whereby God produced the whole universe and the diverse productive and generative processes within the universe? The former is *ex nihilo,* whereas the latter are usually not.[52]

Like Albalag, Abravanel correctly perceives that the concept of agency is crucial. Accordingly, he provides an alternative model of agency, especially as it pertains to the creation story. The first of Abravanel's cosmological postulates is that God is, *pace* Albalag, a voluntary agent.[53] It turns out, however, that since Michelangelo and the neighborhood cabinet maker are also voluntary agents, this standard medieval classification scheme, whereby voluntary agents are contrasted with natural agents,[54] isn't sufficient. Accordingly, Abravanel restructures this schema in order to highlight a distinction between *finite* and *infinite* agents, which is quite close to the approach of Aquinas. There are two kinds of finite agents for Abravanel: (1) artisans, and (2) natural agents, such as fire, water, etc. These agents are finite in so far as their causal efficacy is limited in duration and force. This is obviously not the case with the agent who is infinite. Moreover, a finite agent acts upon or through a substratum, whether it be the material from which a product is made, for example, marble or another body upon which one natural agent acts to bring about some reaction. The infinite agent, however, needs no substratum at all; indeed, in acting it brings into existence the very substrata that all subsequent finite agents will require in their own causal activities. To be "beyond" the use of an instrument or material is precisely to be an infinitely powerful, or omnipotent, agent. Since all the participants in this cosmological debate have agreed that God is omnipotent, creation *ex nihilo* has been shown to be not only logically possible but an essential feature of divine agency.[55]

Abravanel now turns to Gersonides' critique of creation *ex nihilo*. Making use of the arguments of Hasdai Crescas, a late fourteenth-century Spanish-Jewish theologian, Abravanel, claims that Crescas has successfully refuted the vacuum arguments employed by Gersonides. In creating the world *ex nihilo* God made the spatial-material matrix of the world *along with* the world; this matrix did not need to preexist the cosmos itself. And there is nothing to fear if the vacuum argument is supposedly strengthened by adding the Principle of Sufficient Reason, for no infinite body ensues. Even if we were to admit that the space allegedly surrounding the universe is homogeneous, and thus would be uniformly receptive of body, in creating the world God makes the universe just the right *finite* size, according to what His wisdom dictates. Whatever the measurements of the world may be, they are precisely what they *should* be, no more, no less. Nor is it the case that surrounding this finitely large universe a vacuum still remains, as Aristotle and Gersonides believed. For, as Aristotle himself admitted, "beyond" the finite world there is literally *nothing,* not even empty space. Indeed, it is not even appropriate to say that the whole world is "in space" or has a place. Although the various parts of and components within the universe have their places, and thus can be said to be "in space," the universe itself is not anywhere, as again Aristotle had conceded. Thus, there is no space, empty or infinitely occupied, "outside" the universe.[56]

Moreover, Gersonides' notion of eternal formless matter implies cosmological dualism, a doctrine that was rejected and combatted by the rabbis quite early in the classical texts of rabbinic literature. Indeed, such an eternal entity would be of the same rank as the deity and hence might not be subject to the latter's creative power.[57] Finally, if this formless matter were eternal, it would also be a necessary existent since, for the Aristotelians, the predicates 'eternal' and 'necessary' are convertible. But does Gersonides want to admit the existence of *two* necessary existents? Indeed, how could one even conceive of an eternal and necessary existent that "doesn't keep its shape"? The features of necessity and eternity are perfections of a thing; formlessness is a defect. That something which is utterly imperfect could have the ontological status of a necessary existent is a metaphysical oxymoron.[58]

Abravanel's critique of eternal creation is more complicated since this theory was propounded in a variety of ways and with varying degrees of vigor. Among his many arguments two are especially prominent: (1) the argument against the incorruptibility of the universe, and (2) the claim that the very concept of eternal creation is incoherent. Since the first argument has received recent comment,[59] I shall focus upon the second. Maimonides had already noted the peculiarity of saying at the same time that the universe eternally and necessarily emanates from God and that it has or exhibits a design or purpose.[60] Nevertheless, Crescas did not find this criticism convincing and claimed that it is possible for the universe to be both eternal and created purposively.[61] Abravanel is clearly more sympathetic with Maimonides on this score, but he formulates a different argument to support his claim that eternal creation is conceptually incoherent. This argument is based upon his notion of agency.

The defenders of eternal creation are able to minimize and mitigate the deterministic implications of their cosmology by defining freedom in such a way that the necessary emanation of the universe from God becomes a metaphysical virtue, not a vice. Freedom for this theory is simply the absence of compulsion. Since God was not compelled to act or to produce the world, the creation of the world is free, or voluntary.[62] Abravanel contends that this notion of divine freedom is trivially true; of course, God is not compelled to create. After all, *what is there* that could compel Him? All there are and ever were, according to the eternal creation theory, are God and the universe! The absence of a compelling external cause here is obviously true. But such a notion of freedom is empty. What is needed is a stronger notion of divine freedom. According to Abravanel, God is free in so far as He is able to create or not to create; and if He does create, He is free to have created the world differently from the way He has in fact created it. God is free not merely in the trivial sense of not being compelled, since if God were compelled He wouldn't be divine, but in the more significant sense of having live options, no one of which is any more necessitating or even inclining than the others.[63] Had Abravanel read Spinoza, he could have replied to Plotinus, Avicenna, and Albalag that their cosmology is hopelessly confused. Either you assert that the universe is eternal and necessary but without purpose or you say that it is created and purposive; but you cannot say both. If it is the case that something is free to the extent that it acts according to the laws of its own nature and is not caused to act by anything else, as Spinoza claims, then the universe is indeed eternal and necessary. But such a world, Spinoza insists, exhibits no purposiveness.[64] Abravanel agrees, but takes the reverse stand: if the universe is truly created by God, then it cannot be that it necessarily exists. A God who has no option not to create is no God at all. Indeed, the attribution of agency to God is, on the eternity hypothesis, a conceptual confusion. In this respect Aristotle was more consistent: he never describes his Unmoved First Mover as creating or making the world. The notion of eternal creation is really a post-Aristotelian theory that superimposes upon Aristotle the Plotinian doctrine of emanation, along with some biblical voluntaristic connotations. Abravanel is suggesting that we reserve the term 'agent' for a cause that brings about its effect contingently and freely; the term 'prime mover' has nothing to do with this notion of efficient causation.[65]

Having set out the philosophical underpinning for Abravanel's understanding of Genesis 1, I now turn to his exegesis. My exposition will focus upon the first three words of the opening sentence, each one of which expresses an important, indeed fundamental, thesis for Abravanel. The main general point of the story of creation is precisely to tell us that the whole world, both its incorporeal and corporeal citizens, was created by God such that it has finite duration both *a parte ante* and *a parte post.* This thesis is expressed by the very first word of the Bible. The Hebrew term *bereshit* means, according to Abravanel, "at the beginning of time." Thus, time itself has a beginning, a *terminus a quo,* whose first unit is a unique instant having no predecessor.[66] Abravanel explicitly rejects therefore the hypostatic interpretations of *reshit* that construe this term as a noun denoting some kind of entity—such as wisdom—which allegedly plays a role in creation. God needs, Abravanel insists, no instrument or coagent in creating the world.[67] If God did require or even used *ad libitum sui* an instrument, He would be no different from Michelangelo.

Abravanel's analysis of the second word in Genesis 1:1 is directed primarily against Gersonides, who, following the great medieval exegete Abraham ibn Ezra, tried to naturalize the verb *bara,* "create," and to suppress its alleged *ex nihilo* connotation. Ibn Ezra had cited a number of biblical passages in which the verb *bara* occurs *without* connoting *ex nihilo* creation. For example, in Genesis 1:21, the creation of the sea serpents is narrated using the verb *bara.* But what is so special about them? Or, in Genesis 1:26–27 we are told that God created human beings; but, ibn Ezra insists, human beings were created from the dust of the earth.[68] To meet this argument, Abravanel replies by showing that the verb *bara* is used in these cases to connote something strange or extraordinary in the making of these items. This is the derived, or secondary, sense of the verb *bara,* whose primary sense is to make something in such an unusual way that it is in fact a miracle, for example, to make something *ex nihilo.* When the verb *bara* is used in Genesis 1:26–27 to describe the divine making of humanity, the verb correctly connotes the extraordinary origin of human beings, since they alone of all bodily creatures have rational souls, and to this extent are like God. Abravanel asks us to note that in Genesis 2:7, where the human person is described as being made out of the earth, the verb *bara* is *not* used. The human body is *generated* out of the terrestrial elements, just as the worm's body is. No need here to use the term 'create'. In the case of the sea serpents, Scripture uses the verb *bara* to connote the extraordinary size and strength of these animals. Thus, along with Saadia, Abravanel claims that the very meaning of the verb *bara* expresses the *ex nihilo* model of creation.[69]

Unlike Gersonides or Albalag, Abravanel puts special emphasis upon the third word in Genesis 1:1: *elohim,* "God". Even the superficial reader of Scripture knows that there are many different names for the deity. Why should one of these names be singled out and used as the subject of the verb 'create', especially since it is *not* the primary name for the deity? The primary name is of course the Tetragrammaton, the proper name for the deity, and as such cannot be multiplied or transferred to anything or anyone else. It is literally incommunicable. The term *elohim,* however, is a general descriptive name deriving from an adjective connoting *power.* It is thus no accident that this divine name is used in connection with the story of creation. In saying that *Elohim* (God) created the world, the author was virtually uttering an analytic statement, since the subject of the verb is the kind of entity to be productive. The biblical deity, named in Genesis 1:1 as "God," is a being whose nature it is to be productive (*mashpi^ca u-mamtzi'a*), indeed to create. This being has the power to do what the story tells us he does. Had the author used the Tetragrammaton, the reader would have been at a loss to know who and what it is that did create the heavens and the earth. Accordingly, the opening sentence of Genesis should be understood as follows: "At the beginning of time, that is, at the very first instant, the being who has the power to give or not to give reality to others freely created the heavenly and terrestrial domains out of no prior matter and without any instrument."[70]

CONCLUSION

Our exegetical story has been an attempt to illustrate the Maimonidean metaphor of the very wide gates that open up the hermeneutical domain. We have seen how the first sentence of Scripture has been given very different, indeed incompatible, cosmological interpretations by Jewish exegetes throughout the Middle Ages. In this sense the language of Scripture is sufficiently open so as to allow, indeed invite, diverse readings. Admittedly, one such reading became the dominant cosmological theme, but other voices were not altogether drowned out. The Platonic metaphor of a divine craftsman using matter reappears in the fifteenth century in the *Dialoghi D'Amore* of Leone Ebreo, the beloved son of Isaac Abravanel, who wasn't convinced by the arguments of his father.[71] And the Plotinian metaphor of the eternal pouring forth of "the great chain of being" is defended by the seventeenth-century disciple of Galileo, Joseph Solomon del Medigo.[72] These cosmological "heterodoxies" were tolerated because the Torah speaks human language and human beings are the readers and interpreters of the Torah.

NOTES

1. Moses Maimonides, *The Guide of the Perplexed,* part 2, chap. 25.

2. The philosophical mode of biblical hermeneutics was recognized as a distinct style by the popular medieval Jewish exegete Baḥya ben Asher, who distinguished four modes, of which one is the "rationalistic," or philosophical (*sekhel*). Baḥya b. Asher, *Commentary on the Torah* (Jerusalem, 1974), vol. 1, Opening, 4–5.

3. Harry Wolfson, *Philo: Foundations of Religious Philosophy in Judaism, Christianity, and Islam* (Cambridge, Mass., 1948), 2 vols. See especially the preface.

4. See Clement of Alexandria, *The Stromata,* book 1, chap. 5.

5. Already in the twelfth century the exegete Abraham ibn Ezra complained of the increasing use of nonliteral modes of biblical exegesis. See the introduction to his *Commentary on the Torah.*

6. Philo, *On the Migration of Abraham* 89–93; Wolfson, *Philo* 1: 115–38.

7. Philo, *On the Creation of the World* 2. Aristotle, *Physics* 8.1; *On the Heavens* 1.12.

8. Maimonides, *Guide* 2.25.

9. In deciding not to discuss in detail Philo or Maimonides in this essay I take the easy path. Right now there is virtually no agreement amongst modern scholars on the cosmologies of these two thinkers. Wolfson claimed that Philo believed in creation *ex nihilo* (*Philo,* 1, chap. 4); Bréhier saw Philo as a follower of Plato's doctrine of creation out of matter (E. Bréhier, *Les idées philosophiques et religieuses de Philo d'Alexandre* [Paris, 1925], 80–82); and most recently David Winston has argued that Philo advocated eternal creation ("Philo's Theory of Cosmogony," in Religious *Syncretism in Antiquity,* ed. B. A. Pearson [Missoula, Mont., 1975], 157–71). Similarly, Maimonides' "true view" has been a controversial question ever since the Middle Ages. Some commen-

tators inferred from a literal reading of the *Guide* that Maimonides believed in creation *ex nihilo* (Gersonides, *The Wars of the Lord* book 6, part 1, chap. 1); others, both medieval and modern, have read "between the lines" and have detected a doctrine of eternal creation. Among the more recent literature see W. Harvey, "A Third Approach to Maimonides' Cosmogony—Prophetology Puzzle," *Harvard Theological Review* 74 (1981): 287–301; and Sarah Klein-Braslavy, "Maimonides' Explanation of the Verb 'Bara' and the Question of the Creation of the World," *Da'at* 16 (1986): 39–55.

10. Plato, *Timaeus* 48e–53c. See also Seneca, *Moral Epistles* 65, par. 19.

11. Aristotle, *Physics* 4:2. 209b10–12.

12. *Wisd. of Sol.* 11:17.

13. J. Goldstein, "The Origins of the Doctrine of Creation Ex Nihilo," *Journal of Jewish Studies* 35 (1984): 127–35; Saadia Gaon, *The Book of Beliefs and Opinions,* book 1, chap. 2; Wolfson, *Philo,* 1:300–310.

14. David Winston, "The Book of Wisdom's Theory of Cosmogony," *History of Religions* (1971–72): 185–202; Jehudah Halevi, *The Kuzari* 1.67; Maimonides, *Guide* 2.25.

15. Seymour Feldman, "Platonic Themes in Gersonides' Cosmology," *Salo W. Baron Jubilee Volume* (Jerusalem, 1975), vol. 1, 383–405; Jacob Staub, *The Creation of the World According to Gersonides* (Chico, Calif., 1982).

16. Gersonides, *The Wars* book 5, part 2, chap. 2.

17. Aristotle, *Physics* 4:6–8.

18. Ibid., 2.7; *On the Heavens,* 3.2. 302a1–9. Averroes, *Tahafut al-Tahafut* (The Incoherence of the Incoherence) trans. S. van den Bergh (London, 1954), vol. 1, First Discussion, p. 52.

19. Gersonides, *The Wars* book 6, part 1, chap. 17; Aristotle, *Physics* 3.4. 203b27–29; Leibniz, *Letters to Clarke,* 3, par. 6.

20. Aristotle, *On the Heavens* 1.5–7.

21. *B. T. Hagigah* 12a. Maimonides, *Guide* 2.30; Gersonides, *Commentary on the Torah* 9b–10a.

22. Aristotle, *Metaphysics* 5.11. 1019a3–6.

23. Gersonides, *Commentary* 9c, 10a; *The Wars* book 5, part 2, chap. 1; 6.6, part 2, chap. 4.

24. Saadia, *Commentary on Genesis,* ed. M. Zucker (New York, 1984) 210–16; Maimonides, *Guide* 2.30.

25. Gersonides, *Commentary* 9d–10a; *The Wars* book 6, part 2, chaps. 5, 8.

26. Louis Ginzberg, *Legends of the Jews* (Philadelphia, 1913), vol. 1, pp. 13, 16–17.

27. Gersonides, *Commentary on the Torah,* Genesis, 9d–10a; *The Wars* book 5, part 3, chaps. 7–12; book 6, part 2, chaps. 5, 8. On the creation of light as the world of the Separate Intellects Levi refers to the rabbinic discussion in *Midrash Psalms,* Psalm 27.

28. Gersonides' gloss on Genesis 1:1–7 departs considerably and significantly from that of Maimonides. In fact, on certain points he explicitly criticizes the *Rav Ha-Moreh.*

29. Gersonides, *Commentary* 10b,d; *The Wars* book 6, part 2, chap. 7. In both the *Commentary* and *The Wars* Gersonides tries to show that his reading of Gen. 1:6–8 is compatible with several rabbinic discussions found in *Genesis Rabbah* 4.3, 6.6, 12.7–8; *B. T. Hagigah* 14b–15a.

30. Samuel ibn Tibbon, *Yeqqavu Ha-Mayyim* (Let the Waters be Gathered). A useful summary of ibn Tibbon's views is found in C. Sirat, *A History of Jewish Philosophy in the Middle Ages* (Cambridge, 1985), 218–20.

31. Joseph ibn Kaspi, *ʿAmudei Kesef U-Maskiyot Kesef* (Frankfort, 1848), part 2, chap. 13 and chap. 30; Moses Narboni, *Pirqei Moshe,* ed. C. Sirat, *Tarbiz* 39 (1970): 286–306.

32. Isaac Albalag, *Tiqqun Ha-Deʿot,* ed. Georges Vajda (Jerusalem, 1973), chap. 30, p. 41; G. Vajda, *Isaac Albalag: Averroiste Juif, Traducteur et Annotateur D'al-Ghazali* (Paris, 1960), part 1, chaps. 5–6.

33. Charles Touati, "Verité philosophique et verité prophetique chez Isaac Albalag," *REJ* 122 (1962): 35–47.

34. *Midrash Rabbah,* Num. 13:15. Another passage says that there are forty-nine ways to interpret the Torah (2:3).

35. No modern translation or critical edition of this important treatise has yet appeared. See Vajda, *Isaac Albalag,* 7, n.3.

36. Maimonides, *Guide* 1.69; Albalag, *Tiqqun Deʿot* chap. 30 (hereafter *TD*).

37. Aristotle, *Physics* 2.3; *Metaphysics* 5.2.

38. Albalag, *TD,* chap. 30, p. 30.

39. Avicenna, *The Healing; Metaphysics,* First Treatise, chap. 6, trans. Arthur Hyman, in *Philosophy in the Middle Ages,* ed. Arthur Hyman and J. Walsh (Indianapolis, 1983), 2nd ed. 241–44; Maimonides, *Guide* 2.1; Aquinas, *Summa Theologiae* Ia, q.2, a.3; John Duns Scotus, *Philosophical Writings,* ed. and trans. Alan Wolter (Indianapolis, 1962), chap. 3.

40. Averroes, *The Incoherence of the Incoherence,* 96–104.

41. Albalag, *TD,* chap. 30, pp. 30–33.

42. Ibid., pp. 32–33, 46.

43. Ibid., p. 51. See A. Ravitsky's discussion of this idea in some medieval Italian-Jewish thinkers, "The Hypostatization of the Supernal Wisdom (Hebrew), *Italia* 3 (1982): 7–38.

44. Aristotle, *Physics* book 1:7–9.

45. Albalag, *TD,* chap. 30, pp. 38–39.

46. Albalag cites Isa. 45:18–19, Jer. 2:8.

47. Aristotle, *Physics* 1.7–9; *On Generation and Corruption* 1.3.

48. Albalag, *TD,* chap. 30, pp. 40–42. The Muslim falasifa also claimed that the world is eternally created *ex nihilo* in the sense that God did not use anything as a material cause, or stuff, to create the world. As Averroes put it, in creation there was no "out of which," although there was a "from which," God (Averroes, *On the Harmony of Religion and Philosophy,* in Hyman and Walsh, *Philosophy in the Middle Ages,* pp. 305–6).

49. Maimonides, *Guide* 1.65.

50. Albalag, *TD,* chap. 30, pp. 46–47; Maimonides, *Guide* 2.4–6; Pro-

clus, *The Elements of Theology,* trans. E. R. Dodds (Oxford, 1933), propositions 172, 174, 178.

51. Gersonides, *The Wars* book 6, part 1, chap. 18, 7th reply.

52. Abravanel, *Mif'alot Elohim* (Lemberg, 1863), book 4, chap. 3, 32 cd, chap. 5, 34ab.

53. Abravanel, *Mif'alot Elohim,* book 7, chap. 1, 47ab (hereafter *ME*).

54. Jehudah Halevi, *The Kuzari,* book 5, par. 20; John Duns Scotus, *Philosophical Writings,* part 5.

55. Abravanel, *ME,* book 4, chap. 4, 35c–36b; Aquinas, *Summa Contra Gentiles,* book 2, chap. 16.

56. Abravanel, *ME,* book 4, chap. 3, 32a–34a; Hasdai Crescas, *Or Adonai* (Vienna, 1859), book 3, First Principle, chap. 5, 70a. (Crescas' arguments here are reminiscent of Aquinas' discussion in the *Summa Contra Gentiles* 2.35, par. 6, and in the *Summa Theologiae* Ia, q.46, a.1, ad 4.) Aristotle, *On the Heavens* 1.9.

57. Saadia Gaon, *The Book of Beliefs and Opinions,* book 1, chap. 2.

58. Abravanel, *ME,* book 2, chap. 4.

59. H. Davidson, "The Principle that a Finite Body Can Contain Only Finite Power," *Studies in Jewish Religious and Intellectual History: Presented to Alexander Altmann,* ed. S. Stein and R. Loewe (Alabama, 1979), pp. 75–92. Richard Sorabji, *Time. Creation and the Continuum* (Ithaca, N.Y., 1984), chaps. 13–15; Seymour Feldman, "The End of the Universe in Medieval Jewish Philosophy," *Association for Jewish Studies Review* 11 (1986): 53–78.

60. Maimonides, *Guide* 2, chap. 21.

61. Crescas, *Or Adonai,* book 3, First Principle, chaps. 4–5.

62. Aristotle, *Nicomachean Ethics* 3.5. Crescas, *Or Adonai;* Seymour Feldman, "The Theory of Eternal Creation in Hasdai Crescas and Some of his Predecessors," *Viator* 11 (1981): 289–320.

63. Abravanel, *ME,* book 8, chap. 1, 53d; *Shamayim Ḥadashim,* First Essay, 2b, 10a–11a.

64. Spinoza, *Ethics,* Part I, Propositions, 28–36, Appendix.

65. Abravanel, *Shamayim Ḥadashim,* Third Essay, 28–29.

66. Abravanel, *Commentary on the Torah,* Genesis, 11d–12a. Here Abravanel borrows from Gersonides, *The Wars,* book 6, part 1, chaps. 11, 21, 22.

67. Abravanel, *Commentary on the Torah,* Genesis, 12ab.

68. Abraham ibn Ezra, *Commentary on Genesis, ad locum.*

69. Abravanel, *Commentary on the Torah,* Genesis, 5c–6a.

70. Ibid., 7a–8b.

71. Leone Ebreo, *The Dialogues of Love,* trans. F. Friedeberg-Seeley and J. Barnes (London, 1937), pp. 295–96.

72. Joseph Solomon del Medigo, *Novlot Ḥokhma,* in his *Ta'alumoth Ḥokhma,* part 2 (Basil, 1629–31), 102–3; Isaac Barzilay, *Joseph Solomon Del Medigo* (Leiden, 1974), chap. 14.

Creation or Emanation: Two Paradigms of Reason

David B. Burrell, C.S.C.

Those of us who come from traditions highlighting creation find that it makes good sense to pose the philosophical question: why is there something rather than nothing? In fact, we often need to jar ourselves into a mindset where no such question would ever arise. Yet it is the philosophical mindset, I would contend, which is more natural to human inquiry. And the philosopher who posed the question in this form, Heidegger, would support my contention, since it is this very question which introduces one into the mode of reflection proper to metaphysics. And *metaphysics*, for Heidegger, represented an access to the incomprehensible mystery of being which had thus far eluded most ontologists. So the catechetical couplet: "Who made the world? God made the world," embodies a way of looking at our universe which will tax the philosophical resources of those communities which avow God to be "Creator of heaven and earth."

Early Christian reflection spontaneously incorporated the vantage point of Hellenic Judaism, which deemed itself superior to the fruitless philosophizing of "all men who have not known God and who, from the good things that are seen, have not been able to discover Him-who-is, or, by studying the works, have failed to recognize the Artificer" (Wis. 13:1). Paul escalates the charge from ignorance to culpability, presuming that God's "everlasting power and deity—however invisible—have been there for the mind to see in the things he has made . . . ever since God created the world" (Rom. 1:20)! As a result, Paul deems such philosophers to be "without excuse: they knew God and yet refused to honor him as God or to thank him" (1:21). This was a characteristically Jewish response to the wisdom claimed by Greek philosophy, however, and delivered with the edge characteristic of Paul. The author of the letter to the Hebrews would have been more compassionate toward his pagan neighbors, for he avers that "it is by faith that we understand that the world was created by one word from God, so that no apparent cause can account for the things we can see" (11:3).

My own sympathies lie with the author of Hebrews; yet the way to recovering creation as an assertion of faith in God's original gift, eliciting the thanks and praise of a *berakah,* encounters two contrary obstacles. The first, we have noted, may be shared by Jews and Muslims. It amounts to reversing the naive presumption that the universe is simply there, as the context of our life and inquiry, and replacing it with the apparently spontaneous query: whence did all this come? Such an ingrained attitude would assimilate the Genesis story to "true philosophy," and be inclined to find those unable to move their minds "through the grandeur and beauty of creatures [to] contemplate their author" (Wis. 13:5) to be "naturally stupid" (13:1) or even, as Paul did, "without excuse." We might reasonably associate such an attitude with early Christian reflection in Alexandria, which could presume such a vantage point without, it seems, needing to specify more exactly the manner in which the universe originated from its creator. That was to wait until the sixth century, when John Philoponus found it necessary to argue for creation against a highly developed emanation scheme which threatened the faith assertion.[1] But that gets us ahead of our story.

The second obstacle stems specifically from Christian liturgical practice and theological development. Whereas Jewish observance of the *sabbath* offers periodic recognition that the Master of the universe orders and gives life to all things, replacing the sabbath with Sunday—the Lord's day—shifts the focus to Jesus' resurrection as the source of our redemption to everlasting life. And that liturgical replacement received theological confirmation in the thirteenth century, when Philip the Chancellor's distinction of *supernatural* from *natural* made it convenient to distinguish *grace* from *nature,* effectively relegating creation to its pagan status as a *given* rather than a *gift.* These connections are more rhetorical than logical, of course, but one only needs to recall the use to which Luther would later put them to appreciate their immense rhetorical force—or to remind oneself how bereft is Christian liturgy in its capacity to honor and thank the Creator of all, apart from the sacramental vestigia of bread and salt, water and wine. And if we add to all of this the nineteenth-century exaltation of history over nature, we will not be surprised that a philosophical theology which replaces creation by "creativity" can offer itself as a version of Christian theology.

The "distinction" of God from the world, then, which creation is meant to secure, can be jeopardized from two opposing quarters.[2] The first reflects a philosophical oversight, failing to appreciate the kind of reflection needed to articulate such a startling fact about the universe: that it might not have existed at all. The second betrays a temptation peculiar to Christians: to let their preoccupation with redemption overshadow the legacy they have received from Moses, so becoming in practice pagan with regard to nature while espousing a theological anthropocentricism which leaves human beings rootless in an alien world. So our manner of articulating what we believe about creation—as Christians, Muslims, or Jews—will tell mightily regarding our views of God and of humanity.

STRATEGIES FOR CONCEIVING A CREATOR GOD

I mentioned earlier how my own sympathies align with the author of Hebrews: "It is by faith that we understand that the world was created by one word from God" (11:3). It will be my contention that the Plotinian emanation scheme offered a convenient way of obscuring that assertion, by presenting a universe emanating necessarily from the One, and hence originated; yet necessarily coeverlasting with that One, and so effectively indistinguishable from Aristotle's everlasting milieu. As Alfarabi adapted this emanation scheme, moreover, it is difficult to distinguish "the First" from what follows necessarily from it. Thus Islamic philosophers enamoured with eternal emanation were bound to be seen as compromising the majesty of Allah as well as obscuring a cardinal feature of divine revelation: that the universe itself is God's gracious gift. And if the universe comes to be as a free action of God, that coming-to-be may still be described as an *emanation,* since "the universal production of being by God should not be taken as motion or as change, but rather like a simple emanation." Otherwise we would be tempted to think of a free coming forth from "the First" as a *making* of sorts, but clearly "'to become' and 'to make' are used equivocally [when employed to span the] universal production of things as well as other productions."[3] These observations come from Aquinas' commentary on Aristotle's *Physics,* where the intent to reconcile worldviews steers him away from Kalām-type arguments for an originated universe, which rely on a univocal notion of *making.* Yet the introductory phrase—"the universal production of being by God"—fairly broadcasts his differences with the Greeks.

Aquinas will focus on that difference in his treatment of creation, where he introduces the paradigm of practical knowing. But let us first appreciate how natural was the appeal of Plotinus' emanation scheme, wholeheartedly adopted and adapted by the Islamic philosophers, and constantly presumed by Maimonides, who nonetheless found its necessitarian consequences clearly at odds with the Torah. Indeed Maimonides' severe modifications of that scheme culminate in his proposing to us the model of practical knowing—as "an excellent idea, and [one leading] to correct views" (*Guide* 3.21)—an idea, however, which he left quite undeveloped. Nor does Aquinas really exploit the model in his treatment of creation, though his elaboration of the mutuality of intellect and will, as we shall see, offers abundant materials for such a development. But first to the attractiveness of an intellectual emanation scheme for conveying the universe originating from a first principle.

PARADIGM OF SPECULATIVE REASON

Neoplatonism more generally may be said to project onto a world-to-be-known the intellectual patterns which allow us to understand it. We would spontaneously say, "to understand its workings," while they were preoccupied with its order. Hence the strong temptation of inquirers to see there what they would be inclined to find: an order reflecting the logical consequences which constitute valid demonstration. A parallel move would invest logical genera with explanatory power, since one could conclude that all specimens of a certain variety of dog were animals from the fact that all dogs are. Operational questions—how does it work?—were of less interest than ordering questions; and nothing short of divine revelation, it seems, could press one to pose the radical question regarding the origin of it all. So a scheme which derived all things, according to their kinds, from a single first principle, offered a genial *rapprochement* between traditional Hellenists who presumed an everlasting universe, and Jewish, Christian, and Muslim believers who demanded that it originate from a creator God. For the mode of origination respected and reflected a common concern for finding ordering principles, while emanation conceived on the model of logical derivation seemed nicely to finesse questions of freedom, since assent to demonstration cannot be said to be either voluntary or coerced.

Furthermore, we might appreciate this model as something more than a period piece were we to see it as a precursor of the powerful mathematical explanatory schemes of the seventeenth and eighteenth centuries. Neoplatonists were using the formal apparatus available to them; the mathematics developed in the seventeenth century proved more amenable to the empirical temper of the century following, so that the order which they so passionately sought could also be used to explain how things work. But both logicians and mathematicians were intent on finding the world's order. That is in fact the penchant of speculative or theoretical reason. It explains also why Ghazālī's presumption that causal discourse implies an intentional agent was quite beside the point, for formal causality is not agency.[4] Yet Ghazālī's critique did score against believers who hoped that emanation from a first principle would offer an acceptable account of creation. His query whether a first principle from which everything proceeds necessarily need *know* what proceeds from it may sound bizarre until we think of a "logic machine."[5] Necessary emanation follows the pattern of strict deduction, and while the entire activity is eminently intellectual, and hence intentional, the first principles of a demonstration cannot be said knowingly to generate the conclusions which derive from them. As is often the case, Ghazālī's arguments can be found to be weak, but his insight into the matter at hand proves penetrating. The attempt of emanation theorists to explain the origin of the universe by a scheme elucidating its order proved insufficient since it offered too obvious a projection of the formal explanatory mode onto a reality whose very existence had come into question, even though it remains the incontestable context of all we say or do. The religiously unacceptable fact that "the First" thus becomes part of a necessary demonstrative pattern represents a simple corollary of the original projection and indicates where the speculative paradigm will show its fatal weakness as a tool of reconciliation: God's knowledge of particulars.

Should the first principle of all be regarded as itself a knower, and hence circumvent Ghazālī's penetrating query, one then has to inquire what the scheme of emanation allows it to know. Ibn Sina's response here is perfectly consistent: the essences or natures which emanate from it.[6] Maimonides will attribute this position to Aristotle and find it utterly repugnant to the Torah, where covenantal gift and retribution demand that God relate to each individual (*Guide* 3.17–18). He is willing to countenance Ibn Sina's position with regard to subhuman species, where the good of the individual seems clearly to be subordinated to that of the species, but cannot do so for human beings. Gersonides will accuse his mentor of failure of nerve at this point and even link Maimonides' stark insistence on sheer equivocity between human knowing and divine knowing to this impasse between philosophy and revelation.[7] Maimonides locates the impasse precisely at whether God's foreknowledge of particulars necessitates their actions, and the logical inevitability which follows from considering God's knowing on a parallel with our own leads him to insist that God's *mode* of knowing must be completely different from ours. Three chapters later (3.21) he will suggest a proposal tempering that radical move by offering practical knowing as a mode proper to the creator, and clearly analogous to a human craftsman. But so long as knowledge meant "speculative knowledge," he had to insist on sheer equivocity, while his friendly critic Gersonides would take the opposite tack; Gersonides tried to persuade us that knowing things "in the respect in which they are ordered and defined" exhausts the meaning of *knowing,* so believers have no reason to find Ibn Sina's position repugnant.[8] What so obviously dominates this discussion is the paradigm of speculative reason. Yet if creation is to be understood in its own terms, rather than assimilated to emanation, another model for knowing will have to be introduced.

PRACTICAL REASON

Beyond knowing lie doing and making, yet are not these latter activities also a form of knowledge? They are not themselves a "knowing that . . . ," it is true, although they will presuppose much of that to be rightly executed. Yet Aristotle avers that they also qualify as "ways in which the soul arrives at truth" (*Nicomachean Ethics* 6.3. 1139b16). He thus finds specific intellectual virtues associated with each—art (*techne*) with making and prudence (*phronesis*) with doing—since each will involve standards of performance. We must say that artists (or artisans) know what they are doing, certainly, even though they may be quite unable to render that specific knowledge as "knowing that something is the case." Yet our temptation, like the Greeks, is to be led by the linguistic clues to limit knowing to "knowings that," and so effectively nullify Aristotle's distinction by removing making and doing from the realm of knowledge. And that is easy enough to do, since no form of the expression 'to know' occurs in describing such practical knowings. Indeed, that may simply show that Aristotle made a mistake in distinguishing different modes within knowing: theoretical (or speculative) and practical.

Yet we cannot fail to recognize his good sense in doing so, since no one wants to call these actions mindless, nor analyze them as a set of "knowings that" plus certain motor skills. In fact, the more one is inclined to see speculative "knowings that" as involving specific skills (or "know-how"), the more one may be inclined to shift over imperceptibly to *making* and *doing* as paradigms for knowing. Then all forms of knowing would be "knowings-how," much as J. L. Austin's work with performative language began by contrasting "performatives" with mere assertion, and ended asking what sort of performance asserting might be.[9]

What distinguishes making and doing for Aristotle from speculative knowledge is precisely that they have to do with contingent particulars, while science (*episteme*) is concerned with "universal reason" (*Nicomachean Ethics* 6.5 1140a10). And this is the distinction which will appeal to Aquinas, in his effort to move beyond Ibn Sina to affirm God's knowledge of individuals, without however insisting on a radical equivocity between God's knowing and ours, as Maimonides felt compelled to do.[10] In fact, it is the affirmation of creation which guides Aquinas in treating this question. Rather than invoke a paradigm of knowing to offer a scheme intended to account for the origination of all things from a first principle, Aquinas insists that "God does know individuals; [indeed] God must know them [for] God's knowledge has the same extension as [God's] causality" (*Summa theologiae* 1.14.11). Since God is the "source of all things" (1.2 Intro.), God's knowing must be coextensive with "God's active power." The full account begins with an axiom shared by both emanationist and creation accounts—that it is in knowing the divine nature that God knows all that originates from it—but ends by offering a fresh analogy to comprehend existing individuals:

> [God] knows things other than himself through his essence, insofar as it is the likeness of things as their productive principle; therefore his essence must be the sufficient principle for knowing all things that come into existence through him, not merely in their universal natures but in their individuality. The same would be true of the artist's knowledge if it produced the whole thing and not merely the form. (1.14.11; cf. 1.15.2)

So "God's knowledge stands to all created things as the artist's to his products" (1.14.8).

Aquinas will insist that God's knowledge is speculative as well as practical (1.14.16), but the shift has already been made. Following Genesis, the master image is that of a maker rather than an inspector, with the explicit directions on the use of the model that nothing need be presupposed to the activity of this producer. But if "the production of all being from the universal cause" (1.45.4.3) need presuppose nothing at all, what sort of a production can it be? How are we to think of it as a *making*? Aquinas' answer is that we are not, since "'to become' and 'to make' are used equivocally of the universal production of things as well as other productions" (8 *Phys.* 2 2002). So creation is more like an emanation; indeed Aquinas defines it as the "emanation of all *esse* from the universal being" (*Summa theologiae* 1.45.4.1.), according to the formula: "God, in knowing his essence as imitable in this particular way by this particular creature" (1.15.3), brings it into being. Insofar as that primordial activity can be described at all, it is like an emanation, since what is brought forth is not a particular organization of materials but the thing itself in its very existence. So "the effect proper to the first and most universal cause, which is God" (1.45.5), is the very existence of things, and not simply their ordering. It is in this sense, then, that creation, although descriptively more like an emanation than a making, must also be described as a *production* by contrast to a purely intellectual emanation (1.45.4.3), since the intellectual paradigm has been deliberately shifted from speculative to practical knowing.

Such a shift could not have taken place, I would argue, without having distinguished that in the created universe which could be identified as "the effect proper to" God's creative activity: the very existence of things. And it was a Muslim philosopher, Ibn Sina, who first attempted systematically to discriminate existence from essence, in an effort to distinguish the source of all from everything which emanates from it. It is significant, moreover, that no Greek thinker nor pagan commentator had pressed that distinction—inchoately present in Aristotle—so that one seems justified in attributing to Ibn Sina an attempt to offer a philosophical idiom for creation.[11] That is certainly the case with Aquinas' adoption of Avicenna's distinction, in the way in which he recast it as well as the uses to which he put it. What God, "subsistent existence itself" (1.44.1), brings forth in creating is things themselves in their very existence. God does so by an act of knowing at once speculative (i.e., of the divine essence) yet preeminently practical in its mode.

But how is doing or making a mode of knowing? As has been suggested, Aristotle's distinction between "two ways in which the soul arrives at truth"—practical as well as speculative—has been largely overlooked, perhaps because no cognate expression for *knowing* occurs in descriptions of what we are doing or making. Yet we would not want to write off either activity as mindless. Aquinas' elaboration of doing and making involves an ordered reciprocity between the two sides of our intellectual capacity of relating to the world—apprehensive and appetitive (i.e., "intellect" and "will")—better schematized than described. The upshot is to give primacy to the apprehensive side ("intellect") while acknowledging that the appetitive side ("will") does indeed direct our choices, but only after it has received as its proper good the end proposed to it, in an action whose receptive character is conveyed by Aquinas' term *complacentia.*[12] While the will is a mover, it remains a "moved mover," moved by the end proposed to it. So freedom can be drawn or enticed without being coerced—the Platonic legacy inherited through Augustine; thus choosing becomes a proper part of a free action rather than its paradigm.

God's knowing, of course, is not discursive, so the steps will collapse. Yet the structure may be thought to be retained as "God, in knowing his essence as imitable in this particular way by this particular creature" (1.15.3), *consents* to that participation in existence and so executes it in the manner appropriate to each creature "according to its kind." All of this is implied by the pregnant phrase: "as imitable in this particular way." And since the proper effect of God's acting will be at the heart of the creature's existence, there can be no constraint, for "*esse* (to be) is . . . more intimate [to each thing] than all other effects" (*De potentia* 3.7). So it is but a short step to maintain, as Aquinas does, that "everything falls under divine providence, not merely in its universality but in its particularity," *because* "everything comes under God's order as all artifacts fall under the order of art" (*Summa theologiae* 1.22.2). So the transformation is complete: the practical intellect orders as it executes. One may then dispense with an emanation scheme modelled on speculative knowing to image the "emanation of all being from the universal cause, which is God" (1.45.1) by way of a free and gracious act.

One must insist, of course, that a great deal of work remains to be done on practical knowing to bring our understanding of it to a degree of clarity which would allow us to propose even a remotely analogous grasp of God's activity in creating. Moreover, a clearer sense of what it is for existence itself (*esse*) to be the proper effect of that activity is also needed to enable us to picture the universe "in God's hands" without thereby diminishing the freedom proper to rational creatures. This essay is offered as encouragement to such a research program, coming as it does in the wake of a conceptual and historical study of the ways in which Aquinas, with Maimonides' help, transformed the emanation scheme of Avicenna to suggest a different paradigm for creation.[13] It remains to us to determine the reach and the fruitfulness of that suggestion.

NOTES

1. For a penetrating analysis of the philosophical alternatives from antiquity to the early Middle Ages, see Richard Sorabji, *Time, Creation and the Continuum* (Ithaca, N.Y.: Cornell University Press, 1983). For John Philoponus, I am indebted to a recent (and as yet unpublished) essay by Seymour Feldman, "Philoponus on the Metaphysics of Creation," and of course to Her-

bert Davidson's magisterial "John Philoponus as a Source of Medieval Islamic and Jewish Proofs of Creation," *Journal of the American Oriental Society* 85 (1969): 358–91.

2. Robert Sokolowski introduces this pointed use of the "distinction" in *The God of Faith and Reason* (Notre Dame, Ind.: University of Notre Dame Press, 1981), a work whose perspectives have shaped the overall lineaments of my strategy here.

3. Aquinas, *Commentarium in Aristotelis de Physica* 2.2002 (Torino: Marietti, 1950). See David B. Burrell, *Aquinas: God and Action* (Notre Dame, Ind.: University of Notre Dame Press, 1979), p. 136.

4. Ghazālī, *Tahafut al-Falasifa,* ed. Suliman Dunya, 6th ed. (Cairo: Dar al-Maaref, 1980), Discussion 3, pp. 154–64.

5. Ibid., Discussion 11, pp. 198–202.

6. Cf. Michael Marmura, "Some Aspects of Avicenna's Theory of God's Knowledge of Particulars," *Journal of the American Oriental Society* 82 (1962): 299–312; and David B. Burrell, *Knowing the Unknowable God: Ibn Sina, Maimonides, and Aquinas* (Notre Dame, Ind.: University of Notre Dame Press, 1986), pp. 80–83.

7. Norbert Max Samuelson, trans. and ed., *Gersonides on God's Knowledge* (Toronto: Pontifical Institute of Medieval Studies, 1977), pp. 162–73.

8. Norbert Max Samuelson, "Gersonides' Account of God's Knowledge of Particulars," *Journal of the History of Philosophy* 10 (1972): 399–416, and David B. Burrell, "Maimonides, Aquinas and Gersonides on Providence and Evil," *Religious Studies* 20 (1984): 335–51.

9. J. L. Austin, *How to Do Things with Words* (Cambridge, Mass.: Harvard University Press, 1962), pp. 45–91.

10. Aquinas, 6 *Ethicorum* 3.1152 (Torino: Marietti, 1964).

11. Cf. David B. Burrell, "Essence and Existence: Avicenna and Greek Philosophy," *MIDEO* 17 (1986): 53–66; and Charles H. Kahn, "Why Existence Does Not Emerge as a Distinct Concept in Greek Philosophy," in *Philosophies of Existence Ancient and Medieval,* ed. Parviz Morewedge (New York: Fordham University Press, 1982), pp. 7–17.

12. *Inter alia,* see Patrick Lee, "The Relation between Intellect and Will in Free Choice According to Aquinas and Scotus," *Thomist* 49 (1985): 321–42. For more extensive treatments, see Steven A. Edwards, *Interior Acts* (Lanham, Md.: University Press of America, 1986); and Joseph Incandela, "God's Practical Knowledge and Situated Human Freedom" (Ph.D. diss., Princeton University, 1986). Frederick Crowe's "Complacency and Concern in the Thought of St. Thomas," *Theological Studies* 20 (1959): 1–39, 198–230, 343–95, offers an exhaustive and illuminating presentation of Aquinas, while Alan Donaghan's "St. Thomas on the Analysis of Human Action," in *Cambridge History of Later Medieval Philosophy,* ed. N. Kretzmann, A. Kenny, and J. Pinborg (New York: Cambridge University Press, 1982) 2.6, presents a synoptic account.

13. Burrell, *Knowing the Unknowable God.*

Ibn Sina's Theory of the God-World Relationship

Fazlur Rahman

Ibn Sina appears to be the first philosopher to formulate explicitly the concept of contingency in order to introduce a radical distinction between God and the world.[1] Since he could not accept philosophically the idea of creation in time, advocated by orthodoxy, but also took the demands of traditional Islam seriously (far more seriously, at least formally, than al-Farabi), the concept of contingency seemed to him to respond exactly to the demand of religion that God and the world cannot coexist at the same level of being, that between God and the world there is a radical ontological dislocation whereby the status of the world in terms of being becomes purely derivative from that of God. God is the "Necessary Being," that is, self-existing, original, and uncaused, while everything else is caused and brought into being by Him. It is, therefore, not the case that after a contingent thing comes into existence its being is of the same nature or order as that of God. Although Ibn Sina rejected the view that the term 'exist' has two different senses when applied to God and the world and firmly held to the univocality of existence, he still insisted that the original and the borrowed forms of existence can never be the same and that the contingent can never shed its contingency even while it exists.[2] How does our philosopher arrive at this position and what are its implications?

Ibn Sina tells us in practically all his philosophical works that the mark of a contingent being is that when you inspect it, it exhibits that it is in need of a cause to bring it into being and that it cannot bring itself into existence. The mark of the Necessary Being, on the other hand, is that when you inspect it, you see that it is not in need of an external cause and that it has brought itself into being. Ibn Sina's discourse, therefore, *prima facie* seems related to an intuitive perception on our part whereby we can distinguish between the contingent and the Necessary Being:

> Every existent, when you consider it in itself without considering anything else beside it, will either be such that its existence is necessitated by itself or not. If its existence is necessitated (by itself), He is the Real One *per se* whose existence is necessary by itself and He is the Sustainer of all else. But if it is found not to be self-necessary, it cannot be said that it is *per se* impossible after it has been supposed to exist. Rather, if, along with considering it, another condition is added to it, namely, the condition that its cause does not exist, then it is impossible. Or, if the condition of the existence of its cause is added to it, then it becomes necessary. But if no condition is added to it, either of the existence or non-existence of its cause, then it is characterized by the third status which belongs to it *per se,* namely that it is possible (or contingent). Thus, when regarded in itself, it is neither necessary nor impossible. Thus every existent is either necessary by itself or possible (contingent) by itself.[3]

Statements like this are capable of being interpreted as a form of the ontological argument, particularly when we formulate the argument in terms of essence-existence dualism. The formulation would run like this. Every creature or contingent being, on examination, is found to be a composite of existence and an essence, an essence which is its native possession and an existence which comes to it from God. This dualism is the hallmark of the contingent. But the contingent cannot produce itself and cannot be endowed with existence by itself. Save for a being that has existence *per se,* and therefore has no dualism of essence and existence, no contingent could exist. This being, which has no essence and is pure existence, is God. In fact, His existence is His very essence.

But Ibn Sina also presents the above argument from necessary and contingent existence as a standard Aristotelian type of the cosmological argument. This argument states that all contingent existence must end up in a self-necessary, self-caused cause; otherwise, we will have only the last effect (in the present) and the middle chain of cause-effect, but no First Cause, and, therefore, no beginning.

On closer examination, the necessary-contingent and essence-existence argument of Ibn Sina reveals itself to be a reworking of the cosmological argument of Aristotle. Aristotle does not use the term 'Necessary Being', but after stating that the causal chain cannot go back *ad infinitum,* he simply and almost innocently says that therefore this chain must *necessarily* end up in a First Cause.

At this stage, it needs to be pointed out that the modern critiques of the cosmological argument appear to conceive causation in purely mechanical terms. This modern process begins with Descartes, who himself tended to reduce all reality to geometry. Neither Aristotle nor ancient and medieval philosophers—including Ibn Sina, of course—believed in a billiard ball concept of causation. Even the Stoics, who were materialists according to their own claims, believed that the nature of the process of the universe was characterized by *Sympatheia* rather than by a billiard ball impact. For Aristotle and for Ibn Sina—and, indeed, for ancient and medieval philosophy generally—the concept of teleological causation is as fundamental as that of efficient causation. For Aristotle, as for Ibn Sina, God is characterized by self-intelligibility of the highest order. Therefore, to criticize the cosmological argument on the ground that it arbitrarily selects or locates a certain point in the chain of causation and confers upon it the status of First Cause is to totally miss a fundamental point of this philosophy. (More will be given on the details of divine teleology below.)

In the meantime let us return to Ibn Sina. The philosopher tells us after all the proofs he has given for the existence of God, "It is now clear that the First (Being) has neither genus, nor essence, nor quality, nor quantity, nor place, nor time, nor a match, nor a partner, nor an opposite—exalted and great is He. He has no definition. *There is no argument to prove Him, rather, He is the proof for everything.* He can, however, be clearly pointed to by clear indication."[4] This quotation clearly shows that the "proofs" Ibn Sina has given are not strictly speaking proofs—for God is too manifest to be proved—but rather pointers to Him.

Since there are things, then, such that when we contemplate them *per se,* existence forms no essential part of them, there is the Being such that if we contemplate Him *per se,* His existence presents itself to be necessary. When existence thus proceeds from God, the Necessary Being, to other beings, its nature is necessarily ruptured, for it is no longer the original uncaused existence but is borrowed and derivative. This is contingent existence. Contingency is not the same as potentiality, for whereas the latter is destroyed by actual existence, the former continues simultaneously with actual existence. In other words, when the potential becomes actual, it no longer remains potential, but when the contingent actually exists it still remains contingent: even if it exists eternally it remains eternally contingent. In a striking passage, Ibn Sina brings out the difference between contingency and potentiality:

> If something is *per se* the cause of the eternal existence of something else, it is its eternal cause so long as its being persists. If then its existence is eternal, its effect will also be eternal. This kind of cause is most deserving of being called "cause" because it simply prevents absolute non-existence from taking over the effect and bestows perfect existence upon it. This kind of bringing into being the philosophers call *ibda,* which means the bringing into being of a thing after absolute non-existence. This is because the effect considered-in-itself is absolute non-existence while existence comes to it from its cause. Now, that which belongs to a thing-in-itself is prior for the mind essentially but not temporally to that which comes to it from something else. Hence every effect is posterior to its non-being where "posterior" is meant essentially (and not temporally). If, therefore, the term "originated" (*muhdath*) is applied to everything that gets its being (from its cause) after its non being (in itself)—even though "after" does not imply time—then every effect is originated. But if it is not applied in this way, but rather the condition of an originated thing is that it be preceded by a time which is destroyed by its arrival afterwards (i.e., temporally), then its "after" is something which cannot co-exist with its "before." The two must be different in their existence, since they are temporal "before" and "after"—then not all effects are "originated." Rather, the effect that is preceded by time must also be preceded by motion and change, as you know. But we do not quarrel about words. Now, the originated (effect) that does not involve time, either its existence is after an absolute non-existence (like the Transcendental Intelligences), or its existence is after a relative non-existence, that is, after a particular non-existence *in a particular matter,* as you know (like the celestial spheres). If its existence comes after an absolute non-existence, its emanation from the cause in this

> way is called *ibda* ("absolute origination"). This is the most excellent form of the bestowal of existence, for (in this case) non-existence has simply been prevented and existence has been given the sway *ab initio.* If, however, non-existence had found its way before its existence, then its bringing into being would have been impossible except through matter, and the power of creation—I mean the bringing into being of something from another—could have been exercised upon it only weakly, falteringly, and with a fresh start.[5]

This passage of Ibn Sina divides reality or being into a four-tiered hierarchy. First, there is the division between the Necessary Being, God, and the contingent beings. In the contingent, existence suffers a dislocation or a rupture. The contingent beings are of three categories. First are the Intelligences which are pure contingents; they are eternal but throughout their contingent existence, they remain contingent. Their emanation or creation is the best form of creation because they never suffered nonexistence. Next come the celestial spheres which have bodies, although made of ethereal rather than of earthly matter. Now, although celestial spheres are material, their matter did not precede their form like spatiotemporal things whose matter precedes their forms. They are, therefore, eternal. Unlike the Intelligences, they do move; but their motion is circular, which is the most perfect form of motion. Ibn Sina believes that the souls of the celestial spheres are "imprinted" in their bodies. Therefore they have imagination, which is a rational imagination like humans, but unlike humans their Intelligences lie "outside" of them. Thanks to their imagination (in contradistinction to reason), they perform particular movements which are, of course, not movements in locale as in the case of earthly bodies, but only movements in position. Finally, there is the sublunary or the spatiotemporal world where everything that comes into existence also passes away and is always preceded by potentiality and the carrier of that potentiality, that is, matter. Since this potentiality is limited, when the actualized has worked out its limited power it necessarily passes away. Although the power of the heavenly bodies is also limited, these do not face destruction because a "light" from God continues to feed them with ever-new power. This is thanks to the fact that they love God, perpetually move in His love (which constitutes their perpetual prayer to God), and also imitate God and want to become like Him.[6]

In light of this brief analysis, although we started from a four-tiered reality, it really turns out to be a three-tiered one, since Ibn Sina treats the Intelligences and the heavenly bodies as though they were on a par. The only difference is that the heavenly bodies have a motion whereas the Intelligences are motionless. The motion of the heavenly bodies, however, is derivative and follows from their love of God and their attempt to imitate Him.

Corresponding to these three ranks or levels of being, Ibn Sina distinguishes between three kinds of time: eternity (*sarmad*), eternality or perpetuity (*dahr*), and time (*zaman*). In his *Kitāb al-Taʿliqāt* Ibn Sina tells us:

> Reason perceives three kinds of being. One of them is being in time and that is the "when" of things that change and have a beginning and an end, their beginning being different from their end. Indeed, it is always passing away and is always in flow in a condition of lapse and renewal. The second is a being (not in time but) *with* time. This is called *dahr* or perpetuity or eternality; this sort of being encompasses time. Such is the being of the (highest) heaven *with* time, while time is contained within that being since time arises from the movement of the highest heaven. This (*dahr*) characterizes the relationship of the stable with the changing, except that our imagination cannot comprehend it because it tends to see everything as being in time and as a *process* of being consisting of "was" and "will be," that is, being in the past, present and future. It requires a "when" for all things, either past, present or future. The third kind of being is that of the relationship of the stable with the stable; this is called *sarmad* or eternity which contains *dahr* or eternality.[7]

We can see clearly from passages like this, which abound in Ibn Sina, that these three categories of time correspond exactly to the three types of existents that he has distinguished, namely, (1) the Necessary Being, God, (2) the higher contingent beings—the Intelligences and the spheres, and (3) beings that are ever in the temporal flow. He also affirms repeatedly that if there were no world of time, then *dahr* or eternality would not be there as separate from eternity but would be merely a part of eternity, since there would be no temporal flow and succession of moments. As things stand actually, however, eternality has to be sharply distinguished from eternity as that part of eternity which is related to the flux of time.

But at least as frequently, Ibn Sina also says that eternality has to be posited *per se* and in its own right, since it is caused by and contained in eternity just as time is caused by and contained in eternality.

In an earlier essay I attempted to explain Mir Damad's theory of "categorical origination" or absolute creation as a development from Ibn Sina and as conditioned by the development of essentialism in Islamic philosophy.[8] Here I compared and almost identified Ibn Sina's concept of *dahr* with Proclus' notion of "perpetual becoming."[9] There is a certain common factor between the two. Like Ibn Sina, Proclus places this perpetual becoming between eternity and time, and it seems certain that Proclus, for the most part, is thinking of the same sorts of entities as is Ibn Sina: heavenly bodies and time as a whole (and perhaps matter). But there are certain vital differences between the two as well. Perhaps the most important difference is that while Proclus places his "perpetual becoming" squarely *within* time, Ibn Sina explicitly and undoubtedly puts his *dahr* or eternality *beyond* time. This is why the term 'eternality' would translate *dahr* more accurately than the term 'perpetuality'. For Ibn Sina, indeed, *dahr* contains and even creates time just as it is itself contained and created by eternity. Again, while for Proclus perpetual becoming is diffuse since it is always becoming *in time,* Ibn Sina's eternality is not diffuse but, from this point of view, is just like eternity. Whence comes this difference between the two philosophers?

The difference appears to be caused by the sharply defined nature of contingency in Ibn Sina. As we said at the very outset, the concept of contingency is not to be found in thinkers before Ibn Sina. He formulated this concept to mark out God as unique from the rest of the realm of being. There had been, in pre-Islamic times, controversy over the question of the createdness versus the eternity of the world. Aristotle had claimed that he was the first philosopher to have proved the eternity or the "beginninglessness" of the world, since he had proved that motion could not have begun and must be eternal. This thesis, of course, raised a controversy. In the early sixth century C.E., John Philoponus wrote two works against the thesis of the eternity of the world, one against Aristotle and the other against Proclus.[10]

Now Aristotle has no concept of contingency as such, that is, of a being that is *contingent* upon a Necessary Being. Nor does Proclus have one. Neither of these had any interest in or motivation to formulate such a concept. John Philoponus, who was a Christian, does have a strong motivation to set the eternal God apart from a noneternal world and to assert the creation of the latter by the former. But he attempts to prove this by proving the finitude of the creature vis à vis the infinitude of the Creator, which argument is the mainstay of his thesis. Among the Muslim philosophers who inherited this controversy, al-Kindi takes after Philoponus and opts for creationism. For al-Farabi, the world is eternal. Al-Farabi seems to be unique among the Muslim philosophers in that, once he has proved a thesis rationally to his own satisfaction, he cares little for what the demands of the orthodox religion might be.

Ibn Sina is the first great Muslim philosopher who, while being a thoroughly faithful philosopher, cares deeply for what orthodox religion demands and tries to work out a systematic integration between the two. Ironically, just because he tried to synthesize philosophy and religion, he proved to be the *bête noire* of the orthodox, and al-Ghazālī, al-Razi, and other orthodox representatives choose *him* as their unique target, a representative *par excellence* of philosophy.

Ibn Sina could not philosophically accept the theory of temporal creation. But he was also convinced that religion and philosophy have common problems to solve, though their respective approaches to the solutions are different. Religion gives more popular solutions for the benefit of the masses, while philosophy gives intellectual solutions for the elect, solutions which are also embedded in revelation.[11] He thought, as I have said earlier, that although there can be no temporal gap between God and the world, there is surely a gap in the nature of being between the two, a sort of ontological hiatus or rupture which is expressed in the doctrine of necessity and contingency. God is uncaused, self-necessary, and in eternity; the Intelligences and the heavenly bodies are caused, dependent and contingent upon God, and in eternality. God is simple in every way and in all aspects, without any composition or parts whatever, whether parts of being or logical parts—that is, definition. The Intelligences are composites of two factors: a native nonexistence or contingency and necessity-through-God. Heavenly bodies are composites of three factors: contingency-in-themselves and necessity-through-God, form, and matter. Since their matter does not precede their actual existence, they are also in eternality like the Intelligences.

Ibn Sina offers many apologies in defending the eternal status of the heavenly bodies. First of all, their actual existence is not preceded by their matter as is the case with temporal things, which are in flux and which come into being and pass away. Secondly, their motion, unlike that of temporal things, is not inherent in them; it is incidental due to their love of God and their desire to become like Him as much as possible. They are not even aware of their motion for they are simply lost in the love of their Beloved. Finally, although unlike Intelligences they do move through love of God, He bestows continually renewed life and energy upon them whereby they are eternalized, even though *per se* they may not be eternal since they have matter.[12] It is only the sublunary existents which move and change because their actual being is preceded by matter, and because they have a transitory and diffuse existence. Strictly speaking, then, Ibn Sina should have recognized not three but four hierarchical types of existence and four types of time as well, since there seem to be certain drastic differences between the nature of the Intelligences and the hierarchical spheres, including the highest sphere. The Intelligences are fixed and immobile, while the heavens, although they move only in position and not in space, nevertheless do move. Further, although the eternal motion of the heavens occurs thanks to their constant reinvigoration of power injected by Divine Light, Intelligences do not need these injections for their eternal existence, though their dependence upon God is perpetual and they never become independent beings after their initial existence. Accordingly, Ibn Sina might have put God's existence in *sarmad* (eternity), that of the Intelligences in *dahr* (eternality), that of the heavens in *dawam* or *daimūma* (perpetuity), and that of the contents of the sublunary world in *zaman* (time).

To proceed with Ibn Sina's account of creation:

> We often know things that already exist in which case our knowledge is derived from what exists. But in some cases we know and conceive things first and then they come into existence after the pattern on which they were conceived, as a builder first conceives or knows a building and then builds it. Now, the nature of God's knowledge and its relationship to the existential world is of the latter type. The relationship of the entire field of existence to the First In-

> tellect who is necessary existence is such. He knows Himself and what His Self necessitates by way of His consequences, and He knows from Himself how the good in the entire existence proceeds. His intelligible form is then followed by the form of existence exactly (as it is) in the intelligible pattern that is with Him. This does not (mechanically) occur, as light proceeds from the source of light or heat flows from fire. Rather, He knows *how* the system of goodness should exist as a reality and *He knows that all this proceeds from Him.* He knows that His knowledge is such that from it proceeds (all) existence according to the plan which He knows to be a system of good.[13]

It must not be imagined that these intelligibles produce a plurality in God's being by constituting His various parts. First of all, these intelligibles are posterior to His being since God first contemplates His own being. This self-contemplation *is* His being, and His self-contemplation becomes the cause of His contemplating all other things *posterior to* His own being. Secondly, even as His contemplation of all other things is posterior to and caused by His self-contemplation, these other things are contemplated as a structured unity, not *seriatim* as a plurality. They are contemplated in an intellective (intuitive) manner and not in a discursive manner. Furthermore these intelligible forms are intellected as already being intelligible, not like those forms which first exist in matter and are then *rendered* intelligible by abstraction or in some other manner. If this were the case, they would not be intelligible all at once since each would become known to Him as it became available to Him through a process of abstraction.[14]

Now, let us see how we can conceive of the relationship of these intelligible forms to God.[15] If they were posited within His being, His being would become multiple and composite and could not remain a simple unity. If we conceive of them as being posterior to His essential being and concomitants of His being, then He could not remain the necessary being, since these forms, which are contingent, will be attached to Him as His posterior concomitants. If, thirdly, we assume these forms to be separate both from His being and from the being of any other being, and existing by themselves in an arranged and structured manner in the realm of His Lordship, then belief in Platonic forms will impose itself upon us. Finally, let us suppose that these forms exist in some Intelligence, so that whenever God contemplates them they become imprinted in that Intelligence or Mind. That Intelligence or Mind would, then, become a sort of substratum for these intelligible forms. They would thus be intelligible to this Intelligence or Mind in the sense that they are *in* it and they would be intelligible to God in the sense that they are *from* Him (i.e., caused by Him). God will know from within Himself that He is their cause (although they are not *in* His mind). Thus, among those intelligibles, there will be one which will be known to have been caused by God first and without any intermediary, that is, it will be the first to emanate from Him. Also, there will be among them one which will be known to have been caused by God secondarily and derivatively. And so their actual existence will be like their knowability and intelligibility, that is, *seriatim* and causally arranged one after another.

Let us now consider the situation of these intelligible forms. Since they are effects of God, they form part of what God perceives or knows Himself to be the cause or source of. We had previously said that when God knows or contemplates a good, it comes into actual existence. But as it now turns out from our present discussion, that proposition can no longer be held. For what we have now seen to proceed from God is not the actual existence of these intelligibles, but their being simply intelligibles because they have been caused by God to exist in an Intelligence or a Mind. Or, if we choose to call this existence of intelligibles in a Mind a real existence, then we will be caught in an infinite regress, because these so-called existents will be objects of further intellection *ad infinitum,* which is impossible. Thus, they must be regarded as His *intellection* of the good and not as real existents. We are saying here that when God contemplates them they come to exist (i.e., as intelligibles in Mind or Intelligence) and they are not liable to another higher-order intellection. Further, their real existence means no more than that they are intellections. This amounts to a statement to the effect that God intellected them and therefore He intellected them, or that they have emanated from Him and have therefore emanated from Him, which is, of course, absurd.[16]

The upshot of this entire discussion is that the alternative that relates God to a contingent is to be preferred to all other alternatives, and, above all, a multiplicity within God's being must be avoided. For God's being to come into a relationship with a contingent cannot be objectionable. What is objectionable is to introduce contingency into the very being of God, not to relate Him to a contingent. There is, after all, a difference between a form which is at first only potentially intelligible and then becomes actually intelligible, and one that is already intelligible, even though it be a contingent effect of God.[17]

In God, again, there is no separation between His knowledge, power, and will; all three are existentially identical. First of all, it is in us humans that power and will differ since our power is something potential until it is actualized as will. Actualized will is equivalent to an act. But in God there is nothing potential; all is actual. As for the identity of will with knowledge in God's case, this flows from the fact that His knowledge is absolutely perfect. In our case, there is a complicated process between the concept and the action, consisting of opposition, wish, will, and then setting the physical apparatus of nerves, muscles, etc., into motion to work on matter. In the case of God, however, His very intellection of a thing generates its creation and actual existence, and there is no gap between the two—although, as we have seen above, God's intellection of a thing and its actual flow from Him are not the same thing. The fact that God's creation of things presupposes His intellection of them is what constitutes His providence (*ᶜinaya*). If their existential procession from Him preceded His intellection of them, this would nullify this *ᶜinaya* and would also lead to an infinite regress of intellections on God's part. Yet the two are together, since, as was said before, God's knowledge is creative of things without any gap. Ibn Sina says:

> The fact that these forms existentially proceed from Him is His very knowledge of them and His knowledge that they necessarily proceed from Him is the source of their existential procession from Him; the fact that He knows Himself to be their source does not need a higher order or second intellection after His self-intellection.[18]

Again,

> The First (i.e., God) intellects Himself as He is *per se* and also that He is the originator of all existents as His necessary consequence with a simple, undifferentiated intellection. It is not the case that He first intellects Himself, and then intellects Himself to be the originator (or source) of existents in the second place, so that He intellects Him-

self twice. Rather, His intellection of the existents *is* their very existence proceeding from Him.[19]

This self-intellection of God, Ibn Sina calls the identity of the intellector and the intellected *par excellence,* since the objects of His intellection are not extrinsic but intrinsic to Him. In our case, on the other hand, the objects of our intellection still keep something of their extrinsic character and therefore can never be completely identified with the subject so long as we remain in our body.

Why does God create?[20] "Because of His sheer generosity (*jūd*)," answers Ibn Sina. To describe the nature of the creative activity of God, we are in need of a term which is well-nigh impossible to find in human vocabulary. The reason is that whatever we humans do has a certain extrinsic motivation such that the effects of our action redound to us with some benefit for us. We mostly do things for some sort of gain, whether material or nonmaterial. But this is unthinkable in the case of God, since He is already absolutely perfect and hence cannot create for any gain. His activity is purposive, but His purpose cannot be to remedy any deficiency in Himself. His purpose must be intrinsic and not extrinsic, as for example, to benefit His creatures. His creatures do, indeed, benefit from Him, and this is why we have used the term 'generosity' for His creative activity. But this term must not imply either that He needs someone to be generous to or that He gets back something from His generosity. The common person applies the word 'generosity' to describe the activity of a benefactor who expects no benefit in return. Hence Ibn Sina uses the word 'generosity', although most generous persons do benefit in some sense from their generosity, for example, the praise of their beneficiaries or at least the satisfaction and pleasure they themselves derive from their own act of generosity. It is, indeed, in the very nature of God to create and to give generously, provided that from the use of the word 'nature' here we do not understand anything like the nature of natural objects. For example, it is the nature of fire to burn, but fire burns without thought and volition, while, as we have shown earlier, God works through knowledge and volition which, in the case of God, are identical and do not imply a mental-physical process.

Since it is in the very nature of God to be generous and to create, His creation must be eternal. For if He did not create from eternity, this would mean that He withheld His unimpeded generosity and hence was the opposite of "generous." The theory of the eternity of the world is the hallmark of all Muslim philosophers except al-Kindi, while all theologians in Islam are voluntarists and place their entire weight on the side of God's power and will. Ibn Sina in his *Topics* states that the problem of the eternity versus the temporal origin of the world is disputable and neither side of the issue can be demonstrably established. But in his *Metaphysics* and in all his philosophical works, he is clearly and decidedly on the side of the eternity of the world, calling theologians "weak-minded people." This theory of contingency, one which creates an irreparable gap in the nature of being, if not in time, is his way of doing justice to what he perceives to be the genuine demand of religion. His formulation of the concept of contingency, with the allied doctrine of the distinction between essence and existence, had a far-reaching and durable impact on both later Islamic philosophy and medieval Latin thought.

NOTES

1. The concept of contingency (*imkan zati*) in this sense does not seem to exist even in al-Farabi, not to speak of earlier philosophers, including Greek and Christian.
2. Quoted in Mulla Sadra's *al-Asfar al-Arba'a* 1.1, p. 66 (also p. 46).
3. *Kitab al-Isharat* (Istanbul, 1290/1873), p. 197.
4. *Kitab al-Shifa* (Cairo, 1960), vol. 2, p. 354.
5. Ibid., p. 266, line 9–p. 267, line 9.
6. Ibid., p. 389, line 4ff.
7. Quoted in Muhammad Baqir Miz Damadi, *Kitab al- Qalasat* (Tehran, 1977), p. 7, lines 10–17.
8. Fazlur Rahman, "Mir Damad's Concept of Huduth Dahri," *Journal of Near Eastern Studies* 39 (1980): pp. 139–53.
9. Ibid., p. 140.
10. The one against Aristotle seems lost in Greek, but certain excerpts survive in Arabic while the one against Proclus has been published under the title *De aeternitate mundi contra Proclum,* ed. H. Rabe (Leipzig, 1899).
11. See Fazlur Rahman, *Prophecy in Islam: Philosophy and Orthodoxy* (Chicago: University of Chicago Press [reprint], 1979), chap. 2, sec. 2, "Imaginative Revelation."
12. See note 6 above.
13. *Kitab al-Shifa,* p. 363, lines 5–13.

14. Ibid., p. 364, lines 1–6.
15. Ibid., p. 364, line 16; p. 365, line 13.
16. Ibid., p. 366, lines 1ff.
17. See Mulla-Sadra, *al-Asfar al-Arba'a* 3, 1, p. 215, lines 4–6.
18. Ibid., lines 11–13.
19. Ibid., lines 14–16.
20. *Kitab al-Shifa,* vol. 2, pp. 296–98.

PART II

Philosophical Developments and Divergent Theologies

While this section treats each religious tradition in turn, the common concerns of each emerge quite clearly, even if the philosophical problematic may differ from one tradition to another, as the representative thinkers were responding to specific cultural contexts. So the potential for mutual illumination becomes clear to the reader, as it certainly did for the participants who were invited to see in the approaches developed in other traditions complements to their own. It seemed best, however, first to establish the roots of the medieval discussion in the Neoplatonism of the Hellenic period, in which a philosophical monotheism seemed to offer a congenial backdrop for Jewish and Christian philosophical theologians. John Peter Kenney divides the responses of these thinkers into two sorts: demiurgic and nondemiurgic, where the latter would favor a more intellectual emanation scheme rooted in divine ideas. This division, he reminds us, can also be noted in contemporary reflection on the relation of God to the world.

Under the rubric of Judaism, Lenn Evan Goodman shows how Islamic and Jewish thinkers conspired to highlight three dimensions of creation: the contingency of the universe, its eminent design, and its newness of inherent vitality. He then proceeds to suggest how each of these might be understood in our intellectual climate. Tamar Rudavsky elucidates the views of both Moses ben Maimon (Maimonides: 1135–1204) and Levi ben Gershom (Gersonides: 1288–1344) on the central issue: creation and time. While Maimonides' own position on this matter is notoriously difficult to pin down, Gersonides can serve as a useful point of comparison with Christian and Islamic thinkers, and brings a refreshing clarity to the issues. Finally, David Blumenthal essays a current Jewish mode of reflection, which embodies a response to Auschwitz and seeks to root the keen sense of land proper to Judaism in the sovereign will of a creator God.

The first two Christian treatments present divergent patterns for creation. Robert Sokolowski offers a "Christian understanding" explicitly beholden to Aquinas, focusing on a clear "distinction" between God and creatures, while his proposal for a "theology of disclosure" engages the Christian Neoplatonists as well. In more historical fashion, Bernard McGinn suggests a model for understanding creation that tries to show how "emanationist" Christian theologians, such as John the Scot and Meister Eckhart, were anxious to uphold the same values defended by Thomas Aquinas and his followers. Langdon Gilkey, in turn, reprises the doctrine of creation in its classical philosophical setting, suggesting some crucial revisions in that way of expressing the relation of creation to its Creator, so as to leave "'room' of some sort 'alongside' its Creator," reminiscent of the kabbalist teaching of *tsimtsum.*

Eric Ormsby initiates the Islamic section, rooting his exposition in the intellectual journey of the central Muslim religious thinker, al-Ghazālī, who came to a keen appreciation of "the unalterable justice and excellence of things as they are . . . , the perfect rightness of the actual." That intuition followed upon the conviction that actual existence comes forth from the free creative act of God, which lends a poignancy to his sense of contingency. Jane Dammen McAuliffe essays a Muslim understanding of God as Creator in the works of the classical Qur'ān commentator, Fakr al-Dīn al-Rāzī. She notes how his grasp of creation readily translates into an effective mode of worship: the believer's response to so understanding the origin of the universe. Finally, Azim Nanji explores the transcendence/immanence tension with Ismā'īlī thought, which sought to combine an emanation scheme with a sturdy affirmation of God's unique nature, embodied in the classical Islamic notion of *tawhid* (the utter oneness of God).

The actual work of the conference embodied a lively interaction with commentators as each paper was presented for discussion. We have not attempted to characterize that exchange in highlighting the papers themselves, but the comments are as substantive as the essays they critique, and the chapters which appear here have been altered subsequently to accommodate and incorporate some of that dialogue. It is our hope that this mode of interaction will help to establish a paradigm for current attempts to understand issues in philosophical theology whose roots demand the perspective of more than one faith tradition.

Theism and Divine Production in Ancient Realist Theology

John Peter Kenney

Realist theology is rich in its ancient lineage. The theological significance of forms or abstract objects has long been a central issue in Western philosophical theology,[1] with many distinct traditions of monotheism fundamentally grounded upon the notion of an "intelligible world." What I should like to do in this paper is inquire into the incipience of philosophical monotheism and examine several early theories of divine production with their joint realist assumptions explicitly in view.

I have several reasons, both of principle and expediency, for this approach. Chief among them is the hope, tinged perhaps with lingering historicism, that such an investigation may help to clarify the theoretic force which initially obtained behind that theological divergence which we now conventionally discuss by resort to the terms 'creation' and 'emanation'. This seems to be a modest, historical intention; but there can be more involved than just conceptual reclamation. Ontological dependence has always been, and indeed remains, central to the philosophical articulation of monotheistic belief. As such its framing is a fundamental issue across the Western religious spectrum, one which at once divides and conjoins us along philosophical lines often quite distinct from the anticipated confessional ones. Here we own not only to a common problem of conceptual self-definition, but to a set of historically related solutions, each with its own trajectory across the established boundaries of the religious traditions themselves. While this situation should provide historians of religion with much upon which to reflect, its implications for us as students of philosophical theology seem especially important. By returning to the history of our discipline, we can not only recover a once shared discourse, but enrich our understanding of the resources of Western monotheism. It is only when the variegated richness of our theistic patrimony has been restored to contemporary view that the task of assessing its coherence can begin in earnest. My remarks are thus grounded in the conviction that ancient and medieval theism warrant more than just antiquarian interest and that contemporary philosophical theology can profit from this enriched appraisal of its historical antecedents.

I propose then to look into the early development of philosophical monotheism in Hellenistic Jewish, early Christian, and Greco-Roman theology. I want to focus upon a few selected features of this thought in the period before the discussion of divine production hardened into the familiar 'creation-emanation' rubric. This tack may seem somewhat unusual, but if so it is at least eccentrism in the service of a certain stratagem, one which may help to exhibit some important dimensions of the issue. By concentrating upon figures from Philo of Alexandria through Plotinus, we can at least confer upon the thought of these early theists a certain autonomy which it otherwise often lacks, given our prevailing tendency to assimilate their ideas to those of later philosophers or to retroject this subsequent discussion into late antiquity. My plan is to begin (1) with several edicts on terminology and some historical observations on the development of early monotheism; turning then (2) to a review of the salient approaches to the problem of divine production, with particular attention to the foundations of "emanationism"; and finally concluding (3) with some abbreviated remarks on the significance of these early positions for contemporary philosophical theology, in light of the restoration of realism in Anglo-American metaphysics.

1. MONOTHEISM: HELLENIC AND ABRAHAMIC

Theism is a promiscuous concept, indiscriminate in reference but frequent in use. The same might also be said about many other concepts of deity, for example, pantheism or monism.[2] Their employment is often vague and even pejorative: when they are encountered, I am sometimes reminded of the perhaps apocryphal saying attributed to Dean Inge: "Any stigma is good enough to beat a dogma." If we are to make responsible use of such terminology, some initial stipulation seems necessary.

Theism and monotheism are usually used interchangeably within philosophical theology to denote ontological commitment to one ultimate divine principle, transcendent of the physical universe. By contrast, polytheism might be taken as the endorsement of multiple divine principles.[3] Monotheism is subject, of course, to considerable variation of this core thesis, and care must be taken to avoid premature determination of its implications based upon cultural habituation and religious precedence. To assert that there is one ultimate divine principle is to stake a claim about the structure of reality while leaving much unsaid. A key issue is the sense of oneness involved. On a numerical reading, this core thesis would be taken as endorsing the uniqueness of the divine principle: there is a single deity; the class of divine beings has only one member. This is the dominant thrust of what might be called "exclusive monotheism," with its emphasis upon the uniqueness of the deity. So successful has this approach been that we assume this reading and neglect another conceptually possible way to construe this monotheistic thesis, one which turns on a qualitative understanding of oneness. On this account, monotheism would be principally concerned to support a final or ultimate divine unity behind, but distinct from, the world. This unity might be thought of as a special type of reality different from and superior to all others. It would be seen as a unique type of being, rather than a unique being. It would thus not be initially envisioned as a numerically single principle. There is, then, in this qualitative monotheism a final divine unity beyond the multiplicity of the world, a deeper nature behind the physical universe. Divinity seems thus to be the final inclusive unity behind the manifest image of the world's plurality, the ultimate completeness which transcends but resolves its fractured multiplicity. I shall refer to this approach, which emphasizes divine primordiality, completeness, and ultimacy, as "inclusive monotheism."

In noting these abstract, logically possible versions of monotheism, I should hasten to add that they have often been closely interrelated in the philosophical articulation of theism and this is probably because, taken discretely, there seems to be something incomplete about each reading. Exclusive monotheism has the burden not only of articulating the fact that there is one deity, but of explaining why this is so. This type of monotheism would not intend an endorsement of an accidentally unique being: that there happens to be just one God seems not to be its real point. Exclusive monotheism needs, therefore, to explain the numerical uniqueness of the deity and to indicate that the nature of divinity is such that there can be of necessity only one such instance. There is thus some considerable conceptual pressure within exclusive monotheism to develop an account of the nature of divinity construed in a qualitative way. The object is to exhibit the special character of divinity and its unique position in reality, such that the fact of a single deity excluding all others seems to follow conceptually. Inclusive monotheism has, on the other hand, the problem of explaining what the nature of this special underlying quality is. How is this transcendental substance, divinity itself, to be represented? The qualitative uniqueness of divinity is thus in question, and so there is a need for a theoretical discussion of the unique type of being which God is.[4] These two readings thus tend to dovetail and so knit together these conceptually distinct approaches to monotheism. Nonetheless, one can discern in certain theological traditions a disposition toward one or the other version of monotheism, and so we should be alert to these conceptually possible approaches as we begin to review the historical record.

Before taking up the historical project, we need to recognize that, like all philosophically developed concepts of deity, monotheism of whatever sort is not suspended free from a cluster of ontological assumptions; and these are usually so deeply embedded as to be barely separable conceptually from the core monotheistic thesis. This is especially true of the notion of divine production. It might be possible to construe either exclusive or inclusive monotheism as being neutral on the question of ontological generation or derivation. On this view the transcendent divine principle would be just another constituent, albeit a preeminent one, within the inventory of reality. It might be claimed alternatively that God is a unique entity distinct from all others, or that the divine is a special property unlike any other. One would simply prescind from any notion of ontological derivation, so that God would not be an answer to any questions regarding the ontological basis for other sorts of things. Now this is an admittedly odd way to try to think about monotheism, counterintuitive because of our ingrained disposition to conjoin theism with some theory of ontological derivation for the universe. There may be more in this conceptual strangeness, though, than mere habit. Given the conceptual pressure just noted to account for either divine numerical or qualitative uniqueness, there is a clear benefit to be accrued for monotheism by setting the divine principle apart from all reality, as its unique source or ground. By settling upon the divine principle the role of an ontological power which generates all consequent beings, its special status can be more readily construed. As the necessary and suffcient condition of all subsequent beings, the divine first principle can be considered to be numerically unique by position, or distinctive in character because it functions as the unitary source for the universe. This seems to be one important reason behind the tendency for monotheism of whatever sort to include the articulation of an ontological derivation thesis. The drafting of this crucial codicil to monotheism occupied most of the early theists whom I shall be reviewing presently.

I should like now to provide this quite speculative and deliberately abstract discussion with a more historical dimension, making a connection with ancient theological tradition in a manner which is probably already suspected. I have suggested that there are two primary ways to understand monotheism, although any adequate philosophical articulation of one is likely to involve the other. Representation of the numerical uniqueness of God in exclusive monotheism seems to require conceptually some clarification of the special character of such an entity, while the characterization of the unique nature of divinity itself in inclusive monotheism draws in singularity when the finality, ultimacy, and completeness of the divine fundament is explicated. In the former case, exclusivity is vouchsafed by the nature of God; in the latter, the ultimate character of the One merges into its singularity. What we can only separate logically by the attenuation of such theological concepts can hardly be expected to emerge with typological clarity in the history of religious thought. This expectation is not disappointed in the messy business which is the history even of philosophical theology. And yet, as I shall argue, I do think that we can identify a certain preponderance of interest in the more exclusivistic understanding of monotheism within early Jewish and Christian metaphysics, emerging as they did from reflection upon a deposit of scripture in which the numerical singularity and exclusivity of the deity seems especially fixed in the religious imagination. The development of early theories of divine production within these traditions was deeply influenced by the force of such a reading; that will emerge, I expect, as we turn to review the Alexandrians. This process of conceptual clarification within Judaism and Christianity was intimately related to what I think we must see as a different monotheistic tradition, inclusive in its characteristic mode of theological reflection, accepting of the continuation of polytheistic cult, but grounded as well in a developing philosophical understanding of an ultimate divine One. It is the distinctive "Hellenic monotheism" of Greco-Roman philosophical theology and its conceptions of divine production which must be understood in order for us to assess adequately the notion of creation in the emergent Jewish and Christian schools.

I have attempted to make the case for such an analysis of Greco-Roman philosophical theology in late antiquity elsewhere and it cannot be reiterated here; a few points might be summarized for our purposes.[5] Hellenic monotheism was a theology which evolved from spiritual reflection upon the obscure divine fundament behind the surface tale of polytheism. This later monotheism was continuous with elements of ancient cultic polytheism, so that it arrived at an account of divinity that was not exclusive of divine plurality in religious observance or in the interpretation of experience. It sought not to rend the august fabric of ancient cultic polytheism but to revise it, and to shift the focus of its emphasis. It was the ultimate ground of divine unity that mattered to Hellenic monotheists, a unity that could admit of multiple manifestations as proof of its efficacy and primordiality. Hellenic monotheism was thus a theology of divine ultimacy. Throughout this tradition in late antiquity, the gods were not rejected. They were, however, superseded in philosophical theology as interest was focused upon that absolute and transcendent principle into whose fecund unity all gods and divine powers could be resolved, for they were its manifestations at derivative levels of reality. Yet this theology represents a type of inclusive monotheism, for it seems to have been endemically modalistic, ever willing to consider all divine powers as modes of this ultimate divine One. If one is prepared to countenance a broader, inclusive conception of monotheism, then there seems no reason to deny that the Hellenic tradition in philosophical theology which culminates in Neoplatonism was monotheistic. The One of Plotinus is the final divine unity, not so much numerically unique in an exclusivistic sense as distinctive for its position as the ultimate source of all reality. The Plotinian One was single by virtue of its systematic position: the notion of ultimate simplicity as the ontological root of all reality is not an idea which admits of plurality.

We hear the "dead remembered footsteps" of the late antique Hellenes whenever God is represented as the primordial divine One in philosophical theology. It was their inclusive monotheism which first sought to clarify the unique character of divinity as such, for theirs was a legacy of theological discussion based upon notions such as divine being, substance, pure actuality, and absolute simplicity. As such they are co-conspirators in our seminar, a monotheistic tradition lost but for its subsequent absorption into the Abrahamic world. It was their theoretical understanding of divinity which qualified—one might even say tempered—the more exclusive sort of monotheism, providing it with a philosophical vocabulary and an account of divine primordiality. This complex story lies outside my domain, but our understanding of this history, and indeed our appraisal of its contemporary theological outcome, are both critically influenced by how we understand the beginning of the tale.

My experimental suggestion here is that we attempt to think of the early history of Western philosophical monotheism, neither as its progressive emancipation from pagan philosophical polytheism nor as an initially flawed project fraught by the constraints of an essentially polytheistic metaphysics, but rather as the concurrent development of two different types of monotheism, alike in dignity. The Hellenic and the Abrahamic traditions, though clearly distinct in religious origins, culture, and cult, ought to be seen as manifestly related both in their accepted philosophical sources in classical metaphysics and in their parallel efforts to articulate monotheism philosophically. It is on the basis of this revisionist model of the development of ancient philosophical monotheism that I now propose to examine some aspects of the notion of divine production.

2. DIVINE PRODUCTION IN ANCIENT REALIST THEOLOGY

The early development of Western philosophical monotheism owes much to the various Platonic schools of the late Hellenistic and Roman periods, for it is this later Platonism, itself the selective heir of several types of metaphysics, which predominated at the incipience of theistic philosophy. I should like, therefore, to examine some ways in which divine production was understood within this ancient realist theology. Because I am especially interested in exhibiting the discussion which led up to Plotinus' proposal of his theory of emanation, I will be concentrating upon only a few selected features of ancient Platonic theology. This intended focus necessitates my leaving aside two particularly pressing issues: the cosmological debate about the temporal beginning of the physical universe and the especially complicated problem of the preexistence of matter. Suffice it to say that both issues are crucially important, although both are treated by the Hellenes and their Jewish and Christian interlocutors in ways which resist neat divisions along party lines. For example, while most pagan Platonists treated Plato's *Timaeus* as endorsing divine temporal production only for heuristic purposes, some such as Plutarch and Atticus read the dialogue literally.[6] Philo was, of course, much taken (for once) with such a literal account, but he was also far from clear in his position on preexisting matter.[7] Given my remarks on Greco-Roman monotheism in late antiquity, the gradual revision of two opposite principle theories of metaphysics among Platonists and the consequent withering of *hyle* seem apposite topics. I might simply note that most sorts of monotheism by late antiquity endorsed ontological derivation theories which led back to a final divine principle, so that matter became just an abstract pole representative of disorder.[8] On the shared assumptions of Platonic hierarchical ontology, this amounted to a surdal presence, the meontic direction of randomness toward which souls flee as they move away from the Good. Intriguing as this subject is, I want to concentrate on an issue at the other end, as it were, of the ontological hierarchy, one which proved more recalcitrant to general agreement: the relationship of the forms to the deity. Is being itself distinct from God, or ontologically dependent upon God, and if the latter, is the divine will involved in this production?

For late antique realists, a principal desideratum in the monotheist agenda was clarifying the ontological relation between the first principle and the intelligible world. This was a question most pressing in its implications, for the world of being, the forms, were the archetypal foundations of all phenomenal reality and the reference points of all epistemic certainty. We need to reflect for a moment on this ancient realism and its implications in philosophical theology, shedding our natural nominalism and overcoming our academic inoculation to mulling Platonism over yet again. Now, the essential foundation of realist theology is "degree of reality" metaphysics and its postulation of a realm of being. Realist theology entails countenancing the existence of entities separate and superior in their nature and power in relation to those of this world. This commitment to a hierarchical, "degree of reality" ontology[9] clearly distinguishes such theology from those founded upon a weaker, "type of reality" thesis, which might accept such entities only as comprising a distinct ontological category, but certainly not as constituting a superior one. Realist theology is centered, then, upon formal objects which are ontologically superior and which have a greater share of 'being', a claim usually construed as meaning that they are both distinct from the world and free from change and the temporality which follows upon it. Involved as well is a theory of causality, since these ontologically more significant entities are thought to be at least necessary causes for their lower level constituents, which have existence to the extent that they share in the forms. In short, traditional realist theology rests upon selected elements from the metaphysics of Plato's middle period dialogues.[10] We should note, however, that endorsement of a degree of reality thesis does not require the view that these entities be logical universals:[11] while this was often an important feature of later Platonic theology, it is not a necessary one, as discussion of forms of individuals in the school of Plotinus indicates.[12] Neither does realist theology restrict acceptance of forms exclusively to those which are paradigms of value; while not a common position, admission of forms of disvalue remains conceptually open, as both Plato's discussion in the *Parmenides*[13] and Professor Findlay's recent Gifford lectures indicate.[14] Despite these qualifications, it should be clear that acceptance of realism in theology is, and has always been, grounded in a fundamental intuition: that there exists a transcendent world of principles or powers which are the changeless, autonomous, and wholly real foundations for our lower world.

With this abbreviated summary of the constitutive features of ancient realist theology, we can now turn our attention to the development of theories on the relationship of the intelligible world to the principle of divinity. I will identify three basic positions held by pagan

Platonists prior to Plotinus, considering as well how Jewish and Christian thinkers developed their own positions over against these options. While nothing but a sketch can be provided, this will provide some sense of the basic difference involved and establish a context for understanding the theory of Plotinus. The three positions in question are: (a) the demiurgic theology of Philo and the earlier Middle Platonists, (b) the nondemiurgic theology of late Middle Platonism, and (c) the exemplarism of Athenian Middle Platonism.[15]

a. Demiurgic theology

One basic strategy available to ancient Platonists, concerned to explain the origins of the forms or to find some unifying basis for them, was to treat them as ideas in the mind of the demiurge. This approach, derived by creative exegesis of the *Timaeus,* is markedly different from that attributed to Plato by Aristotle,[16] but it was widely accepted in the late Hellenistic period. It maintained that forms were the products of a divine mind, and thus were intradeical principles.[17] While antecedents of this famous divine ideas doctrine might be traced back to Antiochus or even Xenocrates,[18] the position emerges unambiguously in Plutarch, who refers to the ideas as "the thoughts and mental representations of God."[19] With the forms thus firmly identified as intradeical thoughts, God may be considered as himself the paradigm of all things.[20] Probably this identification of the forms with the divine mind had as its polemical intent the strengthening of divine transcendence against Stoicism. It may also have been the result of long established scholastic traditions of *Timaeus* exegesis, or of a philosophical desire for a more conceptually economic approach to the rather diffuse theology of that dialogue. In any case its systematic result was in fact the conjunction of elements kept distinct in the *Timaeus:* the demiurgic intellect and the formal paradigm.[21]

The problem with such conceptualism in early Middle Platonism was the ambiguity involved in this relation of demiurge to ideas, specifically the possibility of subordinating the ideas to divine intentionality. The issue can be seen in Philo, who shows evidence of adopting a conceptualist position, although there are some ambiguities in his writings on the question.[22] It is certain that he used the image of a craftsman's thoughts to describe the ideas within the divine mind,[23] and he also treats the ideas as being generated through this intellection.[24] The dependence of forms upon the divine mind implicit in the intradeical, divine ideas doctrine is thereby made obvious, with these ideas becoming subordinate to divine *noēsis.* While final and detailed specification of Philo's position lies outside my scope, one point is apposite: the divine ideas doctrine had within it the possibility of the abrogation of much of the point of realist theology. Since Philo did not describe the divine ideas with the Platonic ascription "really real," nor as "ungenerated," it is possible to consider forms in his theology to be merely instrumental projections of the divine mind in its productive function. Should the demiurgic aspects of this conceptualism be pressed, then the ideas would cease to obtain as the autonomous and supremely real principles which realist theology takes them to be. To the extent that this implication of conceptualism is emphasized, the force of realist theology is displaced.

The upshot of Philo's position for our purpose should be clear: Philo's tendency is to adapt the divine ideas doctrine such that the line of ontological dependence between the intelligible world and the divine mind is much clearer. Thereby is the deity established with special clarity, not only as the ontological source for true being, but as a distinct and separate power of greater consequence. The imagery implies a numerically single deity, a mind which is not just the collective locus of the forms, but the unique power which produces and sustains these archetypes through the force of its intellection. We must be careful, I admit, not to overinterpret Philo; he is not an especially systematic writer nor is this point of contrast with pagan Platonism one which can be pressed given the extreme paucity of our evidence for the philosophical theology of the period. Nevertheless the deity in Philo's Platonism has a character whose portrait seems distinctive in terms of its intellective production of the intelligible world.

b. Nondemiurgic theology

Besides these demiurgic versions, there is a nondemiurgic position to be found in the later Middle Platonism of the second and third centuries. While founded upon the divine ideas doctrine and so formally conceptualist, this theology revised considerably the analysis of divine intellection and its relation to the ideas, due in part to the influence of Aristotelianism.[25] The evidence for this development is found in Albinus[26] and in Numenius; for the sake of brevity I will concentrate upon Albinus. Now as we would expect, a form is, according to Albinus, a divine thought: "In relation to God, the idea is his thought."[27] So settled has this conceptualist thesis become that he offers a proof of the existence of ideas based upon it.[28] God is, he says, either mind or a being with a mind, and such a being must have eternal and unchanging thought; thus the ideas exist. It is interesting to note parenthetically that Albinus' version of realist theology is in consequence one which emphasizes divine ideas of only a limited sort, for he follows Xenocrates' restrictive definition of an idea as "an eternal paradigm of natural things."[29] The central point concerns his careful elucidation of the relation of ideas to the divine mind. The first principle of his theology is a mind in actuality which is motionless and self-directed, and is thus nondemiurgic. Albinus thus clarifies the nature of this first divinity's self-contemplation through the use of the divine ideas doctrine: in thinking himself, God eternally thinks the ideas.[30]

This type of conceptualism differs significantly from that just reviewed. In this case the ideas are clearly treated as constitutive features of the highest God's own essential nature; they are eternal principles which are the actualization of his own eternal activity. The very nature of the forms, and so of reality itself, is the eternal and immutable product of the inherent intellection of God, and as such is not based upon the instrumental intention of a demiurge. Rather, the ideas are the divine nature itself. I do not think that we would extend this position too far if we were to rephrase it by saying that the notions of divine intellection and the ideas mutually entailed one another in this theology. If this is an accurate portrayal then it should be clear that Albinus' theology has gone to considerable lengths to safeguard the structure of being. Being and divine intellection are, in effect, correlative concepts, inextricably bound up with each other, so that neither can be made subordinate in theological significance to the other. The type of nondemiurgic theology represented by Albinus makes, therefore, an important advance in Platonic theology by insuring against any subversion of the central intuitions of this tradition.[31]

We should note how this type of theology establishes the divine mind as a collective unity, a fundamental power whose essential nature is involved in self-reflection; one consequence of this self-thought is the aspectual plurality of the intelligible world. The richness of the intelligible world, and so ultimately of all lower levels of reality, is based upon the essential nature and function of divinity itself, and it is into that intellective unity that plurality is seen as being ultimately resolved. It is this type of reflection upon the character of divinity and this effort to identify philosophically a final unity which I would see as part of the developing, inclusive monotheism of the Hellenic tradition, although I hasten to add that these Middle Platonists have not jettisoned a materiate principle. At least with respect to the ontological foundations of the intelligible world, these nondemiurgic Platonists were sharply different from those who adopted a demiurgic model, and especially so from Philo. Forms are dependent ontologically upon the divine mind, but this intellection is freed even from the possibility of volition or selection. The production of being itself is a function of the divine essence, its self-articulation. The active demiurgic function is then precipitated down to a lower level, to a second divine principle which is constrained as in the *Timaeus,* to look to the independent forms, now knit into the nature of the first divine principle. I cannot pursue the whole ramified theory of the production of subsequent levels, but I want to underscore the implications of this position for the intelligible world, since it is the starting point for Plotinus.

c. *Exemplarism*

The other major type of Middle Platonist theology which warrants brief review is the exemplarism of Atticus and the Athenian school. Unlike the sorts of conceptualism we have examined thus far, the point of exemplarism is the separation of divine intellect from the forms; the *Timaeus* theology is the principal and most thorough example. While the evidence suggests a continued tendency throughout later Middle Platonism to retain the terminology of conceptualism,[32] some figures, notably Atticus and Longinus, seem to have returned to a modified version of the *Timaeus* model. It is this position which was debated in the Plotinian school according to Porphyry,[33] further evidence of which may be found in *Ennead* 5.5. According to this modified exemplarism, the divine intellect must be treated as the first principle of all reality, while the forms exist at a separate but lower level.[34] Forms are thus extradeical, in this sense that they are outside the supreme deity and distinct from it; indeed, Porphyry cricitized Atticus for this very sense of pronounced separation.[35] One can, I think, understand the attraction of this exemplarist position to some Platonists, especially because it avoided the internal plurality of elements within the first principle which may result in a conceptualist system. From the evaluative standpoint I have been developing, it should be clear that, while not ontologically primary, the forms are certainly treated as the autonomous principles which realist theology requires. Distinct from the divine intellect, the forms remain as the immutable divine paradigms for becoming, and so the central insight of realist theology is assured. Such exemplarism represents, therefore, an important possible solution to the problem of the intellect-forms relation in Platonist theology. On the other hand it is also an odd piece of Platonist traditionalism, rooted in the loosely textured theology of the *Timaeus*. While it may have indeed been an effort to restore a certain simplicity to the divine *nous,* now freed from the plurality of the ideas, it may have done so at some possible expense. It was certainly not part of the monotheistic tendency in Hellenic philosophical theology; indeed, it became the target, as we shall see, of Plotinus on this very point. For the contemporary motto of the Plotinian school will be: "that the intelligibles are not outside the intellect."[36]

I wish it were possible to go beyond this limited conceptual analysis of these versions of Middle Platonism and to show that the nondemiurgic conceptualism of Albinus, or the exemplarism of Atticus, was the result of a conscious rejection of earlier, demiurgic versions of the divine ideas doctrine. The fragmentary state of our evidence makes this impossible at present. I do hope, however, to have indicated that the Middle Platonists did develop positions of genuine systematic significance for philosophical theology, and their thought, when examined from a certain perspective, is indicative of serious reflection upon inherent problems in the Platonic legacy. While the Middle Platonists will doubtless continue to be of interest largely because of their historical influence, we should not allow this fact to obscure the fundamental issues which were being addressed by these figures, who have now all but slipped below the level of history.

Alexandrian Christian Platonism

It is against this complex background that the Christian Platonists of Alexandria must be interpreted. As in Philo, the doctrine of the production of the Logos is directly conjoined with the divine ideas thesis, and once again the problem of its interpretation is central. The doctrine of the divine mind as the "place of the ideas" shows up several times in Clement.[37] The key problem is how this thesis is understood with respect to the activity of intellection. Scholarship on the theory of the Logos in Clement has been focused for some time on the problem of how many stages can be identified in its generation. The alternatives are: (a) a double-stage theory, such that forms within the divine mind are identical with the Logos, which thereafter is projected and becomes a principle inherent within the phenomenal world, and (b) a triple-stage thesis, such that forms are initially within God's reason, but are then generated as a distinct composite being, the Logos, and finally inhere at the phenomenal level of reality.[38] The matter is further complicated by the efforts of Wolfson to construct a similar three-stage theory in Philo,[39] upon which Clement would depend.

Several points seem apposite: While I must confess skepticism in the case of Philo, a three-stage theory seems to me likely in the case of Clement, especially in view of similar theories in Middle Platonists of the second century, e.g., Albinus or Numenius. But for our purposes it is much more important to determine whether Clement viewed the ideas, at whichever level they are located, as produced by the intellection of the Father. Here, as in Philo, Clement seems inclined to treat the intelligibles instrumentally, produced by God for use in a second act of generation, that of the physical world.[40] Clement thus follows Philo in treating the Logos as the generated *arche* which the Father employs as a paradigm for the production of the physical universe. I see at present no certain way to avoid concluding that the intelligibles are the first products of the Father's intention to produce a lower world. If this is so, then we may again be faced with the problem that this theory of the production of the intelligibles is corrosive of their status as autonomous standards and exemplars of true being. They are what the deity intends them to be, pursuant to this deity's specific goals of world generation. No matter what interpretation is put upon their theological level, this instrumental understanding of the intelligibles significantly subverts their status in Platonic theology. And yet despite Clement's dependence upon later Middle Platonism, we have here no clear assessment of the intelligibles as the intrinsic and multiple aspects of the first God's inner life, whose nature is expressed through these intelligibles irrespective of its plans for production. Being itself is instead indexed to the intellective purposes of a first and single divinity; it is to this divine Father, to the unique mind producing the intelligibles, that the balance of interest shifts in such theology.

I must admit reluctance even to treat Origen (the Christian) within so brief a space; neither can he be neglected. Despite the fact that Origen was influenced by nondemiurgic Middle Platonists, e.g., Numenius,[41] did anything in his complex revision of earlier Jewish and Christian philosophical theology significantly alter its emphasis upon the active, demiurgic character of the first divine intellect? Given that the Son-Logos is the 'idea of ideas',[42] and also both distinct from and subordinate to its source, the Father, then passages such as *De Prin.* 1.2.6, where the Son is generated by a deliberate act of the Father's will, underscore this same problem. The fact that this is an eternal begetting, or one that does not wholly separate Father from Son, does not mitigate this concern. At present I see a fundamental continuity from Philo to Origen in Jewish and Christian Platonism based upon their similar representation of the generated status of the intelligible world, founded upon the demiurgic intellect of a unique and single divine first principle.

Plotinian Neoplatonism

I will complete this brief historical sketch with some observations on Plotinus' critical approach to these earlier positions in Platonic theology. Since Plotinus was primarily responsible for initiating what will harden into the doctrine of 'emanation', his views on the ontological basis of the intelligibles are critical. The earliest treatises of Plotinus are especially helpful to this end: 3.9.13, 5.4.7, and 5.9.5. Plotinus criticizes exemplarist, demiurgic, and nondemiurgic theology, and then propounds his own model of the intellect-intelligibles relation, one which marginalizes demiurgic aspects and settles the ideas posterior to a completely simple first principle. At 3.9.1 Plotinus attempts to come to terms with the *Timaeus* and with the exemplarism of Atticus and Longinus. His approach is to criticize the sense of separation between the divine intellect and forms, lacking, as this bifurcation does, any clear explication. He then goes on to review a nondemiurgic system (probably Numenius is in mind) and this fares better, provided that the demiurgic or active intellect be demoted and made subordinate to the ideas. His concern seems to be the one registered earlier: the status of the forms in relation to a volitional and intellective deity; and this naturally allies him with nondemiurgic Middle Platonists, who would view the ideas only as the result of the first intellect's self-actualization. Indeed, Plotinus seems to try out provisionally this thesis for himself in 5.4.2; he clearly prefers this approach to a demiurgic one. His rejection of demiurgic theology is spelled out in 5.9.5, esp. 7–8, where he denies that the divine intellect could produce a form by thinking it up; such theological conceptualism was clearly a problem according to this reading of antecedent versions of Middle Platonism because of its suggestion that being itself is a by-product of the intellective intentions of the demiurge. And yet even the nondemiurgic solution was inadequate on Plotinus' account, because its self-thinking and self-actualizing divine intellect was rendered too plural by the inherence of the intelligibles.

What Plotinus proposes instead is a novel thesis: that forms are themselves each a self-thinking intellect which jointly make up a composite unity, the divine intellect. Priority must always be given to the definitional nature of the forms themselves, not to intellection; there can be no ontological dependence of intelligibles upon an active intellect. Neither is *nous* the first principle, for its composition betokens its lack of self-sufficiency. Ontologically prior to *nous* is the pure simplicity of the One, upon which intelligibles and being depend. As he argues at 5.4.7, 5–17, the first principle must be simple and distinct from all its consequents:

> For if it is not to be simple, outside all coincidence and composition, it could not be a first principle; and it is the most self-sufficient, because it is simple and the first of all: for that which is not the first needs that which is before it; and what is not simple is in need of simple components so that it can come into being before them. A reality of this kind must be one alone: if there was another of this kind, both would be one.[43]

This passage exhibits the Plotinian focus upon an ultimate first principle which is beyond the collective unity of the intelligibles, and indicates the characteristic connection which he then makes with this principle's self-sufficiency. The One is the inclusive final principle, but it is a unity which is so complete that it excludes any sense of collection or composition. We should notice in this passage how the special theoretical character and position of the One, as well as its status as the primordial unity, are used by Plotinus to establish its uniqueness. As the inclusive but perfectly simple first principle, it must be conceived as being unique. Because it is the One, it is alone. At this point the Hellenic approach to monotheism merges into an argument for divine exclusivity.

Plotinus has many different ways to explain the production of *nous* from the One that cannot be examined here. I wish to note, nonetheless, that all his images for this production need to be understood in light of his critical rejection of antecedent Platonic treatments of the foundation of the intelligibles. The self-production of *nous* which shows up even in the early treatises (e.g., 5.2.1, 9–13), is one attempt. The theme of the One's overflowing from the plenitude of its nature is another. These are favored in contrast to volitional models, although Plotinus seems to attempt, in that remarkable later treatise 6.8, to rebut the suggestion that his thesis implies randomness, constraint, or automation. Whatever model or language he employs, it can be said that Plotinus is firm in maintaining that the One is an inclusive though completely simple unity and is the ontological foundation of all reality—including the intelligibles, whose production in no way involves active intellection or volitional selection.

I should like now to bring this abbreviated inquiry into the ancient tradition of Platonic theology to a close by summarizing Plotinus' relation to that long intellectual trajectory. The core of this theology is its belief in a transcendent world of real beings which are the foundations of the existence, order, and value which we find in the fluxion of becoming. Plotinus stands firmly in this tradition, countenancing the existence of such principles, which collectively constitute the intelligible world of being. His metaphysics, however, makes every effort to secure and preserve the insights upon which the postulation of such *onta* depend. A central issue in Platonic thought since the time of Plato himself was the relation between these formal principles and the principle of intellection and cosmic production. Plotinus was faced in effect with a choice among a number of theories: (1) those which emphasized the independence of the forms as paradigms separate from the demiurgic first principle, (2) those which subordinated the forms, construed as ideas, to the demiurgic intellect, and (3) those which treated forms as divine ideas within a first intellective principle, but which demoted the active intellect to a lower level of divinity.

For Plotinus, the second alternative seems to have been unacceptable, too destructive of the force and intent of Platonism as he understood it; his own position emerges as a very complex rethinking of elements from these two other positions. Plotinus was evidently concerned to maintain that the forms constituted a set of inviolable and immutable paradigms which were effective in the structure of becoming. From his standpoint, the exemplarist position (1) seems to have removed the danger of the forms being produced at the intent of the demiurge, but it pluralized the number of explanatory theological principles to an unacceptable degree, and separated them in a way which was problematical as well. The removal of demiurgic intellection from the forms seems to have suggested to Plotinus the danger that the cosmological activities of the demiurge might have been conducted upon an incomplete or erroneous understanding of the real paradigms, so that the forms would cease to be the true principles of the sensible cosmos. Finally, there were difficulties with the last position (3), largely due to the fact that, although considered to be a self-contemplative *nous* at rest whose self-thinking was the forms, its first principle was nonetheless deficiently united to serve in the role of the ultimate principle. These, then, were the inadequacies of earlier realist theology from Plotinus' standpoint.

One final point bears emphasis. If my analysis is correct, then the Hellenic monotheism of Plotinus must be understood to have been developed in opposition to a position in philosophical theology which was characteristic of Jewish and Christian Platonism. It is possible that Plotinus intended his efforts as such. It should be remembered that his greatest work, discerpted into four treatises by Porphyry,[44] was an oblique attack at Christian Gnostics in his own circle. It has also been suggested that 6.8 itself was a reaction by Plotinus to the concept of divine volition in creation which he encountered in the proto-orthodox Christian theology in the mid-second century.[45] It may well have been the case that Plotinus' painstaking efforts to demote the active demiurgic intellect and construct a different account of divine intellection were also initiated in conscious opposition to Alexandrian Christian Platonism, especially his fellow alumnus of the school of Ammonius, the Christian Origen. Whatever one makes of such speculative historical possibilities, the Neoplatonic theology of Plotinus represents a distinctive approach both to realist theology and to monotheism, one which retained its theological force long after the religious tradition in which it developed had become extinct.

3. A CONTEMPORARY CODA

The history of ancient and medieval philosophical theology can be an arcane exercise; this cursory review of ancient theories of the ontological foundations of the intelligibles in God or the One doubtless qualifies. Yet I do think we can find here matters upon which to reflect which pertain to more than just the doxographical record of our discarded theological past. There is, first of all, the persistent question of how we are to represent monotheism. Recollection of this early discussion may jog our recognition of a mode of theistic reflection different from our norm. The inclusive monotheism of the Neoplatonists has been a subtonic tradition in Western philosophical theology since the thirteenth century, especially within Christianity, one which has made its presence felt in contemporary theology with such diverse figures as Tillich, Duméry, and von Balthasar. As we learn more of the Hellenic Neoplatonists themselves, as well as their Jewish, Christian, and Islamic successors, we may begin to discover how different the issue of divine production looks, without the same degree of specific focus on the exercise of primordial divine volition or even active intellection. The highly sophisticated and nuanced position of Plotinus on this question recommends itself, as we attempt to review and understand the whole of our theistic heritage.

In addition, even this record of theories about the relation of the intelligibles to divinity repays consideration, in view of the renewed realism of contemporary Anglo-American metaphysics. Nicholas Wolterstorff has broached this very problem,[46] and while I cannot take up the issue here, I want to register its recurrent significance. Although we may not be faced with the full degree of reality thesis regarding universals from Plato's middle period dialogues, what might be called a lower-case "platonism" has emerged, one which countenances the existence of universals, predicables, or abstract objects, as at least a type of reality. Any inventory of 'what there is' would thus include universals, and so a theist must come to terms with their ontological relation to the divine. Thus the ancient theistic problem of the divine ideas returns in a modified form. Universals, which might be viewed as the foundations of knowledge, the referents of true statements, etc., must once again be given a theological locus. Several options from the ancient discussion are apposite. One could argue for a thesis of divine creation, such that all types of reality, including universals, are dependent upon the intention of the deity. As in ancient demiurgic theology, this implies a specific concept of deity and a willingness to index the structure of reality and the foundations of knowledge to an ultimate divine mind. There is also the thesis that universals are simply a distinct ontological category and so is God. No relation of ontological dependence need be postulated; each is a separate sort of reality. This view preserves some of the force of the ancient exemplarist position from the *Timaeus* or the Athenian Middle Platonists, Atticus and Longinus. Since a modern realist would probably not wish to support the ancient Platonic understanding of intelligibles as self-predicational, there would be no theological point to treating God as looking to these separate universals as perfect paradigms for the production of the physical universe. But universals would be, as in the *Timaeus,* distinct from the divine mind, and ontologically independent. This implies, of course, a particular type of limited theism, one which portrays the deity as a single active intellect but also restrains the scope of divine production in a way very like that of Plato's demiurge. It also assumes that God can be plausibly accounted for as a separate category of entity, disjoint from the other foundations of knowledge and intelligibility. A more radical version of this approach would suggest that universals and God are just different modes of explanation, and these are basically incommensurable. Several other theories are also possible, and while I am tempted to reveal a neo-Neoplatonic solution (to use John Findlay's term), I suspect the reader may not be excited at this point by the prospect.

My final point, then, is that the recapitulation of aspects of ancient realism brings again to the agenda of religious thought the problems of ancient realist theology. The history herein reviewed is thus not vain for an excuse: ancient philosophical theology warrants attention because it can enrich our recognition of the breadth and resources of Western theism.

NOTES

1. I use "Western" in reference to philosophical theology dependent upon classical Greek metaphysics.

2. Cf. H. P. Owen, *Concepts of Deity* (London, 1971); C. Hartshorne and W. L. Reese, *Philosophers Speak of God* (Chicago, 1953).

3. Pantheism might be construed as the thesis that everything is divine; monism, as the view that there is only one reality, so that all multiplicity is illusory.

4. For an especially interesting discussion of this problem in early Christian thought and its foundations in classical philosophical theology, cf. G. C. Stead, *Divine Substance* (Oxford, 1977).

5. "Monotheistic and Polytheistic Elements in Classical Mediterranean Spirituality," in *Classical Mediterranean Spirituality,* ed. A. H. Armstrong (New York, 1986).

6. Aristotle suggests that Plato postulated a temporal beginning for the world (*De Caelo* 1.12; 2.2): Apparently because of their rather resolutely dualistic cosmology, Plutarch and Atticus held that view as well. Cf. Plutarch, *On the Creation of the Soul in the Timaeus;* Atticus, Fr. 4 (Baudry, Paris, 1931). The problem centers on the interpretation of *gegonen* at *Timaeus* 28b. Cf. Calcidius, *Commentary on the Timaeus,* chap. 26 and John Philoponus, *On the Eternity of the World,* preserving the earlier discussion of Calvernus Taurus, the second-century (A.D.) Middle Platonist who distinguished possible readings while siding with the majority view in favor of a merely heuristic reading (145, 13ff., Rabe).

7. In *De Opif.* Philo seems to assume a cosmic production out of no prior material. This is also true of *Leg. All.* 2.2. However *De Prov.* 1.8 treats matter as an eternal principle upon which God is always exercising his ordering function. In a fragment from Eusebius, *Praep. Evan.* 7.21, matter's creation by God seems questionable. At *Heres* 160, we find the traditional Old Pythagorean dualism.

8. The mēontic model seems widely adopted after Plotinus, e.g., Augustine, *Conf.* 7, Pseudo-Dionysius, *D.N.* 4, etc.

9. Cf. in particular Gregory Vlastos, "Degrees of Reality in Plato," in *New Essays on Plato and Aristotle,* ed. R. Bambrough (London, 1965), 1–19.

10. Esp. *Phaedo, Republic, Phaedrus;* cf. W. D. Ross's discussion of the chronology of the dialogues, *Plato's Theory of Ideas* (Oxford, 1951).

11. Cf. A. H. Armstrong, "Platonism," in *The Prospect for Metaphysics,* ed. I. T. Ramsey (London, 1966), 93–109.

12. Esp. 5.9.12 and 5.7; cf. J. M. Rist, "Forms of Individuals in Plotinus," *Classical Quarterly,* N.S. 12, no. 2 (1963): 223–31, and "Ideas of Individuals in Plotinus: A Reply to Dr. Blumenthal," *Revue Internationale de Philosophie,* no. 92, pt. 2 (1970): 298–303; H. J. Blumenthal, "Did Plotinus Believe in Ideas of Individuals?" *Phronesis* 11, no. 2 (1966): 61–80; P. S. Mamo, "Forms of Individuals in the *Enneads,*" *Phronesis* 14 (1969): 77–96; A. H. Armstrong, "Form, Individual and Person in Plotinus," *Dionysius* 1 (December 1977): 49–68.

13. See *Parmenides* 130a–e, *Philebus* 5a, *Timaeus* 51b, *Sophist* 257–58, 266bff., *Laws* 342d3–8 for Plato's views on the scope of the theory; also *Metaphysics* 990b8–17. Cf. Ross, *Plato's Theory of Ideas,* 165–75, and H. Cherniss, *Aristotle's Criticism of Plato and the Academy* (Baltimore, 1944) 1:235–60.

14. J. N. Findlay, *The Transcendence of the Cave* (London, 1967), lecture 7: "The Noetic Cosmos."

15. I have retained herein the standard language for periodization. Stephen Gersh has made some especially interesting remarks on this question in his new study *Middle Platonism and Neoplatonism: The Latin Tradition* (Notre Dame, Ind., 1986), 1–50.

16. *Met.* A, 987b19–988a17.

17. Cf. H. A. Wolfson, "Extradeical and Intradeical Interpretations of Platonic Ideas," in *Religious Philosophy* (Cambridge, Mass., 1961), 27–68.

18. Xenocrates defined an idea as "a paradigmatic cause of regularly occurring natural phenomena," Heinze, *Xenocrates* (Leipzig, 1892), fragment 30. He probably identified them with numbers; cf. *Met.* 1028b24ff. (Heinze, *Xenocrates,* fragment 34). John Dillon suggests that the locus of these idea-numbers is probably at the level of Xenocrates' first principle, the Nous-Monad, which is I think possible but not certain; see *The Middle Platonists* (Ithaca, 1977) 24–30. Antiochus also had some elements of this notion, as Dillon indicates (*The Middle Platonists,* 91ff.), although I am uncertain that the "ideas" in question are sufficiently free from Stoicism to attribute to them a transcendent status.

19. Plutarch *De Plac. Philos.* 882d. Cf. R. M. Jones, "The Ideas as the Thoughts of God," *Classical Philology* 21:317–26; A. N. M. Rich, "The Platonic Ideas as the Thought of God," in *Mnemosyne,* series 4, 7:123–33.

20. *De Sera* 550dff. (De Lacy and Einarson, Loeb edition).

21. *Timaeus* 28c–31a and 39e. In general I agree with Ross's view: "Ideas are not changeable things plastic to the will of a Governor; they are standards to which a Governor of the universe must conform" (Ross, *Plato's Theory of Ideas,* 41).

22. Problems in the interpretation of Philo are considerable and cannot be taken up here. They stem, first, from the nonsystematic character of his writings, and second, from specific ambiguities in doctrine. Cf. in particular H. A. Wolfson, *Philo,* 2 vols. (Cambridge, Mass., 1947), and Dillon, *The Middle Platonists,* 155–66.

23. *Opificio* 16; *Opificio* 20 (Colson and Whittaker, Loeb edition).

24. Cf. Wolfson, *Philo,* 2:207–8.

25. A. H. Armstrong, "The Background of the Doctrine 'that the Intelligibles are not Outside the Intellect,'" in *Entretiens Hardt, 5: Sources de Plotin* (Vandoeuvres-Geneva, 1960), 393–413; J. H. Loenen, "Albinus' Metaphysics," in *Mnemosyne,* Series 4, 9:296–319; 10:35–56.

26. I have used *Albinus* since it remains the conventional name, e.g., in Dillon, *The Middle Platonists.* On the problem see J. Whittaker, "*Parisinus gr.* 1962 and the Writings of Albinus," *Phoenix* 28:320ff. and 450ff.

27. Chap. 9, 163, 10–13 (Hermann).

28. 163, 29–31.

29. 163, 21–22.

30. Chap. 10, 164, 24ff.

31. Also Numenius (E. des Places edition [Paris, 1973]), fragments 12, 15, 16, 17, 22. I cannot examine this complex system here, but cf. Dillon, *The Middle Platonists,* 366–72; E. R. Dodds, "Numenius and Ammonius," in *Entretiens Hardt, 5: Les Sources de Plotin;* J. Whittaker, "Numenius and Alcinous on the First Principle," *Phoenix* 32:144ff.

32. Atticus, according to Porphyry in Proclus, *In Tim.* 1.394.6 (Baudry).

33. Cf. *Vita Plotini* 18; Dillon, *The Middle Platonists,* 256: "This distinction of Ideas from the essence of God seems, on Porphyry's evidence, to have been the doctrine of Athenian Platonism up to Longinus."

34. Cf. Dillon, *The Middle Platonists,* 253–56.

35. *Vita Plotini,* chap. 18, 8–19; chap. 20, 89–95.

36. Ibid., chap. 18, and *Enneads* 5.5.

37. *Strom.* 4.155.2; *Strom.* 5.73.3; cf. Philo *De Cher.* 49.

38. Cf. the most recent reviews of the issue: Salvatore Lilla, *Clement of Alexandria* (Oxford, 1971), 199–211; and Robert Berchman, *From Philo to Origen* (Chico, Calif., 1984), pt. 1.

39. H. A. Wolfson, *Philo,* vol. 1, pt. 4.

40. *Strom.* 5.38.7; and 6.58.1; cf. *Leg. All.* 1.19.

41. References to Numenius: *C. Cels* 1.15, 4.51, 5.57, 5.38.

42. "Idea of Ideas": *C. Cels.* 6.64.

43. *Plotinus,* trans. A. H. Armstrong, vol. 5 (Cambridge, Mass., 1984).

44. I.e., 3.8.30, 5.8.31, 5.5.32, 2.9.33.

45. A. H. Armstrong, "Two Views of Freedom: A Christian Objection in Plotinus *Enneads* VI.8[39]7,11–15?", *Studie Patristica* vol. 18, ed. E. A. Livingstone (Oxford and New York, 1982). J. M. Rist makes a similar suggestion with reference to Christian figures, esp. Origen, in his recent book *Human Value* (Leiden, 1982), 111–12. The Christian background to Plotinus' theology bears further analysis.

46. Nicholas Wolterstorff, *On Universals* (Chicago, 1970).

Response

Paul A. Dietrich

John Kenney's learned and stimulating paper provides us with a carefully nuanced guided tour through the vagaries of late antique Platonism. The exposition of the forms of philosophical monotheism (Hellenistic and Hellenic Greek, Philonic, and Alexandrian Christian) is a helpful historical taxonomy or field guide.

In his prologue he speaks to an implied audience of students of Greco-Roman, Judaic, Christian, and Islamic philosophical and theological traditions when he refers to "a common problem of conceptual self-definition . . . a set of historically related solutions . . . (and) a once shared discourse." In my brief remarks I intend to make several minor observations and raise a larger issue for discussion concerning the status of late antique Platonism as the philosophical codeterminant of the three religious traditions with which we are primarily concerned.

First—some particulars:

1. At the beginning of his discussion of divine production in ancient realist theology he refers in passing to the ontological status of matter in late antique thought. The conception of matter is obviously an essential ingredient in any theology of creation or divine production. He speaks of the "withering" of *hyle*—matter becomes a surdal presence, an abstract pole representative of disorder. Certainly matter means one thing for Plato and the Presocratics, e.g., Heraclitus, and something quite different for Plotinus. Matter *is* devalued in Hellenistic and Roman thought. The cosmic dualism and paranoia of numerous gnostic systems provide extreme examples of a general tendency. And yet there *are* important counterexamples. Calcidius, Theophilus of Antioch, and Augustine help establish the ground work for the reappropriation of matter within a context of Christian Platonism. This tradition reaches its culmination in the affirmation of matter in Book Three of Eriugena's *Periphyseon.* A full account of late antique Platonism must record a fundamental

ambivalence in regard to material reality containing both positive and negative moments.

2. In his sketch of the three species of Middle Platonism Kenney defends using the standard periodization of ancient, Middle, and Neo-Platonism while alluding in a footnote to Stephen Gersh's recent critique of such categorizations. Following the lead of E. R. Dodds and A.-J. Festugière, Gersh stresses the "neoplatonic character of Plato and the Platonic character of Neoplatonism," and argues that the traditional categories retain a chronological utility but are devoid of substantive philosophical content. Given his specialization in the *arcana* of Middle Platonism, we need to know more about how Kenney evaluates Gersh's suggestions. If Gersh is right, it would seem to have implications for the taxonomy given here.

I would now like to turn to that part of the paper which is perhaps of most interest to many of the participants in the symposium. I am referring to the central distinction between Abrahamic and Hellenic monotheism articulated in Part 1 and implicit throughout.

Abrahamic or "exclusive" monotheism represents the religious theism of Judaism, Christianity, and Islam. Exclusive monotheism postulates the *numerical* uniqueness of a single deity and has its roots in the faith experiences of the religions of the Book supplemented by an exposition of divine attributes (unity, infinity, simplicity, immutability, incorporeality, eternity, etc.) derived, in part, from classical metaphysics. The exposition of this dominant and therefore familiar tradition is understandably cursory.

Hellenic or "inclusive" monotheism represents a *qualitative* understanding of oneness. "Divinity seems . . . to be the final inclusive unity behind the manifest image of the world's plurality, the ultimate completeness which transcends but resolves its fractured multiplicity." Like Abrahamic monotheism, Hellenic monotheism is unintelligible apart from its historical context. It "evolved from spiritual reflection upon the obscure divine fundament behind the surface tale of polytheism" and is, in fact, "continuous with elements of ancient cultic polytheism."

Kenney states that both forms of monotheism are incomplete in themselves and imply the necessity of a *rapprochement.* Exclusive monotheism combined with an assertion of absolute divine transcendence with no room for immanence leads to dualism. Inclusive monotheism runs the opposite risk of dissolving into pantheism or monism (or reverting to polytheism). If inclusive monotheism is "endemically modalistic" (shades of Sabellius and Patripassianism!), as suggested, how is divine transcendence preserved?

A few historical and comparative queries about inclusive monotheism:

1. Given the assertion that Hellenic monotheism is "continuous with elements of ancient cultic polytheism," what is the relation of classical theories of divine production to ancient Hellenic myths of creation? The Greek cosmogonies, e.g., Hesiod, recount the involvement of the gods in generation, procreation (*hieros gamos*), fabrication, formation, and violent conflict—all constitutive ingredients in the creation of the world. Is the continuity between Hesiod and Middle Platonism a mitigating factor in the hermeneutical effectiveness of the latter? Or does the history of the effort by the classical Greek philosophical tradition to distance itself (demythologize) from the earliest cosmogonies provide a model for the common project of Jewish, Christian, and Muslim accounts of God and creation?

2. How clear is the distinction between 'inclusive' and 'exclusive' monotheism in practice? Do not these terms, like monotheism and polytheism generally, represent a Draconian embrace if conceived as mutually exclusive? It strikes me that most forms of Abrahamic monotheism from ancient Israel to medieval Christianity and Sufism are theologically exclusive and inclusive in practice. (I am reminded of the assertion that Latin Christianity has always been Augustinian in its head and Pelagian in its members.) I am suggesting this as a possibility for Judaism and Islam; I am certain it is the case with medieval Christianity, which presupposes "a final divine unity behind the multiplicity of the world, a deeper nature behind the physical universe."

The twelfth-century school of Chartres, for example, accepted the fundamental intuition of theological realism given here—"that there exists a transcendent world of principles or powers which are the changeless, autonomous and wholly real foundations for our lower world." Following Boethius—*omne esse ex forma est*—the masters of Chartres identified the forms as archetypal foundations of phenomenal reality. Despite the protestations of William of Conches to the contrary ("Christianus sum, non academicus"), there emerged at Chartres a complex Christian Platonic realism indebted not only to Neoplatonic emanationism but also to Philo's definition of forms as intradeical and the later Middle Platonic notion (derived in part from the influence of Aristotelian intellection and mediated through Calcidius, Macrobius, and Boethius) of the forms and being as the self-articulation of the divine essence. For Thierry of Chartres, God is the form of being (*forma essendi*) of the creature. Thierry describes the enfolding (*complicatio*) of all things in God's simplicity.[1]

In a larger context, historians of religion remind us that Vedantic Hinduism and the Native American Plains Indians represent other traditions combining inclusive and exclusive claims. Kenney's paper offers several suggestions for further thought along these lines that I would like to highlight in concluding. First, Kenney claims that inclusive monotheism has been a "subtonic tradition in western philosophical theology since the thirteenth century" and that it survives in contemporary form in the works of Tillich, Duméry, and von Balthasar. Tillich's definitions of God as the "ground of Being" (derived from Schelling, Boehme, and Eckhart) and as "originating," "sustaining," and "directing creativity" seem to confirm this judgment. It would be interesting to analyze von Balthasar's relation to the inclusive tradition. Finally, the argument for the presence of a lower case platonism in contemporary Anglo-American metaphysics—a return to realism—needs more development. Kenney hints that he is "tempted to reveal a Neoplatonic solution" to our contemporary dilemma. I invite him to do so—and perhaps reverse the protestation of William of Conches.

NOTE

1. Cf. Thierry, *Lectiones in Boethii librum de Trinitate* and *Commentum Super Ebdomadas Boetii* (in *Abbreviatio Monacensis),* in *Commentaries on Boethius by Thierry of Chartres and His School,* ed. Nikolaus M. Häring (Toronto: P.I.M.S., 1971). For a more extensive consideration of the interrelations of Platonism and medieval religious thought, see the McGinn and Burrell essays in this volume.

Three Meanings of the Idea of Creation

Lenn Evan Goodman

Evidence is mounting that would tend to support the thesis that the world is originated.[1] Only a few years ago the "Big Bang" and "Steady State" theories could be presented as near-equal rivals. The "Big Bang" traces the expanding universe suggested by the observed red shift of the radiation emanating from celestial bodies to a point of origin at a tiny speck projected to have existed billions of years ago; the Steady State theory proposes continuous origination of new matter which then diffuses outward to produce the red shift. Both theories, of course, are compatible with the idea of creation: the Steady State theory because it requires the continuous origination of new matter, and the Big Bang because it poses the possibility of instantaneous creation—not of a finished universe at one fell swoop, to be sure, but of an evolving universe, emergent in phases, rather more as suggested in the biblical stories of a phased creation.

Neither theory is compatible with the Aristotelian idea of an eternally ancient universe preserving the same order of events without essential change through infinite ages. Since Galileo, the Aristotelian view has seemed increasingly less plausible, and evolutionary views have exercised more and more authoritative command of the evidence. It is the instantaneous originative act that attracts today's "scientific creationists" to the Big Bang, however, not its evolutionary character. Where such creationists have been put on the defensive in biology by the convergence of the evidence in behalf of biological evolution, contenting themselves with an epistemologically weak search for "alibis"—claims that special creation cannot be ruled out—and critiques of the lacunae in the fossil or taxonomic record of evolution, biblical cosmologists, by contrast, have become almost triumphalist in recent years.

Fred Hoyle, the foremost advocate of the old Steady State theory, has retreated to the defense of an elaborately contrived account of the extraterrestrial origins of life, which, as Spinoza might have put it, demonstrates the brilliance of its author more effectively than the truth of his thesis. Religiously inclined astronomers, and exponents of other sciences as well, write books to show how the findings of astronomy and cosmology have vindicated (or are vindicating) the suppositions of biblical theism. A cover story in *Science News* tells of cosmologists on the brink of solving the ancient Parmenidean and Democritean problem of *ex nihilo* creation by negating the apparent axiom *ex nihilo nihil fit:* if matter and antimatter combine to annihilate one another, could one not achieve something from nothing by segregating "the" nothing into its matter and antimatter components to derive a universe? The magazine's cover pictures William Blake's sinewy God the Father measuring the cosmic *tohu we-bohu* between Alpha and Omega with celestial dividers, while about the figure's bearded head the rotund words echo in the void: "OH I GOT PLENTY O' NOTHIN', AN' NOTHIN'S PLENTY FOR ME." A novelist ironically proposes the case of a somewhat fallen-away theologian (hardly a "divine") contending with a young computer hack who professes to have found God in the recesses of his machine.[2]

Now the idea of a Big Bang does not imply but only allows, as one possible explanation, the idea that God created the universe. An originated universe, it can be claimed, simply originated by itself. Or it might have been originated by some cause less than the supernal and transcendent God whose goodness we agree makes Him worthy of worship. Indeed the evidence for a Big Bang is wholly compatible with one ancient theory of the eternity of the cosmos, the cyclical view. Perhaps, as some have argued, the force of the original explosion will one day be exhausted and gravity will initiate a gradual but accelerating contraction, climaxing in a cosmic implosion, to be followed by we know not what, but possibly another explosion. Perhaps the universe oscillates eternally (or at least repeatedly) between implosion and explosion, and the "Big Bang" which creationist cosmologists of the would-be scientific school claim so eagerly is only one of a series and not the unique instance they were seeking of absolute creation. The Big Bang, in other words, does not imply the world's origination. It allows origination as an explanatory hypothesis. And origination, in turn, can be explained by creation. Some of the rabbis of antiquity used to speculate that the present world was created only after a number of inferior attempts had been discarded.[3] But the riposte was always open: perhaps the world we live in is one of the inferior essays.

To know that the world originated out of a tiny point of matter or out of nothing finite eons ago, is not, we emphasize again, to know that the world is created. Even had we been present or capable of watching from a safe distance—as perhaps we do with telescopes today, peering into the explosive past of the cosmos from the safe distance of the present—we would not have been able to observe an answer to what theology wants to know about creation. We must heed the advice that Saadiah gave us on this question just over a thousand years ago: when we set out to find the cause of all of nature we are not seeking yet another natural phenomenon, but something that transcends time and change and apprehension by the senses, and thus is capable of explaining natural phenomena rather than simply requiring explanation along with them.[4] It was for this reason, Aristotle argued, that the cause of all motion must itself be unmoved. Similarly, Plato reasoned that the ground of all existence must be beyond temporality and particularity, since these are the distinctive marks of existence in nature. Our penchant for seeking sensory evidence should not, Saadiah argues, trap us into seeking the ultimate principles or Principle of nature amongst the very categories we seek to ground. That would be to re-reduce our principle of explanation to the level of the phenomena it was invoked to explain. Sensuous notions of divinity, empiricist conceptions of creation, and what Voegelin called "historicized" symbolisms,[5] all show symptoms of our reductive drive to facticity, which identifies reality with what human beings or our machines can palpate and manipulate. It was not this that the biblical writers or the ancient philosophers and sages were seeking to awaken to us or in us.

When a medieval creationist like al-Ghazali argued that all processes, being temporal, are originated, he could assume that for his readers and hearers the transition from origination to creation was a natural one. The argument came from Plato and was strengthened by Aristotle's analysis of the temporality of process, despite Aristotle's rejection of what he took to be the Platonic notion of creation.[6] If the world was temporal, the world was originated. And if the world was originated, the world required a cause—and that beyond itself, beyond the temporality which was coextensive with its being as a world. It required a God.

Now we cannot simply appropriate al-Ghazali's argument. For we have not necessarily followed Plato quite as far as al-Ghazali did on Plato's "second voyage," into a complete bifurcation of all possible beings into the temporal and originated on the one hand, the eternal and unoriginated on the other. For us to know that a thing exists in time is not (as it was for Plato) proof that that thing had a beginning. Yet neither can we isolate ourselves in a historicist cocoon (because we are "modern" and earlier wonderers were not) from the powerful argument lodged in the rhetorical question asked by so many medieval philosophers: How can any finite thing or any combination of finite things create itself? We have learned from Hume to say that if things did begin, perhaps they simply began of themselves—for no reason at all or for no reason outside their own natures. But we have yet to learn that when we think this way we give up a great deal: we give up the idea that the world can be explained, the rationalist claim that things make sense and that no mere particular or complex of particulars contains within itself, omnicompetently and self-sufficiently, the grounds of all its own determinations.

Consider now the most familiar grounds of our historic division from our philosophic forbears: For our contemporaries the argument that al-Ghazali culled from Plato is lacking, not because they imagine the world in nontemporal terms but because they can imagine origination without creation. Indeed, they have difficulty imagining creation at all. And to the popular sensibility, as Maimonides and al-Farabi pointed out, imagination is an epistemological criterion more powerful, perhaps, than those of logic. The *fashioning* of a world can be imagined pictorially and narrated mythically, and this is what many of our would-be sensualist or neo-mythic theologians cling to, or project upon the minds of others. But absolute creation is not the sort of thing that can be imaged or imagined. It cannot be pictured at all. And even if we had been present at the creation or could watch from a safe distance we would not be able to distinguish divine creation visually or in any other sensuous way from the mere eruption of being out of nothingness or out of something very small. The fact is that our ancestors who conceived the idea of creation and those who accepted it or defended it when they read of it in Scripture did not have the sort of ringside seat or remote access to the spectacle that radio-telescopy may one day give our progeny. Were they jumping the gun, buying the story before they knew its premises or conclusion? Or is it possible that it is we who are settling for an incomplete account? Reason, as Saadiah argues, affords our only access to the idea of creation; and the notions of creation that we accept, reject, or entertain when we envision creation in the cosmogonic vignettes of a Cecil B. deMille movie or a *Nova* broadcast are curiously devoid of the values which the idea of creation once bore rather proudly and explicitly, and by means of which it was rather easier for our predecessors to describe the world as created (without the use of radio telescopes) than it may have become for us. The purpose of this paper is to reawaken some of those values. I shall group them under the headings of contingency, design, and newness.

1. THE WORLD AS CONTINGENT

One of the central values which the idea of creation classically carried was that of contingency. This meant in the first instance that the world was such that if God had not created it, it would not have existed. It was on the basis of this argument—following but universalizing the model of still more ancient myths of origin—that the biblical cosmologists put forward their original and comprehensive version of the cosmological argument, finding grounds to affirm the reality of a transcendent (thus undescribed) God in the facticity of nature and to ascribe goodness, grace, or favor (*hesed*) to that God in virtue of the goodness of His act—for God saw that it was good. God witnesses to the goodness of His work at the cosmogonic opening of His Torah, as later, at that law's close, He calls heaven and earth to witness to the cosmogonic authority of that law's moral dictates.[7]

As Avicenna interpreted the impact of the arguments embedded in Scripture, the concept of creation symbolized in graphic, mythic terms the stark contrast between necessary and contingent being. Only God was necessary, that is, self-sufficient. The world and all things in it were finite, conditioned, causally dependent. For

Avicenna the world's contingency seemed compatible with its eternity, as the ageless product of the eternal emanation of becoming from the Divine. But to other monotheists of perhaps stricter scriptural loyalties or more unswerving devotion to the idea of God's will, it seemed clear not only that if the world was finite it was contingent, but also that if the world was contingent it had begun: a contingent world was not eternal and not the necessary product of some eternal process. As al-Ghazali argued, interpreting the biblical creationism of the *Qur'an,* Aristotelian Neoplatonist philosophers had no grounds to ascribe the world's existence to the authorship of a God if they did not believe the world to be originated. There was no meaning—no operational meaning, as we might say—in the ascription of an effect to a cause when the "effect" was eternal and the "cause" made no actual difference to its existence or character. What sense was there in speaking of the Author (*sani*ᶜ) of a universe which could only have the nature that it had and could never *not* have existed? The intellectualism, emanationism, and eternalism of the philosophers, al-Ghazali argued, made them unwitting or unwilling atheists.[8]

Maimonides judged more gently. His commitment to the idea that biblical theology is taught by symbol, indirection, and suggestion[9] made him unwilling dogmatically to impugn the faith of would-be theists: to be sure, it was possible for an eternalist to believe in God. But the nexus in eternalism between God and nature ontically, and thus between human beings and God epistemically, was attenuated in the extreme. Al-Ghazali's challenge remained sound: What was ascribed to God in calling Him the cause of the universe if God's act made no difference? In Maimonides' version of this challenge the Neoplatonic philosophers were left a narrow ground on which to assume a metaphysical stance: God could exist as the eternal "Author" of the universe if the nexus between God and the world were metaphysical, and the world depended on God ontically by emanation—the dynamic version of Platonic participation, no more amenable to pictorial imagination than was creation. But that view left no alternative case: God's existence became (in our terms) unfalsifiable, and to that extent, the affirmation of His existence and His act was emptied of material content.

Now the creationist claim in principle *is* falsifiable. A creationist can say with a force that an eternalist cannot: if God had not created the world, the world would never have existed. But although such a virtuality is more real in the theory of a creationist than in that of an eternalist, it remains metaphysical in the damaging sense that it is an unknowable possibility. We could never have known the world's nonexistence. This epistemic difficulty points to another weakness of the purely metaphysical approach to contingency: the approach which reduces the contingency of the world to the claim that the world might or might not have existed, and ignores the far richer dimensions of contingency suggested in the scriptural accounts: the dependency of the observable goodness of the world upon God's act, such that one can argue (as Scripture in effect does argue) that had it not been for God's goodness the world's goodness would not exist.[10] In a similar spirit Plato had thought to read God's goodness in the being of things, and it can be read there if the being of things is good. But if the mere neutral unity of each particular is a sufficient mark of its divine ground, then God's existence becomes compatible with any sort of world, and the world's existence and character (if necessitated by God's) give us no sort of insight into God's nature or intentions for it or for us.

Now divine beneficence is as much a feature of eternalist accounts of the world's dependence upon God as it is of creationist accounts. But, as Maimonides and al-Ghazali recognized, God's bounty in the eternalist accounts is reduced to the mere bestowal of being of whatever sort. Moreover, if God were an eternal "Author" the problems of necessitation remained: both God and nature seemed to be subject to a determinism as rigid as that of logic. Species, essences, the heavens were eternal and in principle unchangeable. The movements of the heavens and of all living and nonliving things seemed to be rooted in their courses by the requirement of logic that all things retain their essences, i.e., be what they are. And God's will itself seemed to have no options other than to do what its own nature (and the fixed natures of things) required. If emanation was to be a matter of necessitation from the divine simplicity, even the world's differentiation became unintelligible. In such terms a doctrine of creation seemed both preferable theologically and more probable epistemologically than the seemingly neurasthenic doctrine of God's eternal authorship.[11]

Surely, Maimonides argued, the notion of God's authorship made more sense if there were alternative, unrealized possibilities among which God's goodness chose. The notion of a temporal creation, as distinguished from eternal emanation, left room for such a possibility: there was a time before which the world did not have its present determinate character. The character it has is the one it was given. For Aristotelians and those who came under the powerful spell of the Aristotelian world view, this seemed to imply that matter, potentiality abiding in matter, and time (already measured by the ceaseless motions of bodies made of matter), must have existed even at the juncture of the world's putative creation. The world was formed, some allowed, as in the myth of Plato's *Timaeus;* it was not created. But, as Saadiah pointed out, to maintain a world formed from eternal matter is no different in principle (as a denial of creation) from the direct affirmation of Aristotelian eternalism. And, we may add, it would be no more satisfactory to a true Aristotelian than was a direct affirmation of *de novo* creation.

Maimonides' refutation of the key Aristotelian claim—that a point of origin for change presumes a prior time and thus eternal time, motion, matter, and materially grounded potentiality—was swift and incisive. It was suppositious on the part of Aristotelians, Maimonides argued, to project their notions of matter, time, potentiality, and change—derived from study of the present settled order of nature—onto that radically evolving world which had not yet acquired its settled character, let alone onto the first moment of origination. A perfect man who had no notion of his origins would deny the possibility of living human beings emerging from the womb: surely respiration, nutrition, locomotion, and excretion would be impossible in that environment, he would argue; and how could a human embryo or fetus live in the womb with a different nature than the one we know? Such apriorism, however, is without foundation.[12] Indeed, medieval scientific knowledge of the variety of nature is sufficient to expose the fallacy. The laws of nature have their own necessity, as ordained within the designated order.[13] But they are not matters of logical necessity. The entire system as we know it is just one of the alternative systems of nature God might have chosen.[14] For this reason we can achieve no *a priori* deduction of its principles. God knows the world as the inventor knows a clock, prior to its manufacture, and even prior to its design. But human knowledge, unlike God's, is necessarily *a posteriori:* we take apart the clock and discover the principles of its working.[15]

Plainly, one need not adhere to Maimonides' specific version of the nexus between temporality and modality to recognize the force of his objection to a metaphysic of possibility that allows no scope for alternative possibilities. Freedom, as a value ascribable in different senses to God, to humanity, and to nature, is part of the metaphysical freight of the idea of creation. The value at stake is encountered experientially through those experiences that lead us to affirm the openness of the universe. The necessity of empiricism in science, alluded to in Maimonides' example of the clock, is one such locus of experience.

Al-Ghazali is even more outspoken than Maimonides in linking empiricism with creation, partly because empiricism also has an impact on al-Ghazali's advocacy of mysticism and on his critique of the essentialist account of causality.[16] By the aprioristic principles inculcated in intellectualist philosophy, he argues, one would deny that something no larger than a grain can devour an entire town and then itself. Yet fire has such a nature. Philosophers ascribe the effects of opium to its coldness and say that earth and water are the unmixed elements in which cold is found. Yet pounds of earth and water have not the effect of a single dram of opium. Just as the blind know nothing of color, so those who lack practical experience know nothing of the complexities of nature, the reach of God's power, or the strengths and liabilities of the human soul.[17]

The association between empiricism and creationism, as M. B. Foster and Francis Oakley showed in a pair of now classic articles, was by no means accidental.[18] Part of the message conveyed by the medieval and the ancient ideas of creation was the notion that the world need not have been as it is, indeed need not have been at all. It was not an eternal and self-sufficient substance, nor was it the passive product of fate, extruded from the entrails of the gods or milled between the rollers of the seasons and the heavens.[19] The determinate character of created nature was not a product of inevitability, of lack of alternative, of self-necessity; it was an expression of the living God, whose grace could be encountered in the character of creation. Indeed, a starting point in the natural theology of monotheism was the cosmological move from nature to the thought of God, founded in the recognition that things need not have been as they are and would not have been so, had not God made them so. The theme is echoed clearly by Maimonides and Saadiah when they treat both the causal dispositions of things and the power of free choice in persons as gifts bestowed by God.

Our analysis thus far of the ancient and medieval contents of the idea of creation enables us to take the first two steps toward the development of a modern and indeed perennial interpretation of the idea—an interpretation that does not require us to have perceptual knowledge of the act of creation and is thus in congruence with the limitations on such knowledge that were present in antiquity and the Middle Ages and remain in force today and at all times. First, as in antiquity, we can say that if the world is good, that argues for its creation by a transcendently good God. The argument is not one of entailment but one of evidence. The world's goodness, and any goodness that we find in it, can be taken as corroboration of the thesis that the world is God's act in the sense that the thesis of creation is one appropriate explanation of that goodness: God saw to it that it was good.

Such an explanation of the goodness in the world does not, of course, preclude the world's eternity. Indeed it does not logically exclude any alternative explanation, including an infinitude of bizarre, perverse, outrageous, or tendentiously suppositious explanations. But to the extent that the idea of divine creation is capable (a) of implying what we observe and (b) of ordering the data of observation—noting that in this case they are not neutral data of perception only—in a coherent and well integrated system, those data can be taken as confirming that thesis and as counting in its favor.

Alternative eternalist accounts of the authorship of the world's determinacy and goodness in the Middle Ages point up the relevance of the idea of contingency in the creation concept implicit in the scriptural notion that if God had not created the world it would not exist. In its medieval form this generally tacit bit of scriptural dialectic becomes an argument to the effect that if the world's existence and character are contingent, then the world is created. Eternalist philosophers did not readily give up this language. They saw emanation not as an alternative to but as an interpretation of creation. Defenders of creation against eternalism, like Maimonides and al-Ghazali, did not reject emanation either. They employed it, but sought to strip it of its eternalist connotations. Their insistence on the finite age of the cosmos expresses a desire to point up the contingency of nature. Ibn Tufayl, in seeking to reconcile Avicenna with al-Ghazali, is at pains to argue that the theological implications of creationism and eternalism are no different from one another. Maimonides labors to vindicate a similar claim, worked out in far greater detail, when he derives the principal doctrines of monotheistic rational theology from the assumptions of the Neoplatonic Aristotelian philosophers. The Rambam departs from the position of "the" Philosophers when he treats their eternalism as a postulate distinctive to their system and in fact unwarranted, rather than as a self-evident and universally applicable axiom or a demonstrated conclusion. But he is also careful to show that neither the creation nor the eternity of the world can be demonstrated apodeictically. For any such demonstration would make creation (or emanation) a matter of necessity rather than a matter of fact and rob God of the volition which, in Maimonides' view, it was part of the burden of the idea of creation to preserve and render manifest.

A key thematic premise of the idea of creation, then, was contingency, a linchpin in the Avicennan analysis of scriptural creationism, but a theme which more ardent creationists like al-Ghazali and Maimonides (with a dialectical pointedness aimed specifically at the Avicennan persuasion) argued could be preserved effectively only by the more red-blooded notion that the world's dependence upon God was manifest in the world's finite age. Contingency bespoke creation, and creation rested on contingency.

But how can we form a judgment that the universe as a whole is contingent? Difficult as it is to judge the entirety of nature as to goodness—a difficulty recognized by the biblical authors, who ascribed that judgment to God—it seems even more problematic to claim of nature as a whole that its existence and its character are contingent. Contingency, after all, is a category of the understanding, relegated by many to the description of propositions: not things or states of affairs, we are told, but judgments are what is necessary or possible.[20] But this, it seems, is a mere retrenchment of the understanding based on our inability to use our finite knowledge to pass categorically on the necessity or possibility of diverse states of affairs. Objectively, those states of affairs have a modal status in themselves and relative to their causes—as is assumed in the very claim that our knowledge of them is not absolute but finite and fallible.

As Maimonides' examples of the fetus and the clock, and al-

Ghazali's examples of the dram of opium and the "grain" of fire suggest, one domain of evidence open to us in judging whether the world and the things in it are necessary or contingent is provided by the enterprise of science itself: if all things are necessary categorically, then the necessity of logic is coextensive with that of nature: all real possibilities are actual, and the sciences could legitimately be conducted deductively. But if any part of scientific inquiry is necessarily inductive, so that we cannot infer how things must be because things, in interaction with one another, have been delegated active and dynamic control over their own destinies, then there is contingency in the world: things might have been other than as they are; they are not all fixed eternally in the necessities of their own natures but might have been—might yet be—otherwise.

Now we know in fact that induction is our necessary method of proceeding in the sciences. But we do not know *a priori* whether this requirement arises in the character of nature or strictly in the predispositions and limitations of our understanding. Once again we must say that the necessity of an inductive procedure in the sciences can be explained by the openness of the future, the protean variability of nature, but might also be explained as some manner of reflex of the structure of our minds. To me it seems clear that the former (realistic) explanation is the more credible, since it places being first and makes knowledge dependent on the way things are, rather than vice versa. Indeed, our minds *are* capable of noninductive thinking about nature; they are just not capable of assuring the accuracy of their premises without recourse to experience. The lesson of empiricism, I would argue, is relearned and the theses of empiricism are given new meaning with each new scientific discovery. For me that sort of experience counts as an argument of cumulatively mounting and as yet unchallenged force in behalf of the realistic account of the necessity of induction, and thus, in behalf of the credibility of an open universe. But others, for whatever reasons and in deference to whatever nuances of experience may seem salient to them and unaccountable in terms of real contingency in nature, may draw different conclusions. The fact remains that our failure to discover deductive certainties among the outcomes of experience counts as evidence of the world's contingency, and so of its creation, in one of the important dimensions of meaning that al-Ghazali and Maimonides gave the term. Their arguments, which enliven us to the nexus between empiricism (which their intellectualist eternalist adversaries did not share) and creationism, are indicative not of the inevitability of creationism but of the kind of price one might be forced to pay in apriorism—perhaps idealism or perhaps in positing an overly static or undifferentiated cosmos—if one abandons the creationist mode of explanatory discourse.

From the ancient biblical idea of creation we learn that goodness in the world argues for a divine Creator. From the medieval philosophic analysis of that idea we learn that the necessity of empiricism in science argues the contingency of the world's existence and character, and thus, at a level that parallels the intricate quest for goodness in the world step for step, argues the existence of a Creator once again.[21]

2. DESIGN

Resident within the ambit of the ideas of value and contingency that is generated by the idea of creation is the further idea of purposiveness. The value of the world is bound up with its purpose and the capability of creation or the creatures within it to fulfill that purpose. The idea of the world's purposive design emerges naturally enough from the thought of creation, since accounts of creation are formed paradigmatically on the model of myths: the features of nature are products of the intentions of the gods in much the same way that the features of culture are the products of the designs of culture heroes. Viewed in such a way, whether in a spirit of appreciation or with a more anxious sense of the need for propitiation, nature is scaled to anthropomorphic needs: the cosmos becomes our abode, the heavens a tent over our heads (cf. Isa. 40:22), the seas vehicles for our transport (cf. *Qur'an* 2:164, 10:22, 14:32, 16:14, 17:66, 22:65, 43:12, 45:12, etc.), the meadows fields for our crops, disease the instrument of our chastisement, death and its putative sequel the vehicles of our judgment. Saadiah has not overcome this way of thought when he argues that this world was created as an abode of trial for the human race, to determine whether we will do God's will, so that we may be rewarded or punished accordingly.[22] He reflects the artifactual conception of creation as well when he states that all things are created for human beings, and human beings that we might worship God.[23] Voltaire might archly seek to draw a line in stating that he found no difficulty in agreeing that the human eye was designed for seeing but could not allow that the nose was formed as a perch for a pince-nez. But the Stoics were typically earnest when they argued that a thing as noble as a soul was not imparted to a pig except to keep its meat fresh.[24]

Teleology is notoriously anthropocentric, and the difficulty is not a matter merely of our human tendency to reduce all purposes to our own. It may be that the very category of purpose is inextricably projective. Thus Spinoza's rejection of teleology (at least in its ancient, anthropocentric, and anthropomorphic forms) is founded on the recognition that classical design arguments rest on a *reductio ad ignorantiam;* Hume's rejection of teleology (at least in its modern forms) is based on a recognition that modern design arguments are founded on a suppositious and rather stretched analogy between nature as a whole and a machine. Both Hume and Spinoza are critical of the projection of human purposes onto the principles governing the constitution of nature: Spinoza argues that our ability or inability to recognize the order or disorder of a system is founded in the finite intelligence which serves our human needs; Hume suggests that our notion of the world as a machine, rather than, say, an organism, is at best an imaginative projection of our rather limited experience.[25] Later and more scientistic thinkers than Spinoza and Hume argue less subtly and miss the force of these objections, seeking to show that the world is not a system or that machines are capable of constructing and governing themselves—even of reproducing themselves.

A careful analysis of the idea of creation is as instructive here as it was in the case of the contingency of creation. Foster has successfully contrasted creation with divine artisanship (the ordering and forming of nature and its constituents by a demiurge or craftsman god), using an analogous contrast between crafts and fine (i.e., creative) arts. A craftsman works with a preconceived purpose, by a preestablished plan, and within the limits prescribed by preselected materials. But in creative arts the purpose emerges only with completion of the work: the plan is not preset but is itself a product of the creative act, and the materials (to the extent that this is possible) are not arbitrary and external limits but organically appropriate vehicles and means of the work. Their necessity is determined in the determination of the act rather than being its determinants.[26]

The demiurge god of Plato's *Timaeus* "consults" the eternal pattern of nature in the forms, as a craftsman consults a blueprint, paradigm, or jig, and as a culture hero consults the preexistent needs of presumptive (or presumptuous) beneficiaries, clients, or constituents. A craftsman god worked with preexistent and in some degree recalcitrant materials. But a creator God, like a creative artist, is responsible for the materials as well as for their form or order—radically so, in the case of the one God of monotheism, since He is their originator. A craftsman god must subordinate will to intelligence or design, and any failure to do so is a failing in the world. But in a Creator, the end itself, in Foster's words, is a product of the activity; and thus a will is expressed which is not simply reducible to any prior purpose, our own or that of any preestablished plan.[27] Here we catch again some of the sense behind Maimonides' insistence that there was a volitional element in the divine determination of nature, of existence over nonexistence, and of all the particularizations of nature, law, history, and the powers of human character.

The volitional in God was an aspect that Maimonides associated with matter[28] and thus with the absoluteness of God's creation. The idea of a pattern, design, or plan in nature was not anathema to monotheists, so long as that pattern did not become an independent hypostasis. For Philo, paradigmatically, it was the word or wisdom of God, identified as the logos or rational principle of creation. For our purpose the most pertinent comment on logos theory is found in the famous remark of *Sanhedrin:* that from a mortal craftsman's mold or type, each artifact emerges exactly like the last (but for the recalcitrance of matter!), but when the Holy One, blessed be He, makes human beings, no two emerge identically from the mold.[29] God's universe too is a unique original. Its plan is immanent rather than extrinsically imposed. Thus, as Maimonides argues, it is absurd to seek a general purpose in creation reducible to human terms. Creation, then, is not an artifact like a machine or tool. When Scripture says that God created all things for His glory, it means that (like a creative artist) He created all things for their own sakes—to fulfill their own natures and to manifest aspects of perfection in their own distinctive ways, in accordance with the virtues (that is, strengths) of their own God-given natures. It is in this sense that "the heavens declare the glory of God."[30] "God saw that it was good," surely not *ex post facto* as a discovery, yet objectively, analogous to the satisfaction of an artist witnessing the adequacy of the execution of a plan and knowing that that plan could not be better executed.

Here too, then, two criteria emerge by which we are enabled to judge whether the world has a Creator without being eyewitnesses to the act. The two are associated with our practice of science, although less as its findings than as critical underpinnings, vindicated more by the success of the entire structure which they help support than by any single piece of evidence. They are the intelligibility and the functional autonomy of nature. In keeping with the classic interpretations of the design argument, the fact that nature can be understood, that rational explanations of phenomena are possible, that there are causal regularities that warrant inductive intuitions, is indicative of the appositeness of the idea of creation.[31] Once again, it does not logically imply that there is a Creator. But it can be treated in itself as a datum demanding (although not logically requiring) explanation. It was so treated when Einstein said that the most incomprehensible thing about the universe is that it is comprehensible. The thesis of creation makes possible an explanation of nature's comprehensibility: Nature itself is treated as an act of God, and its intelligibility is an expression of God's wisdom, to which we have an access, then, as broad or narrow as the objectivity or subjectivity of our own understanding and of the world's intelligible limits allow.

The ancients understood this; it was part of what they had in mind when they called the world the product of divine understanding. It was part of what Plato meant when he used the metaphor of a craftsman and a pattern; and the idea was preserved as an analogy by Aristotle, even when he dissolved that metaphor and rejected the assertion that the world was literally the product of any divine work.[32] But again, the medieval analysis refines the idea of creation and renders it more precious and more precise, as when medieval cosmologists pictured the microcosm as an organism rather than a machine. In creationism God's purpose and plan are seen as constituted within and through the work, rather than outside and prior to them and to God's creative act; and matter is seen as integral in what that act provides. For what a Creator creates is not an implement but a creature, whose gift of existence includes autonomy in some measure: the possibility, which each thing contains, of being an end in itself, a being of intrinsic worth rather than a mere means to extrinsic ends, and so testifying to a Creator's glory.

Once again, then, we find indices by which we may evaluate the claim that the world is not merely originated or eternally necessitated but created by a transcendent God: our discovery of intelligibility in the world—the possibility of science, explanation, rational understanding—militates in its favor. It does not prove the world created, for there are alternative accounts of such understanding. But it tends to confirm the thesis of creation, in view of the fact that one account, or one family of accounts, rests critically on the affirmation of the world's creation. The more extensive and elaborate our discovery of intelligibility in nature grows, the more extensively confirmed are those theological models which view the world as a manifestation of divinely transcendent intelligence. Similarly, but again more specifically, the discovery of autonomous value of all kinds—not merely the values of intelligibility, but the full range of the foundations of worth in the beauty, goodness, sheer exuberance, of the works of nature—can be read as an expression of divine creativity.[33] The discovery of such values inherent in the natures of things can, of course, be taken as supporting a kind of radical pluralism, egoism, anarchism. But in the context of the idea of creation, where the natural world at large is taken to be an ordered system, the exuberance of being serves to specify the concept of creation, interpreting it in a direction which regards the divine creative act not, say, as an imposition, but as imparting the freedom, power, and relative independence by which all natural things constitute and existentiate themselves in their natural contexts, and thereby express in their particular and specific ways the pure and universal, yet otherwise unspecifiable, grace and glory of God.

3. THE NEWNESS OF CREATION

According to ancient tradition God created miracles in the twilight of the sixth day.[34] But the imagery of natural creation is that of the morning: creation betokens newness. The biblical writers prescind from a genealogy of the gods or a theomachy prior to the story of the world's origin, partly for reasons of monotheistic chastity but partly to convey the sense of freshness and beginning. The opening word of the Torah is "in the beginning," and it evinces a desire to start the story that will unfold at its logical and ontological opening. There was no prior history. This is a story of absolute origination; and for that reason the poetic chastity of monotheistic imagery suits the naturalistic clarity and metaphysical economy of the account.[35] When the tradition of genesis is addressed by philosophers in the Arabic language, the word they use for 'originated' is *hadith,* which means 'temporal,' but also 'new.' Its opposite, *qadim,* means 'eternal' by application, but 'ancient' literally. The world of the creationist is not old; it is new, young. God is eternal and everlasting. The world is temporal and of finite, measured age, beyond which stands God alone.

When occasionalists endeavored to make creation a rational necessity demonstrable from the logic of finite being, the outcome was an affirmation of continual new creation.[36] Emanation too was interpreted as an affirmation of continuous creation, transferring the newness of the originated universe to a constant renewal of becoming from its ontic Source. Naturally enough, the theme of the world's newness complements and helps to interpret those of contingency and design. For the world is an invention; it did not have to be. Its detailed structure and particularity could not have been predicted *a priori* from a knowledge of God's goodness; and the being of its members and of its system at large serves no need of its Creator but expresses His glory, as a work of fine art (in lesser measure) does not serve the needs of its maker but expresses and embodies the maker's ideas and exists (in some ways) for its own sake.

The ancient meaning of the newness of creation, then, is freedom: God's freedom from constraint in the choice of His creation, and each creature's more limited freedom of self-existentiation, imparted with the imparting of existence. It is because the story of creation is a universal story—the origins of Adam being the origins of everyone, the breathing of a divine breath into the otherwise inert earth of our bodies—that the newness of creation abides with it beyond the initial creative act. No verbal or metaphysical trick like those of *Kalam* occasionalism is needed to achieve this universalization. Nature itself constantly renews itself, and the seasons are symbols not of passing or cyclicity but of rebirth and new growth out of decay.

Once again the ancient idea of newness acquires a new meaning in later hands. But here the authors of the change are modern rather than medieval. New force is given to the idea of newness by the discovery of evolution; and, more specifically, by the idea of emergence. For the existentiation of nature and the creatures in it is not static and passive but active and dynamic—dynamic on the creatures' part. They use the powers and freedoms they find within themselves. They grow, persist, or reproduce, striving to preserve and promote their own being, to express, perfect, and develop their own nature—minimally, to preserve and express that nature. Their essences in this striving are not fixed but evolving, not merely self-actualizing but emergent, that is, susceptible of a redefining in which they themselves as well as their surroundings are agents.[37] It is in this sense (not the passive and external sense of the *Kalam*) that creation is in fact continuous and ongoing. Again this dynamism involves the creativity of the artist rather than that of the artisan: evolution does not work to a preconceived plan but to generate a design that is fully real only in its embodiment and not static even there. Stars emerge from dust, elements from stars, compounds and living beings from elements. No feature of any higher order in evolution is externally predictable from the knowledge of its prior constituents or even describable in their terms; chemical properties are not deducible from the laws of physics or even describable in the terms required to set down those laws. Similarly with biological properties in relation to the principles of chemistry, and with psychological traits, powers, and capacities in relation to biology: the principles of the prior order are their environment; its constituents (to use a Neoplatonic analogy) are their "matter." But at each higher order of integration new capabilities and, crucially, new powers of self-expression and self-direction, new degrees of freedom, emerge. Physics does not "determine" chemistry but sets the stage for it, as chemistry does for biology, and biology for psychology, preparing the ground, as it were, for the emergence of consciousness, intelligence, and the human soul.

The laws of physics do, of course, set parameters for chemistry, and those of chemistry for biology. This is what reductionists refer to when they say that physical laws *determine* chemistry, and that biology is determined by chemistry in turn, the higher order properties being accounted for by reference to a Democritean mystique of complexity. But what is it actually that is called "complexity" in such reductionistic accounts? Subtle atomic interactions generate properties which are not adequately describable in merely atomic terms and whose outcomes are not accurately predictable from the atomic givens. Chemistry emerges from physics synthetically, as geometry might be said to emerge from arithmetic, and similarly, biology from chemistry. The principles needed to derive one from the other could be known only by one who already understood both with an infinitely comprehensive understanding, in which *a priori* and factual knowledge were indistinguishable from one another.

In the electric and magnetic properties of the subatomic particles, to be sure, the basis for chemistry (and thus for biology) was already laid. But it is only with the provision of the social environment of subtly varied constituents of nature that such potentialities are fulfilled. And the complexity that emerges is not the additive product of the nuanced variation of the given constitutions, but their constructive product, in which the dynamics of the more primordial forces take hold of the matter which is their vehicle and build in it new orders of complexity, capable of increasingly self-integrative expression and self-directive activity. Complexity is not the explanation but the outcome of this dynamism. Its explanation is the restless urge toward transcendence present in all things, not an animating *élan vital,* but a far more elementary and immediate presence: the active and dynamic force (*conatus*) which is the essence of each thing. Selves are the emergent product of the evolutionary dynamism which flourishes in our universe and whose efflorescence is manifest not only in our being but even in the commandeering of chemical forces by the biological and in the birth of stars.

In Aristotelian terms the intersection of causal trains among things not regularly related by the internal necessities of their essences is called chance or fortune ("luck"), when it recognizably affects the interests of the participants. Chance in this sense abounds in natural, interactive systems whose members are only moderately complex—so much so that the randomness of their interactions is a principal source of order in nature. Indeed it is of the essence of interaction generally that it contain a large random element, insofar as it relates things not intrinsically related. But it is also of the essence of the dynamism of interaction that it be opportunistic, that entities tend to express their identities upon and through one another. In so doing they enhance the order and complexity of their expression, enhance the information content of their environment, exploit the orderly aspects of random interactions to generate stabler, higher order, and more information-rich complexes, compounds, and communities, capable themselves of still greater enhancement and enrichment. In this sense randomness in nature is not a haphazard thing, and opportunity is not a matter of luck but a natural product of the self-actualizing character of things. It is the dynamism of individual things that pessimists neglect when they argue somberly that all energy flows to disorder. They regard it as somehow accidental that beings can generate order even out of the flow to entropy, as beavers use the energy of flowing water to create their habitats.

Newness in its ancient application refers to freedom from history and determination, the actuality of a fresh and unencumbered start, which belongs to the universe at large and, in some lesser measure, to every creature in it. In more modern terms, newness refers to evolution and specifically to the emergent character of evolution, in which the past is not the sole determinant of the future but present actions and events are determinants as well, and in which the powers imparted to creatures make them in some measure self-transcending, capable of rising above the limitations of their primal natures, self-creative to some degree, imaging the artistic creativity of God. The two notions of unencumberedness are not unrelated: just as we have visible evidence of the world's roundness when we look to the horizon, so we have experiental access to the world's newness when we recognize its unencumberedness even in the sense of discovering the fact of evolution or the possibility of human creativity. The world, we may infer, is still a-building.

We can find the world to be created, then, by discovering its newness—to be sure, in the sense of discovering evidences of its finite age, suggesting but not conclusively entailing its ultimate dependence on an act of God. But marks of another newness which are freighted with significance for us and which add a richer significance to our conception of God's act can be found nearer to hand as well, when we discover the extent to which the world is unencumbered and when we discover the ability of its creatures in their kinds to be true to form not by remaining true to form but by creating themselves—individually, intellectually, generationally, historically, and by species, genera, phyla, and kingdoms. God's creativity here is far more immediate than the distant (and therefore ancient) stars. Its evidences are no less to be found as the objective of a microscope than in the eyepiece of a telescope. They are, in the Qur'anic phrase, nearer to us than our jugular vein.

CONCLUSION

Our analysis of the idea of creation—at least in some of its ancient, medieval, and modern recensions—has given us a great many things to look for which will count as evidences of God's creation of the world. Indeed it has closed off no area of our knowledge or understanding from such explorations. And it has given us some fairly decisive considerations, which rival theses might otherwise account for or attempt to discount or dismiss, but which together form a case for creation while at the same time adding richness to its meaning. A universe in which rational, scientific understanding is possible but in which science is necessarily empirical, a universe in which there are freedom and evolution and in which beings exist for their own sakes according to their own emergent value and plan, a universe in which goals and purposes are inward in the first instance and values in the first instance are inherent or intrinsic, a universe, in short, which can be described as open rather than closed—that is, a universe with an open future, not blockaded by an infinite and overreaching past—is the sort of universe that a transcendent God might be conceived to have created as an expression of His glory. That is the sort of universe, I believe, in which we live.

NOTES

1. Sir John Eccles writes of "Einstein's derivation in 1915 of an expanding universe from his geometric account of gravitation, the General Theory of Relativity. To him at that time with his belief in a stationary everlasting universe, the idea of an expanding universe was highly distasteful, so he introduced a cosmological term into his equations to counteract the derivation of expansion. Then in 1912 the red shifts observed by Hubble in the spectrograms of galaxies produced empirical evidence for the expanding universe.

Forthwith Einstein rejected his cosmological term, calling it 'the biggest blunder of my life', and accepting the distasteful expanding universe.

"The clear formulation of the expanding universe from an initial great cataclysm was first made by Lemaitre in the early 1930s and in 1940 Gamow refined this proposal, and applied the emotive term 'Big Bang' to the cataclysm. However the initial estimates by Hubble for the rate of expansion were too high. They gave a date for the Big Bang, of only 2 billion years ago, which was in conflict with other estimates for the age of the Universe. Hence there was then good reason for the alternative hypothesis proposed by Gold, Bondi, and Hoyle, the steady-state hypothesis: the Universe had always existed; there was no origin in a Big Bang; the observed expansion was exactly compensated by the continuous creation of atomic particles; these particles in time aggregated to form new nebulae. Hence the composition of space was approximately steady, and it was isotropic, despite the continuous recession of already formed nebulae from each other. In terms of Natural Theology it would appear that, in their efforts to escape from a supernatural creation in the Big Bang by a Transcendent God, they had unwittingly proposed continual creation by an Immanent God!

"However, redetermination of the recession rate of nebulae now gives a much earlier dating for the Big Bang, about 19 billion years according to the present best estimates. We shall see that, because of the continuous slowing of the expansion rate by gravitational pull, this figure has to be reduced to 10–12 billion years, which is in good agreement with dates that can be derived for the origin by several methods. Furthermore the evidence for the Big Bang has now become most convincing by the discovery of the predicted faint 'echo' of the Big Bang, as an all-pervasive microwave radiation with a frequency corresponding to the average temperature of cosmic space, 3.0 degrees K" (J. Eccles, *The Human Mystery: The Gifford Lectures of 1977–78* [Berlin: Springer, 1979], pp. 12–13).

2. See R. Jastrow, *God and the Astronomers* (Boston: Norton, 1978). For "alibis" see L. E. Goodman and M. J. Goodman, "Creation and Evolution: Another Round in an Ancient Struggle," *Zygon* 18 (1983): 20–21. See also *Science News,* 3 August 1985; cf. P. W. Atkins, *The Creation* (San Francisco: Freeman, 1981), p. 109, for a nontheistic version; and C. W. Misner, "Cosmology and Theology," in *Cosmology, History and Theology,* ed. W. Yourgrau and A. D. Breck (New York: Plenum, 1977), for a thoughtfully theistic view.

3. *Genesis Rabbah* 9.2.

4. *K. al-Mukhtar fi 'l-Amanat wa 'l-Iʿtiqadat* [Book of Select Beliefs and Convictions] 1, Exordium, ed. Kafih (Jerusalem, 1970), p. 33; trans. Rosenblatt (New Haven: Yale University Press, 1949), pp. 38–39. Hereafter cited as *ED.*

5. See Eric Voegelin, *The Ecumenic Age,* vol. 4 of *Order and History* (Baton Rouge: Louisiana State University Press, 1974), pp. 112–13.

6. For al-Ghazali's argument see his Jerusalem Letter incorporated in

his *Ihya' 'Ulum al-Din* [Revival of Religious Sciences], Qawa'id al-ᶜAqa'id [Bastions of Convictions] Fasl 3; ed. and trans. A. L. Tibawi in *The Islamic Quarterly* 9 (1965): 78–122. And see L. E. Goodman, "Ghazali's Argument from Creation," *International Journal of Middle East Studies* 2 (1971) 67–85, 168–88.

7. Thus there is a structural symmetry between Genesis 1:18, 31 and Deuteronomy 32:1–4.

8. *Tahafut al-Falasifa* [Incoherence of the Philosophers] 3, 4, 10.

9. Maimonides *Dalalat al-Ha'irin* [Guide to the Perplexed], 3.27. Hereafter cited by part and chapter as *Moreh*.

10. For al-Ghazali, as for Maimonides, the empirical goodness of this life was a crucial factor in the argument for its divine creation. It was not just that the world was found to be contingent but that this good world was found to be contingent. Thus al-Ghazali's important departure from theistic subjectivism in holding that "nothing in the realm of possibility is more wondrous than what is." The departure did not go unnoticed by more doctrinaire Ashᶜarites. See Eric Ormsby, *Theodicy in Islamic Thought: The Dispute Over al-Ghazali's 'Best of all Possible Worlds'* (Princeton: Princeton University Press, 1984), and L. E. Goodman, review of *Theodicy in Islamic Thought* by Eric Ormsby, *Journal of the History of Philosophy* 25 (1987).

The present essay is not the proper place to address the problem of evil with the sort of full dress discussion that Josef Stern's allusions to it seem to request. I have reflected on the issues somewhat in my forthcoming books *On Justice* and Saadiah's *Book of Theodicy.* Here I can only remark that I find the claim that the world is not good to be coherent internally but usually radically incoherent with the other judgments of those who demand we entertain it.

As for the claim that Maimonides *wanted* us to believe that God is unknowable and that there is no relation of any kind between God and nature, the first item is refuted by Maimonides' elaborate discussion of the manner in which Scripture uses indirection to convey positive knowledge of God (as the necessary, self-sufficient, all-perfect Being—see *Moreh* 1.1–63 and my discussion in *RAMBAM* (New York: Schocken, 1977), pp. 52–119)—and the second internally. For if we take 'relation' to be as abstract a notion as *we* usually imply by the term, then even being unknowable is a relation between the Infinite and the finite, and Maimonides' statements about relative predications regarding God become incoherent. Alternatively, however, we can recognize that the Arabic term (*nisba*), which we usually translate by our term 'relation', has a rather more restricted reference and refers most specifically to relations of proportion (cf. S. Munk, *Guide des Égares* (Paris, 1856), *1:* 200, n. 1. There is, of course, no proportion or analogy in the strict sense between ourselves and God's unique perfection.

11. Having read Josef Stern's critique of the argument that passes from Avicenna to al-Ghazali to Maimonides and back to the critique of the Avicennan eternalism, I can only confess that I find unintelligible the notion that there is an equivocation operating here between the world's being contingent in itself and its being contingent through its causes. Avicenna is insistent that

all things are either necessary or contingent. Contingent here means capable of existing or not existing. If a thing is contingent (in itself) but actually exists, it must have a cause. It remains contingent in itself but was necessitated by its cause. For Avicenna the world is contingent in character, although necessitated by its cause, as it must be to be actual. Yet Avicenna believes the world's dependence upon God to be eternal. The brunt of al-Ghazali's critique is that the world's contingency is incompatible with its eternity. For Maimonides, the notion of the world's contingency is at least in militant disharmony with its eternity. To hold that the world is contingent in its existence and in other determinations is clearly in no way inconsistent with allowing that the world is necessitated by its cause. All effects are necessitated by their causes. They do not thereby become eternal. The arguments of Maimonides and of al-Ghazali (that claims regarding the contingency of the world are vitiated by claims as to its eternity) connect the Avicennan argument for contingency to the Ghazalian/Maimonidean argument for creation, and appeal to the notion of divine volition as the means of allowing the emergence of diversity and change from perfect unity as well as selecting among the otherwise undifferentiable virtualities of creation.

12. *Moreh* 2.17.

13. For the divinely ordained, or in Maimonidean terms, 'settled' order of nature, see Francis Oakley, "Christian Theology and Newtonian Science: The Rise of the Concept of the Laws of Nature," *Church History* 30 (1961), reprinted in *Creation: The Impact of an Idea,* ed. D. O'Connor and F. Oakley (New York: Scribners, 1969), pp. 54–83, esp. p. 73.

14. See *Moreh* 1.73.10 and cf. L. E. Goodman, "Maimonides and Leibniz," *Journal of Jewish Studies* 31 (1980): 214–36, incorporating Leibniz's reading notes on *The Guide to the Perplexed.*

15. *Moreh* 3.21.

16. *Tahafut al-Falasifa* 17, cf. L. E. Goodman, "Did al-Ghazali deny Causality?" *Studia Islamica* 47 (1978): 83–120.

17. *Al-Muqidh min al-Dalal* [Deliverance from Error], ed. F. Jabre (Beirut, 1959), pp. 50–51; trans. M. Watt, in *The Faith and Practice of Al-Ghazali* (London: Allen and Unwin, 1953), pp. 78–79; cf. Galen, *On Medical Experience* trans. of Hubaysh, ed., and R. Walzer (London, 1944), pp. 47, 122–23. See also Jabre, ed., p. 42; Watt, *Faith and Practice of al-Ghazali,* pp. 64–68 for al-Ghazali's alliance of mysticism with empiricism; cf. Jabre, p. 35; Watt, p. 55.

18. M. B. Foster, "The Christian Doctrine of Creation and the Rise of Modern Natural Science," *Mind* 43 (1934), reprinted in O'Connor and Oakley, *Creation.*

19. See Jacob B. Agus, "If God Be the Élan Vital," in his *Jewish Identity in an Age of Ideologies* (New York: Ungar, 1978), pp. 232–81; cf. C. F. von Weiszsäcker, *The Relevance of Science: The Gifford Lectures of 1959–60* (New York: Harper and Row, 1964).

20. Contingency as a reductive interpretation of creation is a key theme of Avicenna's in which, as we have seen, al-Ghazali finds a rub. Because the

world's possibility is deemed to require a substrate and thus to imply the world's eternity, al-Ghazali goes out of his way to subjectivize modal notions. See *Tahafut al-Falasifa* 1.4, in *Tahafut al-Tahafut,* ed. Bouyges (Beirut, 1930), p. 102: "The difficulty is that the possibility of which they speak comes down to a matter of subjective judgment: Whatever the mind can consider as existent, finding no obstacle to the making of that judgment, we call possible; but if we find such an obstacle, we call it impossible. If we cannot deem it nonexistent, we call it necessary. All of these are subjective determinations with no necessary external reference—as is proved in three ways: (*a.*) if possibility implied an objective actuality correlative to it, and whose possibility it could be said to be, then so would impossibility; but impossibility has no existence of its own nor any material basis in which it inheres. . . . (*b.*) black and white are judged possible by the mind prior to their existence, and if that possibility were correlative to the body in which these accidents were to appear, so that it could be said that its meaning was that this body could possibly become black or white, then the white itself would not be possible and could not be described as such. . . . (*c.*) the souls of men, by their own account, are free-standing substances, without body or matter and are not impressed upon matter yet are originated as conceived by Ibn Sina and other monotheistic philosophers: they have possibility prior to their origination when they have neither identity nor matter. . . ." This is a nominalist and psychologistic account of possibility as we use the term. Cf. Hume, *Dialogues Concerning Natural Religion* 9, but contrast Hume's account of necessity in relation to liberty and al-Ghazali's comparable theistic determinism. Al-Ghazali's critique is put to its intended use when Maimonides argues, as we have seen, that it is suppositious to insist that possibility requires a material substrate.

21. To the claim that if our knowledge were perfect our science would be deductive, I reply that the required perfection of understanding is of the sort that only God and no finite being could have: a finite being will always be in some measure fallible and ignorant. But in God the distinction between induction and deduction is meaningless, since God is a timeless being, and since in God the determination of what shall be done (God's will) and the determination of what is the case (God's knowledge or understanding) are one and the same. Accordingly, relative to God, the distinction between necessity and contingency dissolves. Indeed the distinction is irrelevant to us and other finite beings insofar as we act, and relevant insofar as we are acted upon.

22. See Saadiah, *Book of Theodicy: Translation and Commentary on the Book of Job,* trans. L. E. Goodman (New Haven: Yale University Press, 1987), Introduction, p. 15, etc.; cf. *ED* 9.4, trans. Rosenblatt, pp. 333–34.

23. *ED* 4 Exordium, cf. 3 Exordium.

24. See Chrisippus *ap.* Porphyry *De Abst.* 3.20, "God mingled soul, as if it were salt, with the flesh of this animal."

25. Spinoza *Ethics* 1, Appendix; cf. 2.18 Scholium; Hume *Dialogues Concerning Natural Religion,* 2-3 ed. N. Kemp-Smith (Indianapolis: Bobbs Merrill, 1947), pp. 143, 146; cf. 6-8.

26. See Foster, "Christian Doctrine of Creation," in *Creation,* ed. O'Connor and Oakley, p. 46.

27. For a description of human creativity in the arts and sciences see L. E. Goodman, "Why Machines Cannot Do Science," in *Essays on Creativity and Science,* ed. D. Deluca (Honolulu: Hawaii Council of Teachers of English, 1986), pp. 269–82.

28. See L. E. Goodman, "Matter and Form as Attributes of God in Maimonides' Philosophy," in *Derekh Yeshara: Essays in Honor of Arthur Hyman,* ed. R. J. Long and C. Manekin (Washington: Catholic University Press, 1987).

29. Mishnah *Sanhedrin* 4.5. Note the inference: "Therefore everyone must say, 'For my sake was the world created.'" For Philo's *logos,* see H. A. Wolfson, *Philo* (Cambridge, Mass.: Harvard University Press, 1962), 1:200ff.; David Winston, *Logos and Mystical Theology in Philo of Alexandria* (Cincinnati: Hebrew Union College Press, 1985).

30. *Moreh* 3.13; cf. 2.6 and Aboth 6:11. For Maimonides each thing in nature has its own imparted essence which it exists to fulfill. Cf. the discussion of the delegation of free will in *Mishneh Torah (Sefer Ha-Mada^c), Hilkhot Teshuvah,* 5.2, 5.1, and 5.4.8. (Contrast al-Ghazali *Munqidh* trans. Watt, p. 37.) Cf. L. E. Goodman, "Angels and Emanation," Proceedings of the Seventh International Congress on Neoplatonic Studies, 1988.

31. Here plainly I part company with Foster. My conception of induction (like Aristotle's) is Socratic (based on conceptual intuitions) rather than Humean (based on enumeration of perceptual instances), and I believe (*pace* Foster) that the rational definitions and explanations which such intuitions ground are as necessary as perceptual data to the scientific enterprise.

32. Aristotle writes: "Respecting perishable plants and animals we have abundant information, living as we do in their midst, and ample data may be collected concerning all their various kinds, if only we are willing to take sufficient pains. . . . The scanty conceptions to which we can attain of celestial things give us, from their excellence, more pleasure than all our knowledge of the world in which we live; just as a half glimpse of persons that we love is more delightful than an accurate view of other things, whatever their number and dimensions. On the other hand, in certitude and in completeness our knowledge of terrestrial things has the advantage. Moreover, their greater nearness and affinity to us balances somewhat the loftier interest of the heavenly things that are the objects of the higher philosophy . . . if some have no graces to charm the sense, yet nature, which fashioned them, gives amazing pleasure in their study to all who can trace links of causation, and are inclined to philosophy.

"Indeed it would be strange if mimic representations of them were attractive because they disclose the mimetic skill of the painter or sculptor and the original realities themselves were not more interesting, to all at any rate who have eyes to discern the causes. We therefore must not recoil with childish aversion from the examination of the humbler animals. Every realm of nature is marvellous: and, as Heraclitus, when the strangers who came to visit him found him warming himself at the furnace in the kitchen and hesitated to go in, is reported to have bidden them not to be afraid to enter, as even in that kitchen divinities were present, so we should venture on the study of every kind of animal without distaste; for each and all will reveal to us something natural and something beautiful. Absence of haphazard and conduciveness of everything to an end are to be found in nature's works in the highest degree, and the end for which those works are put together and produced is a form of the beautiful" (Aristotle *De Partibus Animalium,* 1.5,644b26ff., in *The Revised Oxford Translation of the Complete Works of Aristotle* ed. J. Barnes, trans. W. Ogle, [Princeton, N.J.: Princeton University Press, 1984], 2 vols., 1:1003–4). Or, in Ogle's original translation: "If some have no graces to charm the sense, yet even these, by disclosing to intellectual perception the artistic spirit that designed them, give immense pleasure to all who can trace the links of causation, and are inclined to philosophy." Aristotle's artificer is immanent and therefore allegorical. It is because he refuses to make the divine a *deus ex machina* that Aristotle here makes an exception to his usual rule of resolving Plato's imagery, leaving in his account the unresolved analogy of an artificer: there is no better way to describe the effect of nature's work than as a product of design, yet the design is the work of natural causes.

33. One must recognize, of course, that a stronger claim is made here than that of the mere compatibility of divine creation with the world's order and freedom. Although the evidence (being finite and experiential) can never *prove* creation, it can be explained by the hypothesis of creation; and to the extent that the ideas resident in the compact notion of creation more effectively conciliate the data, those data argue in behalf of creation as against rival accounts. The structure of the argument is that of Peirce's abduction rather than that of classical deduction.

Naturally it is no part of our project to seek to choose between volition and intelligence as models of divine creativity. A central theme emergent from Maimonides' investigation is the recognition that too many previous philosophers had needlessly dichotomized these two aspects.

34. *Aboth* 5.9; cf. *Genesis Rabbah* 5.5. See also Maimonides *Moreh* 2.29, who cites Eccles. 1:9 and *Abodah Zarah* 54b ("There is nothing new under the sun" and "The world runs in its accustomed way") in behalf of naturalism.

35. One can even interpret the celebrated prohibition of the rabbis—"Whoever reflects on four things, it were a mercy had he never come into the world: what is above, what is beneath, what is before and what is after" (*Hagigah* 2:1) as a restriction addressed not against metaphysical speculation (which is, after all, invited and encouraged by the Torah) but against a quest for the cause of the Cause of causes, the motives of the purely Good, the genealogy of God, etc.

36. See Majid Fakhry, *Islamic Occasionalism and its Critique by Averroes and Aquinas* (London: Allen and Unwin, 1958).

37. *Emergence,* as I am using the term, does not imply discontinuity

("saltation") in nature and is not confined to the differentiation of levels (e.g., the biological from the chemical). It does involve the non-deducibility (for a finite mind) of outcomes from the preestablished givens and is thus a crucial factor not only in evolution but also in learning, invention, discovery, and all other forms of creative activity. It is because the notion of emergence identifies and seeks to voice the lack of prior givenness of outcomes in the creative processes of nature that it affords a valid interpretation for one dimension of the concept of newness that the idea of creation portends.

For the opposition of self-determination and external determination, see L. E. Goodman, "Determinism and Freedom in Spinoza, Maimonides and Aristotle, A Retrospective Study," in *Responsibility, Character and the Emotions: New Essays in Moral Psychology,* ed. F. Schoeman (Cambridge: Cambridge University Press, 1987).

In response to Josef Stern's request for a vindication of the compatibility or congruence of the values I find within the idea of creation, I can offer the following, drawing upon a suggestive insight of Kant's cosmology: If God's act is eternal, His work should be present at all times. Intelligibility is most evident cosmologically in the past, in the determinate order of nature; creatively, in the future, in the openness of possibility; morally in the present, in the efficacy of human freedom, where determination meets the openness of possibility and marks it indelibly without unique character and stamp.

Response

Josef Stern

Lenn E. Goodman's ambitious paper is a new stab at old-fashioned "experimental" natural theology. However, unlike its eighteenth-century predecessors which Hume attacked in the *Dialogues Concerning Natural Religion,* it takes as its starting point the traditions of medieval Islam and Judaism instead of Christian theism. Nonetheless, I believe that Goodman's account works no better than its forebears and, in some cases, it is subject to the very same criticisms Hume first raised against Cleanthes' argument from design.

Before turning to some of these difficulties, I wish to raise a methodological problem which is posed by the dual nature of Goodman's attempt to argue for creation by appropriating medieval arguments and by locating himself in the tradition of medieval philosophy and theology. On the one hand, Goodman makes it clear that his aim is not, or not simply, scholarship or critical exposition of the views of the medieval authors. He wishes to argue himself for the *truth* of the thesis of the creation of the world. But for this purpose the appropriate arguments and evidence are ones which *we at present* hold true or justified given our current knowledge and beliefs. Claims and assumptions (e.g., those of Aristotelian physics, metaphysics, and cosmology) which the medieval authors accepted on the basis of evidence *then* available to *them* but which *we,* given our *present* knowledge, no longer hold to be true or justified may be historically interesting from this point of view, but they cannot be assumed for the sake of such an argument without significant revision or updating.[1] On the other hand, Goodman—rightly, in my opinion—does not want to consign the medieval heritage to mere historical interest. As he persuasively puts it, for medieval thinkers the idea of creation carried various "values," theological and moral values which they ascribed to the world by describing it as created. By turning to the medieval tradition, Goodman wishes to *reawaken* those same values in and to us—and thereby make the question of whether the world is created or eternal a *live* question of a *specific* kind for us. Now, each of these two aims is attractive, admirable, and unproblematic taken by itself. But when we try to combine them, we open ourselves to a methodological problem: the problem of how to draw on the medieval authors for substantive arguments that bear on the creation/eternity question as it concerned them—and as Goodman would like it to concern us—while, at the same time, remaining true to our current philosophical and scientific knowledge. I do not mean to suggest that this problem is insurmountable. But it is a problem that must be faced by someone with Goodman's joint aims and, as I shall now try to show, it is a problem which he does not entirely surmount. For reasons of space I shall concentrate my discussion on the first section of his paper.

Goodman begins by distinguishing between the two propositions that the world is originated (henceforth: O) and that it is divinely created, i.e., "originated by a supernal and transcendent being whose goodness makes Him worthy of worship" (henceforth: C). Origination, as he explains, is the more general notion and is compatible with both the creation and eternity hypotheses. There is furthermore, he argues, a significant disanalogy between the way the medievals viewed O and C and the way in which we view them. For the medieval philosophers, the burden of argument fell on demonstrating O; but once O was demonstrated, it was a "natural transition" for them to the further conclusion C. For modern philosophers and scientists, however, the situation is reversed: it is now largely agreed that in some sense O is true; the entire burden of argument at present falls on C, the claim that the world is not simply originated but divinely created. Now, if we grant Goodman this disanalogy and his appraisal of the present relative statuses of O and C, then the arguments we would expect to find him addressing to a *contemporary* audience in support of "creation" should be arguments for C in particular—i.e., for divine origination rather than for origination *simpliciter.* Furthermore, if his aim is to argue for the *truth* of C, then the arguments should be philosophically valid and sound given our current philosophical and scientific knowledge. But when we turn to the actual argument Goodman adduces in Part 1, what we find is an argument at best for O, and not specifically for C, and an argument that rests on a modal inference that many contemporary philosophers would probably not accept.

This argument is based on the first value—"contingency"—which the idea of creation is said to have carried for the medievals. According to Goodman, what the ascription of this value meant for them is "that the world [is] such that if God had not created it, it would not have existed." I take him to mean by this—since this value is meant to support C in particular, and not simply O—that if the world were not originated by God *in particular* (i.e., C), not simply if it were not originated in some or another way (i.e., O), it would not exist. Now, this "inference" from contingency to C itself needs more explanation than Goodman gives it but let us grant it for the sake of argument.[2] Still, as Hume pointed out with respect to the design argument, before we argue *from* contingency, we must argue *for* contingency. What is Goodman's evidence that the world *is* contingent? To that he answers: "the necessity of empiricism in science." If the world were necessary, then the "sciences legitimately could be conducted deductively" and, conversely, because a "part of scientific inquiry is necessarily inductive . . . , there is contingency in the world."

The problem with this two-step argument from empiricism to contingency and from contingency to C is that it turns on an equivocation over the meaning of the term 'contingent.' The evidence of empiricism in science only supports contingency in one sense of the term, a sense in which, in turn, it is evidence for O generally rather than for C in particular—which is, after all, not very surprising in light of Goodman's opening remark about the medieval concern with O rather than with C. That the world is contingent in the sense which is relevant to inferring C is a second claim which is itself given no evidence by Goodman. Let me briefly explain these two senses of 'contingent.' As Goodman notes in his paper medieval Muslim and Jewish philosophers following Avicenna generally distinguished between two modes of necessary and contingent existence: the necessity (contingency) of a state of affairs or object *in-itself* and the necessity (contingency) of a state of affairs or object *through-its-causes.*[3] Only God was generally considered to be necessary-in-himself; everything else was assumed to be contingent-in-itself and either necessary or contingent-through-its-causes. The Aristotelians who believed the world to be eternal, accordingly, took it to be necessary-through-its-causes (though contingent-in-itself); those who insisted on temporal creation in time held it to be contingent both in-itself *and* through-its-causes. Thus, the point of disagreement over whether the world was created or eternal was specifically over whether the world is necessary or contingent-through-its-causes; both sides assumed that it was contingent-in-itself. So, to return to Goodman's argument, the kind of contingency which he must show characterizes the world in order to argue specifically for C, and not simply for some kind of origination (which would also be compatible with the necessary existence, or eternity, of the world-through-its-causes), must also be specifically contingency-through-its-causes. This he does not do. The evidence he cites for "contingency," namely, the fact that science is "necessarily inductive" or empirical, only shows that the world is contingent-in-itself, not that it is (also) contingent-through-its-causes. As Goodman states the argument, "because things have been delegated active and dynamic control over their own destinies, *in interaction with one another*, . . . things might have been other than as they are, they are not all fixed eternally in *the necessities of their own natures*" (my emphasis)—i.e., they are not necessary-in-themselves.[4] Hence, Goodman's evidence for the "contingency" of the world is not for the kind of contingency-through-its-causes that he requires in order to support creation. Indeed, one might argue on the contrary that the extent to which there exists a *science* of the world at all, albeit an empirical one, suggests that the world is necessary-through-its-causes and, hence, for the eternity rather than creation of the world!

In sum, then, the first difficulty with Goodman's attempt to utilize the medieval argument for creation from the contingency of the world is that the evidence he gives for such contingency only supports the thesis (O) that the world is originated—i.e., that its existence is contingent-in-itself—a thesis which is compatible both with the eternity and creation hypotheses. However "natural" it was for the medieval philosophers to make the further transition from origination to creation, the argument Goodman needs to move us moderns is still lacking.

Many contemporary philosophers are likely to raise a different objection to Goodman's argument which is also, however, related to the step from the empirical or inductive nature of science to the contingency of the world. Goodman correctly emphasizes that the objects of necessity and contingency are states of affairs, "the world and the things in it," rather than objects of the understanding or judgments; i.e., these modal predicates refer to objective metaphysical properties and not simply to epistemic features of propositions. But if necessity and contingency are *metaphysical* properties of the world, then they are not implied by any *epistemological* claims about the nature of our knowledge of the world, e.g., from the fact that our science is either deductive (or *a priori*) or inductive (or *a posteriori*). As philosophers of recent years have argued, the two metaphysical and epistemological modalities might be kept sharply distinct; in particular, one cannot simply infer that what is known *a priori* is necessary and what is known *a posteriori* is contingent—because there can be shown to exist necessary *a posteriori* as well as contingent *a priori* truths.[5] Hence, even if we grant Goodman the necessarily empirical status of our scientific knowledge, it does not follow that the object of that knowledge, the world, is therefore metaphysically contingent.

A stronger argument for divine creation—"origination by a God whose goodness makes Him worthy of worship"—as distinguished from origination in general is the goodness of the world, another "value" which Goodman does attach to the idea of creation, but which, for reasons that remain unclear to me, he conflates with the value of contingency. The main weakness with Goodman's presentation of this argument is his utter silence about the greatest difficulty for all natural theological arguments for a deity possessing moral attributes: the existence of evil. If, as Goodman says, the creation thesis is an appropriate explanation of the world's goodness, the world's evil is at least equally strong evidence against the same thesis. In other words, what Goodman fails to show in this case is that the world *is* good, an assumption that was never taken lightly, even by the medievals, and which, in light of the Holocaust, at the very least needs some defense.[6] Without some attention to this classical difficulty, Goodman's argument is radically incomplete.

The last comment I would like to make about this first section of Goodman's paper, a comment that bears on natural theology arguments in general, concerns what he calls "al-Ghazali's challenge" both to the Aristotelians who saw God as the first cause of an eternal, or necessarily existent, world and to Maimonides who presents Him as a Neoplatonic metaphysical or ontic cause from whom the world eternally emanates.[7] According to Goodman's al-Ghazali, and as Goodman himself appears to concur, such a conception of God as Creator is "unfalsifiable" and, therefore, vacuous. "The world's existence and character (if necessitated by God's) give us no sort of insight into God's nature or intentions for it or for us." One can *call* such a cause anything one wants, including 'Creator' or 'Author'; but, if the universe is eternal, or necessary, and God's act "made no actual difference to its existence or character," there is no substantive content to the description.

Now Goodman appears to view this consequence as a serious defect of Maimonides' neoplatonized Aristotelianism, but it seems to me to be the very conclusion—however paradoxical—which Maimonides intended for us to draw. The world should *not* offer us any "insight" into the nature of God. For if it did, there would exist some relation, likeness, or association between God and the world, in which case the former being would not be *God* who, in virtue of His unity and incomparability, can bear no relation to the world and must be entirely unknowable.[8] Therefore, only if the cause of the existence and nature of the world is entirely unknowable and unlike it, can that cause be a deity. A similar tension, moreover, underlies all natural theology, "experimental," and design arguments for a deity, a tension well recognized by Hume. Proponents of natural theology attempt to demonstrate the existence of a deity, or creator, by showing that only if we assume that there exists a creator, or author, with a certain nature (e.g., intelligence and various purposes), can we explain various features of the world (e.g., its design or order). Thus, the question of the existence of God on these accounts is inseparable from the question of his nature. The difficulty is that the nature of the being whom we show to exist with such arguments invariably turns out to fall short of our conception of a deity. And, typically, the stronger we make such arguments or inferences for the *existence* of an author of the world, the more the *nature* of that author falls short of a deity. Therefore, to the extent to which we can argue for the existence of a creator from the character of the world, that creator will fall short of having the properties we would want to attribute to a deity. And the more deity-like we make the creator, the weaker the evidence in the world for his existence. This tension seems to me to be the true obstacle in the way of natural theological arguments for a divine creator—and it is this same difficulty to which I think Maimonides is sensitive in the very chapters of the *Guide* to which Goodman refers.

Let me conclude with three brief comments on the last two sections of Goodman's paper and on the second and third "values" of creation.[9] First, throughout the paper, Goodman emphasizes that the values which he believes are characteristic of the world do not logically imply a creation hypothesis, but only serve as evidence for which creation is the best explanation. But this raises the question: how *strong* is this evidence for creation? As Hume might say, at best Goodman shows that the existence and character of the world are logically *compatible* with the existence of a deity; it is, however, much less clear that the evidence he cites is so compelling that, on observing it, we would *infer* the existence of a deity or divine creator.

Second, in arguing from the design of the world for creation, Goodman draws an intriguing distinction between the creative artist and the artisan-craftsman. The design found in the world, he suggests, is that of the former, not the latter: the divine creator of the world is an artist who wills his design in the course of creating the world, not a craftsman who simply makes a product in conformity to a preexistent plan. Now, as this description of the contrast suggests, the artist—as opposed to artisan—conception of the creator emphasizes his volitional side, though (from other comments Goodman makes) it does not seem to exclude a divine intelligence. But what is not then clear is how, as Goodman next claims, the "intelligibility and the functional autonomy of nature" is evidence of the one *rather than* the other. On the contrary, if Goodman's argument for creation is of the form of an inference to the best *explanation* of the data, the more volitional one makes one's conception of the creator, the less it would seem that one thereby *explains* the design in the world.

Finally, to conclude with a question for Goodman: Even if each of his three values "argues for" *a* creator, is it the *same* creator who is argued for by all three? Are the "creators" invoked to explain each of these values in principle mutually compatible? Are the design, intelligibility, and functional autonomy of nature which characterize the second value compatible with the newness, unpredictability, chance, and emergence which characterize the third value? This question is, of course, a question not only about the coherence of Goodman's divine creator but also about "the sort of universe, [he] believe[s], in which we live."[10]

NOTES

1. For a helpful example of such an extension, see Goodman's discussion of design in Part 2 of this paper.

2. Goodman repeatedly states that these "inferences" from the values of the world to C are not logical entailments or implications. It is not, however, clear how strong or weak he means his intended inferences to be; on this, see below. If I understand his position, his idea of an inference is closest to that of an "inference to the best explanation" of the explanadum (e.g., the "values" of the world). In any case, the present objection is independent of this issue.

3. For a detailed discussion of Avicenna's distinction, see Fazlur Rahman's contribution to this volume.

4. For reasons that are unclear to me, Goodman also seems to assume that all necessity is deductive or logical necessity; see, e.g., pp. 00–00. Perhaps this is because he thinks of necessity *simpliciter* as necessity-in-itself and that necessity-in-itself is known *a priori*.

5. The *locus classicus* for such arguments is Saul Kripke, *Naming and Necessity* (Cambridge, Mass.: Harvard University Press, 1980).

6. For one view of the theological impact of the Holocaust on the question of creation, see David Blumenthal's contribution to this volume.

7. This is so in Goodman's interpretation of Maimonides' position. As is notoriously well-known, almost any interpretation of Maimonides is bound to be controversial. Whether Goodman's interpretation is correct is, therefore, a question I will forego here.

8. The paradox, of course, is nonetheless maintaining that there exists a causal relation between God and the world. For some discussion of this point, see Seymour Feldman, "A Scholastic Misinterpretation of Maimonides' Doctrine of Divine Attributes," in *Studies in Maimonides and St. Thomas Aquinas,* ed. J. Dienstag (New York: Ktav, 1976); and Jonathan W. Malino, "Maimonides' Guide to the Perplexities of Creation" (unpublished thesis, Hebrew Union College–Jewish Institute of Religion, 1979).

9. For reasons of space and lack of expertise in the philosophy of biology, I shall not enter into Goodman's arguments for newness which, slender as they are, nonetheless seem to me to conflate (1) questions of strict reducibility among levels of explanation, and the notion of emergence that arises from the synchronic organization of a level of explanation, with (2) questions of predictability in diachronic evolutionary theory (e.g., because of mutation), and the related notion of evolutionary emergence. Although there may be *some* connection between the two sets of issues, it needs much more explication than Goodman gives it.

10. I wish to thank Jonathan Malino and William Wimsatt for discussion of issues raised in this comment.

Creation and Time in Maimonides and Gersonides

Tamar Rudavsky

I. INTRODUCTION

In this paper I should like to contrast the views of Maimonides and Gersonides on the topics of creation and time. It is my hope that this comparison will not only help to shed light on the views of each representative thinker, but will enable us to get a better handle on the status of creation theories in the Middle Ages. I have chosen to concentrate on these two thinkers for several reasons: not only do Maimonides and Gersonides represent the apex of medieval Jewish philosophy, but they reflect a wide variety of responses on many different areas. However, unlike Maimonides, whose works have been scrutinized over the centuries, Gersonides' philosophical writings have been virtually ignored until recent years. Both philosophers regard the problem of creation to be of paramount importance. For both, it represents an apparent clash between an Aristotelian and a theological world view. For Aristotle posits an eternal universe in which time and matter are potentially, if not actually, infinite. That is, Aristotle argues that since there can be no "before" to time, time and the universe were not created, but rather are "beginningless."[1] Jewish philosophers, however, are committed to a theological system in which a divine creator willfully brought the universe into existence. At the same time they want to accept certain aspects of Aristotle's theory of time and universe. Hence both philosophers must reconcile for themselves a number of strands in

Aristotelian thought; most important, they must be able to explain the existence of the universe in time.

The importance of creation cannot be overemphasized, for it is here that the apparent clash between philosophy and theology is most keenly felt. Just as contemporary philosophers are now trying to assess the cosmological implications of the various strands of the Big Bang theory within a theological context, so too did medieval Jewish philosophers have to incorporate the Aristotelian cosmology into their own theological framework.

Could the world have begun to exist at a particular instant in time? In a recent paper, N. Kretzmann has described several options which Scholastic philosophers adopted with respect to this question. Medieval philosophers in general were confronted with two basic responses:

1.1 The world had a beginning; that is, it began to exist at some (theoretically at least) specifiable instant.
1.2 The world has existed from eternity: that is, it is beginningless.

According to Kretzmann, what he terms the "cautious" philosopher is one who claims that (1.2) is not disprovable except on the basis of divine revelation, whereas the "bold" philosopher claims that (1.2) can be disproved on logical or natural grounds. That is, unlike the "bold" philosophers who claim that the world *could not* have existed from eternity, "cautious" philosophers are willing to entertain evidence which supports the view that the world *could* have existed from eternity.[2]

Inasmuch as Jewish philosophers accepted (1.1), or a version of it, on the basis of revelation, they were constrained to argue that (1.2) must be false if only because it contradicts (1.1). Neither Gersonides nor Maimonides, however, is a "bold" philosopher in that both are unwilling to reject (1.2) outright. How, then, might they approach (1.2) from the standpoint of (1.1)? One way might be to refute those arguments which support the "bold" thesis that the world *could not* have existed from eternity. Another way might be to postulate a third option, namely

1.3 The world is both beginningless and created.

Throughout history various versions of (1.3) have been adopted. The most popular has been that of Plato according to whom the Demiurge created the world out of an eternally preexistent matter.[3] Plotinus' cosmology represents a refinement of the Platonic model within an emanationist ontology; this ontology presumed that the world proceeds from the One in a necessary emanation.[4] And finally, Islamic philosophers blended elements of Neoplatonic emanationism with theological components to develop their own conception of "eternal creation".

In general, it can be seen that (1.3), which represents an amalgam of (1.1) and (1.2), describes a world that is *both* divinely created and *beginninglessly* existent.[5] Proponents of (1.3) claim that the universe is eternal without eliminating the need for a divine creator. This creator is the ontological cause or explanation of the universe. In the context of (1.3) the term 'eternity' can be understood in two ways: first, as postulating an infinitely extended world which has no temporal beginning (and possibly no end as well); and second, as postulating a world which is continuously created. It is important to note that although the first sense of (1.3) has affinities with (1.2), the difference between them has to do with the role of a creator. (1.3) will prove important in our subsequent discussion, for I shall suggest that both Gersonides and Maimonides accept a version of (1.3). That is not to say that either thinker rejects a belief in a creator deity. Rather, they will argue both that God is a creator and that the world is beginningless in a particular sense.

My strategy will be the following. After a brief introduction, I shall lay out the major conflicts between Aristotle, Maimonides, and Gersonides. I shall then turn to a brief discussion of Aristotle's theory of time, followed by an elaboration of the views of Maimonides and Gersonides. Although my main concern in this paper is with Maimonides' theories, I shall use Gersonides to elucidate the Maimonidean discussion.

II. THE CREATION CONTROVERSY IN MAIMONIDES AND GERSONIDES

Scholars in recent years have renewed the controversy concerning how to interpret Maimonides' views on creation. As is well known,

Maimonides himself gave impetus to the contention that the ostensibly orthodox views epoused in the *Guide of the Perplexed* are not necessarily his own. In the introduction to the *Guide* Maimonides distinguishes two levels of interpretation, exoteric and esoteric, and suggests that it is sometimes incumbent upon philosophers to conceal their own esoteric position behind the veil of exoteric doctrine.[6] Maimonides further describes seven sorts of contradictions commonly found in philosophical works and suggests that two of these (#5 and #7) may be used specifically to conceal potentially controversial or even heretical doctrines from the masses.[7] He then states that any contradictions found in the *Guide* itself are intentional and are of type #5 or type #7.[8] Finally, Maimonides characterizes the doctrine of creation as a potentially volatile, and certainly an extremely challenging, topic, so that when readers of the *Guide* turn to chapters 2.13–30 devoted to creation, they have already been forewarned by the author to expect at least a modicum of ambiguity at best, or outright deception at worst.

Discussion surrounding Gersonides' analysis of creation is not nearly as controversial; perhaps unwisely, Gersonides did not create around his works such an aura of intrigue and his philosophical corpus was largely ignored until the present century. Writing in fourteenth-century France, Gersonides spent several years in the papal court in Avignon, and may at that time have come into contact with the views of Ockham and other fourteenth-century Scholastics. His major work, *Milhamot Adonai,* is a sustained examination of the major philosophical issues of the day.[9] In this work Gersonides tries to reconcile traditional Jewish beliefs with what he feels are the strongest points in Aristotle; although a synthesis of these systems is his ultimate goal, the strictures of philosophy often win out at the expense of theology.

The problem of creation is a good example of this attempted synthesis. We have already noted that Aristotle posits an eternal universe in which time is potentially infinite. Gersonides, however, will want to argue that both time and motion are finite and created; hence he must eliminate Aristotle's notion of infinitely extended time altogether. Since both Maimonides and Gersonides adhere to an Aristotelian theory of time, let us briefly look at the crucial components of this theory in the context of their respective discussions.

III. ARISTOTELIAN CHARACTERIZATION OF TIME

Aristotle claims in a number of texts that since time is defined in terms of motion, there can be no time without motion. For example, in his work *De Caelo* Aristotle argued that time is an integral part of the cosmos. He had already postulated that there can be no body or matter outside of the heavens, since all that exists is contained within the heavens. Since, however, time is defined as the number of movement, and there can be no movement without body, it follows that there can be no time outside of the heavens.[10]

On the basis of this characterization of time, Aristotle offers a number of arguments supporting (1.2), namely, that the universe is beginningless. Of these, one argument is of direct relevance to us. It has to do with the nature of creation, and can be restated as follows:

[A] Argument from Motion

2.1 If time came to be, it would have come to be in time.
2.2 This would imply a time before the original time.
2.3 Time is inseparable from motion.
2.4 Motion is connected to the moved object (that is, the outer sphere).
2.5 This moved object moves in a single, continuously circular motion, which is itself eternal.
2.6 Since time is inseparable from motion, it too is continuous.
2.7 Hence time is eternal.[11]

From the contention that time is eternal, Aristotle goes on to conclude that the universe as a whole is eternal.

Maimonides' discussion reflects this Aristotelian characterization of time. In the introduction to Part 2 of the *Guide* Maimonides lists twenty-five propositions drawn from Aristotle which purportedly he accepts. Number 15 pertains to time, as follows:

> Proposition 15: Time is an accident consequent upon motion and is necessarily attached to it. Neither of them exists without the other. Motion does not exist except in time, and time cannot be conceived by the intellect except together with motion. And all that with regard to which no motion can be found, does not fall under time.[12]

In positing this definition of time, Maimonides is clearly following the Aristotelian definition of time as the "measure of motion."[13] But does he accept as demonstration what Aristotle would have taken to be an implicit consequence of proposition 15, namely, that the universe itself is eternal? This question, of course, has been and continues to be the subject of extended discussion, but it is important to note that in the introduction to the *Guide* Maimonides does not rule out the *plausibility* of such a thesis. Although he is quick to point out that Aristotle "does not affirm categorically that the arguments he put forward in its favor constitute a demonstration" for the eternity thesis, Maimonides clearly disagrees with the *Mutakallimun* who attempted to demonstrate the impossibility of such a claim.[14] Rather, Maimonides states that "it seems that the premise in question is possible—that is, neither necessary . . . nor impossible. . . ."[15] Aristotle himself, he points out, only considered his theory as probable and not as necessary. This is an important point, the implications of which will emerge shortly. Suffice it to say that at this point Maimonides appears to align himself with those "cautious" philosophers who are unwilling to deny at least the logical possibility of eternal creation.

IV. CREATION MODELS IN MAIMONIDES

The focus of recent discussion has centered around Maimonides' taxonomy of creation and prophecy theories, both of which appear, at least on the basis of Maimonides' word, to be related. In *Guide* 2.13, he describes three opinions on creation, and then in 2.32 he describes three opinions on prophecy, stating that "the opinions of people concerning prophecy are *like* their opinions concerning the eternity of the world or its creation in time."[16] Is the word *like* supposed to posit a one-to-one correspondence between the two sets of opinions? If so, can Maimonides' own position be linked with any one set of correspondences, or is his allegiance split? In answer to these questions, interpreters have suggested every possible combination, and have offered almost every possible strategy for determining which is Maimonides' own view.[17] In this paper I shall not enter the Maimonidean taxonomy controversy *per se.* My main concern, rather, is to elucidate the theory of time/temporality which evolves out of his discussion of creation.

In 2.13, Maimonides summarizes what he considers to be the three standard views on creation as the scriptural, Platonic, and Aristotelian views. The main elements of each theory, as depicted by Maimonides, can be summarized as follows:

3.1 *The scriptural view:* that the universe was brought into existence by God after "having been purely and absolutely nonexistent"; through his will and his volition, God brought into "existence out of nothing all the beings as they are, time itself being one of the created things."[18]

3.2 *The Platonic view:* that inasmuch as even God cannot create matter and form out of absolute nonexistence (since this constitutes an ontological impossibility and does not impute impotence to God), there "exists a certain matter that is eternal as the deity is eternal. . . . he is the cause of its existence . . . and that He creates in it whatever He wishes."[19]

3.3 *The Aristotelian view:* agrees with (3.2) in that matter cannot be created from absolute nonexistence, but concludes that the heaven is not subject to generation/corruption; that "time and motion are perpetual and everlasting and not subject to generation and passing-away."[20]

How do these three views compare to the views adduced earlier? (1.1) and (3.1) are clearly in accord, in that both postulate creation after absolute nonexistence. Harvey points out the importance of distinguishing this theory from creation *ex nihilo;* for whereas the latter may be interpreted to signify continuous creation out of nonexistence, (3.1) implies that *before* creation there was sheer nonexistence. (3.1) is thus incompatible with eternity, whereas creation *ex nihilo* can be made compatible.[21] (3.3) can be seen as Maimonides' understanding of (1.2) in that both postulate an eternally beginningless universe. Finally, (3.2) is a version of (1.3) in that both postulate a creator as well as an eternal substance out of which the universe is created. That is, both (1.3) and (3.2) represent versions of eternal creation.[22] From here on in, I shall refer primarily to Maimonides' rendition of these three positions.

Several observations can be made concerning the relations among these three characterizations. First, contrary to those who "imagine that our opinion and his [Plato's] opinion are identical,"[23]

Maimonides is quick to disabuse those who are tempted to posit a connection between (3.1) and (3.2). The Platonic view, he states, cannot be substituted for Mosaic doctrine, even though there appear to be superficial similarities between the two. Secondly, Maimonides' attitude toward the relation between (3.2) and (3.3) is ambiguous. He first contrasts them on the grounds that the Platonists believe that the entire heaven is subject to generation and passing away, whereas the Aristotelians believe that only the sublunar sphere is subject to such generation and passing away.[24] He then dismisses (3.2) as not worthy of serious consideration on the grounds that

> [both] believe in eternity; and there is, in our opinion, no difference between those who believe that heaven must of necessity be generated from and pass away into a thing or the belief of Aristotle who believed that it is not subject to generation and corruption.[25]

In other words, he dismisses the original grounds for contrast between (3.2) and (3.3) and then argues that if the latter can be refuted, so too can the former be disqualified as a justifiable creation theory. In short, Maimonides appears to equate the positing of eternal preexistent matter with the positing of an eternally beginningless universe. But, as we discussed earlier, clearly there is a difference between the two. Maimonides is equivocating on the various meanings of the term 'eternal' adduced earlier.

Which of these three views is espoused by Maimonides himself? Ostensibly, at least, Maimonides supports (3.1). Having dismissed (3.2) as a weaker version of (3.3), he argues that (3.1) is no more flawed than is (3.3). Then, pointing to the possibility of (3.1), coupled with its Mosaic (and Abrahamic) sanction, Maimonides argues that the very plausibility of (3.1) suggests the nonnecessity of (3.3). In other words, Maimonides employs the stance of the "bold" philosopher by claiming that on the basis of the veridical nature of Scripture, (3.3) must be abandoned. In chapter 25 Maimonides lays out several pragmatic reasons as well for supporting (3.1) over (3.3). The most important of these is that (3.3) would destroy belief not only in the Law but in miracles and prophecy as well:

> the belief in the way Aristotle sees it—that is, the belief according to which the world exists in virtue of necessity, that no nature changes at all, and that the customary course of events cannot be modified

> with regard to anything—destroys the Law in its principle, necessarily gives the lie to every miracle, and reduces to inanity all the hopes and threats that the Law has held out.[26]

(3.2), on the other hand, is not nearly as devastating: for the opinion of Plato would "not destroy the foundations of the Law and would be followed not by the lie being given to miracles, but by their becoming admissible."[27] Why, then, does Maimonides not accept (3.2)? The main reason, as he tells us, is that the Platonic view has not been demonstrated: "In view of the fact that it has not been demonstrated, we shall not favor this [Plato's] opinion, nor shall we at all heed that other opinion [Aristotle's], but rather shall take the texts according to their external sense. . . ."[28]

If we take Maimonides at his word, then, it is clear that (3.1), creation in time of the universe out of absolute nonexistence, is his view. If, however, we are inclined to take seriously Maimonides' original demarcation between an exoteric and an esoteric reading of controversial issues, then it is tempting to dismiss his espousal of (3.1) as an exoteric position and to search for the underlying, or concealed, interpretation which is Maimonides' real view of creation. And as commentators working through the text have demonstrated, there is certainly ample evidence to support either (3.2) or (3.3) as Maimonides' esoteric view.

In fact, there is so much conflicting evidence, all of which can be supported with plausible argument, that S. Klein-Braslavy has recently suggested in a provocative article that perhaps Maimonides is not as definitive in his views as scholars have been wont to believe. In fact, she suggests that ultimately Maimonides upheld a skeptical stance in light of the evidence and did not take to heart any of the three positions. Inasmuch as Maimonides has clearly questioned the demonstrability of each of these views, it is not unreasonable to postulate, she avers, that the true esoteric view of Maimonides is cosmological skepticism.[29] This is not to say that the problem of creation can never be resolved; such metaphysical skepticism is not what Maimonides has in mind. Rather his position is that at present, human intellect is unable to resolve the matter. Portraying Maimonides as a ruthlessly rigorous thinker, Klein-Braslavy suggests that perhaps the moral of these chapters is that when the evidence is conflicting and unsupported by sound Aristotelian demonstration, the only justifiably rational stance is to withhold one's belief until such time as adequate demonstration becomes possible. Yet it should be noted that while such a skeptical view would not be quite so heretical as espousing either (3.2) or (3.3), it still constitutes a provisional rejection of (3.1), which is tantamount to a rejection of the Mosaic theory.

Although I am inclined to agree with the spirit of Klein-Braslavy's assessment, my own strategy is slightly different. I shall argue that, based on considerations of the nature of time, Maimonides recognizes that (3.1) is untenable. He is inclined to accept (3.2) on the grounds that it offers the possibility of reconciling theories of creation and eternity. However, Maimonides has already argued that a stringent reading of (3.2) is tantamount to an acceptance of (3.3). (3.3) would accord with Maimonides' own views on time; it would, however, greatly reduce the need for a creator of the universe. Maimonides is certainly aware of eternal creation as a compromise position, but is uncomfortable with the Islamic formulation of this view.[30] Such a position would best serve his purposes, however, with respect to reconciling a theory of creation with an Aristotelian theory of time. Hence, Maimonides reserves opinion with respect to both (3.2) and (3.3), is clearly uncomfortable with (3.1), and leaves open the possibility of a position close to (1.3) without specifying its details. This position, while similar to (3.2), employs aspects of (3.3) as well; it is closest in temperament to a Neoplatonic version of eternal creation.[31] In support of this contention I should like to offer several considerations based on the nature of time and temporality. Let us turn, then, to four important contexts in which Maimonides concerns himself with time.

V. TIME AND TEMPORALITY IN MAIMONIDES

The first extended discussion of time occurs in 2.13, in the context of delineating (3.1). Having stated that (3.1) involves the creation of all existence, including time, "time itself being one of the created things,"[32] Maimonides raises several puzzles concerning creation and time. The first has to do with how time and motion can be created independently. For if, as Maimonides has already stated in proposition 15, time is consequent upon motion, then time and moving things must be created simultaneously, since neither has any ontological status without the other. But Maimonides does not adopt this route, and does not posit simultaneous creation. Rather, he suggests that "what is moved—that is, that upon the motion of which time is consequent—is itself created in time and came to be after not having been."[33] This statement suggests that first God created time, and then He created moving things in time. It should be noted, however, that this statement contradicts the accepted Aristotelian definition of time which Maimonides accepted in proposition 15.

Secondly, Maimonides raises the issue of the relation between God's actions and the domain of temporality. Surely, he claims, no temporal predicates can be used to describe God's activities or nature *before* the creation, since then there is no time:

> Accordingly, one's saying: God 'was' before He created the world—where the word 'was' is indicative of time—and similarly all the thoughts that are carried along in the mind regarding the infinite duration of His existence before the creation of the world, are all of them due to a supposition regarding time or to an imagining of time and not due to the true reality of time.[34]

Several points are worth noting in this passage. First, Maimonides is suggesting that inasmuch as God transcends the temporal sphere and does not operate in a temporal context,[35] to predicate of God infinite duration has no temporal meaning. Secondly, and perhaps even more important for our purposes, Maimonides' use of the terms 'supposition' or 'imagining' of time (*demut zeman*) brings to mind his dismissal of the *Mutakallimun* on the grounds that they were unable to distinguish between imagination and intellect.[36] Maimonides is suggesting that (3.1) involves one in a crude or vulgar understanding of time based on imagination, one which is contrasted with the "true reality of time." This true reality, of course, is consistent with an Aristotelian theory of time.

The implication of Maimonides' discussion with respect to creation is that "God's bringing the world into existence does not have a temporal beginning, for time is one of the created things."[37] Maimonides does *not* want to suggest that time itself is eternal, for "if you affirm as true the existence of time prior to the world, you are necessarily bound to believe in the eternity [of the world]."[38] But neither will he claim that the creation of the world is a *temporally specifiable* action, for the world, on the Aristotelian definition of time, must be *beginningless* in the sense that it has *no temporal* beginning.

This last point is brought out as well in Maimonides' commentary on the word *b'reshit,* the first word of Genesis 1:1. What does Scripture mean by saying that "In the *beginning* God created . . ."? In order to explain the sense of 'beginning' being used in this context, Maimonides turns in *Guide* 2.30 to an interpretation of the two terms *tehilah* and *reshit,* both of which mean "start" or "beginning." As Klein-Braslavy has pointed out, Maimonides distinguishes between the two on the basis of causal priority.[39] We can specify an event/state of affairs *A* as being causally prior to *B* in one of two ways:

4.1 When *A* is a part of *B.*
4.2 When *A* is not a part of *B* but rather appears simultaneously with it.

In both cases the term *tehilah,* or causal beginning, can be used. In contradistinction, the term *reshit* refers not to a *temporal* priority of *A* to *B,* but rather to its ontological genesis.[40] On this basis Maimonides is able to allow for an interpretation of the word *b'reshit* in such a way as to accord with eternal creation. The *b'* prefix in the word *b'reshit* is not, on this reading, a temporal indicator, but rather fixes the event in question ontologically: it refers not to a temporal beginning but to an underlying ontological state. Thus when we read the statement in Genesis 1:1 ("*b'reshit barah elohim*" = "in the beginning God created"), we should understand it to describe a nontemporal event, one which specifies *that* God is the creator of the universe, that is, its ontological ground of being.

How then does Maimonides interpret those rabbis who understood the creation account in Genesis to postulate a domain of temporality before the creation event? For example, how there can be 'one day', at the beginning of creation, when the temporal indicators, i.e., sun and moon, were not created until the fourth day? In 2.30 Maimonides quotes two rabbinic authorities, Judah ben Simon and Abahu, both of whom imply that "time existed prior to the existence of this sun."[41] Even though he recognizes that their statements support an eternity thesis, Maimonides does not respond directly to them. Rather, he adopts two separate strategies. The first is simply to admit that their comments imply that "*the order of time* necessarily exists eternally *a parte ante.* That, however, is the belief in the eternity *a parte ante* of the world, and all who adhere to the Law should reject it."[42] In other words, one strategy is simply to recognize that these sages were supporting a version of (3.2) and hence to reject their interpretation.

Maimonides' second strategy is to subsume their comments as corollaries of those of Rabbi Eliezer. In 2.13, Maimonides refers to R. Eliezer, whose commentary on creation postulates creation by means of preexistent matter. Maimonides depicts this commentary as admitting "the eternity of the world, if only as it is conceived according to Plato's opinion."[43] Interestingly enough, Maimonides is speechless in the face of Eliezer's statement and his only response to it is to claim that it may "confuse very much indeed the belief of a learned man who adheres to the Law. No persuasive figurative interpretation with regard to it has become clear to me."[44] Uttered by an individual who is generally not at a loss for interpretative prowess, for whom the "gates of interpretation" are rarely if ever closed, Maimonides' stance suggests that he himself is not as uncomfortable with Eliezer's statements as one might expect.[45]

If so, then Maimonides' second strategy with respect to Rabbis Judah and Abahu is similar to his attitude toward Eliezer. Maimonides claims that their comments are "only the counterpart of the passage in which R. Eliezer says, 'Wherefrom were the heavens created.'"[46] Inasmuch as Maimonides is not bothered by the latter, so too can it be inferred that he is not bothered by the former. This, once again, would suggest that Maimonides is at least flirting with a version of (3.2).

It should be noted that Maimonides seemingly discredits these rabbinic comments altogether by questioning the authority of the speakers: "To sum up: you should not, in considering these points, take into account the statements made by this or that one."[47] Here Maimonides seems to be suggesting that in considering the issues of time and creation, one ought not be misled by the opinions of sundry rabbis. If this is so, what sense, then, should we make of Maimonides' overt espousal of (3.1) on the basis of Mosaic authority? At least (3.2) and (3.3) have other considerations in their favor. But if the *sole* basis for (3.1) is authority, then Maimonides seems to be undermining its very plausibility.

Let us turn, finally, to three arguments which were presented by the post-Aristotelians in favor of (3.3), and to which Maimonides must respond. These arguments, summarized in 2.18, all center around the nature of God, and raise the issue of God's activity in time. In all three cases, his arguments will ultimately rest upon two considerations: the intelligibility of his theory of negative predication espoused in 1.51–60, and elucidation of what is meant by an 'instant' of time. The first is beyond the focus of this paper, and I will not address it here.[48] The second, however, is directly relevant to our discussion of temporality. Before addressing these arguments, however, let us turn briefly to an examination of the term 'instant' as it was formulated by Aristotle.

VI. TIME AND THE INSTANT: ARISTOTLE AND MAIMONIDES

In both the *Physics* and the *Metaphysics* Aristotle develops the notion of the instant (το νῦν) as a basic feature of time. The instant is defined as the middle point between the beginning and end of time. Since it is a boundary or limit, it has no size and hence cannot be considered to exist. This characterization of time leads Aristotle to ask whether time is real. Since instants do not in and of themselves exist, it might be argued that time itself does not exist. That is, the past and future do not *now* exist, and the present instant is not a part of time since, as we have already noted, it is sizeless. In *Physics* 8.1 Aristotle claims that because the extremity, or limit, of time resides in the instant, time must exist on both sides of the instant.[49] And in *Metaphysics* 12.6 Aristotle claims that there can be no 'before' or 'after' if time does not exist, for both terms imply the existence of relative time.[50]

Aristotle's basic argument, centered on his definition of the 'instant' as the midpoint between 'before' and 'after', can be summarized as follows:

[B] Argument from the Instant

1. If time came to be, there would have to be an actual instant at which it came to be.

2. But this would entail there being a potential instant before the present instant was actualized.
3. But every part of time has only potential existence, and so no such instant could exist.
4. Hence time cannot come to be.

The main thrust of this argument is that in order to account for the coming into existence of any present instant, there must exist a prior actual instant; but in the case of the first instant, there could be no prior instant, actual or potential.[51]

Against the backdrop of these Aristotelian considerations, Maimonides examines three arguments which support the doctrine of eternal creation. These arguments were directed by the post-Aristotelians against the supporters of (3.1). First, the post-Aristotelians argue that those who claim that God created the world in time "are obliged to admit that the deity passed from potentiality to actuality inasmuch as He acted at a certain time and did not act at another time."[52] The thrust of this post-Aristotelian contention (as stated by Maimonides) can be reformulated as follows:

[C] Argument from Activity

5.1 Suppose that God created the world in time.
5.2 Then the world was created at an instant t_1.
5.3 Then God acted at t_1 and not at t_{1-n}.
5.4 But this implies that at t_{1-n} God was in a state of potentiality to create, and that at t_1 this potentiality was actualized.
5.5 But this move from potentiality to actuality implies change on the part of God.
5.6 God, however, is unchanging.
5.7 Hence, God does not create the world in time.[53]

The thrust of the argument depends upon the Aristotelian conception of action as change from potentiality to actuality. If God is construed as Pure Act, however, he cannot be said to act at an instant.

Secondly, the post-Aristotelians claim that "eternity is shown to be necessary because there do not subsist for Him, may He be exalted, any incentives, supervening accidents, and impediments."[54] This argument actually comprises two main subarguments, which, following Sorabji, we can term versions of the "Why not sooner?" argument and the "willing a change vs. changing one's will" argument.[55] Maimonides' version of the first subargument can be characterized as follows:

[D] The "Why Not Sooner?" Argument

6.1 Suppose that God willed the world at a particular instant t_1.
6.2 Then we are saying that God did not will the world at a previous instant t_{1-n}.
6.3 Then there must have been some incentive or purpose to explain God's willing at t_1 and not at t_{1-n}.
6.4 But in the case of God there can be no incentive or purpose external to his will.
6.5 Hence there is no rationale for his having willed at t_1 rather than at t_{1-n}.
6.6 Hence God did not will the world at t_1.

The second subargument is really a restatement of [C], but this time in terms of will, and can be summarized as follows:

[E] The "Willing a Change vs. Changing One's Will" Argument

7.1 Suppose that God willed the world at a particular instant t_1.
7.2 Then we are saying that God did not will the world at a previous instant t_{1-n}.
7.3 But this implies that at t_1 God willed and that at t_{1-n} God did not will.
7.4 But this implies a change in God's willing, that is, a change in God's nature.
7.5 But God is unchanging.
7.6 Hence God did not will the world at t_1.

There is an additional subargument which is drawn from the nature of God's wisdom, but since it is primarily a restatement of [C] in terms of knowledge, I shall not elaborate upon it here.

Maimonides' reaction to all three arguments draws upon the equivocal nature of God, as well as upon the homonymous nature of divine predicates. In response to [C] he distinguishes two senses of the term 'act': only with respect to material beings does 'act' imply a move from potentiality to actuality. With God or an immaterial being, 'act' does not imply such a move, and hence does not imply change. Similarly, his response to both [D] and [E] is to specify the ways in which divine will is unlike human will. With respect to [D], he argues that God has no need of special incentives to will; that is, God's will does not function like human will in that it is not activated at a particular instant. With respect to [E], Maimonides' point is that, unlike human acts of willing, when God wills a change there is no change in His willing nature.[56]

Clearly, Maimonides has not confronted [C], [D], or [E] head on; nor has he challenged the underlying notions of time, temporality, and acting at an instant which are assumed by these arguments. He prefers to undermine their underlying presuppositions concerning action and the Deity. His main contention has been that these post-Aristotelian arguments rely upon a mistaken conception of the divine predicates. When we turn to Gersonides, however, we witness an attempt to wrestle with the very notions of time and the instant. Although we shall not in this paper be able to examine Gersonides' entire discussion of time and the continuum, nevertheless we shall turn to those arguments which pertain most directly to the topic at hand.[57]

VII. THE GERSONIDEAN CHALLENGE

Gersonides' discussion of time is contained primarily in *Milhamot* 6.1, within the context of his theory of creation. Like Maimonides, he is concerned with whether time is finite or infinite, as well as with whether the creation of the world can be said to have occurred at an instant. In order to uphold the finitude of time, Gersonides refutes the Aristotelian arguments by attempting to demonstrate that time must have been generated. He will argue that just as quantity is finite, so too is time, since time is contained in the category of quantity.[58]

Gersonides' first argument for the finitude of time utilizes the nature of the "when" (*matai*) and can be restated as follows:

8.1 No "when" is infinite, since every proper part of time is finite and the "when" measures only these proper parts of time.
8.2 Since no "when" is infinite, no part of past time is an infinite distance from the present now.
8.3 But if time were infinite, given any past "when," the relation of the time before it to the time between it and the now would be the relation of infinite to finite.
8.4 But time is homogeneous; that is, all its parts have the same ontological composition.
8.5 So (8.3) is impossible, since it implies that time is both finite and infinite.
8.6 Hence time must be finite.[59]

It should be noted that in this argument Gersonides uses the notion of a part of time to correspond to the Aristotelian sense of a 'span'. Medieval Aristotelians generally reflected Aristotle's distinction in the *Categories* between two senses of the term 'part': the first is an interval of time (i.e., instant), whereas the second is a stretch of time (i.e., span). Gersonides uses the second of these two meanings in his argument.[60]

Having shown to his satisfaction that time is finite, Gersonides must now refute those arguments proffered by Aristotle in support of the infinity of time. Aristotle's first argument, [A], we will remember, was that since all generation must take place in time, there can be no beginning to time. Hence phrases like 'beginning of time' have no reference. Gersonides, however, rejects this argument by distinguishing two types of generation. The first is based on Aristotle's notion of a change from contrary to contrary and takes place in time. The second, however, is what Gersonides terms absolute generation and is atemporal; that is, it is instantaneous and does not take place in time. It is in this second sense that Gersonides argues that time was generated. Before this absolute generation, there was no time. Phrases such as 'beginning of time', Gersonides argues, must therefore be understood in an equivocal sense.[61]

Aristotle's second argument, [B], centered around the notion of the instant as the limit between the past and the future. In answer to this argument, Gersonides makes a number of points. To Aristotle's objection that we cannot imagine an 'instant' before which there is no time, Gersonides claims that there are many truths which we cannot imagine (just as many imaginable things are not true). Reminiscent of the Kalam controversy over the doctrine of "admissibility" (*al-tajwiz*), Gersonides' point is that the nonimaginability of a claim is not a sufficient condition for rejecting its truth.[62]

Gersonides' major objection, however, centers on Aristotle's formulation of the notion of the instant. His discussion can be seen indirectly as a response to [C], [D], and [E]. In contradistinction to Aristotle, Gersonides distinguishes two roles of the instant. The first is an initial instant which does not yet constitute time, whereas the second refers to subsequent instants which demarcate 'before' from 'after'. According to Gersonides, these two notions of the instant serve different functions. The former delimits a particular portion of time, namely, continuous quantity, and is characterized in terms of duration. The latter, on the other hand, reflects the Aristotelian function of the instant as characterizing division. Gersonides claims that if there were no difference between these two functions of the instant, we could not distinguish between any two sets of fractions of time—for example, three hours and three days—because our measure of the sets would be identical. Since each period of time would be divided by the same kind of instant, there would be no way of distinguishing three days from three hours.[63]

But how does this distinction resolve the original problem? Gersonides' point is that Aristotle's original objections to the finitude of time obtain only if the instant is understood in the latter sense. When the instant is taken in the sense of an initial instant of a temporal span, we see that there can be a 'first instant' without contradiction. Hence Gersonides' point is that the instant taken in the sense of duration need not be preceded by a past time.[64] That is, when time is first created, the instant does not refer back to any past point, but only forward to the future. In this way Gersonides feels he has resolved the temporal aspect of creation and has allowed for there to be a created universe at an instant.

Having posited that the world was created at an initial instant of time by a freely willing agent, Gersonides must decide whether the world was engendered out of absolute nothing or out of a preexistent matter. Arguing that creation out of nothing is incompatible with the facts of physical reality, he adopts a Platonic model of matter drawn ultimately from the *Timaeus.* The opening verses of Genesis 1 are used to distinguish two types of material reality: *geshem* and *homer rishon.*[65] Totally devoid of form, *geshem* is the primordial matter out of which the universe was created. Since it is not informed, it is not capable of motion or rest; and since it is characterized by negation, *geshem* is inert and chaotic.[66] This primordial matter is identified with the "primeval waters" described in Genesis 1:2 (*tohu, tehom,* and *mayim*). However, Gersonides points out that *geshem* does not itself exemplify absolute nonbeing, but rather is an intermediary between being and nonbeing.[67]

In contrast to *geshem, homer rishon* is the second type of reality. *Homer rishon* is understood in the Aristotelian sense as a substratum which is allied to form. *Homer rishon,* or matter, is inferior to form and hence cannot be known in itself. It contains within itself the potentiality to receive forms yet has no actuality of its own.[68] Inasmuch as it does not contain its own actuality, *homer rishon* is not an ontologically independent entity. Rather, Gersonides is wont to refer to it as "the matter that does not keep its shape".[69] In *Milhamot* 6, part 2, chapter 7, Gersonides compares this matter to darkness, for just as darkness is the absence of light, so too this matter represents the absence of form or shape.

VIII. CONCLUSION

We are now in a position to summarize our findings. Working within a framework which upheld the infinity of time, Aristotle posited an eternal universe which had no temporal beginning. Gersonides and Maimonides, however, are both committed to a cosmology in which the deity willed the universe to exist. Unwilling to reject Aristotle's ontology of time altogether, both philosophers posit a resolution which can be construed as a version of (1.3), eternal creation. We have seen that Maimonides is sympathetic to an Aristotelian theory of time. Much of his effort, moreover, has been aimed at showing that the scriptural view of creation (3.1) is inconsistent with this theory. And yet, Maimonides is unwilling to support Aristotle's denial of creation altogether. His own view, then, is a version of (3.2), which is his interpretation of eternal creation. According to this view, an eternally existing world has been sustained by a creator, but not in a temporal context. In the sense that there is no one instant in which the world is brought into existence, it is eternal; in the sense, however, that God is the ontological ground of the world, it is created.

Gersonides is less willing ostensibly to compromise the temporal beginning of the universe, and so he creatively reinterprets Aristotle's notion of the instant in such a way as to allow for a temporal beginning to creation out of a preexistent matter. In this way he has retained a first instant to the act of creation in light of the notion of an eternally beginningless "substance" whose existence ontologically precedes that of created composites—i.e., matter.[70] Hence according to Gersonides the world is both created at an instant and eternally existent. What has been particularly noteworthy in these two discussions has been the attempt on the part of both philosophers to retain a philosophically defensible cosmology alongside of their theological presuppositions.[71]

NOTES

1. See R. Sorabji, *Time, Creation and the Continuum* (Ithaca, N.Y.: Cornell University Press, 1983), pp. 193ff., for discussion of the notion of beginningless creation.

2. See N. Kretzmann, "Creation *Ab Aeterno:* Can the World Have Been Created Beginninglessly?" (unpublished manuscript).

3. The classic discussion of Plato's cosmology can be found in the *Timaeus.*

4. The notion of eternal creation has been discussed in various contexts. For its importance to Maimonides, see W. Harvey, "A Third Approach to Maimonides' Cosmogony-Prophetology Puzzle," *Harvard Theological Review* 74:3 (1981), p. 293. S. Feldman has characterized the main tenets of an eternal creation doctrine in "The Theory of Eternal Creation in Hasdai Crescas and Some of his Predecessors" *Viator* 11 (1980), pp. 289–320.

5. See B. Kogan, *Averroes and the Metaphysics of Causation* (Albany, N.Y.: State University of New York, 1985) for further discussion of the Islamic development of eternal creation theories.

6. Maimonides, *The Guide of the Perplexed,* trans. S. Pines (Chicago: University of Chicago Press, 1963). Page references will be to this translation. Note the following passages in the introduction to the *Guide:* "For my purpose is that the truths be glimpsed and then again be concealed, so as not to oppose that divine purpose which one cannot possibly oppose and which has concealed from the vulgar among the people those truths especially req-

uisite for His apprehension" (pp. 6–7). Also "God, may He be exalted, knows that I have never ceased to be exceedingly apprehensive about treatise. For they are concealed things; none of them has been set down in any book" (p. 16).

7. The fifth cause of contradictory/contrary statements arises from the necessity of teaching a student difficult and obscure material. Occasionally the teacher must resort to oversimplifying the material "in accord with the listener's imagination that the latter will understand only what he now wants him to understand. Afterwards, in the appropriate place, that obscure matter is stated in exact terms and explained as it truly is" (p. 18). The seventh cause is the most important for our purposes, and is used, when "speaking about very obscure matters . . . to conceal some parts and to disclose others. . . . In such cases the vulgar must in no way be aware of the contradiction; the author accordingly uses some device to conceal it by all means" (p. 18).

8. "Divergences that are to be found in this Treatise are due to the fifth cause and the seventh. Know this, grasp its true meaning, and remember it very well so as not to become perplexed by some of its remarks" (p. 20).

9. In this paper, references to *Milhamot Adonai (Wars of the Lord)* will be made primarily to the Hebrew edition which was reprinted in Leipzig in 1866. References will be to treatise, chapter, and page number. Unless otherwise specified, all translations from the Hebrew are my own.

10. See *De Caelo* 1.9 279a8ff.: "It is obvious then that there is neither place nor void nor time outside the heaven, since it has been demonstrated that there neither is nor can be body there." A similar point is propounded in *Physics* 4.12.

11. See Aristotle *Metaphysics* 12.6 1071b8; *Physics* 8.1 251b10ff.; for discussion of these passages, see Sorabji, *Time, Creation, Continuum,* pp. 279ff.

12. *Guide* 2, Intro., prop. 15, p. 237.

13. In her recent book, *Maimonides' Interpretation of the Story of Creation* (Heb.) (Jerusalem: Israel Society for Biblical Research, 1987), pp. 230–31, S. Klein-Braslavy points out that this definition can mean one of two things: it can mean that (a) time is the measure of all motion whatever, or that (b) time is the measure primarily of the highest sphere. Although Maimonides is ambiguous as to which usage he endorses, she suggests that he seems to accept (b) while not ruling out the possibility of (a).

14. The term 'Kalam' refers to a particular system of thought which arose in Islam prior to the philosopher al-Kindi (d. 873); its exponents, the *Mutakallimun,* were contrasted with straightforward philosophers. For a detailed discussion of standard Kalam doctrines, see M. Fakhry, *A History of Islamic Philosophy* (New York: Columbia University Press, 1983); H. A. Wolfson, *The Philosophy of the Kalam* (Cambridge, Mass.: Harvard University Press, 1976).

15. *Guide* 2, Intro., p. 241.

16. *Guide* 2.31, p. 360. Emphasis added.

17. Representative interpretations can be found in H. Davidson, "Maimonides' Secret Position on Creation," in *Studies in Medieval Jewish History and Literature,* ed. I. Twersky (Cambridge, Mass.: Harvard University Press,

1979) 1:16–40; L. Kaplan, "Maimonides on the Miraculous Element in Prophecy," *Harvard Theological Review* 70 (1977), pp. 233–56. For a discussion of these and other interpretations, see Harvey, "A Third Approach," pp. 288ff.

18. *Guide* 2.13, p. 281.

19. Ibid., p. 283.

20. Ibid., p. 284.

21. See Harvey, "A Third Approach," p. 289, n. 9, for further discussion of this point.

22. It is important to note that not all commentators agree with this reading. Harvey, for example, interprets Maimonides' version of Aristotle's view as a form of eternal creation. Ibid., p. 293.

23. *Guide* 2.13, p. 284.

24. Ibid., p. 285.

25. Ibid.

26. *Guide* 2.25, p. 328.

27. Ibid.

28. Ibid., p. 329.

29. S. Klein-Braslavy makes her case for a skeptical interpretation of Maimonides in her recent article "Interpretation of Maimonides of the term 'create' and the Question of the Creation of the Universe," (Heb.), *Da'at* 16 (1986), pp. 39–55. For additional discussions of epistemological and metaphysical skepticism in Maimonides, see S. Pines, "The Limits of Human Knowledge according to Al-Farabi, Ibn Bajja and Maimonides," in *Studies in Medieval Jewish History and Literature,* ed. Twersky, 1:82–109; see also the unpublished work by J. Stern, "Remarks on a Skeptical Theme in Maimonides *Guide of the Perplexed.*" B. Kogan summarizes some of the other interpretations regarding Maimonides' own view of creation; see note 1 of his essay in this volume.

30. His discussion of the Islamic necessitarian formulation of eternal creation is contained in *Guide* 2.19, in which he reduces the doctrine to an improbable version. There are, however, other plausible versions of this doctrine, as Maimonides himself suggests in later chapters.

31. For a similar interpretation of Maimonides' position on creation, but one drawn from different evidence, see A. Ivry, "Maimonides on Creation," in *Creation and the End of Days,* ed. D. Novak and N. Samuelson (Lanham, Md.: University Press of America, 1986), pp. 185–214. See, for example, Ivry's comment on p. 198: "He [Maimonides] has, accordingly been viewed as either a closet Aristotelian on creation, or a more revealing Platonist. The view which I have adduced . . . puts him in neither camp completely, though brings him closer to that of the Platonists."

32. *Guide* 2.13, p. 281.

33. Ibid.

34. Ibid.

35. In *Guide* 1.54, Maimonides describes the duration or eternity of the Deity in atemporal terms, so as to preclude any temporal predications of Him.

36. For the importance of this passage for subsequent Jewish philosophers, see W. Harvey, "Albo's Discussion of Time," *Jewish Quarterly Review* (1981): 220–21; see also J. Malino, "Maimonides' Guide to the Perplexities of Creation" (rabbinic diss., Hebrew Union College, 1979), pp. 61–62.

37. *Guide* 2.13, p. 282.

38. Ibid.

39. See Klein-Braslavy, *Maimonides' Interpretation,* p. 115.

40. For further elaboration of this point, see W. Harvey, "A Third Approach," p. 296; Klein-Braslavy, *Maimonides' Interpretation,* pp. 81–82, 86–87.

41. *Guide* 2.30, p. 349.

42. Ibid.

43. *Guide* 2.26, p. 331.

44. Ibid.

45. See Klein-Braslavy, *Maimonides' Interpretation,* pp. 235–38 for further discussion.

46. *Guide* 2.30, p. 349.

47. Ibid.

48. Maimonides' theory of negative predication is contained primarily in the *Guide* 1.51–60. For a discussion of the importance of this theory to the present discussion, see Malino, "Maimonides' Guide."

49. See *Physics* 8.1 251b ff.: "Since the instant (το νῦν) is both a beginning and an end, there must always be time on both sides of it."

50. See *Metaphysics* 12.6 1071b ff.: "For there could not be a before and an after if time did not exist."

51. See Malino, "Maimonides' Guide," pp. 64ff., and Sorabji, *Time, Creation, Continuum,* pp. 210ff. for further discussion of this argument in Aristotle.

52. *Guide* 2.18, p. 299.

53. See Malino, "Maimonides' Guide," p. 72 for further elaboration of this argument.

54. *Guide* 2.18, p. 300.

55. See Sorabji, *Time, Creation, Continuum,* p. 269ff.

56. *Guide* 2.18, pp. 300–301.

57. For a more detailed discussion of these topics in Gersonides, see my article "Creation, Time and Infinity in Gersonides," *Journal of the History of Philosophy* (January, 1988).

58. See *Milhamot* 6.1.10, pp. 329ff.

59. Ibid., 6.1.11, p. 343.

60. This distinction is made in Aristotle *Categories* 4. A similar distinction is made in Plato's *Parmenides* where Plato distinguishes similarly between the now (το νῦν) and the instant (γδ ἐξαίφνασ). I owe this latter reference to Professor E. A. Browning.

61. *Milhamot* 6.1.21, pp. 385–86.

62. Ibid., p. 386. For a description of the Kalam notion of admissibility, see the *Guide* 3.15; A. Ivry, "Maimonides on Possibility" in *Mystics, Philosophers and Politicians,* ed. J. Reinhartz et al. (Durham, N.C.: University

of North Carolina Press, 1982), pp. 77ff.; and H. A. Wolfson, *The Philosophy of the Kalam* (Cambridge, Mass.: Harvard University Press, 1976), pp. 43ff.

63. *Milhamot* 6.1.21, p. 387. H. A. Wolfson points out that this distinction can be traced back to Aristotle *Physics* 6.11 219a22–30. See H. A. Wolfson, *Crescas' Critique of Aristotle* (Cambridge, Mass.: Harvard University Press, 1929), p. 653.

64. *Milhamot* 6.1.21, pp. 387–88. See also Klein-Braslavy, *Maimonides' Interpretation,* pp. 126–27, in which she aligns the view of Gersonides with Crescas as well.

65. *Milhamot* 6.1.17, pp. 267–71. In *Milhamot* 6.2.2, pp. 193–94 Gersonides argues that this formless matter accounts for various astronomical phenomena. For general discussions of Gersonides' theory of creation and matter, see S. Feldman, "Gersonides' Proofs for the Creation of the Universe" *Proceedings of the American Academy for Jewish Research* (1967): 113–37; S. Feldman, "Platonic Themes in Gersonides' Cosmology," in *Salo Whitmayer Baron Jubilee Volume* (Jerusalem, 1975), pp. 383–405.

66. *Milhamot* 6.1.17, pp. 367–68, 374. For further elaboration of these arguments, see Feldman, "Platonic Themes," pp. 394–95.

67. *Milhamot* 6.1.18, p. 372.

68. Ibid., 6.1.17, p. 367.

69. Ibid., 5.2.1; 6.6, pt. 2, chap. 4.

70. I would like to thank Professor P. Quinn for this way of stating the matter.

71. I would like to thank Professors B. Kogan, B. McGinn, and P. Quinn for their valued comments on this paper.

Response

Barry S. Kogan

The claims of philosophers and theologians on the question of the world's creation have often been in conflict. Many have attempted to resolve this conflict by devising strategies that would do justice to the arguments of both sides, and one of the best known of these strategies has been harmonization. It suggests that an adequate analysis of all the evidence and arguments will ultimately show that the conflict is more apparent than real and that in some sense the universe is both created and eternal. It is this position which Tamar Rudavsky claims to find in both Maimonides' and Gersonides' discussions of the issue, although she is by no means the first to do so, at least with respect to Maimonides. Elements of the position she defends go back as far as the thirteenth and fourteenth centuries.[1] But she defends it from a perspective which has received relatively little attention thus far, namely, that of time. Specifically, she portrays both figures as committed to the Aristotelian conception of time as the number or measure of motion in a moving body. In the case of Maimonides, that commitment extends to the notion that time is continuous and allows for no instantaneous changes, because the movement of the celestial bodies is likewise continuous. From this she infers that Maimonides rejected the notion of temporal creation *ex nihilo* as untenable, because it represents a radical discontinuity with respect to the existence of time. Accordingly, his arguments on behalf of temporal creation are at most expressions of an exoteric position dictated by theological-political necessity. Maimonides' esoteric position turns out to be a compromise position or an amalgam of the views of Plato and Aristotle. Initially, it reflects a basic cosmological skepticism. For Maimonides not only provisionally rejects temporal creation *ex nihilo,* but also withholds his opinion about the Platonic position, taken by itself, of temporal creation out of a preeternal matrix as well as the Aristotelian view, taken by itself, of the universe as unqualifiedly eternal. It is this stance that is said to leave open the possibility of a theory of eternal creation, in which the world is both beginningless and created, although the details of how this is so remain unspecified.

Gersonides in turn is likewise portrayed as subscribing to the Aristotelian conception of time, but with the qualification that as a manifestation of quantity, which is invariably finite, time cannot be infinite. It must have been generated instantaneously at some point not preceded by past time, although not necessarily *ex nihilo*. From here, Rudavsky concludes that Gersonides too adopts a compromise position, which is likewise a version of eternal creation. But Gersonides' version is that the world had a temporal beginning out of a preexistent matter.

If, indeed, it was Maimonides' goal in the *Guide* to *reconcile* the view that the world was temporally originated with the view that its existence is eternal—and I doubt that it was—then some version of the theory of eternal creation would probably have provided a viable solution. In the Islamic orbit, there were at least two versions of this theory potentially available to Maimonides: an emanationist account developed by Alfarabi and Avicenna, and a nonemanationist account developed by Averroes.[2] But as Rudavsky notes, Maimonides is "uncomfortable with the Islamic portrayal of this view." This, of course, would not have prevented him from developing an independent account. But I do not find one either in the *Guide* or in our speaker's presentation. At most, I believe, we have been offered several considerations for supposing that Maimonides' secret position was identical with Aristotle's eternity thesis.[3] This may indeed have been his view. But to claim that the world always has existed and always will exist as it now does, is not to claim that it is eternally *created,* still less to have shown how it might be. That would require not only filling in certain details, but identifying the basic elements of the theory. Thus we would need to know: (1) Does this creation pertain to the universe as a whole or to individuals within it? (2) Is "being created" identical with "being moved or generated"? (3) Is creation consequent in some sense on nonbeing or not, and in what sense? And finally, (4) is such nonbeing absolute or relative? All these questions need to be answered before we have a viable theory of eternal creation. The same questions would have to be answered in connection with Gersonides. Significantly, Gersonides gives us no reason to suppose he had an esoteric position. Rather, he argues forthrightly and at length that the universe was created instantaneously at a point in the past, but out of an eternal water-like body which does not preserve its shape. This suggests that the world is eternal in one respect and created in another. But it does *not* suggest that the world is eternally created. What Gersonides offers us is in fact a clear version of the original Platonic view of creation. If there is something different in this view, a theory of eternal creation, then its semantics need to be spelled out and justified, and this has not yet been done.

A second concern arises in connection with the use of time as a reference point for explaining or justifying a philosopher's position on the question of creation vs. eternity. It turns out to be a very weak reed. Let us begin with Aristotle's position in *Physics* 8.1. If time is identified as an attribute of movement—namely, its measure or number—then the only valid way for one to determine the duration of time is from whatever can be known about the extent of movement on which it depends. Yet in the argument from the *Physics,* summarized by Rudavsky, Aristotle takes a different tack and argues that whenever the world is assumed to have begun, we can always conceive of a time before its hypothesized beginning and so on *ad infinitum.* Accordingly, time must be eternal. But he then goes on to deduce an eternal movement from eternal time, precisely because time is inseparable from motion. As the late George Hourani once perceptively noted, Aristotle "has reversed his own correct order of reasoning, and instead of inferring the extent of time from the extent of movement, he has inferred the extent of movement from the extent of time—an illegitimate process both on his own assumptions and modern assumptions."[4] The import of this criticism for reconstructing Maimonides' own views on creation is clear. If a philosopher's secret teaching is thought to represent the results of his most critical and independent reflection, then this argument would poorly serve Maimonides' purposes.

But in fairness to him, we should note that he does not *explicitly* deduce either the eternity of time or the universe from the Aristotelian definition of time, and Rudavsky recognizes this. Still, in the absence of an explicit argument, it is suggested that Maimonides indirectly hints at such a theory as part of his summary of the scriptural position (2.13, pp. 281–82). For he states (1) that "what is moved . . . is itself created *in time* [which implies pre-existent time and therefore motion] and (2) that 'God's bringing the world into existence' does not have a temporal beginning" [*lā . . . fi mabda zamānī*], for time is one of the created things, which implies that the creation of the world is not a temporally specifiable action; hence it is without beginning.

Both of these statements are ambiguous; and precisely because they are, they can be read in more than one way, and do not necessarily imply anything about a time before the beginning of time or an eternally created universe. Thus, when Maimonides states that "what is moved [i.e. the sphere] is itself created in time," he adds that it "came to be after not having been." Being created *in* time is here simply a conventional locution for "being created at a point of time finitely distant from the present," and "*after* not having been" need not imply an earlier time in which the sphere was absent, but merely the absence of an earlier time at which the sphere was present.[5] Similarly, if time is one of created things, then to say that "God's bringing the world into existence does not have a *temporal beginning*" does not mean that the world has no specifiable beginning—the Jewish calendar might have been cited as testimony to the contrary—but that the beginning is not part of a preexisting time continuum. In sum, reading intrinsically ambiguous phrases and remarks as supportive of a hybrid doctrine of eternal creation is highly conjectural at best. It certainly yields no proof for any particular position.

Maimonides is quite explicit about the reason why this is so. There simply is no demonstration for any of the three standard positions on the creation/eternity question. But he goes even beyond this and claims further (1.71) that "no cogent demonstration *can be reached* and that it is a point before which the intellect stops" (1.71, p. 180). It seems that Maimonides' principal reason for arriving at this conclusion is his view that "a being's state of perfection and completion furnishes no indication of the state of that being preceding its perfection" (2.17, pp. 297–98). Thus, while Aristotle's claims for the continuity of time and motion might be entirely valid, in terms of the world's realized state at present, they need not be valid prior to the world's having reached its present state. Maimonides argues here in much the same way that Hume did regarding induction, but in the opposite direction. We can no more know that the past was like the present, than we could know, following Hume, that the future will be like the past. For this reason, Maimonides argues that even temporal creation *ex nihilo* is "*not impossible,*" because even in the world as we know it, all things that come to be have a nature after they are fully developed different from that which they have while developing, and different again from that which they had at the outset. That is why a human adult, reflecting solely on the conditions of her *present* existence, would not suppose she could ever have existed as a fetus within her mother's body. In sum, by reasoning from present conditions, she contends we can never really know for sure whether the same conditions obtained in the past.

It is for reasons such as these that I am inclined to think that in the final analysis, Maimonides simply suspended judgment on this question. This suspension is compatible both with a willingness to leave the question open and with some moderate form of skepticism about ever resolving it at all. In either case, if that is his secret teaching, it is surely not particularly heterodox, nor does it destroy the foundations of the Law; and we may well begin to wonder "Why all the secrecy?" Of course, many people are inclined to suppose that if a teaching must be treated esoterically, it must be either theologically or politically destructive of prevailing opinions, and in a direct and obvious fashion at that. But in a little-noted yet important passage of the *Guide* Maimonides denies this.

> These true opinions [referring to the secrets and mysteries of the Torah, of which creation is one (1.35, p. 80)] were not hidden, enclosed in riddles, and treated by all men of knowledge with all sorts of artifice through which they could teach them without expounding them explicitly, because of something bad being hidden in them or because they undermine the foundations of the Law, as is thought by ignorant people who deem that they have attained a rank suitable for speculation. Rather, they have hidden because at the outset the intellect is incapable of receiving them; only flashes of them are made to appear so that the perfect man should know them. (1.33, p. 71)

On this view, the aim of an esoteric writer is to stimulate those of his readers who are equipped to analyze ideas and arguments to discover the most plausible view for themselves. By contrast, his aim for those who are not so equipped is to conceal as much as possible whatever intellectual fare might confuse or disrupt their beliefs. Initially, the incentive for the careful reader of such a work will obviously be to discover the author's concealed opinion. But by examining and reexamining the evidence and arguments, as well as the hints and allusions, such a reader will eventually become more concerned with the truth of the matter, with reasoning clearly, and with discovering what can and cannot be known, than she will be with discovering the author's opinion, whatever it might be. And if that outcome is realized, our esoteric author will have succeeded in his purpose by a kind of gracious ruse, even if his own view on creation or any other recondite subject should remain forever a secret. Robert Nozick expressed the point nicely when he observed that "esoteric texts not only hide doctrine, but by getting the reader to think up the ideas himself, even if only as a hypothesis about what the author really believes, [they] induce him to feel friendly to these ideas because of having (somewhat independently) parented them."[6] That, I suspect, may be the most important secret in Maimonides' secret teaching on creation and eternity.

NOTES

1. See, for example, Samuel ben Judah ibn Tibbon, *Ma'amar Yiqqavu Ha-Mayim,* ed. M. L. Bisseliches (Pressburg, 1837); Moses ben Joshua Narboni, *Be'ur Ha-Moreh;* and Joseph ben Abba Mari Kaspi *'Amudei Kesef U'Maskiyot Kesef* in *Sheloshah Qadmonei Mefarshei Ha-Moreh* (Jerusalem, 1961). Among more recent discussions of Maimonides as an advocate of the eternity of the universe or eternal creation, see Jacob Becker, *The Secret of the Guide of the Perplexed* (Heb.) (Tel Aviv, 1955); Shlomo Pines, "The Philosophic Sources of the Guide of the Perplexed" in Moses Maimonides, *Guide of the Perplexed* (Chicago, 1963), cxxvii–cxxxi; Y. Glicker, "The Modal Problem in Maimonides' Philosophy" (Heb.) *Iyyun* 10 (1959): 177–91; Leonard S. Kravitz, "The Revealed and the Concealed—Providence, Prophecy, Miracles, and Creation in the Guide," *CCAR Journal* (October, 1969): 18–30, 78; L. V. Berman, *Ibn Bajjah and Maimonides: A Chapter in the History of Political Philosophy* (Heb.) (Jerusalem, 1959), 156–63; Abraham Nuriel, "On the Creation or Eternity of the World according to Maimonides," (Heb.) *Tarbitz* 33 (1964): 372–87; and Warren Z. Harvey, "A Third Approach to Maimonides' Cosmogony-Prophetology Puzzle," *Harvard Theological Review* 74 (1981): 287–301.

2. Seymour Feldman, "The Theory of Eternal Creation in Hasdai Crescas and Some of His Predecessors," *Viator: Medieval and Renaissance Studies* 11 (1980): 289–320; Parviz Morewedge, "The Logic of Emanationism and Sūfism in the Philosophy of Ibn Sīnā (Avicenna)," Parts 1 and 2. *Journal*

of the American Oriental Society 91 (1971): 467–76, and 92 (1972): 1–18; Barry S. Kogan, *Averroes and the Metaphysics of Causation* (Albany: SUNY Press, 1985), 203–55.

3. See Becker, *Secret of the Guide;* Nuriel, *Creation or Eternity of the World;* and Harvey, "A Third Approach."

4. George F. Hourani, "The Dialogue Between al-Ghazālī and the Philosophers," *The Muslim World* 48 (1958): 190.

5. Richard Sorabji, *Time, Creation, and the Continuum* (Ithaca, N.Y.: Cornell University Press, 1983), 280.

6. Robert Nozick, *Philosophical Explanations* (Cambridge, Mass.: Harvard University Press, 1981), 651, n. 3.

Creation: "What Difference Does It Make?"

David R. Blumenthal

There is a long tradition of Jewish participation in philosophical theology, beginning with Philo and continuing into this century with Hermann Cohen and Martin Buber. Much of that tradition, however, couched its reflection in the language of essence and existence, being and nonbeing, arguments for the existence of God, systematic answers to the problems of attribution, theodicy, etc. There existed, however, reflection on theological issues before the philosophical tradition joined Judaism and there exists theological thought today which one might call postphilosophic or postmetaphysical. What were and are the categories of such thinking? How does one approach the problem of creation if one does not choose the categories and language usual to such discussion among philosophers and systematic theologians? How does one articulate Jewish thought on creation if one practices a hermeneutics of suspicion toward the metaphysical formulations and a hermeneutics of retrieval toward the nonphilosophic modes of religious reflection?[1]

When the sages of the Talmud found themselves in a bind about the meaning of a text or the thrust of the Law, they often asked: *mai nafka minah* ("What practical difference does it make?") As I review the history of the doctrine of creation in rabbinic Judaism, I ask myself the same question: What difference does it make in terms of concrete action whether God created the universe or not? Does the creationist-evolutionist argument have meaning beyond the confines of the academy and church? Does the cosmological argument for God's existence imply anything beyond itself?

Rabbinic Judaism teaches that there are three major practical implications to the doctrine of creation.[2]

The first implication is clearly stated by the best-known of Jewish Bible commentators, Rashi, in his comment to Genesis 1:1:

> Rabbi Yitzhak said, "The Torah should have begun with the [section dealing with the Passover sacrifice], 'This month shall be the chief month for you . . .' (Exod. 12) because this was the first commandment that the Jews were given. Why, then, does the Torah open with Genesis? The reason is to [fulfill the verse], 'He recounted the power of His deeds to His people in order to give them the inheritance of the nations' (Ps. 111:6). For, if the nations of the world say to Israel, 'You are thieves because you took by force the lands of the seven nations' (Deut. 7:1), Israel can say to them, 'The whole earth belongs to God. He created it and He gave it to whoever seemed fitting to Him (following Jer. 27:5). By His will, He gave it to them and, by His will, He took it from them and gave it to us.'"[3]

The first *nafka minah* of Genesis, then—the first practical implication of the doctrine of creation—is not to be seen in systematic theology, or in cosmology or ontology, but in international politics. Creation means that the claim of the Jews to the holy land is rooted, not in history, not in military occupation, not even in settlement, but in the will of the Creator Who is the only One Who can legitimately dispose of any piece of land. He is the sole Possessor of heaven and earth (Gen. 14:19, 22) and, hence, He alone can determine who has permission to be where.[4]

This runs contrary to the common sense of international relations and to the thrust of power politics where rights are a matter of consensus and possession is, as the popular saying would have it, nine-tenths of the law. It also runs contrary to the claims of liberal ideology where rights are inherent in persons and peoples regardless of the realities of political life. The doctrine of creation proclaims that there is no political or historical "right" to the land. There is no "natural" right to a specific piece of territory. There is only the sovereign will of God Who disposes, as He sees fit, of His possession, creation. For the case of the holy land, He did originally allow others to settle it but then He took it from them and willed it to the Jews. No one can change that act of will other than He—not international consensus, not force, not even the sinfulness of the Jewish people (Lev. 26:44; Deut. 30:5).

To be sure, we would not know to whom God chose to will

the holy land were it not for the twin doctrines of revelation and covenant. Biblical and rabbinic Judaism understand that God did not remain aloof from that which He created; instead, He charged the first persons and various of their descendants with doing His command. In so doing, God constituted a relationship with humankind and, as the story of this relationship progressed, He narrowed His focus to Noah and then to Abraham and Sarah and their descendants in the line of Isaac, Rebecca, Jacob, Rachel, and Leah. It is to them that He revealed His will. It is to them that He provided guidance and a moral standard. And it is to them that He ceded the holy land. Creation thus takes on form and meaning in revelation and covenant.

In this hour this is not an abstract theological issue. Rabbi Tzvi Yehuda Kook, one of the best-known spiritual leaders of the Zionist renewal in the State of Israel today, recalled the evening of the United Nations resolution calling for the partition of the holy land and the eventual creation of the State of Israel as follows:

> Nineteen years ago, on that same famous night, when the news reached us of the positive decision of the rulers of the nations of the world about the creation of the State of Israel, when the whole people flowed into the streets to celebrate with joy, I was unable to go out and join in the happiness. I sat alone and red-faced because a weight was upon me. In those first hours I was unable to reconcile myself with what had been done, with that awful report, because indeed, "They have partitioned my land!" (Joel 4:2). Yes, where is our Hebron? And where is our Shechem? And our Jericho, where is it? Have these been forgotten? They are ours, every clod and divot, every four cubits, every strip of land and plot of earth that are related to God's land. Is it in our hands to concede even one millimeter of them?[5]

Another leader of Gush Emunim, the movement to settle Samaria and Judaea, put it this way:

> Therefore, once and for all, these matters are clear and certain, that there are no Arab territories or Arab lands here, rather Israeli lands, the inheritance of our eternal forefathers. Others came and built on them without our presence or permission, but we never abandoned or were cut off from the inheritance of our forefathers. Always, always, we maintained our conscious connection with them. . . . We

are, indeed, commanded to liberate them, because all this land, in the fullness of its biblical borders, is tied to the rule of the people of Israel.[6]

The authorities cited above may sound extreme. However, even those Jews and Israelis who favor some type of settlement of the territorial claims of the Palestinians, as persons and as a people, do *not* propose that the Jewish people yield its claim to its patrimony. The more cautious voices speak of balancing peace against saving (Jewish) lives, of a temporary yielding of territorial sovereignty in order to achieve the larger and more important purposes of peace and security, of temporary vs. permanent sanctification of certain boundaries, of the inadvisability of war in certain circumstances, etc.[7] Other politically moderate voices speak of the concomitant covenant of justice and its indissoluble link to successful settlement of the land, or of the moral purity of the Jewish people especially in its homeland, or of the need of the Jewish people to be faithful to the word of the prophets who, in God's Name, compel it to justice, etc.[8]

But everywhere the claim of the Jewish people to the whole holy land, though variously defined, is integral. And, while rooted for certain limited purposes of Jewish law in certain conceptions of conquest and settlement, the ground of that claim is the doctrine of creation—in its first *nafka minah,* in its first practical implication, to wit, that God, as Creator, is the sole being who can dispose of any piece of territory; that He did take it from those who had occupied it without His specific authorization; and that He did give it, by an act of His sovereign will, to the Jewish people in perpetuity. A doctrine of creation that does not include this national dimension is not complete or faithful.

COUNTERPOINT

It was Friday afternoon. Israel had just declared its independence. The world, poised between amazement and anguish, held its breath. . . . I was a stateless student living in Paris. . . . At nightfall I made my way to the synagogue for Shabbat services. . . . My teacher, an old man famous for his Talmudic knowledge, pulled me into a corner and asked me point-blank: "From now on will you believe in

> miracles?" "Yes," I answered. "And you will no longer deny God's blessings?" "No." His piercing eyes were watching me, his voice had become harsh and insulting: "Well, then, young man, it takes very little to please you. . . . The present and the future make you forget the past. You forgive too quickly."[9]

The second practical implication of the doctrine of creation has to do with language, metaphor, and life-orientation. A true story points to the problem: the Torah is read weekly in the synagogue and, by tradition, one completes the reading of these first five books of the Bible every year. Furthermore, as soon as one completes the reading of Deuteronomy 34, one starts again from Genesis 1. The day on which this is done, Simhat Torah, occurs at the end of a long holiday season. We have pondered our wrongdoings, we have proclaimed God's kingship, we have trembled in judgment and confessed our sins, and we have tried mightily to feel the joy of God's presence in the sukka and in the other mitsvot of the holiday. The whole season, almost two months long, comes to a climax in the restarting of the cycle of the reading of the Torah, for when we read the Genesis story, we read it without the story of the fall. It is a brief moment of prelapsarian purity, of edenic spirituality.

It was the custom of Rabbi Nahman Cohen of Providence, Rhode Island, to draw attention to this annual spiritual journey on Simhat Torah and then to read the creation narrative in the melody of the Jewish New Year. Before each verse beginning "and there was evening and there was morning," Rabbi Cohen would chant a melody which had been used on Rosh ha-Shana to introduce the part of the liturgy proclaiming God's kingship. What does one think when one reads the prelapsarian Genesis narrative liturgically, pausing at the end of each day of creation to sing of God's kingship? What ought to be in one's mind as music, biblical narrative, and liturgy combine in a moment of striving for untarnished spirituality? One thinks of God. One senses His presence in the creative acts of each of the days as they are read. The meditation is cumulative. The "and behold it was very good" of creation resonates to the fullness of His presence in it. The whole universe trembles and dances before His glory as the reading is read and the song is sung. God is King. Creation makes Him so.

To know that God is King—whether in hearing the liturgy of

Simhat Torah or in reading a Psalm or in any other pondering of the majesty of creation—to experience it is to be filled with joy, spiritual joy. It is to be open to His presence in creation. The second *nafka minah* of Genesis, the second practical implication of the doctrine of creation, then, is that one must expose oneself to God's presence in creation, that one must be willing to see Him as King of the universe. A doctrine of creation which does not include this experiential, spiritual dimension is not complete or faithful.

There is, however, a further step to this implication. To know God as King is to be compelled linguistically, imaginatively, and morally. One must come to terms with His kingship. One must integrate the experience of God as King into one's life and language. One must become a faithful servant of God. This is not an easy matter.

To be a faithful servant is to run directly against the grain of libertarianism and autonomy in modern culture. It is to challenge our deepest beliefs about our right to self-determination. Faithful servanthood evokes a *modus vivendi* of obedience. The question becomes not "What do I want?" but "What does God demand of me?" The text becomes not the human embodiment of a divine inspiration, but the word which must be heard and harkened to. Judging right and wrong becomes not a matter solely of our own thoughts, feelings, judgment, and instincts—though these too become part of the process of the interaction of the Presence, the text, and life—but a matter of discerning and following His will.

Obedience to God's will is a function of the use of moral judgment and in all of creation, only humankind can exercise moral judgment. Nature—that is, creation in its beautiful though mechanical sense—cannot understand and cannot choose. Nature is neutral; it is "very good" in the existential sense, not in the moral sense. Moral action, therefore, cannot be determined from nature. There is no "natural moral law." Hence, humankind cannot look to nature for moral guidance. Creation, however, in the sense of God's kingship over humanity, implies revelation. For having created humankind capable of judgment as part of His world, God must provide a standard since nature itself does not do so. Having included a being capable of judgment in creation, God as King must provide guidelines for the exercise of that judgment—guidance which cannot be derived from the beautiful but mechanical, i.e., natural, aspect of creation. For humans, then, to know that God is King is also to admit God's guidance for humankind *and* to commit oneself to it. It is to agree to measure oneself by the revelation that follows creation. If God is King, we are servants. We are not His constituency, nor is He our elected representative. We live in His world, not ours. We are subjects of His kingdom. We are bound to His will and guidance. The doctrine of creation, therefore, in its second practical implication, imposes upon us the twin realities of kingship and of servanthood—not only as a spiritual experience but also as a commitment to a way of imaging life and of living it.

For example, is homosexuality good, bad, or natural, i.e., morally neutral? It makes a difference what one thinks, for it affects how one votes on certain referenda. To be a faithful servant is to acknowledge His word that homosexuality is an abomination (Lev. 18:22) and to act accordingly. To accept God's kingship into our lives is to say, "Lord, I don't understand it; I even think perhaps You are wrong; but let Your will be done on earth as it is in heaven, in this matter too." To live in God's kingdom is to bear the burden of His will, even when we disagree. We may fall short of this ideal; we may sin (indeed, we do); but proclaiming God's creatorship means accepting the yoke of His kingdom.

The second *nafka minah* of Genesis, the second practical implication of the doctrine of creation, then, is the word 'King' and, with it, openness to the double experience of His powerful presence and of our servanthood. It is an embodiment of our relationship to God and a life-orientation toward the revelation which is implied for us in His kingship over creation. A doctrine of creation which does not include this spiritual, linguistic, and moral dimension is not complete or faithful.[10]

There is a corollary to this implication. If we must live with God as our King, He must live with us as His subjects. Revelation contains reciprocity. Revelation implies covenant. To put it biblically, creation implies Abraham's argument over the destruction of Sodom and Job's defense of his own righteousness. The corollary to God's kingship is that He can hold us to judgment but we can hold Him to standards of righteousness. Justice, which includes love, is thus contained within creation, in the practical implication of God's kingship over humankind. Covenant is a politicoreligious agreement between creature and Creator for the ongoing administration of creation. It is a bond which mutually obligates both sides to loyalty, to compassionate justice, and to the reciprocal exercise of intelligent moral judgment.[11]

DISSONANCE

I Prayed Next to a Survivor
Yom Kippur, 5747

For Alex

We recited confession
I was astounded
What was he confessing, and why?
Who was asking forgiveness from whom?

We recited the penitential prayers
I saw
the shadow that crossed his face
the memories that sprang from the depths.

"Therefore, put fear of You into all Your creatures"—
an anger hidden in his body—
Why were they not afraid?
Why did He not put fear into them?

We recited the *Shma*
I was ashamed
Who am I to recite *Shma* next to him?
What is my faith next to his?

"Our Father, our King"
he has the advantage—
Job, faithful servant—
"How horrible are the terrible deeds You have set aside
for those who fear You;
an eye other than Yours has seen, O God."

"Act for the sake of sucking infants who have not
sinned"—
Were they my children?

Woe unto the eyes that saw such things.
I do not want to see; I cannot
He too does not want to see but he is compelled,
    and I am compelled in his compulsion
My son . . .   my daughter . . .

"If as children, if as servants"–
Lord, we really and truly only wanted to be good children,
    loyal servants
Even now, "we are Your children and You are our Father"
    "we are Your servants and You are our Sovereign"
Have mercy on us; have pity;
    Heal us and we shall be healed.[12]

There are no words in traditional Hebrew for 'ecology' or 'pollution.' Furthermore, the doctrine of creation has no direct practical implication for ecology. The idea that humanity is responsible for creation is subsumed under a completely different rubric—that of normative law, halakha—with concepts appropriate to the inner logic of the law and only indirect roots in the theology of God's creatorship.[13]

Deuteronomy 20:19–20 makes the following provision:

> When you lay siege to a city for a long time in order to capture it, you shall not destroy its trees, setting an axe to them for from them you will eat; nor shall you cut it. . . . Only a tree which you know is not a fruit-bearing tree shall you destroy and cut; you will build siegeworks against the city which is making war against you until it falls.

The text seems, at first blush, to be clear: during a siege, fruit-bearing trees may not be cut down but non-fruit-bearing trees may be cut, presumably for construction of the siegeworks.

The rabbis, however, studied this text very closely and expanded it into the general principle of *bal tashḥit,* "You shall not destroy." The following acts are forbidden: to cut fruit trees during a siege; to cut fruit trees even not during a siege; to deprive fruit trees of water; and, in the broader sense, to destroy something in grief or to wantonly destroy anything valuable such as vessels, clothing, a fountain, food, animals, money, candles, oil, etc. Conversely, it is permitted to destroy non-fruit-bearing trees even if the wood serves no purpose.

Given these guidelines, certain difficult questions can be raised: What if a fruit tree is damaging other trees? Or if it is old? Or if it is needed for building homes? etc. Here, the rabbis are at their analytic best, deciding that, if a greater good for humans is to be gained by cutting down even a fruit-bearing tree, it is permissible to do so. Thus, it is permitted to destroy a fruit tree, and by extension any valuable object, under the following circumstances: if it is damaging other fruit-trees, if the wood is valuable and one needs to sell it to make a living, if it is old and one needs to plant new fruit trees, if it needs to be pruned, if one needs the wood to build a house or needs to clear land for a house, if one needs to warm oneself, if one needs the wood to perform some other commandment (e.g., to build a sukka) or even to enhance a mitsva, and—some say—if one needs to remove such trees so as to reduce guerilla warfare from the besieged city.

The inner logic of the law is easily discerned. The blessings of creation are there for the use of humanity. What is useful may not be destroyed; what has no clear and usual use may be disposed of. In case of conflict, the action which provides the greater benefit to humans is the permissible one. Hence, fruit trees, and by extension anything valuable, may not be wantonly destroyed, but non-fruit-bearing trees, and by extension valueless objects, may be destroyed.

The law is also grounded in sound human psychology, for under no condition may fruit trees be destroyed to spite or cause pain to the inhabitants of the besieged city, i.e., as an act of psychological warfare. Only ill-intentioned people rejoice in acts of wanton destruction; such acts are considered a form of idol-worship and are strictly forbidden.[14]

The law of *bal tashḥit,* "You shall not destroy," in its narrow and in its broader sense, is composed of one, possibly two, mitsvot—"You shall not destroy" and "You shall eat of it." As a Torah-based law, it is enforceable, that is, a violation of it is punishable by flogging.[15]

This normative understanding of the proper utilization of

creation based on its usefulness to humankind is thus rooted in the legal part of the tradition, particularly in the part dealing with human conflict at its sharpest: the laws of war. It is not directly grounded in the theology of creation. The first commandment given to humans, "Be fruitful and multiply; fill the earth and have dominion over it" (Gen. 1:26–28)—that is, that humans are to gain control over nature, to use it intelligently for their common benefit, or as medieval thinkers put it, that humankind is the purpose of creation—is only a general statement.[16] It does not generate the concepts and the rules that govern the use of creation. There are also echoes of this law in the observation that the tabernacle in the desert was constructed of acacia wood, i.e., non-fruit-bearing wood (Exod. 26:15), and in the midrash: "When people cut down the wood of a tree which yields fruit, its cry goes from one end of the world to the other."[17]

If there are no words in Hebrew for 'ecology' and 'pollution,' then there are no words in English for 'sabbatical' and 'jubilee.' Both latter terms are nothing more than anglicizations of Hebrew words drawn largely from Leviticus 25:1–34, which provides that the land shall be left fallow every seventh year, that the land shall revert to its original owners every fiftieth year, and that the land can be redeemed at any time in order to return it to its rightful owners. These laws were incorporated by the rabbis into the halakha and they are very complex.[18]

The medieval authorities differ on the theological root for these laws. The author of *Sefer ha-Hinukh,* in explaining the jubilee (fiftieth) year, writes in #330:

> The root of this *mitsva* . . . is that God wanted to make known to His people that everything is His and that, in the end, everything must go to the person to whom He wished to give it originally because the whole universe is His, as it is written, "The land shall not be sold in perpetuity because the whole universe [land] belongs to Me; indeed, you are strangers and sojourners with Me" (Lev. 25:23).

This author, then, following the simple meaning of verse 23, roots the jubilee law in God's creatorship. However, he goes on to write:

> And by this *mitsva* of counting forty-nine years, they will distance themselves [from evil] such that they will not steal land from one

> another and will not covet it in their hearts because they know that everything must eventually go to the person to whom God wished to give it. (*Sefer ha-Hinukh* 330)

Here the author has introduced a moral-pedagogic reason for the law, one which is not rooted in a theology of creation. In discussing the law of the sabbatical (seventh) year, he follows this latter line of justification—that the purpose of the sabbatical year provisions is "to teach and habituate the people to the virtue of kindness and compassion. . . . We become God's messengers [in this]" (*Sefer ha-Hinukh* 66).

Maimonides construes the jubilee law very strictly, ruling that "the land cannot be sold in perpetuity and, if anyone does so, both parties transgress a negative commandment [and hence are liable to flogging] although their acts have no validity; rather the field reverts to its owners in the jubilee year."[19] Interestingly, Maimonides gives no justification at all in his *Code* for this law. In his later *Guide* he says:

> some of them [the sabbatical and jubilee laws] are meant to lead to pity and help for all men . . . and are meant to make the earth more fertile and stronger through letting it lie fallow. Others are meant to lead to benevolence toward slaves and poor people. . . . Others consider what is useful from a permanent point of view in providing for a living. . . . Consequently, a man's property remains, as far as landed property is concerned, reserved for him and his children, and he can only exploit its produce.[20]

Maimonides, too, then cites the moral-pedagogic motif as the theological ground for the sabbatical and jubilee laws, scrupulously avoiding any connection with a theology of creation.

The inner logic of the law is, again, clear. The usefulness of an object or rule in creating human good is the force that compels moral assent. Put differently, creation does not logically imply the sabbatical and jubilee laws, though, in retrospect, they are a geographical and moral extension of the idea of creation and sabbath. Or again, the sabbatical and jubilee laws do not, except in the exegesis of Leviticus 25:23, imply creation any more than do other laws (e.g., *sukka* or mixing of kinds). Rather, in the final analysis, it is the optimal human use of the blessings of creation that is the theological ground of the normative view. The doctrine of creation as such is present here only as an indirect implication.

DISTURBING ECHO

The Rabbis solved the problem of the chicken and the egg in a very imaginative way. They taught that, when God first created the world in chapter 1 of Genesis, He created everything in the height of its glory. Tulips bloomed together with chrysanthemums. Fall apple trees were heavy with their fruit at the same time that spring cherry trees sparkled with their fruit. Mustard greens were ripe at the same time as corn on the cob. There was no season during the first six days; everything was in its fullness. It is not until chapter 2 that we read of the fruitless plain that is watered, in which a garden is planted from which the richness of creation grows naturally to its fruition. Humanity is charged with working and caring for that garden (Gen. 2:15). What sort of work did Adam and Eve have to do in the Garden of Eden? They were responsible for watering the plants and for keeping the animals from inadvertently destroying them. Even Eden required work, though it must have been pervaded with a deep joy and ease.[21]

We strive mightily to keep the holocaust at the periphery of our consciousness. Nonetheless, relentlessly, the immensity of it penetrates through to our being and casts a pall over our awareness of creation. We tremble before the palpable sense of utter depravity and the terrifying awareness of the unmediated ontological reality of evil. We experience deep fear at recognizing unbridled Jew-hatred, shame at being a fellow human being to the perpetrators, and pain at being a fellow Jew to the sufferers. This is the ghostly, the unbearable dimension of the holocaust; it is the *tremendum.*[22] We cannot integrate it into ourselves.

Yet we cannot really integrate the glory of the King's perfected creation into ourselves either. We cannot sustain the joy of simultaneous spring and autumn. We cannot do prelapsarian work. Rather, we live in a world of both light and darkness. There is only the *nafka minah,* the practical implication—that God as Creator intended to give the Jews a part of His creation, the holy land; that God as King intended us to be open to an awareness of Him, to His kingship over us, and to our servanthood to Him; and that God as Revealer intended us to be guided by His law to use creation for our common benefit while taking care of His postlapsarian garden. And not too far in the back of our minds, we have that reminder that He and/or we can rupture the very fabric of creation and cast all its practical implications to the winds of uncreation.

An interfaith and intercultural post-script:

It may seem strange to write theology in a mode that does not deal with a doctrine and its philosophical ramifications. To write about practical implications, however, is to deal with the experiential and socioreligious realities which a doctrine implies in the actual life of an ongoing community. This seems to me to be a sound way of lending a socially realistic dimension to theology. Ultimate doctrinal truths may or may not be knowable, but life begins *in medias res,* in the concrete implication.

Every theology is particularist, speaking its own language and embodying its own culture. It cannot be otherwise. Yet every theology also has a universal vision, a perspective which encompasses the other. How do we, Jews, begin the discussion with Christians and Moslems? I cannot speak for the dialogue with Islam, having some knowledge but very little experience in an active exchange of views. I can, however, suggest some fruitful possibilities for dialogue between Christians and Jews.

First, it seems to me that, for Christians, the doctrine of creation leads directly to human and natural ecology—that is, to a respect for creation as something not of our doing, as that which must be cared for by us. There must be, however, other practical implications of the doctrine of creation for Christians; what are they? *Mai nafka minah,* What practical difference does it make to Christians whether God created the world or not? To open the dialogue, Christians ought to ask this question, rather than the ontotheological questions, and ought to share their answers with Jews.

Second, I think that Christians could respond to the three practical implications of the doctrine of creation for Jews as I have set them forth. They might do this as follows:

Christians who take seriously the idea of covenant and hence the chosenness of the Jewish people should also take seriously the covenant of land, according to which God gave the Jewish people the holy land in perpetuity. As God promised seed, so God promised the land (Gen. 17:1–9). Though both depend upon obedience, neither can be revoked (Deut. 30). The logical root of both is God's will as revealed in Scripture, which, in turn, is rooted in God's act of creation, as I have argued. Creation alone does not imply chosenness but creation with revelation-covenant does. I think Christians can admit this double chosenness rooted in creation because the incarnation appears to me to be, for Christians, another, deeper revelation which also must ultimately be rooted in creation. Furthermore, as Christians interpret the chosenness of the Jewish people as a sign and foretaste of the election of the church, so they could interpret the chosenness of the holy land as a harbinger and sign of God's promise of physical security (land in general) for all persons and peoples.[23] A Christian doctrine of creation thus could encompass the practical implication of land.

Christians can certainly respond to the practical implication of creation that demands openness to God's presence, acknowledgement of His kingship, and a life of obedient servanthood. For traditional Jews, the obedience is largely embodied in the law (halakha); that is, in deeds which one is expected to do. This could lead to a fruitful discussion of the deeds which one is required to do in Christianity. Another response to this practical implication could be a pondering of the experience and meaning of the kingship of God and a sharing of the requirements and limitations of servanthood (obedience).

The rooting of ecology in normative law must seem strange to Christians, as is perhaps the basing of ecological considerations upon the greatest human benefit. But I think there is a general good in having human behavior firmly planted in the soil of real obligation, one that transcends us. I think that is what 'law' means as a religious concept. Do Christians have a sense of religious law? What are the *mitsvot* (commandments) of Christianity and in what sense are they commanded and not just recommended?

I am not sure that practical implications are philosophically verifiable, or that there is an effective way to adjudicate differing implications. The way for interfaith dialogue, however, is open, on the specific and the general aspects of this theology of creation.[24]

NOTES

1. For Heschel's critique of the metaphysical formulation of theological issues, cf. A. J. Heschel, *The Prophets,* vol. 2 (New York: Harper and Row, 1962, 1971). For my own early effort, cf. D. Blumenthal, "Speaking About God in the Modern World," *Conservative Judaism,* 33:2 (Winter, 1980): 49–59. Cf. also the critique of the liberation theologians (e.g., R. Chopp, *The Praxis of Suffering* [New York: Orbis Books, 1986]) as well as the Derridean critique of the ontotheological tradition (J. Derrida, *Margins of Philosophy,* trans. A. Bass [Chicago: University of Chicago Press, 1982]).

2. By 'rabbinic Judaism' or 'the tradition,' I mean that organic understanding of biblical and rabbinic religion which, over the centuries, has become known as "Judaism." In response to Jonathan Malino's critique, I acknowledge that there are many streams within this Judaism: philosophical, mystical, legal, etc. (cf. D. Blumenthal, "Religion and the Religious Intellectuals: The Case of Judaism in Medieval Times," in *Take Judaism For Example,* ed. J. Neusner [Chicago: University of Chicago Press, 1983] 117–42); that there are modern nontraditional forms of Judaism; and that even within talmudic or classical (i.e., nonphilosophic) Judaism there are many variations. Nonetheless, as Jacob Neusner has amply demonstrated and as the tradition itself testifies, there is both variety and continuity in the concept "rabbinic Judaism," and I accept that. To "be faithful" to the tradition, then, is to faithfully explicate rabbinic Judaism, broadly construed. With David Tracy ("Religious Values After the Holocaust: A Catholic View," in *Jews and Christians After the Holocaust,* ed. A. Peck [Philadelphia: Fortress Press, 1982] 87–88), I see this as part of the task of the theologian. It would not be possible to write a theology of creation that took into account all the intellectual variations within Jewish religion.

3. The source for this Rashi is unknown but it is a comment learned by all Jewish children brought up in a traditional religious school setting.

All translations are my own unless otherwise indicated.

4. As we, at the end of the twentieth century, ponder humanness in its divine context, we must confront the claim that the language of Western culture, Jewish civilization included, is largely male-dominated. I, for one, think this is true and, in an attempt to restore the universal human meaning of the divine in religious teaching, I have chosen to use egalitarian language throughout this article. Purists in style may object but the aesthetic should never take precedence over the spiritual; that itself is part of Jewish theology.

There is one exception to my choice of the egalitarian mode of expression: pronouns referring to God. Here, I have chosen always to use the traditional masculine form. There are several reasons. God uses that language of Himself according to the tradition. The connotation attached to the use of female pronouns is one of idolatry; it is not just the strangeness of it. And perhaps there is a remnant sexism in me; I feel better with the male pronouns when talking about God. I encourage, though, women colleagues to write their own theologies in their own style and with their own issues. Theology grows through serious discussion.

In preparing a text, an author-editor has to make decisions about punctuation, capitalization, etc. These may seem to be outside the spiritual but nothing is outside the scope of the divine Presence. I had been capitalizing many words when I stumbled upon "the Golden Calf." The absurdity struck me. How can one capitalize the very embodiment of idolatry? And yet I had done it. But, if one does not capitalize idols, what does one capitalize? That is, to what does one give capital status?

I have decided, therefore, that as a matter of spiritual principle, only the following shall be capitalized: God, pronouns referring to Him, and words which are substitutes for Him such as 'the Presence,' 'Name,' 'Glory,' 'Infinite,' 'King,' 'Ayin,' 'Nothing,' etc. Everything else is not He and does not deserve to be capitalized—even though one usually does so in English—such as 'holocaust,' 'messiah,' 'temple,' etc. (The word 'presence' is capitalized when it stands alone but not when it occurs together with 'God's' or 'His.') I have, however, retained the usual English usage of capitalizing names of books, places, and holidays. This has been an interesting exercise in finding and redeeming a divine spark in the mechanics of English grammar.

I think, too, that scholarly and interfaith dialogue has reached the point at which Hebrew words which are part of the usual vocabulary of the discussion of Jewish religion should not be italicized or otherwise set off. I have followed this policy.

5. F. D. Levine, *Territory or Peace: Religious Zionism in Conflict* (New York: American Jewish Committee, 1986), 1.

6. Ibid., 14.

7. D. Bleich, *Contemporary Halakhic Problems* (New York: Ktav Publishing, 1983), 2:169–221.

8. Y. Landau, ed., *Violence and the Value of Life in Jewish Tradition* (Jerusalem: Oz veShalom Publications, 1984), vol. 2; L. Hoffman, ed., *The Land of Israel: Jewish Perspectives* (Notre Dame, Ind.: University of Notre Dame Press, 1986).

9. E. Wiesel, *One Generation After* (New York: Avon Books, 1965), 164–65.

The problem of how to reflect theologically after the holocaust is the most oppressive problem of our age for Jews and Christians alike. Susan Shapiro ("Failing Speech: Post-Holocaust Writing and the Discourse of Postmodernism," unpublished), following E. Fackenheim ("The Development of My Thought," *Religious Studies Review,* 13:3 [July 1987]: 204–13), has commented that one way of responding, in some measure, to the presence of the holocaust among us while still doing literary (or theological) writing is to break up and disperse moments of the holocaust into our work. This conveys the fragmented sense of reality that must pervade everything we do. It creates a theology that is never whole. "The word, thus, requires the breaking of the Word (breaking closure and completion into the openness of incompletion)." I have consciously chosen to follow Shapiro's advice and, hence, intersperse my theological reflections on the practical implications of the doctrine of creation with fragments from the kingdom of night.

10. Cf. Maimonides *Guide for the Perplexed* 2.25, cited in D. Hartman, *A Living Covenant* (New York: Free Press, 1985), 23, 98.

I acknowledge Malino's criticism that I have used a property model for understanding the doctrine of creation. I believe it, however, to be theologically authentic. I acknowledge, too, the possibility that the doctrine on homosexuality may be rooted in the law of "mixed-kinds." However, the tradition does not root it there, so I leave it where it is—in the laws on sexual purity and dominance. Finally, the link between acknowledging God's kingship and accepting revelation is experiential, a function of the phenomenology of the living faith (with W. C. Smith); it is not logically formal, as Malino would wish it.

11. On this, see D. Blumenthal, *Faith and Grace* (Austin, Tex.: Center for Judaic-Christian Studies, 1985); and "Mercy," in *Contemporary Jewish Religious Thought,* ed. A. Cohen and P. Mendes-Flohr (New York: Scribners, 1987), 589–96.

12. D. Blumenthal. The quotations are from the liturgy.

13. This discussion is based upon *Encyclopedia Talmudit,* "Bal Tashḥit," 3:335–37. Cf. also Maimonides, *Code of Law,* "Laws of Kings," 6:8–10, translated in A. Hershman, *The Book of Judges* (New Haven: Yale Judaica Series, 1949), 3:222–23; and the rabbinic commentaries to Deuteronomy 20:19–20.

The discussion of contemporary halakhic issues has concentrated largely on biomedical problems, sabbath observance, war and peace, the sabbatical year in Israel, and matters of personal status. There is practically nothing on that which Western civilization calls ecological issues. The *Index to Jewish Periodicals* notes only several articles on Israeli beaches and the more scholarly *Index to Articles on Jewish Studies* lists a few articles on smoking and one on vandalism. The column by D. J. Bleich, "Survey of Recent Halakhic Periodical Literature," in *Tradition* and the *Journal of Halakha and Contemporary Society* are probably the best places to watch for such issues to begin surfacing.

14. *Sefer ha-Ḥinukh* 529.

15. Ibid. Some say everything but the fruit tree provision is rabbinically based and hence subject to a different type of flogging.

16. Cf. J. B. Soloveitchik, "The Lonely Man of Faith," *Tradition* 7:2 (1965), pt. 1, and Nahmanides on Gen. 1:28. For the contrary view, cf. Maimonides *Guide for the Perplexed* 3.13.

17. *Pirke de Rabbi Eliezer,* chap. 34, trans. G. Friedlander (reprint New York: Hermon Press, 1916, 1970), 254. Note also the strange provisions: "When a woman is divorced from her husband, her voice goes forth from one end of the world to the other, but the voice is inaudible. When a wife is with her husband at the first coition, her voice goes forth from one end of the world to the other, but the voice is inaudible."

18. Maimonides, *Code of Law,* "Hilkhot Shemiṭa ve-Yovel" ["Laws Pertaining to the Sabbatical and Jubilee Years"].

19. Ibid., 11:1.

20. Maimonides *Guide for the Perplexed* 3:39, trans. S. Pines (Chicago: University of Chicago Press, 1963), 553.

21. Rashi to Gen. 1:25; Ha'amkek Davar to Gen. 2:5; Ibn Ezra to Gen. 2:15.

22. A. Cohen, *The Tremendum* (New York: Crossroad, 1981).

23. The provisional statement, "A Theological Understanding of the Relationship Between Christians and Jews," adopted for study by the General Assembly of the Presbyterian Church (U.S.A.), June 16, 1987, has begun to think in this way. The earlier draft of the document, done under the auspices of the former Presbyterian Church in the United States, was especially clear and forward-looking on this matter.

24. Malino's criticism that the practical implications which I have outlined "are neither obvious nor universally plausible"—particularly, that they do not speak for, or appeal to, non-Orthodox Jews—needs further attention.

I reply, first, that theological insight need not be either obvious or universally plausible. That expectation is a distortion added to the Jewish, Christian, and Muslim traditions by the philosophical, ontotheological tradition (see note 1 above). Theological insight need not be consistent in a logical sense; historically, it has not been. Theological insight must rather be a fruitful explication and extension of the teaching and experiential realities of the living tradition. Thus it is the experience of the intimacy of chosenness that leads to the first implication. It is the experience of the royal creative Presence and its concomitant moment of servanthood which lead to the second implication. And it is the experience of halakhic consciousness that leads to the third implication. None of these follow in strict logical fashion from assumed rational premises.

I reply, second, that the decision to accept or to reject any particular teaching is a function of a vast array of factors which include intellectual training, emotional attitudes, personal psychology, ethical impulses, the ability to sense the holy living presence of God, communal affiliations, etc., as well as one's reasoning processes. The decision to adhere or to observe is, thus, emotional, affective—indeed, political and social in the best sense of the words. The exercise of various types of reason is only part of such sociopolitical and experiential decisions. 'Non-orthodox' is a political-social term, not a philosophical category or even a theological construct. There certainly exist "non-Orthodox" theologies and even secularist worldviews within Judaism. This essay, however, is not an attempt at the "rhetoric of persuasion." Nor is it intended to represent all the views within Jewish religion. It is, rather, an example of the "rhetoric of explication" for a specific stream within Judaism. It fulfills the responsibility of the theologian insofar as it allows the voice of the tradition to resonate in the intellectual and affective space between persons. To identify with it is another matter.

Response

Jonathan W. Malino

For centuries, the question of creation was pivotal to the task of constructing a philosophical theology true, at once, to philosophical scruple and religious tradition. Not surprisingly, discussions of creation were thick with metaphysical subtleties about time, infinity, causality, and a host of other weighty concepts. In this light, one can easily sympathize with the impatient tone of David Blumenthal's central query, "What difference does it make *in terms of concrete action* whether God created the universe or not?" (emphasis added). This is, I think, an instance of the foundational and troubling question whether philosophical (and especially, metaphysical) affirmation has any genuine bearing on religious life. In its general form, and in its application to creation, it is a question which deserves to be pressed and honestly confronted. For this we owe Professor Blumenthal our thanks. As will emerge, however, I am less happy with Professor Blumenthal's response to his query.

Let me begin with a word about method and genre. In the oral summary of his paper delivered during our symposium Blumenthal noted its lack of philosophical language, attributing this to the postphilosophical climate in which his paper took shape. My comments, in contrast, are decidedly *not* postphilosophical. I hope that rather than merely missing Blumenthal's point, they will serve to provoke reflection on the very idea of postphilosophical discourse.

To assess Blumenthal's efforts, we must grasp the vantage point from which he pursues his query. Though he is not sufficiently explicit on this point, I take him to be both describing "the" rabbinic view of what creation practically implies, as well as endorsing this view. For his paper is utterly devoid of any indication that when he speaks of the rabbis, he is speaking of an "other." There is no critique, no questioning, and, for much of the paper, no overt marking of boundaries between author and subject. The rabbis, it seems, even if they never explicitly formulated Blumenthal's question, provided an unmistakable and essentially accurate answer to it.

Since Blumenthal's focus is on the implications of creation rather than on the doctrine itself, it is imperative that we have an adequate understanding of implication. Blumenthal seems to be aware that the term 'implication' has its ambiguities, but true to his nonanalytic style, he is reticent about making the ambiguities explicit. We will, nonetheless, be well served by trying to do so.

Most basically, a set of propositions Gamma implies a proposition P if, and only if, it cannot be the case that the members of Gamma are true and P false. So, necessarily, if the members of Gamma are true, then so is P. This concept of implication, as a timeless and absolute relation among propositions, is the province of formal deductive logic and is referred to simply as logical implication. Often, however, when we say that one thing implies another we have a less severe notion in mind. What we intend, then, is that Gamma, *when supplemented by additional evident, reasonable, or otherwise epistemically acceptable propositions,* logically implies P. This second notion of implication is perhaps best referred to as mediate epistemic implication, because the relation between Gamma and P turns into logical implication when Gamma is joined by mediating assumptions with some epistemic cachet.

Unlike logical implication, mediate epistemic implication is neither timeless nor absolute. It is defined, in part, in terms of epistemic notions which are themselves sensitive to the evidence available to a person (or group) at a particular time. To be sure, and as we shall see this is of some moment in the case at hand, the appropriate relativizations are frequently left unspecified; but logically speaking, they are no less essential for that.[1]

We are ready now to consider Blumenthal's first claim about the practical implications of creation. Blumenthal is quite clear that the relation that holds between creation and the idea that the land of Israel belongs to the Jews is, in our terms, a mediate epistemic implication. For he notes explicitly that the implication requires that the doctrine of creation be supplemented by the doctrines of revelation and covenant, which are completely absent from the biblical stories of creation. But given the epistemic relativity of this notion of implication, assessing Blumenthal's claim requires that we go on to ask, Relative to whom is this implication intended to hold? To whom, that is, is Blumenthal claiming that these doctrines of revelation and covenant are epistemically acceptable?

We need only formulate this question to realize that even among those who affirm the doctrines of creation, revelation, and covenant, there is wide divergence over the epistemic status of particular versions of these doctrines. Blumenthal may well be correct that *for the rabbis,* in view of their epistemic attitude toward their own ideas of revelation and covenant, creation mediately implies that the land of Israel belongs to the Jews. Such a claim would much less obviously be true for Christians and Muslims, however, given their very different views of revelation and covenant. Indeed even for contemporary non-Orthodox Jews, for whom rabbinic interpretations of revelation and covenant are problematic indeed, this implication would be suspect, or at the very least, controversial.

What we should conclude from these observations, it seems to me, is that it is highly misleading, if not tendentious, to talk of this first "practical implication" of creation without specifying explicitly for whom this implication is meant to hold. There is undoubted rhetorical power in lines like "everywhere, the claim of the Jewish people to the whole holy land, though variously defined, is integral," and "a doctrine of creation that does not include this national dimension is not complete or faithful," but the power is dissipated if the claims are, *sotto voce,* relativized to "the ancient rabbis" or "contemporary Orthodox Jews." If, on the other hand, these relativizations are otiose because, as we suggested earlier, Blumenthal is endorsing rabbinic views of revelation and covenant, then the power is potential only, awaiting the not inconsequential task of justifying these views.

One final point on the first "practical implication" of creation. Just as we have to be sensitive to concepts of implication, so must we be fully aware of the significance of the term 'practical'. Once again, Blumenthal seems well aware of a distinction which, nonetheless, warrants explicit formulation, namely the distinction between a *prima facie* and an *all things considered* judgment. Even if one accepts the implication that the land of Israel belongs to the Jews, how one should *act,* now or indeed ever, remains undetermined. The reason is that the claim about a right to the land of Israel at best leads to *prima facie* judgments about what to do. Granted, this does not rob the putative implication of the status "practical," but it does remind us of the complexities of any practical reasoning which issues in a call to action. And though Blumenthal certainly has not summoned us to endorse any policy on Israeli-occupied territories, his overall concern with practice over theory, coupled with his disinterest in explicit distinctions, could easily mislead.

Let us turn now to the second "practical implication" of creation. It seems to consist of three claims: that one ought to respond joyously to creation; that one ought to see God as King; and, as a consequence of the second claim, that one ought to become a faithful servant of God. Each is a mediate epistemic implication, the first, for example, requiring at least some mediating assumptions about the goodness of God and the presence of his goodness in creation. Since the mediating assumptions of the first claim have been so worked over in the philosophical and theological literature, I shall limit myself to observations about the assumptions which mediate the second and third claims.

To get at what mediates the second claim, it is sufficient to ask, "Why should the divine have the right of kings?" The answer presumably rests with an assumption (essential, as well, for the earlier "practical implication" about the land of Israel) that creation entails "property" ownership, which in turn entails the right of the owner to dispose of the property, and, if appropriate, to issue it commands. But how convincing is this view of the relation between creator and created? Perhaps, once again, it is in keeping with rabbinic attitudes, but need *we* accept it? How else might a creator be bound to his creation? And will it matter, in answering this, whether we regard God as masculine or feminine (or neither)? In his endnotes, Blumenthal makes some puzzling remarks about the use of nonmasculine language in Jewish theology. On the one hand he seems to want to restore "the universal human meaning of the divine in religious teaching." On the other hand, he is unwilling to endure the inevitable linguistic dislocation this would seem to require. But surely if one is serious about the presence of male imagery in theology, one cannot move from "creator" to "king" to "property owner" with nary a glance at the inevitable weight of masculine social models. Here, it would seem, we have a prime target for egalitarian thinking in theology.

Suppose, however, that we grant Blumenthal's mediating assumptions about property. Since these very assumptions embody norms about the right to dispose of and to command what has been created, it would seem that, contrary to what Blumenthal claims, there is a moral dimension to the universe which is independent of God's will. We do not, therefore, fully depend on God's guidance for moral knowledge.[2]

If this is correct, then there must be a flaw in the bold argument which Blumenthal mounts for the claim that affirming God's kingship entails accepting revelation as the only source of morality. A quick review of the argument does indeed reveal a flaw. For the argument, in part, seems to be that since moral guidance cannot be derived from "the beautiful but mechanical, i.e., natural, aspect of creation." God must have provided guidelines which we are bound to obey. But surely those who believe that moral judgment can be grounded in other than divine will do not limit themselves to those aspects of nature to which Blumenthal seems to be alluding, nor necessarily to nature at all. We need only think of Aristotle and Kant to conjure up alternatives to the limited options which Blumenthal must pretend are exhaustive if his conclusion is to be forthcoming.

But let us grant, finally, that creation entails kingship and kingship, revelation. In what sense, then, are we God's servants? And precisely how does servanthood conflict with autonomy?[3] These are large and slippery questions, and it would be unfair to expect Blumenthal to provide much guidance in a short essay. Surely, though, no suggestion that revelation commits us to an unreflective acceptance of the Torah's injunction about homosexuality can do justice to rabbinic notions of revelation, servanthood, and individual autonomy, to say nothing of more recent conceptions. Rabbinic tradition's own account of its internal development, with its recognition of the necessity and power of interpretation and the inevitable conflict this spawns, undermines any simple antithesis in rabbinic thought between the rational self and revelation. Reason has its limits, for the rabbis, but nowhere near the surface, as Blumenthal's example of homosexuality would suggest.

Once again we are forced to conclude that Blumenthal has failed to make his claims about the practical implications of creation convincing. His "implications" are neither obvious nor universally plausible. And once again, the difficulty stems from the mediating assumptions, which are uncertain and vague. If one is interested in the implications of creation, practical or otherwise, there would seem to be little alternative to patient philosophical investigation.

In concluding, let me note my appreciation for Blumenthal's sensitivity to the Holocaust, and for the moving "fragments from the kingdom of night." Who can fail to acknowledge with Blumenthal that "we must live in a world of both light and darkness"? And yet we are left wondering, what are the practical implications of this for our ability to affirm a God who is Creator?

NOTES

1. These unspecified relativizations should not be confused with the specific mediating assumptions and the specific epistemic concepts which are existentially generalized in the definition of mediate epistemic implication. Unlike the relativizations, these assumptions and concepts need not be specified in the truth conditions of statements about mediate epistemic implication. Of course the inferential processes by which we determine which relativizations are intended on a given occasion may be the same as the processes by which we determine the intended mediating assumptions and epistemic concepts.

2. For an excellent discussion of the relationship between God's commanding authority and his being a creator, see Baruch A. Brody, "Morality and Religion Reconsidered" in *Readings in the Philosophy of Religion,* ed. Baruch A. Brody (Englewood Cliffs, N.J.: Prentice Hall, 1974), 592–603.

3. I am not certain how consistent Blumenthal himself is on the relationship between servanthood and autonomy. On p. 159 he strongly emphasizes our dependence on God's guidance, while on p. 160 he insists that revelation contains reciprocity.

Creation and Christian Understanding

Robert Sokolowski

I. INTRODUCTION

Creation can be understood in a narrow and in a wide sense. In the narrow sense, creation is the divine activity in which the world—everything that is not divine—is made to exist. In this narrow sense, creation refers only to the beginning of the relationship between the world and God. The continuation of this relationship would be called preservation.

But we can also discuss creation in a wider and fuller sense. We can discuss it not in its character of being a beginning, but as establishing a distinction and a relationship, a distinction and relationship that remain after the beginning. We can discuss creation as that which defines how we are to understand God, how we are to understand the world, and how we are to understand the relationship between the world and God. By discussing creation in this way we also discuss God as Creator and the world as created.

Creation, in this fuller sense, is not merely one teaching among many in Christian belief. It is not one in a list of teachings along with, say, those concerning grace, the Eucharist, the Church, the inspiration of Scripture. Creation is related to such other teachings in a way that is logically distinctive. We could say that the teaching about creation enables these other teachings to be believed, in something like the way that the introduction of a mathematical interpretation of nature enables us to have Newtonian physics, quantum theory, relativity, and computer science. The teaching about creation opens the logical and theological space for other Christian beliefs and mysteries.

Furthermore creation, as well as the creature and the Creator, have a special meaning in Christian belief. They are not understood in the same way as they are taken in many other religious traditions. It is not the case that, say, creation and monotheism constitute a common ground, a common genus for Christianity and many other religions or philosophies, and that the specific difference that distinguishes the Christian religion from the others is to be found in the other Christian teachings, such as those concerning the Holy Trinity, the incarnation, and the Church. Rather the Christian understanding of God and creation is itself given a special tone by these other beliefs. What appears as the more specific has an effect on what appears as the more generic. What appears in the foreground has repercussions on the background. It is not the case that the doctrine of creation simply enables the other elements of Christianity to become believable but remains untouched by them, as a neutral background to them. Rather the doctrine of creation is affected by the beliefs that it enables, but it is affected in a way different from the way it affects them.

To pay attention, systematically, to relationships such as those I have just described is part of what I would like to call the theology of disclosure. It could also be called the theology of manifestation or a theology of epiphany, a theology of apparition. It is not just a psychology of religious experience; it does not examine simply the subjective consciousness we happen to have of religious realities. Rather it examines how the religious reality presents itself, indeed, how it must present itself, how it must differentiate itself, in its own manner of being differentiated, from whatever is other to it. To reflect on the epiphany is to think about *how* something appears, but it is also to think about *what* discloses itself in the manifestation, and it is also to think about *ourselves* as the datives for this revelation, as those to whom it appears.

Traditionally, one of the tasks of theology has been to bring out the relationships, the nexus, among the various revealed truths. This task can be pursued in regard to not just the truths themselves, but the way the truths become presented. It is not just the truths that are interwoven; their ways of being disclosed are also interlaced, and we can better appreciate the truths themselves by reflecting theologically on how the truths come to light. In the course of this essay we will carry out such reflection in regard to creation and its relationship to other Christian mysteries, but first we must determine what the specifically Christian sense of creation is.

II. THE CHRISTIAN SENSE OF CREATION

The distinctive sense of creation that is held in Christian belief can be described as follows. Let us call "the world" everything that is not God. The world, obviously, does exist. We start with that. But in Christian belief the world is understood as possibly not having been. The world becomes understood as existing in such a way that it might not have existed. And, in the Christian understanding, if the world had not been, God would still be. Furthermore, God would not be diminished in any way, in his goodness and perfection, if the world were not. While the world is understood as possibly not having been, God is understood as not being perfected in any way, as not increasing in goodness, by virtue of the actual existence of the world. Both the world and God become understood in this special way.

At first sight these understandings might seem to drain the world of its goodness and perfection. It might seem that the being of the world is said not to add anything to God's perfection because the world is understood to have no value in itself. Clearly we would resent this implication. But the reason the world does not add perfection to God does not lie in any poverty of the world; the reason is that God's goodness, perfection, and independence are understood to be so intense that nothing could be added to them. God is so understood that it would be meaningless to say that creation added to his goodness, that he created out of any sort of need. It is because of the greatness of God, not because of any worthlessness of the world, that creation does not better the perfection of God.

To bring out the novelty of this understanding, let us compare it to the sense of the world and the divine that is reached by natural religion and by philosophical thinking, as such religion and philosophy are found, say, in the classical poets and philosophers of Greece and Rome, in many religious writings, and in many beliefs that are current now, and that will doubtlessly always be current, among scientists, intellectuals, and people who have religious convictions.

According to the natural and spontaneous understanding, the

divine and the nondivine form parts of a larger whole. The divine may be recognized as the exemplary, the controlling, the encompassing, the best, and even in some sense the origin, but it is not normally conceived as that which could be, in undiminished goodness and excellence, even if everything else were not. Natural religious thinking and experience, as well as philosophical thinking about the whole, do not attain to this extreme turn of the dial.

It is characteristic of natural and spontaneous thinking to accept the world as simply there. The initial understanding of the world as dense and ineluctable, as unquestioned in its existence, is not a deficient form of thinking. It is the appropriate beginning. It is sound and robust. At the recorded inception of Greek philosophy, in the poem of Parmenides, the goddess who addresses Parmenides is quite correct in prohibiting him from looking for an origin for what is in that which is not (Fragment 8). To accept things as simply and necessarily there is the way reason should start. We *ought* to be impressed by the density of the nature of things. Even the Christian understanding of the being of things needs this natural stability as its counterpart and ever-present foil. The Christian understanding would not be appreciated as revelation without it. But over against this pagan and spontaneous understanding, Christian belief distinguishes the divine and the world in such a way that God could be, in undiminished goodness and greatness, even if everything else were not.

The Christian understanding introduces a new horizon or context for the modes of possibility, actuality, and necessity. Each of these modes is understood in a new way. The being of things is now questioned in a new setting. Questions are raised that are different from those that, say, Aristotle would raise. If we were to think as Aristotle thought, we might ask how it is that the elements and powers of the world—of the world which is always there—become congealed into being this animal or that building, and how they acquire the centeredness and intelligibility of being one substance or one artifact. This is how Aristotle would inquire into the being and substance of things. But in a Christian understanding one can ask why the animal or the building exists at all. Things are profiled not against the world and its elementary forces, but against not being at all. Their possibility is rooted not only in the potentialities of what already is and always has been, but in the power of God to make them be. The necessity against which their contingency is contrasted is not the iron bonds of fate that border the world, but the still more extreme necessity of the self-subsistent God whose choice is the source of everything else that is, everything that is now understood as not having to have been. The introduction of this sense of creation introduces a new slant on being, on what it is to exist, and on all the modalities of being.

It also introduces a new slant on ourselves. We to whom this understanding occurs come to understand ourselves in a way different from the self-understanding of a pagan or a secular philosopher. A pagan would consider himself as coming to be from the actions of his parents and his people, from the process of evolution, and from the physical and psychic necessities of the world. He would be grateful to his parents and his people, with a filial piety and loyalty, for they were responsible for his coming to be.

But even if a pagan accepted a divine principle in the world, he would not have the kind of gratitude toward that divinity that a Christian would have toward God. He would not consider himself as having been chosen to be, he would not consider his being as having been bestowed, in the way that a Christian would. His attitude toward the divine would be more like one of admiration and reverence rather than one of gratitude, because according to his pagan understanding there is something in him that is not due to the god, something that precedes both him and the god, something for which the god is not responsible. To some degree the pagan does stand on his own over against the divine in a way that one who believes in creation does not. For the pagan the whole is essentially prior to both the divine and the rest of being, but for the Christian the divine could be the whole, even if it is not, since it is meaningful to say, in Christian belief, that God could be all that there is.

This understanding of the whole has an impact on how we understand ourselves, since we have such a prominent place in the whole of things; we are the ones for whom the whole is an issue, and the way we take the whole will modify how we take ourselves. The issue of creation is not just a question about things but a question about ourselves as well.

It is interesting to note how the metaphysical and the personal become blended in this Christian understanding. If the world is understood as possibly not having been, then its being is the outcome of a determination that selects between possibilities. Before the beginning there was something like an indeterminate future; before the beginning the world might be, but it also might not be. Its actual being is then the outcome of something like a choice, something like the determination of an undetermined situation that contains possibilities that invite a decision. The play of metaphysical modalities, of possibility and actuality, calls for something like a choice, something like a personal transaction. Creation is not simply emanation from possibility to necessity; if it were, it would no longer be creation. And just as the modes of possibility, actuality, and necessity, when examined on this scale, are only analogous to the modes we experience in our worldly involvements, so also the choice to create is only analogous to what we are familiar with as choices; but there is nothing more appropriate for us to use than choice as we attempt to speak about the actual but nonnecessitated existence of the world. And because something like choice is involved in creation, something like gratitude is our appropriate response to it, not just for the being of things, but for our being as well. The fact that we are is the outcome of a personal transaction, not the outcome of chance or necessity, and it calls for a personal reaction on our part.

Finally, it should be apparent that what seemed like a kind of indifference of God toward the world, in the claim that God is not perfected by creation, is really the condition for a greater generosity and benevolence in creation. If God is not perfected by creating, then he does not create out of any sort of need, and his creating is all the more free and generous. There is no self-interest and no ambiguity in the goodness and benevolence of creation. And the pure generosity of creation tells us about the nature of the giver of this gift. The nature of the action tells us what the agent is like, and along with the generosity of redemption, it establishes the context for our own response in charity, first toward God and then toward others.

III. CREATION AND OTHER CHRISTIAN MYSTERIES

Let us now discuss the relationship between the Christian understanding of creation and some other Christian beliefs. I want to claim that the final determination of the Christian sense of creation is achieved as an implication of the Christian understanding of the Incarnation. In the councils of Nicaea, Ephesus, and especially Chalcedon, in response to controversies about the being of the Redeemer, the church stated that Christ was one person and one being with two complete natures, the human and the divine, and that neither of these natures was in any way diminished or changed by virtue of their union in him. Christ was fully human and fully divine. He was one being but two kinds of being. In stating these things, the church claimed to be restating the understanding of Christ that is found in the New Testament.

In the natural order of things, a union such as that of the Incarnation is impossible, and to assert such a union would be to state an incoherence or an inconsistency. In the natural order of things, each being is one kind of being. In being what it is, each thing excludes other kinds of being. A human person is not and cannot be a tree; a lion is not and cannot be a diamond. And since the divine as part of the world is one of the natures in the world, in the natural order of things a god, as understood by pagan thinking, cannot be human. A god could become human only by becoming less than a god, or not fully human, or by being only apparently human or only apparently divine, or by becoming some new kind of thing different from both the divine and the human. One being could not be fully human and fully divine.

Therefore the doctrine of the Incarnation implicitly tells us something about the nature of the divine. For the Incarnation to be possible, the divine nature must not be conceived as one of the natures within the whole of the world. It must be conceived as so other to the world that the union in the Incarnation would not be an incoherence. Thus the Jewish emphasis on the otherness of God, which provided the background for the life, teaching, and actions of Christ, was ratified and intensified by the belief in the Incarnation.

The doctrine of creation is also related to belief in the Holy Trinity. First, just as in the Incarnation, the special sense of the divine that the doctrine of creation introduces opens the possibility of a new union and a deeper communion, the union of one nature and three persons. In worldly being, it would again be incoherent to speak of three persons in one nature or one being, to speak of three persons in one substance. Each agent or person we experience is one being. But when we conceive of God as so different from the necessities of the world that he could exist, with no loss of excellence, even if the world were not, then we cannot say that the triune God is not possible. The limitations and definitions we are familiar with from our experience of the world and of agency within the world no longer apply without qualification.

Secondly, the doctrine of the Holy Trinity confirms the understanding we have of the transcendence of God through belief in creation. A pagan religious thinker might raise an objection to the understanding of God that we have proposed, of God as the one who could be all that there is, even without the world. He might object that this is too extreme a projection of unity. It seems to remove the involvement of difference, otherness, multiplicity, relation, and exchange from the highest being, and it seems to remove any sense of community from the divine. It seems to remove the tasks that ought to be involved in being. Unity seems to be carried to excess. It is as though someone were so impressed by the beauty of Plato's One that she wanted to project nothing but the One in sheer isolation. The good seems to be discarded in favor of the best. One aspect of being seems intensified to the exclusion of other principles that are equally necessary, even for the One and the Good to be what they are.

This is an objection that could be made if the divine were merely distinguished from the world and left in solitude. But part of the Christian understanding is that community, exchange, relation, and divergence are to be found within the divine nature, in the life of the Holy Trinity. The exchanges, relations, and divergences, as well as the community, are not the kind we are familiar with, and in no way do they subordinate God to a need for exchanges with the world; quite the contrary. Because of the abundance of the life of the Holy Trinity, God becomes even more independent in his nature of any involvement with anything that is not divine. This independence of nature, of course, does not become indifference; rather it defines both creation and redemption as all the more generous and unnecessitated.

The Christian distinction between the world and God is also important in regard to the doctrine of analogy. Traditionally, Christian theology has claimed that discourse about God is analogous discourse, that is, that a word like 'good' or 'one' when applied to

God is meant in a way that is analogous to its usage in worldly applications. The unity of God is not the same kind of unity as that, say, of a human being or an animal. Rather, there is an analogy of proportion in the two uses. The divine unity is to God as human unity is to a human being, or as organic unity is to a living thing. Such an analogy allows us to say that we know something of what the word means when it is applied to God, and that we can apply the term meaningfully, even though the full and literal sense of the term is beyond our comprehension.

Now there is no problem with the analogous use of terms within the confines of worldly experience. We find analogous structures everywhere. For example there is an analogy between the way scales are to fish, and feathers are to birds, and hair is to mammals. There is an analogy between the way the past is presented in memory and the way the past is presented in a historical treatise; the term 'the past' is used analogously, not univocally, in the two cases. There is even a rather uncontroversial analogy between, say, the wisdom of the divine principle in the world, and human wisdom, and animal cunning. Even a secular thinker will attribute a kind of ingenuity to evolution that is analogous to human prudence. All these are worldly analogies that possess an intelligibility and provide an illumination peculiar to them as analogies.

But in the Christian distinction between the world and God, a new and more radical analogy is both introduced and required. A new kind of nonworldly difference is introduced, a new distance that a new analogy is supposed to span. This distance becomes so great, and the difference between the worldly and the divine becomes so radical, that at first it would seem that nothing could span it at all. It would seem that nothing coherent could be said about the divine, because the divine is so out of reach of our discourse. However, this extreme of obscurity, this excess of darkness which is an excess of light, is complemented by the belief that the world does have its being from God and that traces of the hidden God will be found in it, and that they support analogous discourse about the Creator.

Language arises as an outcome of our power to distinguish, and the syntax of language arises as we bring back together, into various kinds of wholes, the things and features we have discriminated.The special distinction that occurs in the Christian understanding of God and creation, the distinction between God and the world, with the special form of negation and affirmation that it implies, gives rise to an appropriately modified language, to the terminology and syntax of theological analogy.

IV. CREATION AS A DISTINCT DIMENSION

Belief in creation is not simply belief in a fact or an item of information that is added to all the other things we know and hold as true. Belief in creation introduces what I would like to call a dimensional difference, a new way of taking things. It introduces a new way in which the world as a whole, and everything in the world, can be interpreted.

There are other forms of thinking that also introduce new dimensions, and if we examine them briefly, we may be helped to appreciate the special character of creation. Consider, for example, the difference introduced when we learn what names are, or when we learn how to use names. If we learn that things have names, we are not merely given one more fact about the world, one more feature of things. Rather, when we appreciate things as nameable, everything in the world, and even the world as a whole, takes on a new aura. Everything takes on a new mode of being presented, and we ourselves take on a new form, not only because we expect ourselves to have our own name, just like everything else, but because we surface as the ones who use names, who can supply the name of a thing or who can look for its name if we do not know what it is. If things are nameable, it is partly because we or someone like us can give names. The presentational form of being named is a form for things, but a form for us and for our intentionality as well.

Likewise a dimensional difference is introduced when things are appreciated as measurable and countable. This too is not simply a new fact, but a new way in which things can be presented. Moreover, in introducing measurability and countability, we are not just making a change in our psychological and intellectual powers. We are saying something about how beings can be presented and intended. We are saying something about the being of things and about ourselves as the datives for the presentation of things.

Still another dimensional difference occurs when we appreciate the articulations of time, when we entertain not just what is immediately going on, but the distant future and the past. When this happens, we do not merely annex a future and a past to an unperturbed present; it is not the case that we begin with a complete present and then add two more dimensions to it. Rather the present itself becomes established as the present in its contrasts with the future and the past.

Now a religious attitude, even a pagan one, also introduces a dimensional difference into the way we take things. A religious attitude is not merely the addition of a divine principle to everything else. It is also a new way of taking the "everything else," a distinctive way of appreciating things. Things, in the religious attitude, are taken as being governed or influenced or known or judged by an agent or a mind that is different in kind from our own. Our own perspective on things becomes contrasted to a perspective that is radically different, and the things we know and experience are appreciated as also known and influenced by the gods.

But the Christian distinction does not simply fit into the religious perspective. It introduces a further dimensional difference into the natural religious understanding. All the things that are, including ourselves, are now appreciated as known and chosen by the God who allowed them to be. The whole context, even the whole religious context, is changed. The gods or the divine is replaced by God, and everything looks different when this happens. What had seemed to be the whole—the whole made up of the gods and the world—now is seen not to be the ultimate whole. God alone could be all that there is. God alone could be the whole. The sense of the whole itself changes.

And this dimensional difference pervades all the other presentational forms, so that language and names, for example, now become activated in a context that is not like that of the context of the world. The names of God, and discourse about God, are not like the speech we use in expressing the things we know in the world. To mention another example, the presentational form of picturing takes on a new dimension, since a depiction of the divine, understood as it is in Christian belief, is not a normal image of an object, nor is it an idol; it is rather an icon, and the theology of icons, with the importance it has had in the Eastern Christian tradition, can be fruitfully developed against the setting of both creation and Incarnation.

I want to emphasize that unless this new sense of the whole, this rather formal change in the way we take being, is introduced, other descriptions of God and of the relationship we have to God will not be properly understood. For example we may believe in divine providence, but unless everything is appreciated according to the sense of creation that we have discussed, the providence of God will not be properly interpreted. The context for what is meant by providence will not have been correctly established, and the difference between the biblical providence of God and, say, the Stoic sense of providence, will not have been secured. Christian discourse about God remains vulnerable to distortion so long as the context of creation, and the logic that follows from this context, have not been clarified.

V. THE THEOLOGY OF DISCLOSURE

The dimensional difference introduced by belief in creation establishes a new setting within which everything we are familiar with is understood in a new way. Everything is identified within a new set of differences and everything thereby takes on a new tone. Another person, for example, is no longer only our brother or sister or friend, but is someone who exists through the generosity and choice of God. This truth about the person makes us act toward him or her in a new and appropriate way. If the being of other persons is God's gift, other persons are more emphatically understood as ends in themselves than they would be if they had simply the dignity, great as it is, that comes from being rational agents, fellow citizens, members of our family, or neighbors or friends.

Now it is one thing to introduce this dimensional difference and to live in and according to it. That is done by someone who lives in Christian faith. It is another thing to reflect thoughtfully on the new dimension and to think about it, as clearly and systematically as we can. It is another thing to think about it as a dimension—in the way it comes forward, in the way it differentiates itself from the original and spontaneous religious dimension, in the way it sheds light on things and allows us to appreciate things and persons in a new context, in the way it calls for and legitimates a new analogical language, in the way it changes the sense we have of the whole and the world and the divine, in the way it modifies the modalities of being, the actuality, possibility, and necessity of our experience, in the way it introduces new forms of negation, distinction, and assertion, in the way it calls for an appropriate response in our self-understanding, deliberation, and action, in the way it introduces the possibility of sacraments and icons. To carry out such investigations is to pursue a theology of disclosure, to think theologically about the epiphany of God in our world.

This theology of disclosure is a supplement to the Scholastic theology that has been the dominant form of theology, in Catholic circles at least, since the Middle Ages. Scholasticism reflected on the existence and nature of God, and on the world in its relation to God, but it carried out its work within the horizon set by the Christian distinction between the world and God. It did not examine the emergence of the distinction itself. It took the presence of the distinction for granted.

Furthermore the theology of disclosure is an appropriate and positive response to issues that have been raised in modern, post-Scholastic thinking. During the European philosophical age set by the late Scholastics, Machiavelli, Descartes, Hobbes, and modern science, the issue of appearances has surfaced as the central philosophical concern. Appearances have been interpreted as coming between ourselves and the things we want to know. We have been led generally to be sceptical of appearances and to separate them as phenomena from the things in themselves, from the noumena, that are known through scientific inference and not directly through perception and received opinion. In religious thought there has been a corresponding tendency to turn within, to find our contact with the divine more through immanence and subjectivity, and not in the world. In this turn to subjectivity the sacramentality of the world has been allowed to fade away.

The theology of disclosure is an attempt to publicize religious appearance. It is concerned with a distinction that occurs in regard to the world, not just with a subjective experience. It seeks to discover an indication of the divine even in the materiality of the world. In doing this it attempts to validate appearance and remove the suspicion we have toward it. It also emphasizes history, whether biblical, ecclesiastical, or secular, as the place in which the Christian distinction occurs, but it interprets this history speculatively. It sees it not simply as information about the past, but as serving the truth that the distinction brings to light.

Thus the theology of disclosure supplements Scholastic ontology by introducing subjectivity and appearance in a more systematic way, and it responds to modernity by thinking about appearance in terms of distinction and being. And the religious issue that it brings to the fore, the central concern that allows it to speak about faith and reason, and grace and nature, and the world and God, is the issue of creation. The theology of epiphany turns to creation not as a problem but as light, a light that both itself appears and allows other differentiations to take place, a light whose brilliance is glimpsed by human reason and revealed in the word of God.

Response

David Tracy

It is a pleasure to provide a brief response to the important paper of my friend and former colleague, Robert Sokolowski. In keeping with the role of respondent, I shall briefly comment on merely a few aspects of his fine and complex analysis.

In harmony with his philosophical work in phenomenology, Professor Sokolowski develops a theology of disclosure or, more expansively, a phenomenological theology of disclosure. Hence he provides us with a paper which, like his book, *The God of Faith and Reason,* presents a genuine alternative to several more familiar ways of understanding Christian theology in our period. This is the paper's great strength and its challenge. For most Christian theologies of creation in our period—whether the "turn to the subject" transcendental theologies of Rahner and Lonergan, or process theologies, or different dialectical theologies like those of Barth, Bultmann, and Tillich—do not take the phenomenology of disclosure approach of Sokolowski. Here his position is both original and bold: clearer, it seems to me, than his natural theological allies such as Hans Urs von Balthasar and Joseph Cardinal Ratzinger; bolder in his insistence that the very category most suspected by most of modern thought (viz., 'appearance') is, in fact, the central philosophical category needed for a new theology of disclosure.

This philosophical move frees him to argue that it is not only a *beginning* that the doctrine of creation allows to appear. Fundamentally, creation allows the appearance of the central *distinction* between God and world and the proper understanding of that relationship. In sum, a theology of disclosure, once articulated through a phenomenology of appearance, allows for the emergence of the radical distinction between God as Creator and all else as created. Thereby can we clarify for thought: (1) that God appears; (2) how God appears; and (3) how that appearance affects the notion of subjectivity. This central notion of disclosure is clarified and even radicalized by Sokolowski's further reflections on the doctrines of Incarnation and Trinity, as well as what new analogical language may be suggested by that appearance of creation.

I realize that this brief summary hardly communicates the full complexity of the development of a theology of creation via a philosophy of disclosure-appearance in Sokolowski's paper. However, his own customary clarity as well as his precision in making distinctions encourage me to believe that his paper itself communicates its argument very well indeed. I shall, therefore, raise a few points for further discussion.

1. For the comparative theological purposes of this conference, I believe that Section II, entitled "The Christian Sense of Creation," could, without loss of any content, be entitled "A Jewish-Christian-Muslim Sense of Creation." This is not the case, of course, for those parts of Section II where the Christian doctrines of Incarnation and Trinity are claimed to provide additional understandings of creation and thereby of the relationship of God and world.

Some questions suggest themselves here:

(a) What is the exact meaning of the verb 'intensify' when Sokolowski claims that the Christian understanding of Incarnation both ratifies and intensifies the Jewish understanding of the "otherness" of God?

(b) Does not the biblical understanding of 'covenant' already suggest such philosophical notions as difference, otherness, relation, and exchange in the biblical understanding of God? Or are we to believe that an adequate theology of disclosure need reflect only in such philosophical informed doctrines as Trinity and Incarnation and not in the originating Christian biblical symbols? I see no intrinsic reason why the answer need be yes, but continue to be puzzled by Sokolowski's silence here—a troubling silence given the importance of the relationship of scriptural symbol and doctrine in the Christian tradition alone, and even more so far as Jewish-Christian-Muslim dialogue.

2. I remain intrigued by the fruitfulness of Professor Sokolowski's theology of disclosure or epiphany in developing, first, a philosophical-theological reflection on the mystery of creation in its appearance, and, second, a reflection on the possible interconnections of the mysteries of creation-Incarnation-Trinity from this

perspective. The particular ways he develops the analysis, however, lead me to ask two questions:

(a) Does not the use of the analogous term 'choice' for understanding creation suggest that there is also some kind of "turn to the subject" (however muted and Aristotelian, not Kantian) in the use of what has traditionally been called the "analogy from nature" in Catholic theology? Does not the very use of 'choice' (allied to the critique of emanation) suggest that this analogy from nature is in fact an analogy from human nature, i.e., from the peculiar human ability to choose?

(b) Allied to this first question is a more strictly theological question: Granted the great need and import for a theology of the sacramentality of nature (even matter) that this theology of disclosure can produce, and granted that an overconcentration on redemption and history and thereby on anthropology can impoverish a proper understanding of the Christian's relationship to the natural world, we are still left with many central scriptures, doctrines, and theological traditions that demand more attention to the creation-redemption relationship than most pure theologies of disclosure seem willing thus far to undertake. The theological issue is this: insofar as Western Christians distinguish creation and redemption—and, within redemption itself, incarnation-cross-resurrection—they have been driven, since Augustine forward, to work out theologies not only of nature-grace but also of grace-sin and theologies not only of incarnation but of incarnation-cross-resurrection. The radical negativity in human beings disclosed in the Christian understanding of sin and the radical negativity disclosed in the symbols of the cross and kenosis suggests the need for a more explicitly dialectical understanding of the relationships among the mysteries than most theologies of disclosure (like von Balthasar's) attain.

Just as most modern (and, on the whole, Augustinian) theologies need the kind of corrective which the more cosmic theologies of disclosure typically insist upon, so too the theologies of disclosure, in fidelity to their own demand to encompass all the mysteries of faith, need to pay greater attention to the unsettling disclosure of the negativities manifested in the doctrines of redemption, cross, and sin.

Such an inner-Christian conversation, moreover, seems promising for comparative theology as well, insofar as the God-world relationship becomes distinguished in all three traditions in their distinct ways as God-cosmos-history-self in each of these great traditions of the Creator God. To these further distinctions, a full theology of disclosure must address itself.

Do Christian Platonists Really Believe in Creation?

Bernard McGinn

Do Christian Platonists really believe in creation? The history of Christian thought indicates that this is a real, not just a rhetorical, question. Over the centuries, both in the East and in the West, difficulties have been raised about the presentation of the doctrine of creation found in some Christian theologians whose thought has been influenced by Platonism. Even today, especially from the perspective of Christian philosophers and theologians who stress a strong distinction between the pagan world view and the Christian creation-centered one,[1] Christian Platonists are suspect for smuggling in pagan notions of "emanation" that imply that God is part of a necessary and eternal universe. Are Christian Platonists really willing to entertain the possibility that all we see and experience might not have been, but was created out of nothing in time by the decision of a wholly transcendent God whose being and goodness are in no way increased or altered by the existence of the universe?

My answer to this question will be in three stages. The first part will involve a brief analysis of the presentation of creation in the thought of Meister Eckhart, a Christian Platonist who was explicitly condemned for his views on creation. The second will be an even briefer comparison of Eckhart's views with the thought of John the Scot, called Eriugena, another Latin theologian in the Platonic tradition who became suspect, among other things, for what he had to say on God as Creator.[2] Finally, I will close with an attempt to test the adequacy of Eckhart and Eriugena's thought in terms of four essential characteristics of the traditional Christian view of creation.

Meister Eckhart's explicit treatment of creation, as might be expected, is primarily to be found in his technical scholastic works. His vernacular sermons and treatises, while always presupposing his profound thoughts on the *exitus* or *ûzbruch* of all things from their divine source, are more explicitly concerned with the return of the soul to God. Although the Dominican's teaching on creation pervades the Latin works, there are four passages that conveniently summarize the major lines of his doctrine.[3]

These four passages reveal the fundamental principles that govern Eckhart's teaching in this area.[4] First, as might be expected of a Dominican Master, Eckhart is traditional in his formulae concerning the definition of creation. Following Avicenna and Aquinas, he defines *creatio* as "collatio esse," "productio ex nihilo," "productio rerum ex nihilo," "collatio esse post non esse," and "dare esse ex nihilo."[5] Like Thomas Aquinas, he insists that the whole meaning and purpose of the act of creation is to confer *esse,* the act of existence, upon all that is.[6] *Esse* is both the "ground of creatibility"[7] and the purpose, or final cause, for which God acts. He makes all things "that they may be." Eckhart's understanding of the "collatio esse," however, has a character of its own. In a passage in his *Commentary on the Gospel of John,* he notes that *esse* serves as the "principle" (*principium*) of creation insofar as it expresses the notion of "the One" (*ratione unius*).[8] These two key terms, *principium* and *unum,* reveal what distinguishes Meister Eckhart's doctrine of creation from that of his master, Thomas Aquinas.

In his literal *Commentary on the Book of Genesis* Eckhart insists at the outset, "You must recognize that the 'principle' in which 'God created heaven and earth' is the ideal reason (*ratio idealis*). This is what the first chapter in John says, 'In the principle was the Word (the Greek has 'Logos,' that is, 'reason')."[9] The conflation of the "in principio" of Genesis 1:1 with the "in principio" of John 1:1 had been achieved a millennium before Eckhart wrote. With roots deep in an originally non-Christian intradeical interpretation of the Platonic Forms or Ideas,[10] this theme became central to Latin theology in the fourth century with Ambrose and Augustine.[11] Eckhart's understanding of creation in the "Principle," or "Word," however, was both original and daring.

The Meister's analysis of the nature of the *principium,* that is, the source or origin, is found throughout his works, especially in his extensive comments on the Prologue to the Gospel of John.[12] His explicit treatments of creation return again and again to the central message that the key to understanding creation is to grasp that it takes place *in Principio*—in the Divine Logos, or in God himself (*in seipso*).[13]

For Eckhart creation is best understood as one of the three essential modes of what we can call "principial activity," as is made clear in an important passage in Latin Sermon 49.[14] *Bullitio* ("inner boiling"), the mode of production of the three Divine Persons in the Trinity, is a formal emanation in which the Divine Principle through reflexive conversion emanates its perfect Image, something one and the same as itself. *Ebullitio* ("boiling over"), though isomorphically similar insofar as it proceeds from a principle, is the production of something different from the principle that takes place in the realm of efficient causality. It is of two kinds, *creatio,* the production of something from nothing, and *factio,* the making of one thing from another.[15] In the wake of the condemnations of the Latin Averroists, Eckhart emphasizes God's free decision in creating;[16] nevertheless, the essential relationship he sets up between the procession of the Divine Persons and the creation of the universe has seemed problematic to many.[17]

Even the scriptural basis for Eckhart's understanding of creation is unusual. One of his favorite texts was an unlikely passage from Psalm 61:12, "God has spoken once and for all, and I have heard two things," which he interpreted as signifying that in one and the same eternal speech-act God is responsible for the emanation of the Persons within the Trinity (*bullitio*) and the creation of the whole universe (*ebullitio*).[18]

The God who creates the universe as its Principle is identified with *esse absolutum, ipsum esse subsistens, esse indistinctum.* While Eckhart's formal analyses of creation for the most part are conducted under the rubric of transcendental *esse,* the John Commentary's insistence that "esse sub ratione . . . unius principium est . . . totius entis creati" provides the important clue that Eckhart understands the relation between creating and created *esse* according to a dialectical model most clearly expressed in some of his explorations of how God is said to be *unum,* or Absolute Unity.[19] "Thus the term 'one' adds nothing beyond existence (*esse*), not even conceptually, but only according to negation. . . . For this reason it is most immediately related to existence in that it signifies the purity and core and height of existence itself, something which even the term 'existence' does not do."[20] The import of this intimate relation between *esse* and *unum* will be taken up below. Some significant related questions, such as whether or not Eckhart's sometime exclusion of the related transcendental predicates of *vivere* and *intelligere* from the realm of creation indicate that these terms were meant only to signify the uncreated realm in the human soul, will not be taken up here.[21]

From these fundamental themes, which we may characterize through the terms *collatio esse, principium,* and *unum,* the remaining principles of Meister Eckhart's doctrine of creation can be deduced. Four of these principles are particularly important: (1) creation as eternal (what I will call the *nunc stans* principle); (2) creation as two-leveled (the virtualiter/formaliter principle); (3) creation as formally nonexistent (the *nihil* principle); (4) creation as a one-to-one relation (the "*uni-versum*" principle).

In both his Latin and in his Middle High German works, Eckhart always affirmed that if God creates, he must do so "now" (*nû, nunc*) that is, in the timeless present moment (*nunc stans*) of his divine being.[22] God's creation in the ever-present *nu* of eternity is the ground for many of Eckhart's most problematic statements about the nature of creation.[23] Nevertheless, he was convinced that the point could not be denied. Not only is it metaphysically impossible for God to act otherwise than in the present moment of eternity—no past or future being possible to him[24]—but Christian tradition, especially Augustine in a text Eckhart loved to quote,[25] had always taught the same. However, Eckhart also insisted, and not just when taken to task by his inquisitors,[26] that creation has a beginning in time. "Exterior creation is subject to time which makes [things] old."[27]

How did Meister Eckhart put together these two seemingly contradictory aspects of his teaching on creation? The answer lies in his distinction between two levels of creation and therefore of the existence of created being: the virtual and the formal. As a passage from the Wisdom Commentary puts it: "All things are in God as in the First Cause in an intellectual way and in the mind of the Maker. Therefore, they do not have any of their formal existence until they are causally produced and extracted on the outside in order to exist."[28] Of course, these dual levels of existence are just another way of talking about existence *in principio*.[29] It is also evident that the relation between virtual, or intellectual, existence and formal existence constitutes one of the most complex and problematic aspects of Meister Eckhart's thought, and that all that can be attempted here is an introductory presentation, not a real explanation, let alone a defense.

The unusual character of Eckhart's view of this relation is immediately evident in what I have called the *nihil* principle. Both the Latin and the vernacular works are full of statements that creatures in themselves, that is, in their formal existences, must be said to be nothing. The Meister's vernacular formulations are perhaps the more radical,[30] but the scholastic works are also replete with texts that insist, "Every created being taken or conceived apart as distinct in itself from God is not a being, but a nothing."[31] A typically Neoplatonic form of this view of created being, frequent in the major texts on creation, is the presentation of descent from the Absolute Unity of the One as a form of metaphysical "fall" (*casus, descensus*) into number and numeration.[32] Also Neoplatonic in origin is one of the most striking of Eckhart's expressions of the nothingness of creatures through the invocation of the metaphor of reflection in a mirror. Just as a face is always a face, whether or not a mirror is present, and just as the image of a face in a mirror is always being created by the face looking into the mirror without any effort or change in the face itself, so too does creation reflect the reality of God.[33]

According to Eckhart, God the Creator is, above all, the One God. Thus, the final principle of Eckhart's teaching on creation is that God and the created universe must be fundamentally conceived of according to a one-to-one relation. In a typically unusual, but revealing, etymology he interprets *universum* as *universum,* that is, the whole that is directed to the *unum,* God insofar as he is Absolute Unity.[34]

This principle helps explain Eckhart's position on some of the important debates about creation that disturbed his era. God as one can only produce what is one.[35] The German Dominican often dwells on how God's creative intention immediately looks not to individual beings as such but to the single universe of which they form integral parts. This enables him to show the deficiencies in Siger of Brabant's attacks on the traditional understanding of God's creation of the unity-in-multiplicity that is our universe,[36] and also to criticize Avicenna's view of creation as mediated through a First Supreme Intellect that alone is worthy to be the product of the Primary Cause.[37] Finally, this principle is the source for his extensive, if not completely original, reflections on how the inequality of creatures contributes to the harmony of God's one creation.[38]

Eckhart's teaching and preaching aroused considerable opposition toward the end of his life. This culminated on March 27, 1329, when Pope John XXII condemned twenty-six propositions drawn from his works, the first fifteen as guilty of heresy. The first three of this group, drawn from the commentaries on Genesis and the Gospel of John, deal with the duration of creation.

> The first article. When someone asked him why God had not created the world earlier, he answered then, as he does now, that God could not have created the world earlier, because a thing cannot act before it exists, and so as soon as God existed he created the world.
>
> The second article. Also, it can be granted that the world has existed from eternity.
>
> The third article. Also, in one and the same time when God was, when he begot his coeternal Son as God equal to himself in all things, he also created the world.[39]

Although the Pope's difficulties centered on the Dominican's teaching about the eternity of creation, a glance further down the list shows propositions that seemed to threaten the distinction between creature and Creator as well. Article thirteen, a passage from one of the German treatises, claims that because whatever is proper to God is also proper to the just and divine person, "this man performs whatever God performs, and he created heaven and earth together with God, and he is the begetter of the Eternal Word."[40] Finally, the first of the appended heretical articles, one which Eckhart denied making, at least in this form, but which clearly reflects many passages in his works, provides the root for his startling elevation of the human person to the status of cocreator by asserting, "There is something in the soul that is uncreated and not capable of creation."[41]

It is instructive to see how Eckhart defended himself when questioned about his teaching on creation in the trials held at Cologne and Avignon. Most of the debate centered on the duration question—was the world eternal or not?—but other issues were also revealed. Considerable opposition was directed at Eckhart's teaching that every activity of God takes place in the simple now of eternity and that therefore if creation is truly God's work it must be eternal from the divine perspective. In response he invoked the Aristotelian distinction between *actio* and *passio* to defend the temporal character of the created universe—from an eternal *actio* it does not follow that the created *passio* must be eternal. In one of his Latin Sermons he had said, "The created thing is always coming to be according to that existence which in itself precedes motion, though the thing is not always being created."[42] He repeated this at Avignon: "It is the same now of eternity in which God creates the world, in which God exists and in which God generates his coeternal Son. But it does not follow that because God's action is eternal that the world is eternal, because God produces the world from the start and out of time and in the now of time in such a way that the world and its creation is a reception [*passio*] in time, and the now of time and creation as reception are not in God but in the creature."[43]

Thomas Aquinas would not have been happy with this analogy, since he had underlined the importance of recognizing that creation must be conceived of not according to the paradigm of change as analyzed by Aristotle, but as the beginning of a relation of dependence.[44] The Avignon inquisitors also rejected this, saying that *creatio,* even actively considered, must be a temporal action because *actio* and *passio* are simultaneous aspects of the same production. According to Aristotelian analysis, motion is formally in the thing moved; hence creation, formally speaking, is in the creature and not in God.[45]

Eckhart's invocation of Aristotelian categories to help explain his teaching on creation here was clearly not helpful. In his major creation texts, *actio* and *passio* frequently appear as the two fundamental *extrinsic* principles of the universe.[46] One wonders why in the Defense he appears to have confused natural causality, explained through the categories of *actio* and *passio,* with the divine *collatio esse.* A passage in the literal *Commentary on Genesis* had put the matter much more clearly in saying that God "is not so much the cause of things or beings, but rather the *ratio causae.*"[47]

This suggests that Eckhart would have been much truer to the principles of his own thought had he defended himself through the invocation of the distinction between the different modes of reality predicated of things, the formal and the virtual, or the "real" and the ideal. Both Eckhart and his critics admitted that the *in principio* of the beginning of Genesis could be interpreted as signifying that God created all things "in the Word and *Ars* full of the living Ideas,"[48] but for the Dominican this virtual ideal existence of all things in the Word as Principle was central, whereas his critics appear to cite it only as a bow to tradition. If Eckhart invoked the distinction between the eternal character of the virtual existence of all things in the Divine Word and the temporal nature of their formal existence in the created world at this point in his defense, it is not reflected in the texts that survive to us save by implication; but it was fundamentally this principle which allowed the Dominican to be so bold in his use of the language of eternity to speak about created things.

Eckhart's ways of talking about the two levels of being present in creatures led to further difficulties. In condemning his statements about the absolute nothingness of all creatures (one of these became article twenty-six of the papal Bull), the Avignon inquisitors insisted that there must be something "really real" about formal existence. "Even though God and creature are not greater than God alone, there are still many existing things (*res*), just as a line and a point are not greater than the line alone, though there are many points (*res*)."[49] Throughout the Defense, Eckhart poured scorn on his attackers for thinking that creatures were other than sheer nothing. "To say that the world is not nothing in itself and from itself, but is some slight bit of existence is open blasphemy. If that were so, God would not be the First Cause of all things and the creatures would not be created by God in possessing existence from him."[50] For Eckhart, if *esse* is to be really predicated of God, then it cannot belong to creatures in themselves; conversely, if creatures are spoken of as possessing *esse,* then this form of *esse* must be denied to God.

Thus, Eckhart's view of creation was attacked from two different directions. The first line of attack condemned statements about the eternity of creation that the Dominican based upon the principle that the true reality of all things is the principial or virtual existence they enjoy in the *nunc eternitatis* of the Divine Principle. The second attacked statements about the nothingness of formal temporal existence considered in itself apart from the Divine Principle.

The oppositions suggested by these attacks point to the fundamental basis for the whole of Eckhart's metaphysics. Implied in his defense, and explicitly formulated in a number of places in his writings, is a profoundly dialectical understanding of the God-world relation. The mysterious conjunction of virtual, principial existence and formal, particular existence in Eckhart's doctrine of creation is most truly grasped through his dialectic of distinction and indistinction. Insofar as God and the creature are distinct, the formal existence of creatures is temporal and empty. For Eckhart, however, what makes God distinct, that is, the distinguishing feature of his being, is precisely that he alone is indistinct, that he is the inner existence, the eternal *esse indistinctum* of all that is. The relation between these two aspects of God is not mere connection or some form of analogy, but a dialectic that forms a paradoxical new "logic" of its own whose basic rules Eckhart once put as follows:

> Everything which is distinguished by indistinction is the more distinct the more indistinct it is, because it is distinguished by its own indistinction. Conversely, it is the more indistinct the more distinct it is, because it is distinguished by its own distinction from what is indistinct.[51]

It is clear from reading the documents relating to Eckhart's inquisitorial proceedings at both Cologne and Avignon that his inquisitors did not share his dialectical approach to theology.[52] Although the Meister's Neoplatonic dialectic had its roots in texts hallowed both by the odor of sanctity (as in the case of the Pseudo-Dionysius), and the musty smell of academe (as with the *Liber de causis*), this form of language about God was not ultimately compatible with the more empirical theological trends that were increasingly evident in fourteenth-century thought.

Before asking about the adequacy of Eckhart's daring views on creation, it may be helpful to look at one other Christian Platonist who got into trouble for his teaching on creation, the ninth-century Irish scholar John the Scot. John was a controversial figure in his day, but it was not until 1225 that his great work, the *Periphyseon (De divisione naturae)* prompted a papal attack. In the wake of the 1210 condemnation of Amaury of Bené and his followers for pantheism, Pope Honorius III ordered the bishops of France and England to send all the copies of the book to Rome to be burnt.

Subsequently, the first modern edition of the *Periphyseon* was placed on the Index in 1684.

The differences between Eriugena and Eckhart are many, but their similarities are also striking.[53] The Irishman's dialectical understanding of how God is related to the world led him to formulae which seem to compromise the distinction between the two and to suggest that the universe is an eternal and necessary part of God.[54] It can be argued, however, that John's teaching on creation is more subtle and complex than such easy generalizations allow.[55]

Unlike Eckhart, who explicitly condemned those who said that the world was a necessary product of divine activity, John says little about the free character of the divine decision to create, though he insists that "everyone of the things that are made He willingly made."[56] For the Irishman, creation is fundamentally divine self-manifestation, or theophany. This is the root of the twin aporiae that govern the exposition of his teaching on creation—the claim that God both creates and is created,[57] and its corollary, that all things are both eternal and made.[58]

The explanation of how God can both create and be created is closely related to the well-known four species of the genus *natura* that John understands as embracing both that which is and that which is not (*quae sunt et quae non sunt*). In simplified fashion, we can say that the nature that creates and is not created is God as the efficient cause of all, the nature that both creates and is created is the exemplary unity-in-multiplicity of the Divine Causes or Ideas (*rationes*) in the Logos, the nature that is created and does not create is the world understood as the divine manifestation, and the nature that neither creates nor is created is the hidden God, the final cause of all things. To say that God both creates and is created also implies, as John notes, that the deepest meaning of *creatio ex nihilo* is that creation proceeds from the superessential Nothing that is God.[59]

Like Eckhart, John argued that God's activity in making must be coeternal and coessential with his being. We can thus find in his writings formulae about the eternity of the universe very similar to those for which Eckhart was condemned.[60] Also like Eckhart is his insistence that created natures do not possess being in themselves. His emphasis on God's immanence and omnipresence in creation led him to the famous claim: "So when we hear that God makes all things we ought to understand nothing else than that God is in all things, that is, that He is the Essence of all things."[61] To many interpreters the characterization of God as the *omnium essentia,* something John took over from Pseudo-Dionysius and communicated to many subsequent thinkers, including Eckhart, has seemed pantheistic.[62] But, as Etienne Gilson and others have shown,[63] it is difficult to convict John of pantheism (though not perhaps of a certain monism). The Irishman insists that although God is the essence of all things, we cannot reverse the formula to say that all things are the divine essence, because the absolute simplicity of the unknown divine nature remains transcendentally distinct from its composite created manifestation. In other words, while it may well sound pantheistic to say "God is all things," is this statement still pantheistic when it is dialectically coupled with the assertion that "God is not all things"? The Eriugenean dialectic, like that of Eckhart, manages to combine outrageous expressions of identity between God and the world with ringing affirmations of the absolute difference between the two. The question to be investigated is whether this is a form of verbal subterfuge or a true *docta ignorantia.*

Although Eriugena's initial announced concentration on the four species of *natura* undergoes considerable development in the later books of the *Periphyseon,* the shifts in focus do not make basic changes in the way in which John presents the God-world relation. Book 2 is a digressive analysis of how the creation account in Genesis, properly interpreted, reveals the mode of production of all things from the hidden God. Book 3 continues this and is especially important for its treatment of the aporia of how things can be both eternal in God's Wisdom and also made from nothing—"There is no more profound question than this that seekers after truth should investigate," as he says.[64]

The way in which Eriugena deals with the "eternal-yet-made" character of creation is similar to Eckhart, though his expositions are more detailed. His initial strategy is to distinguish two understandings of creation: "'Creature' can be understood in two ways, the one relating to its eternity in the Divine Knowledge, in which all things truly and substantially abide, the other to its temporal establishment which was, as it were, subsequent in itself."[65] Throughout the *Periphyseon* he emphasizes that real existence is to be found in the former aspect, that is, on the ideal or virtual level. "For in so far as we are, we are nothing else but those reasons of ours which subsist eternally in God."[66] Like numbers, which are eternal in the Monad but made in their multiples,[67] opposed predications can be made of all things in the universe. "'There was not a time when they were not', because they subsist always in the Word of God," that is, causally, "and 'there was a time when they were not' because in time they began through generation to be that which they were not, that is, to become manifest in forms and species."[68]

Like Eckhart, John is also compelled to move beyond the level of merely opposed predication to the level of true dialectical thinking when he turns to the issue of how all things are *simultaneously* created and made in the Word. Here his language tends to create a series of paradoxical expressions that fuse the divine and created together in single enunciations, as when he says "the Eternal begins to be," or "their [creatures'] eternity was created and their creation is eternal," or "they were never eternal and not made, or made and not eternal."[69] While John does not develop the circumincession of dialectical language as explicitly as his thirteenth-century successor, the essential lines of his presentation of the relation of the divine ground to its created manifestation are remarkably similar, as is his ultimate appeal to negative theology: "But how or why the Word of God is made in all things which are made in Him eludes the sharpness of our mind."[70]

But does this all have anything to do with the Christian idea of creation? Or is it merely another example of how powerful intellects are able to delude themselves about the basic sources of their inspiration? John the Scot frequently noted that the Scriptures had revealed the truth about creation that was hidden from the philosophers,[71] and Meister Eckhart attacked non-Christian thinkers who taught the necessity of creation. But in their stress on the eternity of creation and the way in which they insist upon the identity or lack of distinction between God and creature do they not evacuate the true Christian content of the words "In the beginning God created heaven and earth"?[72]

In trying to analyze the adequacy of the view of creation found in Meister Eckhart and John the Scot as representatives of the more suspect side of Christian Platonism, I will proceed by asking how well they express what I take to be four basic constituents of the idea of creation, at least as found in Christian theology. (In medieval number symbolism, four is always the number signifying created reality, while three denotes the divine.) I am not claiming that these four aspects, which for mnemonic reasons I shall describe as the four *D*'s—dependence and distinction, decision and duration—exhaust the intelligibility of what we mean by creation. I will be satisfied if they provide us with a heuristic device for raising some of the right questions.

Christian theologians, like their Jewish and Muslim counterparts, held that the world must be conceived of as both contingent and dependent on God. This implies, as Robert Sokolowski has shown, a decisive break with the pagan world view which accepts the universe as a given and sees the divine, however conceived, as within this total order, that is, as one of the things to be distinguished within it.[73] The world is neither given nor self-explanatory from the perspective of belief in creation. By its very nature it requires a ground of being that is other than any of the things that constitute it.

Absolute dependency has important implications for the nature of the distinction between God and the world. Again, Sokolowski's analysis is helpful in pointing out not only that the God-world distinction is the foundation for all else that follows, but that the distinction itself need not have been, since God would be God even if the world had not existed. The reality of the world adds nothing to the reality of God, that is, God and the world are not more than God alone, as we have seen Eckhart's inquisitors pointing out.[74]

It follows that the existence of the distinction between God and the world is in some way based upon "decision" in God. If a world is to exist, it must necessarily be distinct from God. That a world does actually exist, depends upon God's decision to create it. What exactly is meant by talking about "divine decision" is not only difficult to understand, but is also especially prey to the dangers of anthropomorphic projection, psychological and otherwise, upon the divine nature. God's freedom cannot be conceived after the analogy of human choosing between alternatives, but must be some deeper form of absolute freedom about which we can have only hints. One of the elements that the "decision" character of the Christian notion of creation brings to the fore is the personal relation of God to the world. Both the Hebrew Scriptures and the New Testament emphasize the way in which God as Creator "addresses" the world, and Christian theology has always insisted that God's relation to the world must be understood in personal rather than in impersonal terms. To say that God "decides" to create means that he is related to the world in a personal way.

If the absolute dependence of a distinct world flows from the decision of its divine Creator, then it also follows, as Thomas Aquinas argued,[75] that the duration of the world is a function of the decision. That is, reason cannot exclude the possibility of a universe eternally dependent on God's will, but faith tells us that God's decision was to create the universe in time as a more fitting way of demonstrating his almighty power. However, as we have seen, Platonist Christians, and indeed all classical Christian theologians, insisted that the beginning of the universe in time did not imply any change or mutability in God. There was, then, an eternal "aspect" or "deep reality" of all things in God, and the way in which all Christian theologians down to William of Ockham expressed this "deep reality" was through the affirmation of the existence of the Divine Ideas in the Word understood as God's eternal unitary awareness of the manifold ways in which his simple existence can be manifested. All classical Christian theologians admitted an eternal aspect to creation; it was in how they related this eternal aspect to the temporal one that significant theological differences emerge.

In what ways, if any, did Meister Eckhart's and John the Scot's understanding of the relation between the manifest creation and its eternal archetype in the Divine Ideas compromise these four notes or characteristics of the classical Christian doctrine of creation? In relation to the first dyad of dependence and distinction, I would argue that there should be little doubt that both authors strongly affirm the absolute dependence of the whole created realm on its transcendent source or ground in God and that both also insist that from one perspective God and creatures are totally distinct. For them God is not the first in a series from which all else flows; he is the transcendent ground of this or any other series that could be conceived. In terms of the metaphysics of the One so dear to Christian Platonists, the One is not the first number; it is the source of all numbers.

The issue of distinction is difficult to adjudicate, because both Eriugena and Eckhart believe that distinction can never be properly understood apart from indistinction. Every Christian theology of creation has to insist not only that God is absolutely different from creation, but also that he is related to it in an essential way. God is closer or more intimate to things than they are to themselves; indeed, he is the reality of all things, for what can exist apart from him, what can be added to, or counted along with, God? In other words, the doctrine of creation has to be able to express as best it can the paradox of how God is not only utterly distinct from all things, but also completely indistinct from them (to use Eckhart's terms), or how God is both transcendent and immanent. Thomas Aquinas's subtle and original handling of the transcendence-immanence relation in terms of the metaphysics of *esse* and *essentia* has been well studied in our century.[76] The way in which Christian Neoplatonists like Eriugena and Eckhart have attempted to deal with this fundamental issue has been less appreciated.

Our two Christian Platonists treated this fundamental issue in terms of a dialectical mode of thought whose origins go back to problems posed by Plato and whose explicit development owes much to the thinkers described as Neoplatonists, especially to the dominating figure of Plotinus.[77] It is here perhaps that too strong a division between a pagan and a Christian view of creation begins to break down, or at least to become more fluid, and where the possibility of a *praeparatio evangelica* raises its seductive head. Christian theologians have been divided on this issue since at least the second century, when Justin welcomed the idea of such a preparation and Tertullian subsequently asked what Athens had to do with Jerusalem. Here I would question Sokolowski and those who find in the very proximity of Platonism to Christianity a danger because it may prevent the novelty of the message of creation from becoming evident.[78] This may be a question of optimists and pessimists viewing the same half-filled bottle, but I would suggest that it goes deeper than that. The theoretical exposition of Christian belief in creation did not begin from a cultural *tabula rasa,* but was from the start forged within the context of a dialogue with systems of Greco-Roman speculative religious thought. The great intellectual effort of thinking out and expressing the Christian message of creation within the framework originally provided by the pagan Platonic tradition not only transformed this tradition in essential and not accidental ways through the creation of distinctive forms of Christian Platonism,[79] but it also became an integral and not merely an adventitious part of Christian theology of creation. That is to say, the transformed *praeparatio* became part of the message.

It is true that some Christian Platonist views of the God-world distinction have been among the more controversial in the history of Christian thought, not so much because they lacked the resources to give adequate voice to the transcendental distinction between God and the world, but because their dialectical fusion of distinction and indistinction has seemed to many to err on the other side. Some of the dialectical thinkers, like John the Scot and Meister Eckhart, were condemned, perhaps mistakenly; others with structurally very similar answers to the issue of transcendence and immanence, such as Maximus the Confessor in the East and Nicholas of Cusa in the West, were not. The intention of Christian Platonism, like other forms of Christian theology, is to give true expression to both divine immanence and transcendence. Its distinctive mode of achieving this is by insisting that the God-world relation is utterly distinct from every other relation because it alone is truly dialectical, that is, God is more transcendent the more immanent he is.

If it is possible to argue that Christian Platonists like Eriugena and Eckhart do give adequate expression to the dependence and distinction of creation, it may well be that they have more difficulty dealing with the second dyad of characteristics, the issues of decision and duration. God's distinct-indistinct relation to creation may suggest that creation is really necessary, that God needs to create in order to complete or manifest himself, that creation is the "other side" of God. Perhaps the root of the difficulties that Eriugena and Eckhart encountered because of their stress on the eternal dimension of creation reveals a necessitarian undertow in Christian Platonism despite the surface avowals of God's freedom of action.

The reciprocal relation between God and creation that characterizes Christian Platonism does lend color to this line of objection, but whether it makes creation an absolute necessity and removes the personal character of the relation of God to the universe remains a debatable question. Aristotelians might well want to distinguish between the "absolute" necessity implied in the deep reality of creation, that is, that it is impossible to conceive of the Christian God save as a being who is eternally aware of his infinite imitability, and the "hypothetical" necessity realized in the actually existing universe which we know God did choose to create.

The Christian Platonists, like Eriugena and Eckhart, approach the question from other perspectives. For all the fundamental similarity of their metaphysical structures, there are interesting differences in emphasis between our two authors here. In trying to give some meaning to the question "Why did God create?" John the Scot follows a resolutely intellectual path, while Meister Eckhart, for all the intellectualism of his thought, leaves an important place for the divine will.

For the Irish scholar God creates, or manifests himself, in order to express himself, or to come to know himself. Donald Duclow has spoken of the "expressionist paradigm" that governs John's understanding of the *analogia entis:* "John thus consistently views creativity, in both God and man, as formative self-disclosure in word and symbol."[80] Prior to creation God cannot be said to know himself, because for John, as for the ancient Greek philosophers, knowledge implies distinction and limitation. Knowledge is always of something, and God is not a "something." However, John insists that it would be impious to say that God is ignorant prior to creation. While he does not "know" himself, he is always transcendentally aware of his Nothingness and its capability of being multiplied through the Divine Ideas. The actuality of this multiplication necessarily demands the transcendental categories of space and time and therefore a universe that *as known* must be both multiple and temporal. As such, this adds nothing to God. It is what God "chooses" to do in order to become aware of himself through his self-expression.[81]

In one of the most famous of his vernacular sermons, Meister Eckhart invited his hearers to true poverty by analyzing three levels of disinterest: wanting nothing, knowing nothing, and having nothing.[82] Each of these levels invites us to a "breaking-through" (*durchbrechen*) to the divine realm. This is most forcefully put on the level of "having nothing," where the soul no longer even has a "place" in which God can work in it. Here the soul attains the God beyond the "God" who is understood as the Creator of the universe, that is, the God who would still be God and in no way diminished even if the universe did not exist. In this "breaking-through" the identity of God and human is fully realized and the one creative will alone is at work—"There I myself was, there I willed myself and committed myself to create this man."[83] Elsewhere, Eckhart equates the breakthrough with the ability to live "without a why" (*âne war umbe,* or *sunder war umbe*),[84] that is, a sheer spontaneity of life flowing out of identity with the divine ground, our sharing in the inconceivable freedom in which God created the universe.

Theologians have often appealed to the image of artistic creativity as an analogy for God's activity in forming the world. The world is not made "for" something else; the act of creation is its own realization and the source of the joy the Creator takes in it. Perhaps the Christian Platonism of Eriugena and Eckhart, for all their suspect views, has important contributions to make here. John the Scot invites us to consider divine creativity as a transcendental form of self-expression or, perhaps better, self-discovery. His fundamental analogy is rooted in the human experience of our imperfect attempts to manifest our minds to ourselves and others when we express ourselves in speech. Meister Eckhart, on the other hand, at least in his invitation to learn to live as God does, "without a why," suggests another analogy, that of absolute spontaneity, a state in which we will without willing, in which we act without any consciousness of further goals, but merely to express our being and enjoyment. Perhaps the unself-conscious, totally committed, and supremely happy play of children is the best human model. Creation is God at play.

NOTES

I would like to take the opportunity to thank Paul Dietrich, Donald Duclow, and Frank Tobin, all of whom made valuable suggestions about aspects of the treatment of Eriugena and Eckhart found in this paper. The selectivity and limitations of my use of their observations is due solely to my own pertinacity.

My greatest debt, however, is to my friend and colleague Zachary Hayes, whose perceptive response to the initial version of this paper follows. In meditating on Professor Hayes's response and the discussion it promoted, I have come to what may seem like too easy a conclusion. Insofar as Professor Hayes's observations about Bonaventure serve to confirm my own positive approach to the incorporation of Neoplatonic metaphysics into Christian theology, I see his response as a confirmation of my plea for the pluralism of the past. But insofar as he has deftly put his finger on the issue of the reality of matter and history as a far more serious problem for Christian Platonism than that of supposed pantheism, and insofar as he has quite correctly observed that Eriugena and Eckhart, at first blush (and perhaps even at last blush), leave matter and history in an ambiguous position, he has raised an issue of such moment that only a whole new paper could even begin to respond. The response would be easier to make for Eriugena than for Eckhart.

1. E.g., Robert Sokolowski, *The God of Faith and Reason: Foundations of Christian Theology* (Notre Dame, Ind.: University of Notre Dame Press, 1982).

2. It would be interesting to perform a comparative analysis with the doctrine of creation found in some of the "safer" Christian Platonists, especially Augustine and Bonaventure in the West.

3. All references to Eckhart's writings will be made to Deutsche Forschungsgemeinschaft edition, *Meister Eckhart: Die deutschen und lateinischen Werke* (Stuttgart and Berlin, 1936–). The abbreviations LW (*Lateinischen Werke*) and DW (*Deutschen Werke*), together with the respective volume and page numbers, will be used throughout. The LW volumes include section numbers (abbreviated as n. or nn.). The four texts on creation are: (1) *Prologus generalis in Opus Tripartitum* (hereafter abbreviated *Prol. gen.*) nn. 12–22 (LW 1, pp. 156–65); (2) *Expositio Libri Genesis* (hereafter abbreviated *Comm. Gen.*) nn. 1–28 (LW 1, pp. 185–206); (3) *Liber Parabolorum Genesis* (hereafter *Par. Gen.*) nn. 8–40 (LW 1, pp. 479–507); and (4) *Expositio Libri Sapientiae* (hereafter *Comm. Sap.*) nn. 19–40 (LW 2, pp. 339–62). The translations used here, unless otherwise noted, are taken from *Meister Eckhart: The Essential Sermons, Commentaries, Treatises and Defense,* trans. Edmund Colledge and Bernard McGinn (New York: Paulist Press, 1981) (hereafter cited as *Essential Eckhart*); and *Meister Eckhart: Teacher and Preacher,* ed. Bernard McGinn, with the collaboration of Frank Tobin and Elvira Borgstädt (New York: Paulist Press, 1986) (hereafter cited as *Teacher and Preacher*).

There are, of course, many other important texts that would need to be studied to plumb the depths of Eckhart's views. Among these are *Prol. in op. prop.,* esp. nn. 11 and 23 (LW 1, pp. 171–72, 179–80); *Comm. Gen.* n. 112 (LW 1, pp. 265–67); *Par. Gen.* nn. 47–77, esp. nn. 53 and 69 (LW 1, pp. 521, 535–38); and *Comm. Jn.* nn. 213–22 (LW 3, pp. 179–86).

4. Eckhart himself lays down four basic principles regarding the interpretation of Gen. 1:1 in *Prol. gen.* n. 15 (LW 1, pp. 159–60). My enumeration is meant to be more inclusive in the light of consideration of all the major texts.

5. E.g., *Comm. Gen.* n. 14 (LW 1, p. 197); *Par. Gen.* n. 9 (LW 1, p. 481); *Comm. Wis.* n. 25 (LW 2, p. 345); *Prol. gen.* n. 16 (LW 1, p. 160) and *Comm. Wis.* n. 19 (LW 2, p. 340); *Prol. gen.* n. 12 (LW 1, p. 157).

6. This is exhaustively analyzed in the treatment of the final cause of creation laid out in *Comm. Wis.* nn. 19–35 (LW 2, pp. 339–62).

7. *Comm. Wis.* n. 25 (LW 2, p. 345).

8. *Expositio Sancti Evangelii secundum Iohannem* (hereafter *Comm. Jn.*) n. 514 (LW 3, p. 445): "Restat videre quomodo esse sub ratione sive proprietate unius principium est et ab ipso procedit universitas et integritas totius entis creati."

9. *Comm. Gen.* n. 3 (LW 1, pp. 186–87). Translated in *Essential Eckhart,* p. 83.

10. For an introduction, see Harry A. Wolfson, "Extradeical and Intradeical Interpretations of the Divine Ideas," *Religious Philosophy* (Cambridge, Mass.: Harvard University Press, 1961), pp. 27–68.

11. See Augustine, *De diversis quaestionibus 83,* q. 46.

12. *Comm. Jn.* nn. 4–51 (LW 3, pp. 5–43). See my remarks in the "Theological Summary," *Essential Eckhart,* pp. 38–41.

13. E.g., *Comm. Gen.* nn. 3–5, 20 (LW 1, pp. 186–89, 201); *Par. Gen.*

n. 10 (LW 1, p. 482); *Prol. gen.* n. 17 (LW 1, pp. 160–62); *Comm. Wis.* n. 122 (LW 2, p. 459); *Sermo* 23 (LW 4, p. 208); *Comm. Jn.* n. 56 (LW 3, pp. 46–47).

14. *Sermo* 49. 3 (LW 4, p. 426). Cf. *Par. Gen.* nn. 9–20 (LW 1, pp. 479–91); and *Prol. gen.* n. 17 (LW 1, pp. 16–62).

15. On *bullitio* and *ebullitio,* see *Essential Eckhart,* pp. 37–41; and *Teacher and Preacher,* index under *emanatio* (pp. 391–92).

16. For Eckhart's attacks on the necessitarianism of the Muslim philosophers, see, e.g., *Comm. Gen.* nn. 6, 10–11 (LW 1, pp. 189, 193–95).

17. It is worth noting that even Thomas Aquinas admitted that "processiones Personarum sunt rationes productionis creaturarum inquantum includunt essentialia attributa, quae sunt scientia et voluntas" (*STh* 1a, 45, 6). Cf. *Comm. in Rom.* 1.6. Cf. also Bonaventure, *In I Sent.* d. 6, art. un., q. 3, resp.; and d. 10, a. 1, q. 1 (*Opera Omnia* Vol. 1, pp. 129b–30a, 195a).

18. For some uses of the text in this sense, see *Essential Eckhart,* pp. 85, 99, 148, 205.

19. Especially, *Comm. Wis.* nn. 144–57 (LW 2, pp. 481–94); *Sermo* 29 (LW 4, pp. 263–70).

20. *Comm. Wis.,* n. 148 (LW 2, p. 486), trans. *Teacher and Preacher,* p. 167.

21. See *Comm. Gen.* n. 112 (LW 1, pp. 266–67).

22. Among the vernacular works, we find this theme in Sermons 5a, 9, 10, 38, 50, as well as in the *Liber Benedictus* (DW 5, p. 42?).

23. These are spread throughout the Latin works, e.g., *Comm. Gen.* n. 7 (LW 1, pp. 190–91); *Prol. gen.* nn. 18, 20–21 (LW 1, pp. 162–63, 164–65); *Comm. Wis.* n. 33 (LW 2, p. 354); *Comm. Jn.* nn. 213–18 (LW 3, pp. 179–84); *Sermo* 45 (LW 4, p. 380), etc.

24. Perhaps the most extensive analysis of why there can be no past or future in God occurs in the midst of a discussion of the trinitarian processions in *Sermones et Lectiones super Ecclesiastici* n. 23 (LW 2, pp. 249–51). There is also an important discussion of why all God's gifts can only be given in an eternal fashion in Eckhart's response to the twenty-seventh of the articles brought against him in the second list of errors at Cologne. See G. Théry, "Edition critique des pièces relatives au procès d'Eckhart contenues dans le manuscrit 33b de la Bibliothèque de Soest," *Archives d'histoire doctrinal et littéraire du moyen àge* 1 (1926), pp. 129–268 (pp. 229–35 for this text). This work will be cited hereafter as Théry (for a partial translation, see *Essential Eckhart,* pp. 71–77).

25. Augustine, *Confessiones* 1.6.3, cited, e.g., *Prol. gen.* nn. 18, 20 (LW 1, pp. 163–64); *Comm. Wis.* n. 33 (LW 2, p. 354); *Comm. Jn.* nn. 580, 638 (LW 3, pp. 508, 554).

26. See the conclusion of his response to the List of 49 Articles as found in Théry, p. 206.

27. *Comm. Jn.* n. 323 (LW 3, p. 271).

28. *Comm. Wis.* n. 21 (LW 2, p. 342). Cf. *Comm. Wis.* nn. 22, 32 (LW 2, pp. 343, 352–53); *Comm. Gen.* n. 77 (LW 1, pp. 238–39); *Comm. Ex.* n. 175 (LW 2, p. 151); *Comm. Jn.* nn. 37–38 (LW 3, pp. 31–33).

29. Another related mode of analysis can be found in Eckhart's discussions of how the *esse* of creatures is both *ab alio* as the Boethian *id quo* and *propria* as *id quod est.* E.g., *Comm. Gen.* nn. 2, 14 (LW 1, pp. 186, 197); *Par. Gen.* n. 34 (LW 1, pp. 501–2).

30. The passage which was eventually condemned appears to have been taken from Predigt 4 (DW 1, pp. 69–70), but numerous other examples could be cited.

31. *Comm. Ex.* n. 40 (LW 2, p. 45). Cf. *Prol. gen.* n. 22 (LW 1, p. 178); *Comm. Ex.* n. 135 (LW 2, p. 124); *Comm. Wis.* n. 34 (LW 2, p. 354); *Comm. Jn.* nn. 215, 308 (LW 3, pp. 181, 256); *Sermo* 31 n. 323 (LW 4, p. 283).

32. E.g., *Comm. Gen.* n. 26 (LW 1, pp. 205–6); *Par. Gen.* nn. 11, 16–18 (LW 1, pp. 482, 486); *Comm. Ex.* n. 141 (LW 2, pp. 128–29); *Comm. Wis.* n. 38 (LW 2, p. 446). Once again, it is worth noting that there are texts in "safe" authors that Eckhart could easily appeal to as making similar claims, e.g., Thomas Aquinas, *STh* IaIIae 109. 2. ad 2: "Unaquaeque autem res creata, sicut esse non habet nisi ab alio, *et in se considerata est nihil.*"

33. Pr. 57 (DW 2, pp. 600–602). Cf. the use of the mirror image in Plotinus, Macrobius, et al.

34. *Sermo* 44.3 n. 445 (LW 4, p. 372).

35. *Par. Gen.* n. 10 (LW 1, pp. 481–82).

36. *Comm. Gen.* nn. 10–13 (LW 1, pp. 193–97). Siger seems to be referred to in n. 10.

37. *Comm. Gen.* n. 21 (LW 1, p. 202). Cf. *Comm. Wis.* n. 36 (LW 2, p. 356); *Sermo* 36 (LW 4, p. 314).

38. Cf. especially *Comm. Wis.* nn. 35–40 (LW 2, pp. 355–62).

39. The text of the Bull may be found in M.-H. Laurent, "Autour de procès de Maître Eckhart: Les documents des Archives Vaticanes," *Divus Thomas* (Piacenza), Ser. 3, 13 (1936), pp. 435–46. For an annotated translation, see *Essential Eckhart,* pp. 77–81.

40. Ibid., p. 79.

41. Ibid., p. 80.

42. *Sermo* 15.2 (LW 4, pp. 147–48).

43. See the *votum theologicum* of the Avignon Commission as edited by Franz Pelster, "Ein Gutachten aus dem Eckehart-Prozess in Avignon," *Aus der Geisteswelt des Mittelalters: Festgabe Martin Grabmann* (Münster: Aschendorff, 1935), p. 1109. Eckhart's responses to attacks on his view of the eternity of creation are found throughout the Defense documents; cf. Théry, pp. 186–87, 194, 208–9; and especially Pelster, pp. 1109–11.

44. E.g., Thomas Aquinas, *STh* Ia, q. 44, aa. 1–2. Eckhart does, however, make use of two of the other basic principles of the Thomistic teaching on creation: (1) the distinction between universal and particular cause, e.g., *Comm. Gen.* nn. 149–50 (LW 1, pp. 300–301); *Comm. Ex.* nn. 48–50 (LW 2, pp. 52–53); and (2) the distinction between a natural and a voluntary cause, e.g., *Comm. Gen.* nn. 6, 10 (LW 1, pp. 189, 194); *Par. Gen.* n. 44 (LW 1, pp. 510–11).

45. Pelster, p. 1110.

46. E.g., *Comm. Gen.* n. 24 (LW 1, pp. 203–4). *Par. Gen.* nn. 21–34

(LW 1, pp. 491–502) discuss (a) *actio/passio* as the extrinsic principles of created being; and (b) *forma/materia* and *esse/essentia* as the two pairs of intrinsic principles.

47. *Par. Gen.* n. 62 (LW 1, p. 228).

48. Pelster, p. 1110.

49. Ibid., p. 1113.

50. Théry, p. 207 (*Essential Eckhart,* p. 75). Cf. Théry, pp. 205, 208, 218, 247–48; Pelster, pp. 112–13.

51. *Comm. Wis.,* n. 154 (LW 2, p. 490), as translated from *Teacher and Preacher,* p. 169. On Eckhart's dialectical thought, see Bernard McGinn, "Meister Eckhart on God as Absolute Unity," in *Neoplatonism and Christian Thought,* ed. Dominic O'Meara (Albany: SUNY Press, 1982), pp. 128–39.

52. For an analysis of the trial, see Bernard McGinn, "Eckhart's Condemnation Reconsidered," *The Thomist* 44 (1980), pp. 390–414.

53. Eckhart certainly knew some works of Eriugena directly, such as his commentary on the Johannine Gospel (frequently circulating under Origen's name). Although he never mentions the *Periphyseon* directly, it seems likely that he was acquainted with it.

54. Some modern scholars have argued that the Irishman taught that the universe was necessary, e.g., Rodolfo Rini, "Dio come 'essentia omnium' nel pensiero di G. Scoto Eriugena," *Rivista di Filosofia Neoscolastica* 62 (1970), pp. 101–32.

55. Two of the most helpful recent studies of Eriugena's view of the God-world relation are Donald Duclow, "Divine Nothingness and Self-Creation in John Scotus Eriugena," *Journal of Religion* 57 (1977), pp. 109–23; and Stephen Gersh, "Omnipresence in Eriugena: Some Reflections on Augustino-Maximian Elements in the Periphyseon," *Eriugena: Studien zu seinen Quellen* (Heidelberg, 1980), pp. 55–74.

56. *Periphyseon* 3.17. For the first three books of the *Periphyseon* I shall make use of the edition and translation of I. P. Sheldon-Williams, *Iohannis Scotti Periphyseon (De Divisione Naturae)* (Dublin: Institute for Advanced Studies, 1968–81), but also cite the column number of the edition in J. P. Migne, *Patrologia Latina* vol. 122. Thus this text is to be found in vol. 3, p. 151 (673B).

57. God as creating and created appears throughout the *Periphyseon.* For one important discussion, see 1.12, vol. 1, pp. 62–66 (453C–455B).

58. There is a lengthy discussion of this in 3. 7–17, vol. 3, pp. 70–162 (638C–679A).

59. 3.19–21, vol. 3, pp. 166–68, 172, 178–80 (680D–81C, 683C, 686C–87A). See the discussion in Duclow, "Divine Nothingness," pp. 114–15.

60. 1.72, vol. 1, p. 208 (517CD): "N. Deus ergo non erat prius quam omnia faceret? A. Non erat. Si enim esset facere omnia ei accideret, et si ei accideret omnia facere motus et tempus in eo intelligerentur."

61. 1.72, vol. 1, p. 208 (518A).

62. John himself recognized that to say that God is both maker of all things and made in all things could easily be construed as pantheism, e.g., 3.10, vol. 3, p. 98 (650D).

63. Etienne Gilson, *History of Christian Philosophy in the Middle Ages* (New York: Random House, 1955), pp. 116–17.

64. 3.7, vol. 3, p. 71 (638C).

65. 3.17, vol. 3, p. 159 (677A). Cf. also 639C.

66. 3.8, vol. 3, p. 75 (640A).

67. 3.10 and 12, vol. 3, pp. 112, 118 (656C, 659A).

68. 3.15, vol. 3, p. 133 (655C).

69. 3.16, 17, vol. 3, pp. 163, 141, 145 (678D, 669A, 670D).

70. 3.16, vol. 3, pp. 145–47 (671C). This brief account has prescinded from the important issue of the role of *ratio hominis* in creation that is taken up in Book 4.

71. E.g., 3.5, 14, 17, vol. 3, pp. 68, 130, 146–48 (637B, 664D–65A, 672C).

72. John, for instance, seems to give everything away with statements like the following: "Proinde non duo a se ipsis distantia debemus intelligere deum et creaturam sed unum et id ipsum" (3.17, vol. 3, pp. 160–62 [678C]).

73. Sokolowski, *The God of Faith and Reason,* chaps. 1–3.

74. Ibid., chap. 4, esp. pp. 33–34, 38–39.

75. Thomas Aquinas, *STh* Ia, q. 46.

76. That is, God's *essentia* is identical with *esse,* while in all creatures *essentia* is distinct from *esse* as a limited and contingent participation.

77. Stephen Gersh traces the pagan evolution in detail in *Middle Platonism and Latin Platonism: The Latin Tradition* (Notre Dame, Ind.: University of Notre Dame Press, 1986), 2 vols.

78. Sokolowski, *The God of Faith and Reason,* pp. 49–51.

79. Thus, some of the things that Sokolowski establishes as differences between Christianity and Platonism (e.g., God as only "distinguished" and not "involved," God as the source of unity but not of multiplicity, etc.) are explicitly reversed in the Christian Platonists.

80. Duclow, "Divine Nothingness," p. 121. Cf. the discussion on pp. 122–23. Bonaventure's doctrine of creation can also be described as deeply "expressionistic," e.g. *Breviloquium* 2.11: "primum principium fecit mundum istum sensibilem ad declarandum se ipsum" (*Opera omnia* 5, p. 229a).

81. For this aspect of Eriugena's thought, see Bernard McGinn, "The Negative Element in the Anthropology of John the Scot," *Jean Scot Érigène et l'histoire de la philosophie* (Paris: CNRS, 1977), pp. 315–25; and D. Duclow, "Divine Nothingness," pp. 111–13.

82. This is the famous vernacular Sermon 52, "Beati pauperes spiritu" (DW 2, pp. 486–506). It is translated in *Essential Eckhart,* pp. 199–203.

83. Ibid., p. 202.

84. On this theme, see *Essential Eckhart,* pp. 59–61; and *Teacher and Preacher,* "Glossary," under *âne war umbe* (p. 400).

Response

Zachary Hayes

Alfred N. Whitehead once described Christianity as a "religion seeking a metaphysics."[1] In many ways, this is an apt description of the historical road taken by Christianity in its centuries-long engagement with the great philosophical visions of reality. Through this dialogue between a religious tradition and philosophical visions of reality, key theological concepts have been shaped and philosophical positions have been reformulated in ways that made them more acceptable within the world of Christian faith.

The relation between Christianity and Neoplatonism is a specific and very important instance of this dialogue. So deeply has the dialogue shaped Christian theology that numerous theological concepts bearing the strong stamp of Neoplatonic philosophy have acquired a certain self-evident status in Christian theological circles even though they are not without a problematic side. In selecting the work of Eckhart and Eriugena, Professor McGinn has singled out two of the most problematic representatives of this interaction between Christianity and Neoplatonic philosophy.

McGinn's paper highlights elements in the thought of Eckhart and Eriugena that have given rise to the accusation of pantheism. By assessing the presentation of both these authors in the context of the four *D*'s (dependence and distinction, decision and duration), this paper shows in what sense and under what limitations the synthesis of Christian creation-faith and Neoplatonic metaphysics can be said to be successful, at least in these two authors. The highlighting of the strongly dialectical thought pattern in both authors sheds important light on the question of the distinction between God and the world, and on the paradoxical language which makes both of these authors so difficult to interpret. In doing so, the paper not only suggests in what sense these authors might be seen as orthodox in their understanding of creation theology, but also how they might be related to other representatives of the Christian Neoplatonic tradition whose orthodoxy has never been questioned seriously. In doing so, the paper raises questions about the broader implications of this dialogue between Christianity and Neoplatonic philosophy. To what degree was it successful for Christian theology, not only in Eckhart and Eriugena, but even in its less controversial proponents? Does Christian theology in its Neoplatonic transformation lose something of fundamental significance in the biblical tradition?

An example might help to make this point. Eckhart gives great emphasis to the virtual existence of all creatures in God. In so far as God's existence is existence in the fullest and absolute sense of the word, in comparison with which the existence of creatures is best seen as nonexistence, that mode of existence which creatures have in God is more real, by far, than their existence in themselves as finite entities. This is not to deny that finite creatures do exist in themselves. And if one should argue that the word 'existence' applies properly to such finite beings, it would be appropriate to say that God does "not exist." Given this starting point, it becomes more understandable that Eckhart should make statements which give clear priority to the virtual existence of creatures in God; and—in view of the fact that this virtual existence is eternally immanent to God as the eternal speaking of the Father in the Word—that he should readily speak of the fundamental identity of God and creature when the creature is viewed in terms of its ground. Put in terms of the human person, Eckhart can write: "I discover that God and I are one." Or: "If my life is God's being, then God's existence must be my existence, and God's is-ness is my is-ness, neither less nor more."[2] What "I" am in the deepest sense is identical with what "I" am in my virtual existence in God. There is a precreational oneness of the creature with God which constitutes the truest reality of the creature.

Viewed in the light of the heuristic structure suggested by McGinn, this view of Eckhart can be judged to be at least as orthodox as the views of other Christian Neoplatonists who expressed similar views but never with the radical-sounding language used by Eckhart. For example, in commenting on Distinction 36 of the first book of the Sentences, Bonaventure treats the issues involved in McGinn's paper: whether and in what sense, if at all, creatures can be said to be in God. Bonaventure clearly affirms the distinction between

God as the efficient, productive cause, and creatures which are produced by God "ex nihilo." Viewed from this perspective, argues Bonaventure, the creature is "nihil omnino"; what is "in" God is the power to produce the creature from nothingness. But the God-world relation can be viewed from another perspective, namely, that of "expressive, exemplary causality." From this perspective, all actual beings as well as all things knowable to God (whether actual or possible) must be said to be living reality in God in as far as God is exemplary cause. In this way, Bonaventure offers a metaphysical commentary on the Gospel of John: "Quod factum est in ipso vita erat" (John 1:4).[3]

Continuing his commentary, Bonaventure distinguishes a triple existence of creatures: they exist in the eternal exemplar, in the created intellect, and in their actual existence in the world. In the first two, creatures exist in so far as their similitude exists in the divine and in the human intellect. In the third case, creatures are viewed as existing in their own finite reality in the concrete world. In which of these modes is the creature said more truly to exist? When the matter is viewed in terms of the relation between the creature and its likeness, the position of Bonaventure has a tone strikingly similar to that of Eckhart. Here, he argues, the similitude of the creature has an existence in God that is more true and more noble than the existence of the creature itself as it is found in the world. In a corollary to this, Bonaventure extends his argument to say that even the existence of the similitude of the creature in the created intellect represents a more noble mode of existence than does the existence of the material being in the concrete world. In this respect, he appeals to the authority of Augustine: "The knowledge of a body is greater than the body which is the object of the knowledge. For knowledge is a mode of life in the knowing mind, whereas the body is not life; and any life is greater, not in extent but in power, than any body."[4]

With this in mind, we might ask: If the Christian Neoplatonist tradition, as represented in this paper by Eckhart and Eriugena (and in my remarks by Bonaventure and Augustine), can be seen to provide a satisfactory account of the relation between God and the "other" that constitutes creation, what sort of "other" are we dealing with? If the world, in its most perfect mode of being, is the world as it exists in the mind of God, and if the world in its best mode of existence "outside" God is the world as it exists in the finite knowing subject, what sort of judgment is made on the world as it exists in the objective reality of material-temporal beings? And if the world as it exists in the finite knowing subject is ontologically better than the world of material beings, why did God not create a world of created spirits without a material cosmos? We have the impression that the Neoplatonist version of creation theology could give a better account of a purely spiritual creation than it can of a creation that includes both material and spiritual dimensions. The question raised by this theological model, then, is not so much the question of pantheism as it is the question of idealism.

This question may be highlighted by viewing it in terms of the eschatological dimension of theology. What is the final destiny of the created realm? With this, we raise not only the specific question about materiality but also the implied question about temporality and history. It is my conviction that the biblical tradition, in its vision of the future, looks to the salvation of the world of God's creation. The theological symbols of absolute origin and absolute end are connected by a sense of time and history. I take this to mean, further, that something comes about through history that is not simply given at the beginning of history, at least not in any actualized form. If it is true to say that the biblical tradition of creation theology is intrinsically related to eschatology and, therefore, to a theology of history, it is not sufficient for a theology of creation that it give an account of the absolute origin of creation in God in such a way as to avoid pantheism. It must also be able to give an account of the relation between the world and God which is the divine aim in creating, and which comes about not simply through the divine act of creating but also through the response of creatures to God's creative activity in the history through which the material/spiritual creation is brought, by God's grace, to the goal for which God intends it in creating.

It is from this perspective that it might be helpful to look at the "end of the journey" of creation as it appears in the Neoplatonists. What, for example, is meant by Eckhart's breakthrough to the desert where God will speak to the heart of the creature "one with one, one from one, one in one, and in one one everlastingly"? Reflecting on the final depth of the soul's relation to God, Eckhart writes: "Henceforth I shall not speak about the soul, for she has lost her name yonder in the oneness of divine essence. There she is no more called soul: she is called infinite being."[5]

Christian antiquity had employed a circular symbol to express a particular understanding of history: "Omega revolvit ad alpha." In the end, the circle closes on its beginning. In Hellenistic philosophy, the circle was the symbol of perfect movement since "nothing really changed." Beginning and end are the same. Taken as a symbol for history, the Hellenistic symbol of the circle expressed a negative assessment of historical/temporal reality. For early Christian writers, on the other hand, this circular symbol was interpreted by means of a typological understanding of history. There is a typological correspondence between the "structure" of the beginning and that of the end. But the "content" embraced by that structure is different, the difference being accounted for by history. Thus, in a sense, the end closes on the beginning. But in another and very significant sense, the end is different from the beginning because it involves the actualization of that which was only potential in the beginning. This ancient Christian symbol, while at one level apparently the same as the Greek symbol for history, appears at another level to express quite a different perception of history, and one that is quite in harmony with the biblical tradition.

The circular symbol is common in medieval authors of the Neoplatonic persuasion. But it is not clear precisely what the meaning of the symbol is in this instance. Is a problematic aspect of Neoplatonist creation theology hidden in the principle which affirms that "the end and the principle are the same"? What does it mean when we view the "end" as a union not of two things that remain distinct, but as an absolute unity in which there is simply the One. "He who is one with God is 'one spirit' with God, the same existence." That is strong language. As a description of the end, it seems to coincide with what Eckhart had envisioned as the point of departure for his system: the undifferentiated Godhead, the mysterious origin of life. If creation emerges from a precreational oneness in the undifferentiated Godhead and returns to a final "postcreational" undifferentiated oneness on the Godhead, what is being said about history? If all is the same as "it was" after history is over, is history just so much "sound and fury"? God gains nothing from it, for by definition, this is impossible. The creature seems to gain nothing from it, for it already "was" what it "becomes." What, then, is the point of creation and history at all?

While the work of Eckhart and Eriugena seems to fall short in dealing with history, a more detailed comparison with the thought of Bonaventure could help clarify the matter. Even though the Neoplatonic influence is very strong in Bonaventure's theology, the fact that Bonaventure's world clearly has a history and that this history makes a difference for the final condition of created reality not only distinguishes his thought from that of the two Neoplatonists discussed by McGinn in this paper. It suggests also what some of the limiting factors might be in the dialogue between Christianity and Neoplatonism. A strong argument can be developed about the meaning of history in the Christian vision of reality before the question of modern historical consciousness is raised. In so far as a historical vision involves different sorts of emphasis, it suggests a vision of reality significantly different from an ahistorical vision of reality. It is my suggestion that the question of history and Christianity needs to be studied in greater detail before a fuller judgment may be made concerning the adequacy or inadequacy of Christian Neoplatonism in its various forms.

Looking over these remarks, I might summarize my observations by saying that it is not clear to me who has won in the dialogue between the biblical tradition and the philosophical tradition. Though the Christian Neoplatonists may be exonerated from the charge of pantheism in their account of origins, it is not clear: 1) what sort of world they best account for, and 2) what difference the existence of the world makes in the final analysis. Has the systematic power of the One gained the victory over the sense of history? How is the medieval conflict between history and metaphysics resolved in Christian Neoplatonism?

NOTES

1. A. N. Whitehead, *Religion in the Making* (Cleveland, 1969), p. 50.

2. *Meister Eckhart: The Essential Sermons, Commentaries, Treatises, and Defense,* trans. Edmund Colledge and Bernard McGinn, Classics of Western Spirituality (Mahwah, N.J.: Paulist Press, 1981), p. 33.

3. Bonaventure *Commentary on the Sentences* 1 d. 36, a.1–3 (I.619–29).

4. Augustine *De trinitate* 9 c.4, n.4.

5. F. C. Happold, *Mysticism: A Study and an Anthology* (London: Cox & Wyman, 1970), p. 275.

Creation, Being, and Nonbeing

Langdon Gilkey

There is little question that the symbol of *creatio ex nihilo* and its direct correlate, the "naming" of God as Being, Pure Being, or Pure Actuality, have been both crucial and predominant in Christian theology. Not since the Gnostics and not until process theology have significant groups within the general range of Christian reflection questioned this identification of God with Being Itself. God as Being, the source and ground of finite being, seems as established and durable a part of our symbolic repertoire as incarnation and resurrection, and more durable even than sin! Nor is its other direct consequence, the positive affirmation of time, space, nature, human being (both individual and social), and history—that is, finite being in all its scope—any less persistent. In fact, one finds this affirmation of "the world," if not of the flesh and the devil, a major assumption not only of theologies (e.g., process) that relinquish *ex nihilo* and so deny that God is the source of being; even more, it is also enthusiastically seconded by a variety of secular viewpoints that scarcely know what either *ex nihilo* or God as Absolute Being might mean.

This paper will not seek to repudiate the legitimacy of any one of these three symbolic assertions: *creatio ex nihilo,* the naming of God as Being or Being Itself, and the affirmation of "the world."[1] It will, however, question the way we have (and I include my own previous reflections) thought of these symbols, and it will begin to articulate the paradoxical suggestion that "nonbeing" be included, in ways it has previously not been, in the consideration both of creation and of God. Let us begin, then, with a brief summary of the traditional approach, starting with the clear assets of this tradition and then moving to some of its now apparent liabilities.

GOD AS BEING AND THE AFFIRMATION OF THE WORLD

Since the important interrelation of the symbol of creation, that is, *creatio ex nihilo,* with God as Absolute or Pure Being and with the affirmation of the world is familiar doctrinal territory to us all, I shall only summarize here. If, as Christian convictions made plain, God is the *sole* source of all that is and, being God, is the *spiritual* source of all that is, then the other two follow at once.[2] On the one hand, as the sole principle of the being of things (the First Cause of Being, as Thomas said), God must represent Absolute or Unconditional Being, Nondependent Being, or Being Itself. On the other hand, all that is must have intrinsic value—since it is the purposed creation of God—or, as Bible and tradition have put it, it must "be very good." With regard to the first, God as Unconditional Being, the primary meaning of *ex nihilo* was the denial of dualism, *non ex materia sed ex nihilo;* God did not create out of matter but on the contrary posited *all* of finite being, matter as well as form, into being from nothing. Thus is God the source and ground of finite being in its entirety. As a consequence, God is neither an example among others of the ontological structure of finitude (as in Whitehead), nor is God the former or fashioner of finitude out of a given material (as in the *Timaeus*). And as their source, God transcends all the factors within finite being that depend upon and limit each other: matter and form, creativity and eternal objects, nonliving and living. As transcendent to every sort of dependence and limitation, therefore, God is First Cause and without cause, Unconditional or Absolute Being (Absolute Causality, as Schleiermacher said), or Being Itself—and so, as the patristic theologians stated and the tradition has reiterated, eternal (not temporal), incorruptible (not mortal), independent (*a se*), necessary (noncontingent), and omnipotent (without external limit). One notes that these "attributes" are more negative than positive in their meaning. Like the formula *ex nihilo* itself (*non de Deo et non ex materia sed ex nihilo*), they represent more an explicit denial of the experienced and known limitations of creatureliness than a positive, cognitive grasp of the meaning of these transcendent terms. In any case, the transcendence of God over the limitations of finitude follows directly from the affirmation of the divine creation of all things.

In the same direct way, the positive affirmation of the world (as "good") is correlated with the belief in the divine creation of the world. In an epoch when the goodness of finitude, its potentiality of meaning and fulfillment, was by no means assumed, and frequently repudiated, this was a novel rather than a conventional assertion. It is not that God the Creator was believed to be good because God's creation was known as good, but the reverse: the creation, despite its evident and deep ambiguity, was affirmed to be good because the God who made it was known in the covenant and later in Christ to be good. This implication of creation, therefore, which in periods of optimism seems unnecessary and redundant, became spiritually significant in difficult times, when life otherwise might have been regarded as futile, meaningless, and even evil. It is also important to record that the basis for this affirmation of goodness—repeated over and over again in the Genesis account—is, as we noted, the *spiritual* character of God and, further, what Calvin called "the divine benevolence" known in the covenant and in Christ. Thus the patristic theologians emphasized that creation was an *intended* and *purposive* act of God, not a "mere" metaphysical necessity of the divine nature—neither an automatic emanation nor an act of divine self-fulfillment. For in both of these cases finite being would have value not in and for itself but only for its ambiguous divine source. Thus the spirituality of God, and the nonconstrained and so purposive ("free") character of the act of creation, are symbolic grounds of the goodness affirmed of the world and its life.[3] Needless to say, the spirituality of God was also very important in the conception of the human entailed in the creation: a spiritual God created men and women in the divine image, as analogously "spirit" (and so as both intelligible and responsible—and *we* would add "creative") as well as analogously "living"—though the latter tended to recede in importance. As, therefore, God is unconditional being, life and spirit or freedom, so nature represents finite existence and life and so humans represent conditioned or finite being, life, and freedom; all of finite being is, in its own way, therefore, "good."

In the symbol of creation, however, both the ontological transcendence of God and the goodness or value of creation were qualified by their apparent opposites—the divine immanence in the world and the ambiguity of creation—and hence results the richness (to some) and/or the confusion (to others) of this cluster of religious symbols. If all the creation is essentially and so permanently *dependent* on its source (that is, non-self-sufficient or non–ontologically autonomous), then God is necessarily continually present in and to finitude, preserving it from moment to moment on the one hand, and on the other (again as spirit) giving to it a renewed—and so refashioned or revised—order and purpose. The *immanence* of God in creation follows as a polar concept to the divine transcendence, as the symbol of providence is entailed in that of creation. God is both transcendent to creation and therefore absolute, and at the same time immanent and participating in or relative to creation. Or, to put this in another way, God is absolute but God is not all that there is, since there is also the real and relatively autonomous creation. Christian understanding does not, therefore, represent a monism in which plurality is unreal, shadowy, or abrogated. On the other hand, God is the source of finite reality and not another finite factor over against and balancing finitude; this is not a dualism or a pluralism of finite principles. Theologians of creation have all teetered on a thin line between monism and dualism, each leaning towards one or the other of these poles. Some have emphasized more the *presence* of God in creation and so the continuing and pervasive dependence of finitude on God, towards monism (Augustine, Luther, Schleiermacher, Tillich). Others have emphasized the *distinction* between the transcendent God and creation and thus tended towards dualism (Thomas, Calvin, Barth). All alike, however, have in the end illustrated the dialectical, paradoxical notion implicit in creation: the world is totally and essentially dependent on God (*non ex materia*), and yet the world is not identical with God (*non de Deo*). Correspondingly, God transcends the world as distinct from it, and yet God is immanent within the world as the source of its being, as the principle of its life and order, and as the ground of its hope for fulfillment. As creator, God transcends and is "independent" of the world; but as creator, God also participates in and so is in relation to the world. Both consequences are essential for our topic, although they have hardly received equal emphasis at all times![4]

The goodness and value of the world has also been vigorously qualified in the tradition—though it has never been denied. For vast ranges of common experience deeply challenge that goodness, and these too represent important aspects of the Hebrew and Christian "worlds"—not least since both, as noted, begin with unexpected experiences of rescue from apparently overwhelming evil. For neither tradition does belief in creation originate as the result of a rationally responsible survey of the order and goodness observable in ordinary, common existence. The depth of this experience of "estrangement"—as Tillich put it—emphasizes, therefore, the *distinction* between God and our world. It is the deepest and continuing ground of the *non de Deo*. The world is not God because the world is suffused with an evil in which we all share; and yet it is "of God" and thus is its undeniable evil neither essential, necessary, nor unredeemable. As a consequence, the evil is made possible on the one hand by the ontological distinction between Creator and creature. On the other hand, evil is effected by the historical enactment of creaturely freedom or spirit; its "cause," as Augustine said, is not "nature" but freedom, namely, the capacity of freedom to estrange itself from the God on whom it is nevertheless totally dependent; ontologically, therefore, evil has no cause. The paradoxical symbol of creation—we are dependent on God yet distinct from and even free over against God—grounds the possibility of the Christian interpretation of sin and redemption. Sin is possible because we are not God but relatively autonomous; and sin is destructive because "we are made by and for God," that is, absolutely dependent on God. Correspondingly, redemption is "necessary" because we are estranged from God, and it is possible, because, again, we are made by and for God. It was Augustine who first wove all this together into the fundamental symbolism of our common tradition: the transcendence of the unconditional and eternal God, the immanence of God in creation, the consequent goodness of time and of the world (of "nature"), and yet the possibility and the actuality of the Fall due to freedom—and hence both the need for and the possibility of redemption in time. A junior edition of this synthesis, showing the interrelations of creation, divine transcendence, world affirmation, sin, and redemption, appeared in my own earlier work on creation. One may well ask, therefore, if all this was good enough for Augustine, and if a modern revision was possible, why should we suggest a further and even more radical rethinking?

Before we turn to that point, however, let us note the important interrelations between God, the human, and nature that the symbol of creation implied. Through the mediation of God the Creator of both, nature and humankind are implicitly and deeply related to one another: both have value as God's creation; both reflect the divine life, order, and "glory"—if not the divine image—and both participate in the divine purpose of redemption and reunion. The human is, to be sure, distinguished if not separated from nature: as "spirit" humans are creative and responsible—creators of culture and of cities, and responsible to be obedient to the divine law through their freedom, just as nature is obedient through its regularities. Implicitly in this vision, nature shares in its own ways with humans the creativity, the order, the life, and the value for itself which the infinite power and purpose of God have given to it. Unfortunately, however, much of this remained at best implicit, at worst forgotten and overlooked. The relation of life and fertility radically receded (almost as quickly as did the Baalim); the role of nature as merely the "theater" for redemptive history came to the fore; and the predominant relation of the human being to nature was at best that of responsible steward and at worst that of a dominating sovereign. The clear affirmation of time, of world, and of history—of the rationality of nature and the meaning of history—involved in creation remained as one of the predominant "assets" of the Western inheritance; and the high evaluation of the human, as rational, responsible, and creative—as therefore of "infinite value"—represented perhaps the most precious part of this inheritance. But both of these assets (history and the human) eclipsed the admittedly subordinate role and value of nature in the symbolism of creation, leaving us with the question: how can we reevaluate radically the status, role, and value of nature, which we have overlooked, and yet preserve the affirmation of history and of the human—on which most of our culture's real values rest?

THE APPARENT NEMESIS OF GOD AS ABSOLUTE BEING

Let us turn now to the reasons why in the present this traditional interpretation or reading of the symbol of creation—both vis-à-vis God and vis-à-vis the world God made—seems unsatisfactory, in need, if not of rejection, at least of radical revision. No symbol or set of symbols represents the most *fundamental* causes of an epoch's major dilemmas; "sin," expressed through greed, aggression, hostility, dominance, and exploitation, does. But symbols channel and encourage estrangement and self-love, or they can "break," criticize, and reshape them. Thus do they have a creative or destructive, healing or disintegrating role in history. If, then, creation as an interwoven *Gestalt* or cluster of symbols has seemed to have gone awry, in what way has it done so?

My suggestion may be put as follows: the belief in creation resulted in an undialectical and thus an unqualified affirmation of being, first with regard to God as Creator, and then with regard to creation, to the world and especially to humans within the world. Let us begin—as this history does—with regard to God. That God transcends the creation that has its sole source in the divine being, life, and purposes, is, as we have seen, intrinsic in the symbol. This has led in part to a sense of the intrinsic *mystery* of God. God is not, therefore, a being among the beings of the world, and thus God cannot be experienced or thought of as are those other beings. Since, then, all our words and categories come from such experience of the finite, none of them can apply directly (univocally) to the divine that transcends the finite; all must at best apply "symbolically" or "analogically." In this sense, among others, God remains essentially mysterious: the more God is revealed, the more is the divine veiled; the more we understand God, the more we understand that God's mystery is quite beyond our understanding. Hardly a major theologian has denied this implication of transcendence; and the greatest have made it central.

Another implication of transcendence, however, has tended—so it seems now to me—to overshadow this first one. This is the transcendence of God expressed by means of the absoluteness of God's being. Here the creative being of finitude is not transcended in a mystery that, so to speak, transcends even being; rather, the relative being of finitude is transcended in terms of an absolute degree of being, namely, the absoluteness of God's being. This is, of course, by no means an unequivocal error: God *is* or *exists* in a different way than creatures *are,* if God is their source and ground. Nevertheless, if the emphasis is put here, on the transcendence of finite being into absolute being, then God's nature becomes defined by its unconditional and absolute character rather than by its mystery, and the dialectical nature of the relation of that mystery to the being that is God is lost—as the continual relatedness of God the finite being is also sacrificed. God becomes, so to speak, unequivocally absolute in being: *a se* or independent, necessary, changeless, timeless, actual, unrelated—or, as in Protestant orthodoxy, undialectically sovereign in absolute power. The divine nature comes to represent, in other words, the transcendent *glorification* of being rather than the *transcendence* of being and thus the principle of being's transmutation. In turn, this undialectical glorification of being contradicts rather than buttresses or supports important other elements of the Christian vision.

In the first place, the God who is undialectically changeless, necessary, impassible, and hence unrelated, comes soon enough to contradict the God who creates, preserves, and guides a changing world, the God who comes into and participates in that world, and above all the God who shares in some mysterious way in the suffering, vulnerability, and even mortality of all creatures. But these latter aspects of God—God's presence in temporal being and changing experience, God's participation in the ambiguity of our existence, and God's revelation of God's self in and through weakness—these aspects are the basis for our *knowledge* of God, even our knowledge of God as Creator and so as transcendent in the first place. Without God's presence in and through time and change, God would not have been known as eternal and changeless; without the light of God's participation in weakness and death, God would not have been known as the eternal giver of life and of glory. Thus (as both Barth and Rahner saw), in such an order of knowing, it makes no sense at all so to define the divine order of being as to preclude both the divine participation in finitude and the divine sharing in vulnerability and nonbeing. The church's two-fold answer to this, namely, that such relations of God to change and finitude are not "real" relations, and that it is only the creaturely nature of Christ that shares the weaknesses of temporal being, are no answers at all. In both cases the divine nature has been defined so as to contradict other fundamental aspects of that nature: namely, as one capable of revealing itself in time and as one present to our world in redemption. It is small wonder that most twentieth-century theologians have followed Barth in questioning the priority of this extrachristological definition of God as Absolute Being and have empathized with Moltmann's effort to understand the divine nature also in terms of the divine suffering present in and revealed through the crucifixion.

These intrasymbolic tensions within the Christian doctrine of God are, however, by no means the end of the story. With the

Renaissance and especially with the Enlightenment, the affirmation of the reality, goodness, and potential meaning of the world—grounded as noted on the confidence that it had been established by the good God—grew apace: more and more it was commonly apprehended that whatever there is that is real is located *here,* in the midst of temporal change; that goodness alone inhabits that temporal world, its tasks and vocations; and that fulfillment is increasingly possible in historical time. For such an apprehension or self-understanding a persistent sense of deity is in any case precarious; but *a fortiori* in such a situation any sense of the reality, the goodness, and the relevance of a deity quite transcendent to time and change tends to erode. And erode it did; the categories of aseity, changelessness, and necessity became mere "words," inapplicable and empty in real experience. Moreover, whenever the absolute deity reappeared, through orthodox proclamation (Catholic or Protestant) or in cultic memory, it seemed to many only to threaten the waxing and deeply treasured sense of autonomy in modern culture. The God who was originally experienced as the principle of the establishing, undergirding, and fulfilling of an ambiguous creaturely creativity, had now become the heteronomous negation of all such creaturely creativity. The absoluteness of God was not the sole cause of the deity's reported "death," but it surely did nothing in the eighteenth and nineteenth centuries to put that event off!

The story goes on. We have suggested that the definition of God as Absolute Being represents an undialectical affirmation of finite being applied to God and thus transmuted into unconditional being—and that this move did not "fit" the major emphases and themes of Christian belief. Now the point is that as the reality and relevance of the *divine* receded from modern Western consciousness, this undialectical affirmation of finite being did not recede. In fact, with the growing autonomy, knowledge, and power of God's human creatures (at least Western ones—but then they were sure they stood for "man"), this self-affirmation only increased. As a consequence, as Marx might have put it, the undialectical affirmation of finite being moved down from heaven to earth, from the sacred to the secular, worldly realms. The autonomous self—the cognitive self as scientific knower, the emotive self driving toward fulfillment and happiness, the deciding self legislating its own values—this autonomous self is now undialectically affirmed in relation to a world whose potentialities for value are also undialectically affirmed.

Such an unqualified affirmation possesses (as Augustine saw) an infinite dimension; it sees itself as innocent and benevolent, but in fact it is driven by the powers of alienation, domination, and infinite thirst, by concupiscence. It sweeps, therefore, without limit across every previous horizon. Western thinkers gloried in this descent of infinite power and purpose onto earth and into their hands. It was, so they reflected, the fitting reward to peoples blessed with an absolute God, an absolute revelation, and (later) an absolute civilization. Looking at this process from the inside, our history books continue to speak glowingly of newly "expanded" horizons, of the "opening up" of whole new regions and realms of possibility: of geography, of knowledge, of techniques, of goods, of experiences, of fulfillment.

From the outside, however, from the perspective of those who were overrun, this was not so much an expansion of horizons as an expansion of the imperial ego. Those wider horizons meant in historical fact newly achieved and newly organized empires, a conquest, possession, and exploitation that soon encircled the globe. And the glory of the infinite God—harnessed to this lively creaturely ego—meant that crosses accompanied gunboats and traders to every corner of earth.

The empires have now receded; the West is proceeding to pay the bill. But concurrent with that political expansion, and gaining momentum in our century as the empires waned, has been a corresponding imperial conquest of nature, which, as we now see, will in the end present us with an even more devastating bill to pay. Once undertaken, this unqualified affirmation of our selves, equipped with ever more efficient knowledge and techniques, and so holding out ever more alluring promises of satisfactions, is almost impossible to stop. It presents us, therefore, with a particularly clear disclosure of the self-destructive possibilities of intellectual, scientific, and technical creativity—if that well-armed autonomy is driven by what the Buddhists call "desire." Expanding selves, united in a community of self-love, and driven by concupiscence, present a vivid image of historical nemesis. Finite being, unqualifiedly affirmed and transmuted into absoluteness, results in the imperial and so the oppressive, not to mention the self-destructive, ego. Was God *flattered* by this name we gave to God: *Absolute Being?* Was not the very point of the revelation we treasure that an affirmation of being is *ambiguous,* that the first shall be last and the last first? One suspects that an undialectical affirmation of being represents, from a Christian perspective, an *overaffirmation* of being, an expansion of power, interest, and will untrue to the Gospel and a nemesis for both self and world.

THE MYSTERY OF GOD AS A POLARITY OF BEING AND NONBEING

The positive thesis of this paper is that creation can more coherently and faithfully (adequate to Christian sources) be understood as also the disclosure of the divine nonbeing. Or, more precisely, in the act of creation God revealed God's self as a *polarity* of being and nonbeing rather than as Absolute, Unconditional, and Necessary Being. In our tradition the nature and will of God are disclosed through the divine activity: creation and providence, incarnation and atonement, resurrection, justification and redemption, and so on. In all of these—so we suggest—this polarity of being and nonbeing is disclosed. As one moves from one divine activity to the other, however, the relations of being to nonbeing seem to change. The proportion, so to speak, of being is greater in the act of creation, less in the "kenotic" event of incarnation, and least of all in the act of atonement. Correspondingly, as one moves through this series of revelatory actions to their center, incarnation and atonement, where weakness, vulnerability, and even death are paramount, the presence of nonbeing increases in intensity, apparently contradicting (as we have noted) the divine power of being manifest at creation. This apparent contradiction has long baffled church theology: how does God as being share in the weakness and suffering of the Son? If God does not share in this, are these events of redemption—and they are central—then not revelatory of God; and is not the divine redeeming love on which all of Christian faith depends even more intimately related to these acts disclosive of nonbeing than it is to those other divine acts more disclosive of being, e.g., creation and providential ordering?

Our suggestion is that these fundamental puzzles of Christian theology—and of the texts on which that theology is based—are more appropriately understood if we view the divine mystery as a polarity of being and nonbeing rather than as a mystery of absolute being. A full discussion of the divine nature as manifesting such a polarity, and of the ways this mystery is unveiled in the full scope of divine activity—providence, incarnation, atonement, resurrection, and sanctification—extends far beyond the limits of this paper. Our concluding task is to show that even within the activity of creation, God reveals God's self as a mysterious dialectic or polarity of being and of nonbeing.

As we noted, modern experience and so modern reflection on experience have become more and more aware of the reality and the value of the finite, creaturely, and historical realms which we humans now inhabit. This is—again as noted—in part due to the Christian heritage. One effect of this increased awareness has been a new appreciation for, even celebration of, change, potentiality, and novelty on the one hand, and human autonomy, freedom, and self-direction on the other. In fact, these two—change and autonomy—represent the foci of modern culture, its fixed points of concern; its lodestars. But as philosophy has always understood, change and autonomy bafflingly represent nonbeing as well as being, a "mixture," as Plato put it. As a consequence, in other epochs they were frequently disvalued and even feared. Concentration centered on the "being" aspects of finitude; and despite incarnation and atonement, theology separated God as radically as it could from these "negative" elements of creaturely existence. Unfortuntely, however, the being and the nonbeing aspects of finitude are quite inseparable. And above all the reality and goodness of creaturely life are as essentially interwoven with these elements of nonbeing as they are with the elements of being. There can be no finitude without nonbeing; finitude as both real and good is a paradoxical union of being and nonbeing, a *creaturely* polarity of these two apparent opposites.

Nothing is so essentially characteristic of finitude, of the creaturely as creaturely, as temporality (actually spatiotemporality) and change. Both are also disclosive of nonbeing: temporality represents the banishing of the present and of all that inhabits the present; change represents the replacement of what is by what is not, a present actuality by future potentiality. These "negative" aspects of finitude dominated pre-Christian consciousness: time and change represent continual loss and ultimately signal death. How *could* they characterize the divine as well—even if God had entered them to share in them and transform them? But these elements of nonbeing *also* represent the reality and the value of finitude: temporality is the possibility of the new, of a new birth and a new life, and change can represent growth, growth in grace and in wisdom. Being and nonbeing dialectically penetrate one another in temporal and changing finite or creaturely reality: neither can be or be of value without the other. The question is: is this polarity of being and nonbeing, or is it not, a disclosure of the nature of God?

The same baffling polarity of being and nonbeing characterizes spirit or personhood as this dimension appears in creaturely life. It too is characterized not so much by changeless continuity as by temporality and change, by a continual openness to the new as well as the continuation of character. Above all, each self, to be itself, must achieve "distance," relative separation, relative otherness—from its own past, from its present self, from its community, from its world—if it would become a self, knowing itself in its world, constituting and directing itself, and relating freely and intentionally to others. And essential to this process of self-transcendence—a transcendence of self, community, and world—is a continuing presence of alternatives, of genuine possibilities, of "not yets" that may nevertheless be. Such real alternatives or possibilities are the necessary conditions for authentic decisions, and so for the possibility of self-constitution and self-direction, for the reality and value of the person. Also, the self is hardly a changeless substance, if it would be a self, that is, genuine, authentic, and autonomous; thus, these possibilities cannot be already *actual* if they would be genuine possibilities for decision. In sum, nonbeing appears in every crucial interstice of finite being: in temporality and spatiality, in change, in self-transcendence, and in decisions for the future—precisely at the points where finite being possesses both reality and value. Again the question of the relation of God to the nonbeing essential to the reality and goodness of creaturely existence arises—if God be the sole source and ground of that existence.

We can, however, push this argument one step further, namely, to the implications of the mysterious act of creation itself. God, we say, brings the world into being out of nothing; or more precisely—as Irenaeus and Tertullian put it—God establishes the world in being, positing it into existence, and positing thereby a real, autonomous, and yet dependent "other" than God's self. Creation is neither a part of God, *de Deo;* nor is the ground of its reality separated from God:

ex materia. It is of God and so absolutely dependent; and yet it is also real and self-constituting. This is an almost fiercely paradoxical set of relations. Not only is "*ex nihilo*" paradoxical; the assertions that creatures are dependent and yet real, dependent yet "over against," dependent yet autonomously rational and autonomously responsible, dependent yet self-constituting and self-directing—all these are equally paradoxical, or at least dialectical or polar, apparent opposites that mutually sustain each other. True creaturely life is neither ruled by an alien sovereign nor is it self-sufficient, *a se;* it is "theonomous," constituting itself as spirit yet constituting itself in an Other, as Kierkegaard put it. We are not our own, as Calvin reiterated; yet we must ourselves so choose, if we would be God's. Every generation of theologians has puzzled out these paradoxes, and reexpressed them in their own terms.

However we choose to state this central relation, established by creation, between the real creature and its Creator, this relation necessitates "room" of some sort "alongside" its Creator. The creature is "there" in and of *itself* as well as of *God.* Thus is the absoluteness of the Creator qualified in creation. Creation represents not only the positing of being but the self-negation, the self-limitation, of God in order that authentic, finite being be. God "steps back" in creation, as Kierkegaard put it. Or, put in terms of our images, creation reveals or discloses a polar aspect of nonbeing as well as of being in God, a dialectic of being and nonbeing.

Modern theology since Schleiermacher has—as is well known—had difficulty in distinguishing creation from providence. Although there are interesting and valid reasons for this, I think the distinction is still important and have implied it in this account: creation concerns the bringing of a dependent yet real, finite existence into being solely by the activity of God. Providence, on the other hand, represents the divine relation to the creaturely so constituted, the continuing relations of God to God's creatures as dependent yet real, preserving and ordaining or directing being the main elements of the classical doctrine of providence. This relation, however, as we have noted, is to a self-constituting finitude in passage, a finitude laced with elements of nonbeing as well as being. Again, therefore, the divine creative activity, in preserving and directing such a creaturely world, must make increasing "room" for the aspects of autonomy and possibility, of genuine self-constitution ushering into novelty, in order precisely to create and preserve the creaturely creativity that characterizes the reality and the value of that world. Again, in providence the absolute power of deity is radically limited; the relation of God to possibility as possibility asserted; the responsiveness of God to novelty in history acknowledged—all of them polar aspects of nonbeing, of divine self-limitation, balancing the traditional aspects of being, of divine self-assertion.

Both as Creator and as providential Lord of history, God *limits* God's self in relation to a dependent yet real creation—and that self-limitation is a disclosure of the polar nature of God as a mysterious dialectic of being and nonbeing. These "negative" elements, moreover, increase in intensity and in significance in the deeper revelation of God through incarnation and atonement; here the contrast to the absolute, changeless, and necessary God becomes itself almost absolute. God "comes" to an alienated and desolate world; God "appears" in and through finitude, weakness, vulnerability, and suffering—and God even shares in the final negations of anxiety, lostness, and death, in order precisely to refashion and transform God's creatures to what is neither pure being nor pure nonbeing but the divine unity of both.

NOTES

1. I had better not! My first book, written thirty years ago this winter and spring, gave unqualified affirmation of all of these three and sought to articulate their "meaning" in modern terms: *Maker of Heaven and Earth* (Garden City, N.Y.: Doubleday, 1959).

2. When I say "follow" I mean to explicate the *order of being* of these concepts or symbols, not the *order of knowing*. With regard to the latter, it is almost universally recognized that the affirmation of God's creation of the world followed as a consequence the Hebrew experience of the divine rescue and the divine covenant relationship, at Exodus and at Sinai; God was first known as redemptive actor in history and then known as Creator of people, history, and nature. The logical order of concepts, however, the order of being, goes the other way: because God created the world, including nature, history, and men and women, therefore 1) God is able to act in revelation and in redemption within nature and history, and 2) time and creation alike were known to be "good."

3. This point is overlooked in modern attempts to render this account "more rational" by showing the necessity of creation to the nature or comple-

tion of God: cf. Hegel and Whitehead especially. To both of them, the goodness of creation was inherent in creation itself, and so obvious to reason. Thus, God's goodness was made more rational, more secure, and more meaningful, if it can be shown that God's nature entails God's creative activity in producing or fashioning this good world. If, however, the value of the world is (as it is to us) ambiguous, and if that value is dependent on the divine purpose for the world and love of it—both being notions that involve freedom—then the nonnecessity of the act of creation and so even its metaphysical contingency seem to follow.

4. As an illustration, when I reread, as I have perforce done, my own *Maker of Heaven and Earth,* I am mildly horrified at the way that essentially Niebuhrean viewpoint minimized, nay, even overlooked, the immanence of God in creation. From my later, more Tillichean perspective, this seems bizarre indeed.

Response

Charles Kannengiesser

Langdon Gilkey's proposal is written with the simplicity and the religious sensitivity proper to the homiletic genre. It is an invitation to meditate over God and divine creation in reasserting the human self with the kind of awareness common to enlightened thinkers.

With a graciously Hegelian pattern of thought Professor Gilkey leads us through the three stages of the proposed inner journey.

First, the "symbol of creation," as he puts it, is contemplated in itself. This symbol implies a) the basic affirmation of God's *radical transcendence* over all things, an affirmation introduced here as proper to the Jewish and Christian traditions; b) the affirmation of the positive *goodness of the world;* c) the recognition of a *divine immanence* in the world, so that "God is both transcendent to creation and therefore absolute, and at the same time immanent and participating in or relative to creation"; d) a "world . . . suffused with an *evil* in which we all share," because "the evil is made possible on the one hand by the ontological distinction between Creator and creature. On the other hand, evil is effected by the historical enactment of creaturely freedom or spirit." Augustine, who seems once more to be the church father best known in this country, is the patron of Gilkey's vision of creation. Thus we are plunged into the midst of the Christian myth which, in its theoretical assumptions, remained critically unexamined by the Christian theologians and exegetes at large until Rudolf Bultmann's demythologizing intervention.

The second stage of Gilkey's inner journey toward a more rational sense for God as creator focuses on the "radical revision" which, he thinks, is needed by the symbol of creation. Gilkey scrutinizes what he calls "the apparent nemesis of God as Absolute Being." He denounces at first the confusion made through the centuries by the unexamined traditional understanding of God as it shifted from the "transcendence of God" to "the absoluteness of God's being." This confusion is erroneous, because "the definition of God as Absolute Being represents an undialectical affirmation of finite being applied to God and thus transmuted into unconditional being." The ontological error, as denounced here, opened a way for a fatal development in the Western history of thought. With Karl Marx one may observe that "the undialectical affirmation of finite being moved down from heaven to earth, from the sacred to the secular, worldly realms." The "expansion of the imperial age," in its political and economic realization, produced colonialism. It ends today in technological madness and alienation. Gilkey summarizes his "vivid image of historical nemesis" without mercy: "Finite being, unqualifiedly affirmed and transmuted into absoluteness, results in the imperial and so the oppressive, not to mention the self-destructive, ego."

The third stage of the journey seeks to surmount the negativity of the antithesis explored in the second stage. We are now contemplating "creation . . . as also the disclosure of the divine nonbeing." In God's incarnational and salvific revelation, and in "the activity of creation" as well. "God reveals God's self as a mysterious dialectic or polarity of being and of nonbeing." God reflects God's *own* being in the *creaturely* life which God produces. I may go straight to the final conclusion: "Both as Creator and as providential Lord of history, God *limits* God's self in relation to a dependent yet real creation—and that self-limitation is a disclosure of the polar nature of God as a mysterious dialectic of being and of nonbeing."

As my personal reaction to this paper, I would start rather bluntly with a question of common sense: Is it appropriate to claim that the notion of God, considered as absolute Being, is irrelevant and fatal, and to offer as an alternative the notion of God's paradoxical nonbeing? If the category of being becomes absolutized when applied to the nature of God, the same should happen with the category of nonbeing. In fact, I would not see any problem at all in it, except that in both cases the reality of God continues to be announced in substantialist terms by affirmation or negation. For if one concludes that the Christian salvation narrative postulates a "disclosure of the divine nonbeing," one continues nonetheless to make a statement about God's absolute being.

A friend of mine in Cambridge, England, Christopher Stead,

has devoted much of his time to clarifying such statements, as he found them repeated in chorus by the many theologians of the patristic era. He entitled a recent collection of his essays *Substance and Illusion in the Christian Fathers* (London: Variorum Reprints, 1985), the illusion being the use of substance language in the Christian God-talk. Should we still be victimized by the same illusion?

At the time of the Reformation, the omnipotence of God, as Creator and Judge, became a burning issue for theologians. The same bias seems still to linger in Gilkey's proposal. God's very nature is less at stake in it than God's unlimited power considered for itself. But who wants to engage in debate over such an outdated problematic?

Even if we may doubt Dietrich Bonhoeffer's prediction of a "religionless" Christianity, we are inclined today to share his criticism of what he called Karl Barth's "positivism of divine revelation." The "negative" theology proper to the present time tends to become "a-theistic," in relegating theistic ontologies to the peculiarities of a vanished culture. To simulate today speculation based on one of these past and long-forgotten ontologies would be, at best, comparable to the electronic life given for the time of a short flight to the fossil bird which hangs now in the National Air and Space Museum in Washington, D.C.

So much has been written since Gregory of Nyssa on human finitude and divine infinity, and on the incomprehensible transcendence of God understood in Christian terms, that it would seem trivial to insist on it here. There is only one real question imposed on us in this matter: How should we catch precisely the everlasting tradition of negative theology in our postsubstantialist Western culture of today?

Perhaps I can be allowed, in regard to this fundamental question, to express my frustration, as an expert in patristic theology, at the fact that not one of the founders of the Christian theology of creation—neither Origen of Alexandria, nor Gregory of Nyssa, nor Augustine—is discussed in his own right by the speakers and in the papers of this symposium. It would have been worth investigating how far they transcended the paradoxes of their substantialist language when they christianized their cultural "theos".

Thus I have brought my response from a consideration filled with ontological presuppositions to the modest level of a more common intellectual self-evaluation. What do we really mean in stating any opinion about God? Can we use our mortal language for such a purpose? Does "creation" allow us to scrutinize "God," without holding us hostage in a circular non-sense? These questions and many others of the same kind call not for what Gilkey calls a "radical revision," but rather for a revision of our theological patterns. Our task would not consist, then, in replacing the traditional "symbol of creation" with another one: a post-Kantian or a Hegelian one like the symbol of God's double "polarity." It would rather mean that we have to elaborate the notion of creation, like all the foundational notions of the Jewish-Christian tradition of faith, along with our own hermeneutical conversion, as believers who still enjoy faith in an a-theistic world, after Auschwitz, and despite the atomic crimes currently committed against creation.

Creation in Time in Islamic Thought with Special Reference to Al-Ghazālī

Eric L. Ormsby

No distinction is so fundamental to Islamic thought, nor perhaps so all-encompassing, as that between the eternal and the created-in-time. The eternal is applied properly only to God, whereas the created-in-time applies to everything else without exception, from the stars in their seemingly enduring courses to the least scratching of an ant upon a stone at our feet. It is the contrast, the opposition itself, which is instructive and fertile for reflection. "Things are explicable through their contraries" (*bi-ḍiddihā tatabayyan al-ashyā'*).[1] Through the created and contingent we come to recognize the eternal and self-subsistent. The impermanence of the world reminds us unceasingly that there is another permanent and unceasing world. The contrast between the eternal God and mere transient and contingent being is nowhere more vividly and poignantly expressed than in certain old Muslim graveyards where the gray, tilting, columnar tombstones are exquisitely incised with the stark and confident affirmation: "God is the enduring one" (*huwa al-bāqī*). Mere dust, the hidden remains of the pious bear witness by their very insubstantiality to an equally invisible but unchanging reality which cannot decay.

The vast disparity between eternal and temporal prompted a number of questions which traditional Islamic thinkers pursued with great interest over centuries. It is not possible to explore the topic in any exhaustive way here; instead, I wish to trace certain aspects, if only briefly.

In traditional Islamic theology, especially as it came to be codified from around the twelfth century onwards, creation-in-time is denoted by the Arabic word *ḥudūth,* and anything created in time is termed *ḥādith.* This contrasts with *qidam,* or "eternity," and that which is *qadīm,* "eternal." The distinction is Qur'ānic, though different terms are used there, e.g., "All that dwells upon the earth is perishing, yet still abides the Face of thy Lord, majestic, splendid" (55:26; trans. Arberry). Or, as in the beautiful and famous verses: "God, there is no God but He, the Living, the Everlasting [*al-qayyūm*]. Slumber seizes Him not, neither sleep; to Him belongs all that is in the heavens and the earth" (2:255).

The term *ḥādith,* though non-Qur'ānic, from an early date came to denote the "created-in-time" and that which may be termed "contingent" (also represented by the term *mumkin,* among others), i.e., that which can both be and not be, equally. In the Thomistic formulation: *quod potest esse et non esse* (*S.T.,* Ia, q. 86, a. 3). Further, the noun *ḥudūth* is defined as "a thing's needing something other than itself in order to exist."[2] This is, of course, preeminently true of the world itself, the very contingency of which serves to signal the existence of an eternal and self-subsistent originator—a *muḥdith* or *mūjid* who brings something into existence for the first time, or who produces existence (*wujūd*)—and this can only be God.

The term *ḥudūth* is glossed in other, related ways. It is explained as that which has beginning, a "firstness" (*awwalīyah*); it is that which commences after it was not. It is that the existence of which is preceded by nonexistence. And so, *ḥudūth* means "to exist after not existing."[3] It is "an existence preceded by non-existence."[4] This is termed "essential contingency" (*ḥudūth dhātī*)[5] and, in the words of a glossator, it denotes "temporal contingency" (*ḥudūth zamānī*),[6] i.e., the term emphasizes a thing's appearance in time, rather than its mere causation. The created-in-time is characterized essentially by this "being-preceded-by-non-existence" (*masbūqīyah bi'l-ʿadam*). The great philosopher and theologian Naṣīr al-Dīn al-Ṭūsī (d. 1274) expresses the distinction with unsurpassed succinctness when he notes that what is "not preceded by anything else, and not by non-existence, is eternal; otherwise, it is contingent (*ḥādith*)" (Ṭūsī, *Tajrīd* in Shīrāzī, *al-Qawl al-sadīd* 41). It is in the very nature of what is *ḥādith* that it be preceded, for its existence is not conceivable except as the result of some "preceding thing" (*amr sābiq*).

The great "Scholastic" theologian Aḍud al-Dīn al-Ījī (d. 1355) summed up the matter in his usual magisterial fashion in his *Mawāqif* where he states:

> *Ḥādith* is something that is preceded by non-existence, i.e., its non-existence was before its existence. Hence, it possesses a first, before which it was non-existent. And this is termed 'the temporally contingent' [ḥādith zamānī]. (4.2,3)

By contrast, the eternal is "that the existence of which is not preceded by non-existence."[7] Furthermore, the eternal entails a "negation of firstness" [*awwalīyah,* i.e., "commencement"].[8] Moreover, again in the words of al-Ṭūsī, "non-existence is inconceivable in connection with it, either because of its intrinsic necessity or because it depends on [something intrinsically necessary]." As his commentator explains, *qadīm* may apply either to God, who is necessarily existent in Himself, or to something necessarily existent *propter aliud,* e.g., the world (Shīrāzī, *Qawl,* 67).

Nevertheless, in the strict sense, "there is no eternal other than God" (Ṭūsī, *Tajrīd* in Shīrāzī, *Qawl,* 66). Just as God is the only naturally necessary being, so, too, is He alone the uniquely eternal being. What exists may be divided into God and all that which is not God (*mā siwā Allāh*). "What is not God" is everything transient, evanescent, contingent, everything temporal; as though all mutable and transitory reality might best be described purely by what it is not—the "not-God," a kind of apophatic theology in reverse. In the creedal affirmation of the great theologian Abū Isḥaq al-Isfarā'inī (d. 1027) whose work has now been made available by Professor Richard M. Frank, one must "believe that 'world' [*ʿālam*] is the term for everything but God."[9]

Everything except God is subject to certain inevitable laws. Everything that is not God is radically perishable. At its root, it is mere fictive being. What we are pleased to call "reality" is for much of Islamic theology a "supreme fiction"—to borrow the expression of the poet Wallace Stevens. According to the great theologian Abū Ḥāmid al-Ghazālī (about whom more later), God represents the only genuine (ḥaqīqī) reality; all else is merely "figurative" (majāzī).[10]

The essential "nonexistence" of the world—the notion that intrinsically and of itself, the world has no basis for existing—is explored in certain of its implications by the great theologian Sayf al-Dīn al-Āmidī (d. 1233) in the following syllogism:

> Since the world is contingent (*mumkin*) with respect to its essence, then its existence is an accident derived from another, while its non-existence is essential to it [and] derived from its own nature (*dhāt*). Whatever is essential to a thing precedes what is accidental in relation to it. Therefore, the world in its existence is preceded by an existence which is necessarily existent *per se* and whose priority is established because of its very nature (*li-dhātihi*). But whatever possesses beginning and whose existence is preceded by non-existence in an essential precedence—how can its existence be coterminous with an existence which has no beginning to its existence and which non-existence does not precede? (*Ghāyat al-marām,* p. 259)

But, of course, the issue is not so simple. What is not God may possess only figurative reality in contrast to God, whose existence alone is genuine; but it does possess nonetheless a certain form of reality. Questions about creation arise in part because of the ambivalent nature of reality. If contingent creation were sheer illusion and nothing more, certain of these issues would immediately lose all significance.

Islamic theology often seems poised most fruitfully on certain prolific antinomies. The complicated and perennial debate over the import of human acts is perhaps the most conspicuous example; one of the earliest, and most divisive, of theological issues in Islam, it continued to inspire debate and discussion for centuries up until modern times. The present instance may provide another example, though the issues are rather more tacit. Contingent creation is insubstantial and virtually fictive over against God, and lacks even the semblance of self-subsistent reality. To be contingent, after all, means that it is absolutely equal whether a thing be or not be. What is not God can be and it can not be, and there is no reason whatsoever within the contingent—there is no compelling intrinsic factor—why a thing should be or not be. This is the real import of contingency—not merely that a thing be caused in its existence or non-existence by another, but that *within itself,* in its very nature, there be no impelling reason for its existence or nonexistence.

On the other hand, this nondivine "reality" may be figurative, or fictive, but it would be wrong to term it illusory. It is real enough, but what reality it possesses it receives from God, and only from Him. It is the work of His hands. It issues from Him. It is specifically designated by His will. It is effectuated by His power. Because of this, so contemptible a contingency as the world, so drastically evanescent an entity as the whole of created being, is also inescapably necessary. In itself contingent, in itself, as it were, inert to the possibilities of existence and nonexistence, the creation is nevertheless necessary because of the prior will and knowledge of its Creator. To suppose otherwise is either to posit a defect in divine foreknowledge, as though God hesitated or were uncertain or imperfectly foresighted in His creation; it is to inject a suspicion of inadvertence into what must be consummate omniscience. Or (and even worse), it is to suppose that the world is itself necessary and coeval with God. The world is necessary because it results from God's eternal decree; the world is contingent because it requires another for its existence which has been preceded by nonexistence.

The insight into the world's double nature—contingent *per se,* necessary *propter aliud*—goes back to Ibn Sīnā (Avicenna, d. 1037) and was later elaborated in a new direction by al-Ghazālī (d. 1111), to whom I shall return shortly.

This familiar but profound perception serves a double purpose. It is satisfying and has a certain logical elegance about it. At the same time, it forms part of an effort to reconcile warring conceptions of created reality: on the one hand, the ancient doctrine of the world's eternity, on the other, the orthodox Islamic belief in creation *ex nihilo.* The world thus assumes a borrowed necessity; it is intrinsically contingent but extrinsically necessary. It is hardly surprising that this notion took deep root in Islamic theology, especially following the work of al-Ghazālī. The world as the product of an omniscient and omnipotent creator cannot be dismissed as a meaningless trifle, or as something created whimsically and out of caprice; as the Qur'ān notes, God did not create "frivolously" (*ᶜabathan:* 23:115). Nothing He does is without its hidden wisdom or purpose (though Ashᶜarite theologians recoiled vehemently enough from Muᶜtazilite insistence on God's unfailing purposefulness to deny that He acted out of any discernible motive).

If the world did not always exist—and the very supposition of the world's eternity was profoundly repugnant to orthodox Muslim theologians—then at some moment in time it began to exist when previously it had not. This apparently indisputable fact prompted a series of questions. For example, what did God do in His beginningless eternity before He created the world? Was He somehow prompted to create the world? Conversely, if nothing prompted, or could prompt, Him to create at one moment but not another (either earlier or later), why was He not always and incessantly creating? Was there some reason, some "preponderating factor" (*murajjiḥ*), which led Him to select one moment rather than another? Furthermore, did God "defer" creation? Did He create "later" than He might have? In fact, is not any creation in time inescapably a "deferral" of creation (*ta'khīr al-khalq*)?[11] And does not this putative deferral cast a shadow of suspicion across the radiant munificence of God? If creation was a good—and may we suppose otherwise?—was it not miserly, was it not tight-fisted, to withhold creation? Did God "hoard" His creation the way a miser hugs wealth? Unthinkable, and yet. . . .

Such questions, and many others, occupied theologians concerned with the doctrine of creation in time. Let me deal briefly with certain of these here, before turning to a discussion of how the very notion of contingency underwent a certain characteristic alteration at the hands of al-Ghazālī.

The question as to what God did before He created the world is an old and bitter chestnut which Western theologians from Augustine onward have felt compelled to dismiss with some petulance. Albertus Magnus might remark mildly that "this seems to me a foolish question" (*videtur mihi esse stulta quaestio* in *Opera omnia* [Paris, 1893], 36.391), but the poet John Milton, full of *ira theologica,* would snap: "Anyone who asks what God did before the creation of the world is a fool; and anyone who answers him is not much wiser" (*Christian Doctrine* in *Complete Prose Works* [New Haven, 1973], 6.299). The great Ismāʿīlī poet and philosopher Nāṣir-i Khosraw also records the dismissal of the question as "meaningless palaver" (*guftār bī-maʿnā: Zād al-musāfirīn* [Berlin, 1341], p. 276) on the grounds that before the creation of the world, time did not exist. Time itself begins with creation, and the succession of moments up to that Last Hour, when time and the world will cease, has been foreseen and foreordained by an all-powerful Creator.[12] Time, itself created, is resolutely linear and terminal.

But the response to the question among Muslim thinkers may have had other causes. To ask what God did before creating the world may be a legitimate question, but it smacks of a possible impiety.

The question seems full of presuppositions, not all of them well concealed. In discussing such questions, one must always be aware of what larger and more threatening issues lie just out of sight. In this case, it is clearly the whole vexed question of the world's eternity, or, more broadly, the question of whether anything might be coeternal with God. First of all, the question raises the disturbing dilemma of whether God was inactive and then became active, i.e., whether a change took place within the divine nature. Secondly, it suggests that God prior to the creation of the world had not realized His full creative power, and that creation in some obscure way "fulfilled" Him. Thirdly, it presupposes a temporal continuum, as though creation occurred at one instant in an unceasing succession of such instants. It thus posits a "before" to creation when something other than God existed with Him. The question in this sense reveals possible affinities with such doctrines as those repudiated beliefs of the "materialists" or *dahrīyūn,* who upheld the eternity of entities other than God: the soul (*nafs*), prime matter (*hayūlā*), space (*makān*) and time (*zamān*) (cf. Nāṣir-i Khosraw, *Zād,* p. 275).

The question bears as well on the doctrine of contingency. Implicit in the notion of creation in time is the distinct sense that God chose one moment rather than another. According to al-Ghazālī, "God knows that the world's existence in the moment in which it existed was possible and that its existence after that or before that was equal to it in possibility because these possibilities are equal" (*Iqtiṣād,* p. 92). And, as we know, God does nothing frivolously; but did He choose this moment, and no other, for some wise purpose? Creation in time seems to confer upon the actual moment of creation a distinction not enjoyed by other possible moments.

Discussion of this question leads directly to the doctrine of the divine will (*irādah*), as presented in traditional Ashʿarite *kalām.* I wish to present here a synopsis and brief discussion of this doctrine as it appears in the systematic theological treatise of al-Ghazālī entitled *al-Iqtiṣād fi'l-iʿtiqād.* I will then seek to show how al-Ghazālī modified this doctrine—or rather, made it peculiarly his own—in certain of his later mystical (Sufi) works.

The treatise in question is a product of al-Ghazālī's "middle" period, and was written around 488 (i.e., 1095 C.E.). He was then at the height of his public renown; he enjoyed great esteem and official favor. He lectured regularly to enthusiastic crowds of students in the Niẓāmīyah *madrasah* in Baghdad, a position to which he had been appointed by the Seljuq vizier Niẓām al-Mulk. It was during this period, however, that al-Ghazālī was also exploring a variety of schools of thought in a restless quest for certainty—a quest prompted by an early siege of skepticism in which he came to doubt all the bases of knowledge.[13]

The treatise is also important in the history of the development of *kalām,* and represents something of a turning point. Many influential arguments presented in the work will become normative for later theologians; the form and arrangement of the treatise will also have a strong influence on later treatises.[14]

The divine will (*irādah*) is one of seven "attributes of essence" (or "existential attributes").[15] Like the attributes of power (*qudrah*) or knowledge (*ʿilm*), will is said to be "superadded" (*zā'id*) to the divine nature. In the customary formulation, God wills "by virtue of a will" (*bi-irādatin*). That is, His will is not indistinguishable from His nature (as the philosophers would hold), but is separate and distinct. On the other hand, it is not created simultaneously with its object; it is not a "created" will (*irādah ḥādithah*), as certain deviant sects would aver. In the characteristic formulation, the divine will "is not God and is nothing other than God." For al-Ghazālī, the essential character of God's will is conveyed in the statement: "What He wills, is and what He does not will, is not." This maxim has certain far-reaching consequences, as we shall see.

The divine will serves a precise function. Possibilities are by their very nature equal with regard to existence and nonexistence; they have within themselves no predisposition either to be or not to be. Hence, there must be something extrinsic to them that determines their status. This cannot be the divine nature itself for it, too, is "one in relation to opposing alternatives."[16] Nor can it be divine power, for it is undifferentiated and does not determine at what moment a thing may be or not be: power merely effectuates existence or nonexistence. There is thus a need to posit for some attribute the function of determining when and how things shall be; and this attribute is will. Its unique function is termed "the specifying action of the will" (*takhṣīṣ al-irādah*).

Now the philosophers asserted that the world exists through God's very nature (*bi-dhāt Allāh*). They denied that there is any attribute such as will superadded to His nature. Since God's nature is eternal, the world is also eternal. It is related to the divine as effect to cause: it is like light cast by the sun or the shadow which a person projects.

Against this, Ashᶜarite theology, and al-Ghazālī particularly, affirmed that "the world comes to be at that time when the eternal will stands in nexus with its coming-to-be." And yet, the will of God is eternal and suffers no alteration *qua* eternal attribute when it determines the creation of the world in time. Al-Ghazālī formulates the underlying problem as follows:

> Why does the divine will stand in nexus with temporal creation at a specific time (*fī waqt makhṣūṣ*), neither earlier nor later, despite the fact that the relations of [various] times to the will are equal?[17]

With their doctrine of the world's eternity, the philosophers could avoid this difficulty. But they could not escape the evidence for the "specifying effects of the divine attributes" (*khuṣūṣ al-ṣifāt*), for these are plainly manifest in the world itself. "The world is specified in a specific measure and a specific position" (*al-ᶜālam makhṣūṣ bi-miqdār makhṣūṣ wa-waḍᶜmakhṣūṣ*).[18] The eternal nature cannot be said to conform better to some possibilities than to others. Even so, the world as we experience it is in fact "specified." Certain things exist but not others. The fact that certain things exist, and in a certain specified way, demonstrates that the world has indeed been specified. Therefore, there must be something which specified the existence of things as they are, as well as that which does not exist and remains as a mere possibility in the mind. It is this specifier that we call "will." Through will, things created in time come to be when they do.[19] The will distinguishes these things from other similar or opposite things.

The world bears witness to the determining and discriminating action of the divine will. But a further perplexity arises. Why does this will choose one thing and not another? Are not both opposing things equal with respect to possibility? In his reply, al-Ghazālī provides the answer to his first and more fundamental question: why does the will act at one time rather than another? The question, he claims, is itself misguided. It is like asking, why does knowledge entail disclosure of the knowable (*inkishāf al-maᶜlūm*)? This is tantamount to asking, why is knowledge knowledge? The acts of distinguishing and specifying are the acts of the will par excellence.

To ask why it distinguishes or specifies one time or one thing rather than another is to ask, why is it a will, or, why is will will? It is these actions that constitute will: "the true nature [of the will] is to distinguish a thing from what is like it."[20]

Whatever exists has been created by God's power; but in order to exist at all, a thing stands in need of the divine will "in order to direct power to its object and specify [the object] for [power]." Every object of power is at the same time an object of will: *kull maqdūr murād.* Things that exist in time are objects of power, or possibilities. Therefore, things created in time are also objects of will: *kull ḥādith murād*—"everything that is created in time is willed."[21]

To summarize: the world is a realization of one possibility among many possibilities, all of them utterly equal in respect to God. With respect to itself, the world could as easily not exist as exist; and this inescapable fact applies to every object and event in the world. The corollary of this is that whatever does exist is a product of the divine will: "every contingent is willed." Nothing exists, or can exist, which God has not expressly willed, and willed from all eternity. So, too, whatever does not exist, does not exist because its nonexistence God has knowingly foreordained and willed. Nothing is random; nothing is happenstance; whatever exists, whatever occurs, is intended.

Now the consequences of this position, which I have here briefly sketched, are immense and far-reaching; but they become evident only later, in those ardent writings of al-Ghazālī's "Sufi" period, i.e., the latter part of his life from his crisis in 1095 C.E. until his death in 1111.

In July, 1095, al-Ghazālī suffered a severe crisis attended by disabling psychosomatic illness which led him, agonizingly and after six months of conflict, to renounce his prestigious position for a life of seclusion, poverty, and meditation. He slipped out of Baghdad intending never to return. During the next decade or so, he wrote certain of his most famous and influential works, including the *Iḥyā' ʿulūm al-dīn.*

The nature and circumstances of al-Ghazālī's crisis remain puzzling, even though these have been much discussed. Whether he experienced an inner transformation or suffered a nervous breakdown or even went mad (as one of his own pupils and earliest biographer would claim) need not concern us here. What matters is that in some fundamental way he underwent an experience of momentous intensity which left its traces throughout his later works. It appears in certain cardinal themes, such as the "oneness of existence" (*waḥdat al-wujūd*) which would have an influence on many later mystics, and in certain seemingly personal notes repeatedly struck, e.g., the almost obsessive concern with sickness and with healing, a timeworn topos in religious texts which al-Ghazālī's persistent elaboration somehow lends an unexpected urgency and force. It should not be forgotten either that al-Ghazālī, especially in the *Iḥyā',* writes with a gaze fixed steadfastly on the swiftly approaching fifth century of Islam, that turning point which should call forth its own "renewer" (*mujaddid*). He refers explicitly to this fact in his "autobiographical" work *Deliverance from Error,* written some five years before his death.[22]

The result of all this is manifest in the rather extraordinary way in which al-Ghazālī appropriates whatever he deems useful for his own proselytizing purposes. He draws and borrows freely from every subject at his disposal, not merely scripture and tradition but folklore and poetry, Sufi manuals and compendia, philosophy and logic, medicine and anatomy. He borrows wholesale from numerous predecessors, and not only such acknowledged Sufi masters as Abū Ṭālib al-Makkī, al-Muḥāsibī, and al-Qushayrī, but also, and more significantly, from such philosophers as Ibn Sīnā.

This is not the occasion to deal with al-Ghazālī's immense indebtedness to Ibn Sīnā.[23] The philosopher's influence permeates his later work to such an extent that one might justly claim that al-Ghazālī's reading of Ibn Sīnā was the most decisive and formative of his intellectual experiences. This is true despite his unequivocal repudiation and refutation of Ibn Sīnā's principal metaphysical doctrines in the *Tahāfūt al-falāsifah.*

During his ten years of seclusion and prayer, al-Ghazālī seems in some way to have experienced a profound intuition of the unalterable justice and excellence of things as they are, what I have called elsewhere his conviction of "the perfect rightness of the actual."[24] He formulated this intuition in a memorable dictum, which carried echoes of various antecedents among ancient and Islamic philosophers and theologians, but which was also very much his own: "There is nothing in possibility more wonderful than what is" (*laysa fi'l-imkān abdaᶜ mimmā kān*). In my view, this represents a perception on his part of what in more philosophical terms he expressed by the phrase "contingency of the world." It embodies the realization in immediate, personal terms with compelling implications for the individual.

Within the realm of possibility, or contingency, i.e., in the realm of that which can equally be and not be, whatever actually does exist at a given moment represents the best possibility that can exist. The realm of the contingent extends beyond actual existents to merely possible or conceivable entities. Possibility thus comprises conceivable beings, "what exists in the mind" (*fi'l-dhihn*): *entia rationis*. What exists in the mind does not represent a genuine alternative to what actually exists; or, rather, since it does not exist, it is already a rejected, an excluded, alternative.

Contingency is paradoxical. Whatever exists could always be other than it is. In its very nature, it is characterized by an "intrinsic possibility" (*imkān dhātī*).[25] Furthermore, what God can do is unlimited and the objects of his power (*maqdūrāt Allāh*) are infinite; this is axiomatic. At the same time, things could not be otherwise, for whatever is has been specified by an eternal will. A thing's very existence betokens its extrinsic necessity. Its occurrence in time signifies that it has been predestined, willed, and effected by an eternal and omniscient creator. It is thus logically correct and permissible to affirm that our world could be different than it is, but it is not theologically correct and permissible—indeed, it is impious—to assert that our world could be better than it is. The world in all its circumstances remains unimpeachably right and just, and it is unsurpassably excellent.

This is not in any sense to suggest that God selected the best possible world, or the best possible moment for its creation, out of an infinitude of possible worlds and possible moments (as Leibniz argued). There is no best possible world; there is no best possible moment for the world, for any world, to exist, or not to exist. The excellence justly ascribed to this world accrues solely from the fact that God created it and the moment of its creation was the "best" only because it was the moment at which God created, not because of any excellence inhering within it. (As the Bach cantata has it, "Gottes Zeit is die allerbeste Zeit"—though the context is of course different!) This world did not present itself *in potentia* to the mind of God as the best of a range of possible worlds, each of which might be ranked in terms of some intrinsic excellence. The world became, instantaneously and irrefutably, "the most wonderful" at the instant of its realization, and by virtue solely of that realization.

Because of this, we are justified—indeed, we are obligated—to scrutinize and to study the realm of created contingency, for within it we may discern hidden instances of the divine wisdom which will reveal to us how nothing could be better than it is. We do not study creation in order to sit back and congratulate God on His acumen and cleverness for selecting a particular set of contingencies rather than others; we approach creation after the fact to learn the depths and intricacies of divine wisdom as it discloses itself irresistibly in contingent things.

Throughout his later work, al-Ghazālī draws on a number of examples taken from anatomy and natural history, among other subjects.[26] By these examples he seeks to show the wonders of divine wisdom in created beings. On one level, this is a familiar homiletic device used by preachers from time immemorial. But on another level, it reveals a view of the world radically contingent and yet governed in design down to the most minute and fragile particular by a necessary wisdom. The world is a "mirror of God" and what exists there reflects some fragmentary aspect of Him. Moreover, this world becomes increasingly transparent to the schooled perception. Al-Ghazālī can dismiss the lore of physicians and anatomists—two of his favorite targets—with hearty contempt: "The physician considers [the bones] so that he may know a way of healing by setting them, but those with insight consider them so that through them they may draw conclusions about the majesty of Him who created and shaped [the bones]. What a difference between the two who consider!" (*Iḥyā',* 4:372; cf. also 3:3).

It would be easy to adduce numerous examples of the way in which al-Ghazālī raids other disciplines not merely to pluck handy illustrations for a particular thesis, but as a way of appropriating the very substance of the discipline. Often when he does this, he attempts to personalize and internalize his borrowings within a Sufi context. This characteristic procedure seems at times to take on the appearance of a spiritual exercise. To give one example: in discussing the divine name *al-muṣawwir* ("He who forms") in his treatise on divine names entitled *al-Maqṣad al-asnā,* he recommends a certain mental exercise through which man may realize a "share" in this divine appellation. A person, he says, should gain within himself the form of all existence with regard to its form and its arrangement, until he may comprehend the form of the world and its order as though he were looking at it, and then descend from the whole to the specific parts (*tafāṣīl*).[27]

In proceeding thus, one must come to know the human form and its organs and limbs with their measure and number; and one must come to appreciate the particular wisdom of their corporeal disposition. Then one must extend the process to the animals and the plants. And the final object of this exercise is to obtain "a picture of the all and of its form in one's mind" (*naqsh al-jamīᶜ wa-ṣūratihi fī qalbihi;* p. 83). This is desirable because "knowledge is a form in the soul corresponding to the thing to be known" (ibid.). The human portion remains a figurative participation in the process of formation (*taṣwīr*) in that human beings can merely create pictures of things in their minds, whereas God's knowledge of forms effects their very existence. But the exercise of fashioning a picture within one's mind of the world in its general and particular aspects, as a means to greater spiritual perfection and insight, constitutes a typical example of the way in which al-Ghazālī drew on a well-known and traditional conception of knowledge—the correspondence theory—in order to create a rather novel form of spiritual and devotional practice.[28] The *Iḥyā',* it must be noted, is full of examples of this "exercise" put into rather elaborate and ingenious practice.

This "internalization" of the cosmos for mystical purposes has other reasons. There are numberless parallels between the created world and human beings. Al-Ghazālī's fondness for pointing out microcosmic affinities, which is itself a common theme in Islamic mystical literature, is carried at times to fantastic lengths.[29] For our purposes here, it is enough to note that such analogies are also strategically significant. It is a way of driving home in an immediate and compelling way the notion of radical contingency. Thus, in his anti-Bāṭinī treatise entitled *al-Qusṭās al-mustaqīm,* written during his years of seclusion, he draws the analogy explicitly:

Man is not created in time by himself, for he has a cause and a creator. . . . We know that he has a creator and that his creator is knowing. If we say, "Every possible has a cause and the specification (*takhṣīṣ*) of the world, or of man, in the measure in which he/it has

> been specified, is possible" (*jā'iz*); therefore, it follows from this that he/it has a cause. . . . (*al-Qusṭās*, p. 37)

The parallel between world and human existence is drawn so finely that the grammatical antecedent is ambiguous (the pronoun here could refer either to 'world' or to 'man').

On the one hand, humanity is like the world itself: both have been created and caused, and both are essentially contingent. Human beings must acknowledge their created status. The very wonders in their bodily structure and in their nature, like those of the world itself, bear witness to this createdness. And yet, "man is the most amazing of animals, but he is not amazed at himself" (*Iḥyā'*, 4:376). The creation of the human race "from a drop of dirty water" compels astonishment, and creation in time is both inimitable and in the end, unfathomable:

> Turn now to the drop of semen and consider its state at first and what it then becomes. Reflect that if *jinn* and men had joined together to create for the drop of semen, hearing or sight or intellect or power or knowledge or spirit, or to create in it bones, veins, nerves, skin or hair—would they have been able to do that? Assuredly not! Even if they wished to know its real nature, and how it took shape after God created it, they would be incapable of that. (*Iḥyā'* 4:373)

At the same time, such a perception lends a charged significance to every aspect of human existence, for whatever occurs, whatever suffering or joy befalls one, has been willed. Everything that happens has been intended. And this encompasses even the least, seemingly inconsequential actions:

> God wills existing things and sets things created in time in order, for there occur in this world and in the transcendent world neither few nor many, small nor great, good nor evil, benefit nor harm, belief nor unbelief, recognition nor denial, gain nor loss, increase nor diminishment, obedience nor disobedience, except as a result of God's decree and predestination and wisdom and will. What He wishes, is; what He does not wish, is not.
>
> Not even the casual glance of a spectator nor the stray thought in the mind come to be outside the sphere of His will. He is the originator. He causes recurrence. He is the effector of what He wills. (*Kitāb al-arbaʿīn*, p. 6)

Finally, it must be noted that however inscrutable God's purposes—if, indeed, He may be said to have "purposes" at all, from a strict Ashʿarite viewpoint—His creation of the world and of human beings remains the first and paramount sign of His unique compassion. God need not have created the world at all; He need not have created human persons. He might have created no world, or a world purely of inorganic matter. And He would still have remained utterly just and generous in so doing. Al-Ghazālī notes in commenting upon the divine name *al-raḥmān,* applied exclusively to God, that His compassion is manifest "first, in creation (*ījād*); secondly, in guiding to belief and the means of happiness; third, in making possible the bliss of the next world; and fourth, in granting the vision of His noble countenance" (*al-Maqṣad al-asnā,* p. 67).

The notion of contingency which al-Ghazālī received from his theological predecessors emphasized the nature of the world as the temporally caused product of an eternal cause; the world served as a sign of an eternal creator. The notion of contingency had served principally in proofs of God's existence, or of God as Creator, *a contingentia mundi.* The concept was deepened and refined considerably in the work of Ibn Sīnā, coming to denote that which can both be and not be, as well as that which is caused by another. This notion al-Ghazālī accepts outright, as in his well-known logical treatise *Miʿyār al-ʿilm* (e.g., p. 249 of the Beirut, 1978 ed.), but later he seeks to apply it within a Sufi context. It seems to become almost a guaranty of the unfailing efficacy of the divine will, such that every event in human life, not merely the momentous and significant, but even the seemingly random and trivial happenings, come to be charged with meaning. Such a perception entails a constant awareness of the divine agency in the world. It also necessitates a response, a response of complete and unquestioning acceptance of whatever befalls one.

This is allied with the Qur'ānic injunction to "trust in God," e.g., "So trust (*wa-tawakkal*) in the Living One who does not die" (25:58). As is well known, the precept to "trust in God" (*tawakkul*) also became one of the principal Sufi tenets, and is discussed in all the standard manuals and treatises.[30] Al-Ghazālī himself devotes a major book of the fourth part of his *Iḥyā'* to this.

It seems probable, in my view, that al-Ghazālī appropriated such notions as contingency, in the Avicennian sense, not only because he was profoundly impressed with their truth, but because he found them useful. They had the force (though also the controversial reputation) of logical concepts; they appealed to the reason. Al-Ghazālī is no despiser of reason, as he is so often portrayed. Demonstration (as he makes clear in the *Munqidh*) remains one of the fundamental approaches to truth. The notion of contingency, with its characteristic jargon borrowed from his philosophical predecessors, served to strengthen and to rationalize what otherwise might have remained at the level of mere exhortation. It could appeal to those of a skeptical bent more than accumulations of scriptural quotation or lists of exempla.

Al-Ghazālī wishes to persuade, to convince, to change his readers.[31] To this end, he preaches, argues, harangues, cajoles; he relies on anecdote and legend; he draws up syllogisms; he marshalls evidence from a dozen disparate disciplines. He is an eclectic not for the sake of eclecticism, but in order to convert and transform his auditors. He is a man filled with proselytizing zeal. There are states of the soul of such purifying intensity that they seem to gather and concentrate all that went before in an individual's past history and focus it on one overriding objective. I believe, though I cannot prove, that something of this sort occurred to al-Ghazālī. After his own transformation, he sought to transform all that he knew into a new form of knowledge which could be experienced with all the immediacy of sense experience.

As he acknowledges, there are various ways to the truth and the validity of each differs. But in the end, the highest approach is that which reconciles action and knowledge within a single act of perception. To express this, he employs the term 'taste' (*dhawq*).[32] Only those truths which are somehow "tasted," i.e., known and experienced in one's inmost being, are fully genuine. The abstract notion of contingency, of createdness-in-time, must somehow be experienced directly; it must be made one's own and internalized. It thus affords the possibility of experiencing in one's own person the blessedness of created existence.

NOTES

The present paper draws on my book *Theodicy in Islamic Thought* (Princeton, 1984) but develops certain themes in a new direction, albeit tentatively. The most thorough discussion of the subjects of eternity and temporal creation is Ismāʿīl Vāʿiẓ Javādī, *Ḥudūth va qidam* (Tehran, 1347/1968), a work which should be translated into English.

1. ʿAyn al-Quḍāh al-Hamadānī, *Muṣannafāt* (Tehran, 1962), p. 187.
2. Zakarīyā' al-Anṣārī, *Fatḥ al-wahhāb* (Garret Arabic MS H454/4), 27a, 1. I am indebted for this reference and for those in notes 3–6 and 8 to the late Professor Rudolf Mach.
3. Al-Māturīdī, *K. al-tawḥīd* (Beirut, 1970), p. 13.
4. Al-Baydawi, *Ṭawāliʿ al-anwār* (Cairo, 1323), p. 60.
5. Ibid.
6. Ibid.
7. Al-Ghazālī, *al-Iqtiṣād fi'l-iʿtiqād,* (Ankara, 1962) p. 39.
8. Al-Shahristānī, *Nihāyat al-aqdām* (London, 1934), p. 46.
9. I am grateful to Professor Frank for giving me a copy of his as yet unpublished work. The phrase occurs on p. 1 of his edition of al-Isfarā'inī's *ʿAqīdah* (creed): *al-iʿtiqād bi-anna al-ʿālam ʿibārah ʿan kull shay' siwā Allāh.*
10. Al-Ghazālī, *Makātīb-i fārsī-yi Ghazzālī* (Tehran, 1333), p. 20.
11. See Ormsby, *Theodicy,* pp. 76f.
12. L. Massignon, "Le Temps dans la pensée islamique," in *Parole donnée* (Paris, 1962), esp. p. 354.
13. See J. van Ess, "Skepticism in Islamic Religious Thought," *al-Abḥāth* 21 (1968), pp. 1–18. The highly artful and self-conscious literary structure of al-Ghazālī's own account of his crisis in the *Munqidh min al-dalāl* should not impugn his sincerity or the genuineness of his "crisis." I plan to deal with the literary qualities of the *Munqidh* in another place.
14. See L. Gardet and M. Anawati, *Introduction à la théologie musulmane* (Paris, 1948), pp. 157–60.
15. See the discussion in Ormsby, *Theodicy,* pp. 192–96.
16. *Al-Iqtiṣād fi'l-iʿtiqād,* p. 101.
17. Ibid., p. 104.
18. Ibid., p. 106.
19. Ibid.
20. Ibid., p. 107.
21. Ibid.
22. *al-Munqidh min al-dalāl* (ed. Jabre), p. 49: "God promises the revival of His religion (*iḥyā' dīnihi*) at the begining of every century."
23. This is shown explicitly in work in course of publication by Professor Richard M. Frank and should also become obvious when the long-awaited book on Ibn Sīnā by Professor Dmitri Gutas appears. I thank both Professors Frank and Gutas for their comments on this influence.
24. See Ormsby, *Theodicy,* pp. 32–91.
25. Ibid., pp. 266–67.
26. Ibid., pp. 44–51.
27. *Al-maqṣad al-asnā fī sharḥ ma'ōni asmā' Allāh al-ḥusnā,* ed. Fadlou Shehadi (Beirut, 1971).
28. For "correspondence," see J. van Ess, *Die Erkenntnislehre des*

ᶜ*Aḍudaddīn al-Icī* (Wiesbaden, 1966), pp. 70–71. For knowledge as representation, see (among many possible examples!) Mītham ibn ᶜAlī ibn Mītham al-Bahrānī (d. 1300 C.E.), *Qawāᶜid al-marām* (Qum, A.H. 1398), p. 21: "huṣūl ṣūrat al-shay' fi'l-ᶜaql."

29. See Ormsby, *Theodicy,* p. 106.

30. The exhaustive treatment of this is Benedikt Reinert, *Die Lehre von tawakkul in der klassischen Ṣufik* (Berlin, 1968). See also Ormsby, *Theodicy,* pp. 43ff.

31. See V. Poggi, *Un classico delia spiritualità musulmana* (Rome, 1967), p. 17.

32. *Al-Munqidh,* pp. 35–41. Cf. also Poggi, *Un classico,* pp. 188, 203–5. I deal with the subject of *dhawq* in a forthcoming article entitled "The Taste of Truth," *Islamic Studies Presented to Charles J. Adams* (Leiden: E. J. Brill, 1990).

Response

Paul A. Hardy

We are very much indebted to Professor Ormsby for his illuminating discussion of creation in time in Islamic thought, in general, and in al-Ghazālī, in particular. The distinction between the eternal (*qadīm*) and the created-in-time (*ḥādith*) is an almost constant theme in falsafa, kalām and tassawuf and bears a slightly different meaning according to how each thinker viewed God's relation to the world. In the theological context, for example, the term *ḥādith* refers to the temporal beginning of the world. But in philosophy, it denotes contingency (*'imkān*) exclusive of its temporal dimension. Thus, the distinction represents Islam's unique contribution to the metaphysics of creation. As Charles Kahn noted, Muslim thinkers thematized existence in a way that was foreign to Greek thought.[1] Influenced by the Qur'ān, they developed a notion of radical contingency. This was not simply the old Aristotelian idea that things might be other than they are but that the entire universe might not have existed at all.

Because of the different contexts in which we find the distinction between *ḥudūth* and *qidam* used, it is impossible to agree with Ormsby's assertion that in Islamic thought "the eternal is applied properly only to God whereas the created in time applies to everything else without exception." This is certainly true for al-Ghazālī. But the situation is somewhat different for other thinkers. In the following comments I shall suggest at least two exceptions to Ormsby's general characterization of the distinction between the eternal and the created-in-time. These are the philosopher Ibn Sina and the Sufi Ibn Arabi. Let us start with the philosopher.

In Ibn Sina, the First Intelligence emanates from the Necessary Existent, the First Cause (*al-sabab al-'awwal*) as a result of a continual and eternal act of self-intellection (*taʿaqqul*) and knowledge (*ʿilm*) of its own essence (*dhāt*).[2] From this First Intelligence, the other Intelligences proceed extending down to the Tenth or Agent

Intelligence in continuously replicated acts of self-intellection. The Tenth Intelligence then produces human souls and the four terrestrial elements and thus establishes a connection with the sublunary world. The universe is in this way a manifestation of God's eternal knowledge of Himself.

One must not imagine a temporal delay between the First Cause and its effect since Ibn Sina believes that when the proper cause obtains, the contingent effect must follow without delay. And if the effect of the First Cause cannot be delayed, it becomes, in a certain sense, necessary like its cause. By the same token, if the First Cause is eternal, its effect, the First Intelligence, and even subsequent ones also become eternal.

But if both the universe and God are eternally existent, how is one to distinguish between them? Ibn Sina found a solution by distinguishing between the different modes of being found in the two cases of the Deity and that of His creation. This was the distinction between the eternal (*qadīm*) and created in time (*ḥādith*), the necessary existent (*al-wājib*) and the contingent (*al-mumkin*). But unlike al-Ghazālī, Ibn Sina thought that eternality (*qidam*) and necessity (*wujūb*) are not applicable only to God but also to the Intelligences (*ʿuqūl*) and celestial spheres (*'aflāk*). Unlike the contingent beings of the sublunary world, the intelligences and the celestial spheres do not come into existence after nonexistence since a cause's effect must come into existence forthwith and without delay. They are for that reason necessary in a certain sense and exemplify a type of entity which is not necessary in itself (*al-wājib bi-dhātihi*) but is necessary through God (*al-wājib bi-ghayrihi*).[3] In themselves, they can only be possible (*al-mumkin bi-dhātihi*). It is clear then that Ibn Sina's formulation of the *qidam/ḥudūth* and *wujūb/mumkin* distinction points to his doctrine of the eternity of the world. This position naturally puts him at variance with al-Ghazālī who, as Ormsby has said, applies the eternal only to God and the created-in-time to everything else.

Behind al-Ghazālī's formulation is his perception that a conflict existed between the emanationist model of a nondeliberative and eternal process of creation found in Ibn Sina and the image of the autonomous Agent/Creator evoked by the Qur'ān. An eternal universe suggested a deity bereft of will. But if the world could be supposed to have a beginning in time, then a decision on the part of the Creator to bring it into existence at a definite moment could be readily inferred. This is what, in his opinion, the Qur'ān clearly suggested. To al-Ghazālī's mind, emanation was no more than a phenomenon of nature. It implied a Necessary Existent governed by the objective laws of its nature which were reflected in the natural order. Moreover, since Ibn Sina's God cannot act in an arbitrary way by intervening to alter those laws and yet remain true to His nature, for al-Ghazālī it followed that the laws governing the cosmos are independent of His will.

It is true that Ibn Sina couched his theory of divine volition in negative terms. Divine volition meant no more than the fact that God is not unwilling that the world should proceed from Him (*kullu fiʿlin yasduru ʿan fāʿilin was-huwa ghayru munāfin lahu fa-huwa murāduhu*).[4] But emanation, according to him, was not simply a process of nature because creation involved an act of self-reflexion absent in natural processes.[5] If emphasis upon volition is absent in Ibn Sina's account, it is because he does not separate it from the total cognitive/conative creative process. This is because, in his view, the divine attributes of knowledge, power and will are identical. But what this means is that God's relation to the world is reduced to being essentially cognitive.

With al-Ghazālī the situation is quite different. God's relation to the universe is voluntative in nature. This is because the locus of contingent things is located in the divine will, not in their mode of being as it is for Ibn Sina. What fascinated Ibn Sina was the fact that we can rearrange entities in any way we choose and even invent new things. Yet our actions never produce existence. But to al-Ghazālī what was striking was that the arrangement of things might always have been otherwise. Thus, he reasoned that the essential feature of every thing created in time is that it is an object of the divine will (*kullu ḥādithin murād*). In al-Ghazālī's world, then, what gives us contingency is that the actual is constantly threatened by permutation through divine volition.

Another variation on the distinction between the eternal and the created-in-time is found with Ibn Arabi. Like Ibn Sina, his doctrine of creation is built upon a theory of existence. But within this theory he deploys the notions of eternity (*qidam*) and temporal origination in a rather unique way.

Ibn Arabi accepts an emanation model of creation and uses

the Arabic term for emanation, *fayd,* synonymously with his own technical term *tajalli* or self-manifestation. But this *tajalli* or 'Most Holy Emanation' (*al-fayd al-'aqdas*), in its first instance, means for Ibn Arabi the manifestation of the divine attributes as the Necessary Existent achieves self-consciousness. The divine attributes, the contents of consciousness, denominate the universal forms of things in the sensible world. At this level, however, they constitute entities *in potentia* (*al-mawjūdat al-mumkinah* or *al-mawjūdat bi-al-quwa*). Indeed, from the standpoint of the sensible world, these essences of possible things (or *aᶜyān thābitah,* "permanent archetypes," as Ibn Arabi calls them) are nonexistent. In his words, "they have not smelt the fragrance of existence."[6] Ibn Arabi says that the "*aᶜyān thābitah*" are nonexistent (*maᶜdūm*) in order to contrast them with entities of the external world. In fact, before their actualization through the process of the "Holy Emanation" (*al-fayd al-muqaddas*), they occupy an intermediate position between Absolute Existence and the delimited being of sensible reality. Ibn Arabi expresses the intermediary status of the Permanent Archetypes by the term 'Third Thing'. This entity is something which can be described neither as existent nor as nonexistent, neither as created in time nor as eternal. It is conjoined to the eternal absolute reality eternally and to the world temporally.[7] This third level or "Third Thing" thus joins together eternity and creation in time (*jamᶜ li-ḥudūth wa qidam*). Emanation for Ibn Arabi thus becomes a veritable "coincidentia oppositorum" forming the core of his solution to the problem of God's relation to the world.

But the real basis of Ibn Arabi's solution is found in his theory of existence. In contrast to the philosophers and the Muᶜtazila (except Abū al-Husayn al-Basrī), yet together with the Ashᶜarites, Ibn Arabi rejects the view that existence and nonexistence are qualities superadded to entities and nonentities.[8] Rather, a thing and its existence are identical. To identify something is, in a certain sense, to countenance it in one's ontology:

> Existence and non-existence are thus expressions for the affirmation of the identity (ᶜain) of a thing. . . . When its identity has been affirmed, then it can be characterized by existence and non-existence at the same time. This is in the sense of a relationship: for example, Zayd who exists in his identity can exist in the market but not exist in the house. If non-existence and existence were qualities with which

> one referred to the entity and non-entity like blackness and whiteness, then it would be impossible for the referent to be described by both existence and non-existence. On the contrary, if it were non-existent, it could not be existent just as if something is black it cannot be white. But it can be described by both existence and non-existence at the same time. This is relational existence (*wujūd idāfī*) . . . after the formation of a thing's identity.[9]

In Ibn Arabi's view, a thing can exist and not exist at the same time because 'existence' has more than one sense: (1) concrete existence in the external world; (2) existence in knowledge; (3) existence in linguistic utterance; and (4) existence in writing. Reasoning in this manner, Ibn Arabi concludes that the "Permanent Archetype," the essential forms of the divine names, can exist and not exist at the same time, just as Zayd can exist "in knowledge and speech but be non-existent externally, for example."[10]

Ibn Arabi's willingness to accept the reality of eternal entities besides the eternal God puts him at variance with the orthodox party of the Ashᶜarites who, as Ormsby has shown, wanted to make everything, save God, contingent or created (*mumkin* or *majᶜūl,* i.e., "made"). In fact, Ibn Arabi's notion of *aᶜyan thabitah,* or "Third Thing" as he sometimes calls it, owes a great deal to the Muᶜtazilite view that *maᶜdumat* ("nonentities") are yet something and he acknowledges this debt in several places.[11]

But because this Third Thing mediates between the level of the divine essence (*dhāt*) and sensible reality, Ibn Arabi refers to it as the level of relatedness. For this level of the Godhead (*martabah 'ulūhiya*) always presupposes what is not God. Indeed, Ibn Arabi holds that 'God', in the sense of the divine name "Allah," is inconceivable without that creature for whom He is God (*ma'lūh*). Similarly, the divine name 'Lord' (*Rabb*) is inconceivable without that being for whom He is Lord (*marbūb*). Were the Divine Essence to have remained in a state of nonmanifestation, He would not be able to be called God. This is why Ibn Arabi says that

> if the divine essence were abstracted from all the relations, it would not be a god (*'ilah*). Ourselves are what causes these relations to come about in time. For we make them a God by virtue of Him being a God for us. Absolute Existence (*al-Ḥaqq*) cannot become known until we ourselves become known. The Prophet said, therefore, "He who

> knows himself, knows his Lord," and he is the most knowing of God among mankind. Some of the wise—Abū Hamid [al-Ghazālī] is one of them—have claims that God can be known without any reference to the world. This is erroneous. Yes, the essence, eternal and everlasting, cannot be known until the object exists for whom it is known. For the latter is the indication of the former.[12]

The divine names and attributes then denominate the infinite number of relations in which Absolute Existence stands to the world. All of these are, at first, *in potentia* within the divine mind but become *in actu* because we ourselves turn the Absolute Existent into a God. Accordingly, temporal creation (*ḥudūth*) and eternality (*qidam*) are also relative because, as Ibn Arabi reasons, if the world should cease to exist, we too could not apply to the Necessary Existent the name 'eternal' (*qadīm*) or 'created-in-time' (*ḥādith*).[13]

Here it is interesting to contrast Ibn Arabi's idea of relations with those of al-Ghazālī and Ibn Sina. Al-Ghazālī's view that God is the sole agent of change in the universe made it impossible for him to countenance the objective reality of relations. This is evident in his argumentation against the rational basis of causal connections between things.[14] Underlying his views, of course, is Ashʿarite atomism in which God brings the atoms and their attendant relations into being from one moment to the next. If God is simultaneous with every temporal thing, then it becomes crucial not to involve Him with the mutability of temporal matters. Hence, relations between things in general as well as things with God in particular can only have a subjective status.

Ibn Sina also was anxious to keep the First Cause aloof from the mutability of temporal affairs. Yet he did this by a different strategy. While vigorously maintaining the objective existence of relations in things, he pointed out that some relations are an accident of one term only with no corresponding accident in the correlative.[15] An important example of this type of relation for Ibn Sina is that which obtains between God and His creation since His creation of the universe effects no corresponding modification in God.[16]

Ibn Arabi's strategy differs from both of these. While he does not deny the objective existence of relations outright, he maintains that if there were no human creatures, there would not exist those aspects of Absolute Existence which express its relations to creation. This Third Thing, the level of relational names, in the schema of emanation, has then the quasi-existential status of subsistence (*thubūt*). Describing it, he concludes:

> This thing appears as eternal with the eternal and originated with the originated. Therefore, if you were to say this thing is the world, you would be right. If you were to say that it is God the eternal, you would be right. And if you were to say that it is neither the world nor God but some additional factor, you would also be right.[17]

But with regard to the relations, Ibn Arabi differs from al-Ghazālī and Ibn Sina not only in the peculiar ontological status he gives them. Earlier, it was suggested that al-Ghazālī stressed the voluntative as opposed to the cognitive aspect of God's relation to the world. For Ibn Arabi, however, the opposite was the case. This is clear from his view that, within the hierarchy of divine attributes, will is subordinate to knowledge.[18] This is because volition can take place only when its object is known:

> For His will is a relation . . . directly consequent upon knowledge and knowledge is a relation which follows up on the object known and you and your circumstances are the object known. For knowledge has no effect upon the object known. Nevertheless, the object known has an effect upon the knower.[19]

In contrast, al-Ghazālī believed that the proof of divine knowledge is divine will and the proof of the latter is the temporal origination of the world which presupposes an act of will. That is, God's knowledge is inseparable from the act of will itself. It is not, in any case, something in the mind of God by which His will is guided.

This, of course, is erroneous from Ibn Arabi's viewpoint because it tends to equate being, in its most absolute sense, and will. But divine will can never be on the same level as Absolute Existence. Never can it be more than relative for the simple reason that it always presupposes a level which is not God, the level of creatures over which it exercises choice and deliberation. At the same time, the divine essence or Absolute Existence must, of necessity, limit the actuality of divine volition. For Absolute Being is the source of the will's existence. But more importantly, it is a function of the *a'yān thābitah,* the "permanent archetypes," which structure its articulation throughout creation.

This is why Ibn Arabi said that "knowledge follows its object and the object is you and your circumstances." He means that our essences and their consequents within the divine mind determine the way God's gift of being becomes manifest in us. For being itself is ever the same. Creatures receive it, however, according to their different modes and degrees of preparation (*istiᶜdād*) and commensurate with their *aᶜyān thābitah,* the "recipients of being." But this mode of reception, according to Ibn Arabi, places a constraint upon Absolute Existence just as Absolute Existence constrains them.

Here we come to one of the more surprising aspects of Ibn Arabi's views of the God-world relationship: the idea of a mutual constraint between God and creation. It is an idea that differs from Ibn Sina's view. He, we recall, maintained divine aloofness from change by construing God's relation to the world as unilateral in nature. Ibn Arabi, on the other hand, asserts a general bilateral relationship between the universe and deity and says a certain constraint takes place between them because of it. God constrains the world just as the world constrains God. This constraint of God by the world cannot of course be that which we find when a being of greater power constrains one who is of lesser might (*taskhīr bi-al-irādah*—i.e., constraint by will).[20] The constraint Ibn Arabi has in mind emerges because of the mode of reception (*qabūl*) peculiar to the archetypes of created things. It is what Ibn Arabi calls "taskhīr bi-al-hall," the constraint of circumstance, the constraint monarchs suffer because they are charged to defend and protect their subjects. Their capacity (*istiᶜdād*) forces the Absolute Existence, as it were, to bestow being according to determinate structures, fixed for all eternity.

From this, it might seem that Ibn Arabi denies the idea of contingency. In fact, he does say that in the realm of being there is nothing possible or contingent at all. This is because God is one who wills (*murid*) but he is without choice. But for Ibn Arabi there are levels of divine willing corresponding to the strata of divine emanation. At the highest level of the divine personality, Absolute Existence is without choice because He does not deliberate between alternatives, as if someone were to say of the Creator: If He willed, He could have brought the world into being, and if He did not will He would not have brought the world into being.[21] According to Ibn Arabi, the particle *law,* meaning "if" in Arabic, is a grammatical device expressing some theory actually impossible. If the Absolute

Existence wills what He is, He cannot be whatever He wills. He cannot, that is, will to be other than what He is. Here *wujūd* or being becomes synonymous with necessity *wujūb,* as Seyyed Hossein Nasr has suggested in our discussion. Yet at the level of Godhead (*martabah 'ulūhiya*), the level of the *aᶜyān thābitah,* we may, according to Ibn Arabi, speak of possibility. Refusal to note this difference has led "certain theorists of weak intellect" to deny the category of possibility (*imkān*) and assert that there are only two ontological categories, necessity by itself (*wujūb bi-al-dhāt*) and necessity by another (*wujūb bi-al-ghayr*). But those who know God admit the category of possibility (*imkān*) and realize that although, in the final analysis, it represents a kind of necessity by another, this does not obliterate its unique ontological status.

Enough has been said in order for us to see some of the nuances of the distinction between the eternal and the created-in-time as it was applied in Islamic thought. We observed, on the one hand, how Ibn Sina's formulation reflects his doctrine of the world's eternity and how contingency signified a certain mode of being. The consequence of his views was the postulation of a God who operates by certain rational necessity with no real choice. This is why he could say that contingent things like the Intelligences and celestial spheres, while possible in themselves, are yet necessary from the standpoint of God. All of this stands in contrast to al-Ghazālī, who stressed the voluntative aspect of God's relation to the world. For him, the contingency of created things lies less in their mode of being than in the fact that they are objects of an autonomous divine will. On the other hand, Ibn Arabi's perspective on these matters was seen to be different from that of Ibn Sina's. If, in the philosopher's view, the necessity of things comes from another and they are only possible in themselves, for the Sufi thinker, things are, in the final analysis, necessary. Neither necessity nor existence comes to things. They have them simply by being what they are. The categories of eternity, created-in-time, possibility emerge because of the relation which Absolute Existence has to its human creatures. 'Eternity' and 'created' *qua* relations subsist (*thābit/thubūt*) but do not exist *in concreto.* By positing this intermediary realm of being, Ibn Arabi can affirm the reality of the divine attributes of volition and knowledge. This was impossible for Ibn Sina because volition, knowledge, power are identical within the divine essence. In Ibn Arabi, the essence (*dhāt*) and attributes (*sifāt*) are distinct levels of the divine personality's self-manifestation. The moral and axiological implications of these doctrines are immense and are certainly a topic for fruitful discussion. But, by now, at any rate we have some inkling of some of the consequences which follow upon how we conceive the relation between eternity and time.

NOTES

1. Charles Kahn, "Why Existence Does Not Emerge as a Distinct Concept in Greek Philosophy," *Archiv für Geschichte der Philosophie* 58 (1976): 323–34.

2. Ibn Sina *al-'Ilāhiyyāt,* in *Kitāb al-Shifā',* ed. G. C. Anawati and Sa'id Zayed (Cairo, 1940), pp. 402–8.

3. The reasoning behind Ibn Sina's view has been lucidly set forth in Fazlur Rahman's essay in this volume, "Ibn Sina's Theory of the God-World Relationship."

4. *Kitāb al Taᶜliqāt,* ed. ᶜAbd al-Rahman al Badawi (Cairo, 1973), p. 17, 1.11.

5. Cf. *al-'Ilāhiyyāt* in *al-Shifā',* ed. Ibrahim Madkour (Cairo, 1960), p. 402. Cf. *Taᶜliqāt,* p. 17.

6. *Fuṣūṣ al Hikam,* ed. A. Affifi (Cairo, 1946), p. 76.

7. Ibn Arabi, *Kitāb Inshā' al Dawā'ir,* ed. H. S. Nyberg in *Kleinere Schriften des Ibnul ᶜArabi* (Leiden, 1919), p. 16.

8. Jami, Abd al-Rahman, *al-Durrat al-Fākhirah,* ed. Nicholas Heer and A. Musavi Behbahani (Tehran, 1980), p. 2.

9. *Inshā' al Dawā'ir,* p. 6.

10. Ibid.

11. See *al-Futūhat al Makkivah* (Cairo, A. H. 1329), vol. 2, p. 232, 1.12 and vol. 3, p. 47, 1.30.

12. *Fuṣūṣ al Hikam,* p. 81.

13. *Inshā' al Dawā'ir,* p. 16.

14. Al-Ghazālī, *Tahāfūt al Falsafa* in *Averroes' Tahāfūt al Tahāfūt,* trans. Simon van den Bergh (London, 1954), 1, pp. 316ff.

15. Ibn Sina, *al-'Ilāhiyyat* in *al-Shifā'* pp. 152–60. See also *Die Metaphysik Avicennas* in *Das Buch der Genesung der Seele,* trans. M. Horten (Halle, 1907), pp. 228ff.

16. A view similar to Ibn Sina's has come down to us in the Thomistic doctrine that the relation of creatures to God is real but that of God to creatures is unreal or *relatio rationis.* On this see *Summa Theologica* Ia, q.13, art.12, ad 3um; and Ia, q.85, art.1, ad 1um.

17. *Inshā' al Dawā'ir,* p. 17.

18. *Fuṣūṣ,* p. 153.

19. Ibid., p. 82.
20. *Fuṣūṣ,* pp. 193–94.
21. Cf. Jami, Abd al-Rahman, *Sharh 'alā fuṣūṣ al-ḥikam,* in the margin of al-Nabulisī's commentary (Cairo, A.H. 1303–1323), pp. 15ff.

Fakhr al-Dīn al-Rāzī on God as al-Khāliq

Jane Dammen McAuliffe

INTRODUCTION

References to God's creative activity are spread generously throughout the entire Qur'ān. Few themes are more persistent or more central. Few topics have occasioned more theological and philosophical disputation than that cluster of questions about the Creator and His creation, questions of time, of particularity, of divine knowledge, of endurance and sustenance. As a source for the Islamic adjudication of these issues the Qur'ān has proven, to generations of its exegetes, to be both tantalizing and frustrating. The very multiplicity of Qur'ānic *āyāt* (verses) about creation, and their broad dispersal through the canon, militate against developing the sort of tidy doctrinal statement dear to the hearts of systematic theologians of whatever religious persuasion. The Qur'ānic depiction of creation is fluid and diffuse, an exegetical challenge and conundrum stubbornly resistant to reductive schematization.

Even from the lexical point of view, variety is a hallmark of the Qur'ānic portrayal of creation. No single Arabic stem, in either its verbal or nominal forms, suffices. A plurality of terms is used to denote the Creator and His creative activity.[1] Three active participles may be noted in particular, their prominence highlighted by a combined appearance in *sūrat al-ḥashr* 59.24: "He is God, *al-khāliq, al-bāri', al-muṣawwir;* His are the most beautiful names (*al-asmā' al-ḥusnā*)." Much philological exegesis has attempted to explicate the particular connotations of these and the other Qur'ānic expressions which announce aspects of creation. Certainly the most conspicuous stem, however, the one most frequently encountered, is the triliteral *KhLQ*. References to God as *al-khāliq,* to forms of the verb *khalaqa* and to the verbal noun *al-khalq* occur well over two hundred times in the Qur'ān.[2] Not unexpectedly, then, it is precisely this conflux of terms which has provoked the most extensive exegetical analysis.

To choose but a few passages for particular attention invites, of course, the charge of systemic methodological distortion.[3] Yet any attempt to survey all the uses of *khalaqa* and its derivatives is equally doomed, this time on grounds of inevitable superficiality. There is thus no escape from the need for selectivity, albeit a justified selectivity. In light of such considerations, this work will focus upon the exegetical analysis of two uses of the verb *khalaqa, sūrat al-baqarah* 2.21 and *sūrat al-ᶜalaq* 96.1–2. The first of these passages is the initial Qur'ānic use of the stem *KhLQ,* while the second is often cited as the earliest revelation to Muḥammad. Within the corpus of Qur'ānic *tafāsīr* (commentaries), the first mention of a key term or concept is not infrequently the occasion for extended discussion of it. In the case of *khalaqa,* there is the further qualification that the notion of 'first mention' may carry either a textual or a chronological signification. In the order of the text, therefore, the use of *khalaqa* in *sūrat al-baqarah* 2.21 is primary. Within the traditional account of revelatory chronology, however, precedence is given to its use in *sūrat al-ᶜalaq* 96.1–2.

The further choice of which among the abundance of extant exegetical materials would likely prove most enlightening was dictated by this volume's thematic concern for philosophical reflection, be that broadly or narrowly defined. Qur'ānic commentaries are traditionally classified into two categories. The first of these, *al-tafsīr bi-al-ma'thūr,* represents interpretation based largely on transmitted materials (*ḥadīth*). The second, *al-tafsīr bi-al-ra'y,* is commonly understood (and to some extent denigrated) as interpretation based on one's own reflections and opinions. Perhaps the most illustrious member of this latter group is the twelfth-century *tafsīr* (commentary) published under the titles *Mafātīḥ al-ghayb [Keys to the invisible]* and *al-Tafsīr al-kabīr [The great commentary].*

Its author, Fakhr al-Dīn al-Rāzī, was born in Rayy, a city which has now been absorbed by the urban sprawl of Tehran. His birthdate is usually given as 543/1149 or 544/1150, little more than a century before the final Mongol incursions into Transoxania and western

Asia.[5] This exegete's early education was under the direction of his father, who was himself a noted preacher.[6] His more advanced work included study in both Rayy and then further west in the Adharbayjānī city of Marāgha.[7] Through his studies he became conversant with the traditional Islamic sciences as well as with the Islamic philosophical tradition.[8]

Fakhr al-Dīn put this education to wide use both intellectually and geographically. Not only was he a master of many fields of knowledge, his career as a teacher and preacher took him all over central Asia and perhaps into India as well.[9] His preaching and lecturing were frequently aimed at such controversial groups as the Muᶜtazilīs and the Karrāmīs.[10] His vigorous defense of Ashᶜarī Sunnism aroused such hostility in Khwārazm that he was forced to flee.[11] After similar experiences in Transoxania and trips as far afield as Samarqand and perhaps northern India, he finally settled in Herāt. This city, in present-day Afghanistan, was to be his primary residence for the rest of his life. In Herāt he became generally known under the title of *shaykh al-islām* and reaped the full benefit of his growing prestige and political connections. Under the patronage of the Sulṭān of Ghaznah, Ghiyāth al-Dīn, Fakhr al-Dīn was permitted to open a *madrasah* (school) within the precincts of the palace.[12] There his success against the dissident Karrāmīs was evidently better than it had been against the Muᶜtazilīs of Khwārazm and elsewhere: many of the former group "reverted to the *ahl al-sunnah.*"[13] According to his biographers he died on the day of *ᶜĪd al-fiṭr,* 606/1209, in Herāt.

The commentary on the Qur'ān known as either *Mafātīḥ al-ghayb* or *al-Tafsīr al-kabīr* is al-Rāzī's magnum opus. It is a massive work of thirty-two volumes (in the most widely available printed edition) and has been both extravagantly praised and roundly damned.[14] To repeat two pithy, but opposing, evaluations of *al-Tafsīr al-kabīr* has become a commonplace in al-Rāzī studies. The commentary was dismissed by Taqī al-Dīn b. Taymiyyah (d. 728/1328) as containing "everything but *tafsīr.*"[15] Abū al-Ḥasan ᶜAlī al-Subkī (d. 756/1355) retorted that it contained "everything else in addition to *tafsīr.*"[16] In terms of method and arrangement the closest, near-contemporary Western parallel to *al-Tafsīr al-kabīr* could be the *Summa Theologiae* of Thomas Aquinas. In a manner analogous to the structure of that work, Fakhr al-Dīn frequently divides his analysis of a particular verse into a series of "questions" (*masā'il*). Each *mas'alah* may then be further subdivided to present a full range of possible interpretations. His biographer, al-Ṣafadī, has remarked on the originality of Fakhr al-Dīn's method: "He was the first one to devise this arrangement in his writings. He accomplished in them what no one before him had done, for he stated the question (*mas'alah*) and then proceeded to divide it and to classify further these sub-divisions. He drew conclusions on the basis of such probing and apportioning and no relevant aspect of the *mas'alah* eluded him. He defined the basic principles and determined the scope of the *masā'il*."[17]

Sūrat al-baqarah 2.21

> *yā ayyuhā al-nās uᶜbudū rabbakum alladhī khalaqakum wa-alladhīna min qablikum laᶜallakum tattaqūna* (O you people, worship your Lord who created you and those before you so that you may be godfearing.)

It would be very difficult adequately to understand or to appreciate al-Rāzī's treatment of this Qur'ānic passage without knowing something of the exegetical tradition out of which his own work grew and to which, in many ways, it was a response. Even to classify *al-Tafsīr al-kabīr* as solely *al-tafsīr bi-al-ra'y* is ultimately misleading. Many of his concerns echo those of traditionalist exegesis, to whose most notable early exponent attention must now be turned. Abū Jaᶜfar Muḥammad b. Jarīr al-Ṭabarī's (d. 310/923) *Jāmiᶜ al-bayān ᶜan ta'wīl al-Qur'ān* introduced the classical period of Qur'ānic exegesis. In this monumental work, the author collected and arranged the exegetical material of the first three Islamic centuries. The concern which dominates al-Ṭabarī's treatment of 2:21 is quasi-juridical in nature. It centers upon the imperative *uᶜbudū rabbakum* (worship your Lord), specifically upon those to whom that imperative is addressed.[18] Al-Tabarī's response is to make such worship universally incumbent, applicable to believer and nonbeliever alike.[19] Worship itself is understood by this exegete as obedient submission. He refused to follow Ibn ᶜAbbās (d. 68/686) in glossing *uᶜbudū rabbakum* as *waḥḥidū rabbakum* (testify to the oneness of your Lord), a paraphrase which al-Ṭabarī's contemporary,

Abū Manṣūr al-Māturīdī (d. 333/944), forcefully defends in his own *tafsīr.*[20]

The twelfth-century Ḥanbalī preacher, Abū al-Faraj b. al-Jawzī (d. 597/1200) shares al-Ṭabarī's concern. In his *Zād al-masīr fī ʿilm al-tafsīr* he expands the possible identification of those addressed to four. This *tafsīr,* which functions as a kind of exegetical handbook, is written in almost shorthand form. Thus in summary fashion he lists the possibilities culled from prominent names among the earliest exegetical strata as: (1) everyone, (2) the Jews only, (3) the nonbelievers among the Arab *mushrikūn* (idolators) or (4) the *munāfiqūn* (hypocrites) and the Jews.[21] Ibn al-Jawzī's third category, i.e. the *mushrikūn,* recalls the *sabab al-nuzūl* (occasion of revelation) offered for this verse by Abū al-Ḥasan al-Wāḥidī (d. 468/1075).[22]

For al-Ṭabarī identification of those addressed by the divine imperative is but a prelude to specifying the object of worship. The one to be worshipped is, of course, the one who creates. He alone is worthy of adoration by virtue of the fact that He alone is capable of the creative act.[23] Ibn al-Jawzī, who glosses the verb *khalaqa* with the term *ījād* (bringing into existence), reinforces this stress. In fact, he adds to al-Ṭabarī's emphasis by finding in the phrase *min qablikum* (those before you) a further refinement of the focus on God as the sole creative agent.[24]

Chronologically intermediate between these tenth- and twelfth-century works lies the Muʿtazilī commentary of Abū al-Qāsim Maḥmūd b. ʿUmar al-Zamakhsharī (d. 538/1144). Al-Zamakhsharī's commentary, *al-Kashshāf ʿan ḥaqāʾiq ghawāmiḍ al-tanzīl,* is noted for its attention to lexical and grammatical issues.[25] His treatment of the verse under discussion thus characteristically centers on such questions as the particular form of the vocative used and the reason for its use with this imperative. Like the traditionalist *tafāsīr* of al-Ṭabarī and Ibn al-Jawzī, al-Zamakhsharī specifies those addressed by this command. Yet he shapes the issue somewhat differently. For those who already believe, the command to worship is a command to adherence and intensification. For those who do not believe it is a command which includes the order to believe, just as—to use al-Zamakhsharī's example—the obligation of the *ṣalāt* (the prescribed prayer) includes that of ritual purification and conscious intention.[26]

Following his customary philological interest, al-Zamakhsharī deals with *khalaqa* both lexically and syntactically. As synonyms he offers the terms *al-taqdīr* (determining, decreeing) and *al-istiwā'* (straightening, leveling). Further he remarks that the phrase *alladhī khalaqakum* (who created you) functions as a *ṣifah* (adjectival phrase) both to clarify and to exalt the preceding *rabbakum*.[27] Al-Zamakhsharī's emphases form an important prelude to Fakhr al-Dīn al-Rāzī's own exegetical analysis of the verse. While the latter has drawn explicitly on the former, he has reversed the relatively minor attention paid to *khalaqa* and taken that as the keystone fitted to bear the weight of this verse's interpretation and far more besides.

Fakhr al-Dīn's treatment of *sūrat al-baqarah* 2.21 begins in a manner congenial to contemporary analytic modes—it begins with a structural analysis. Al-Rāzī is, in fact, unique among the classical *mufassirūn* (exegetes) in the degree of consideration which he devotes to understanding the contextual placement of the particular verse under discussion. While others may draw a perfunctory connection between a verse and that which immediately precedes or follows it, Fakhr al-Dīn's interest in contextuality ranges far more widely. In the present instance, he takes the full *sūrah* (chapter) up to this point and delineates it as a triadic composite of the three possible human responses to divine revelation: belief, unbelief, and hypocrisy.[28] Each group of respondents has been divinely described beginning with the *mu'minūn* (believers) in verses 2–5, then the *kāfirūn* (unbelievers) in verses 6–7, and finally a lengthy description of the *munāfiqūn* (hypocrites) in verses 8–20.[29]

Abruptly, al-Rāzī notes, the *sūrah*'s focus shifts. Yet once again a triadic pattern emerges. This time the component elements are not responses to revelation but rather the basic elements of that revelation: affirmation of the nature of God (*al-tawḥīd*) in verses 21–22, the fact of prophecy (*al-nubuwwah*) in verses 23–24, and the life to come (*al-maᶜād*) in verse 25.[30] The pivotal phrase, the fulcrum upon which these two triads swing, is the introductory invocation of this verse, *yā ayyuhā al-nās* ("O you people"). Grammatically the shift is striking because it moves the *sūrah* from the third to the second person, thereby echoing the intercessory vocative of *sūrat al-fātiḥah* 1.5. But of even greater significance is the honor accorded humankind by this first Qur'ānic usage of divine direct address. Al-

Rāzī comments that it is as if God were saying to his creation: "At first I placed the Messenger as an intermediary (*al-wāsiṭah*) between you and Me. Now I am further honoring you and drawing you closer by addressing you without an intermediary. Thus may you receive both the guiding indications and the dignity of being addressed and spoken to directly."[31] The sense of distinction thus conveyed eases acceptance of this first *amr* (command), of this first *taklīf* (imposed duty). Drawing upon the analogous human master-servant relationship, al-Rāzī concludes his contextual analysis by complimenting the psychological acuity displayed by the *malik al-mulūk* (King of kings).[32]

The verse then moves immediately from the vocative to the imperative. After discussing issues both synchronic and diachronic, e.g., whether the command is variously applicable to the *mu'minūn* and the *kuffār* (unbelievers), whether it applies to future generations or only those directly addressed, Fakhr al-Dīn confronts the central phrase of the verse, *rabbakum alladhī khalaqakum* ("your Lord who created you"). This, the first Qur'ānic mention of the most commonly used verb for creation provokes from the exegete an elaborate and extended justification for the use of critical reasoning. Here he claims his right and duty to address the Qur'ānic text with those God-given powers of discursive intellection which so distinguish the human creature.

The logic of this justification develops in a sequential, but somewhat elliptical fashion. The first step is, of course, the divine command to worship. The imperative's objective phrase, *rabbakum alladhī khalaqakum,* identifies the focus of that worship precisely in his function as Creator, as Maker (*al-sāniᶜ*). To know the Creator, one must reason from the evidence of creation, or, as Fakhr al-Dīn insists: "The only way to know God is through *naẓar* (reflection) and *istidlāl* (rational, discursive thought)."[33]

At this point in the argument, al-Rāzī employs a device familiar to students of Christian scholastic philosophy, i.e., the erection of an *adversarius.* In this instance the role is played by a group, loosely defined as al-Ḥashwiyyah, who denounce the epistemological priority of *naẓar* and *istidlāl* as *bidᶜah* (heretical innovation).[34] While Abū Muḥammad ᶜAbd Allāh b. Muslim b. Qutaybah (d. 276/889) classes the Ḥashwiyyah among those *aṣḥāb al-ḥadīth* (traditionists) who are more zealous to collect than to comprehend, Fakhr al-Dīn applies the epithet al-Ḥashwiyyah in a much more general sense.[35] Inasmuch as no individual members of this group are cited by name, it functions as a kind of dialogical "straw man," useful, nevertheless, in providing due cause for Fakhr al-Dīn's detailed defense of reasoned theological discourse.

That defense first seeks to establish the unparalleled superiority of such knowledge and then to argue that the means to its attainment, i.e., *naẓar* and *istidlāl,* are justified on the grounds of both traditional teaching and individual reasoning (*wujūh naqliyyah wa-ᶜaqliyyah*). With his penchant for numerical ordering, al-Rāzī adduces seven reasons for the preeminence of *ᶜilm al-uṣūl,* the foundational science of theological reflection. Of these, two are of particular interest, one for the self-reflective evaluation he makes of his own task as exegete and the other for its relative ranking of Qur'ānic verses. To prove the priority of *ᶜilm al-uṣūl,* Fakhr al-Dīn cites the work of the *mufassir* (exegete) as a derivative occupation: "The *mufassir* simply investigates the meanings (*al-maᶜānī*) of God's *kalām* (speech), an activity which presupposes the existence of the Maker (*al-sāniᶜ*), the Speaker (*al-mutakallim*)."[36]

Al-Rāzī's second noteworthy argument for the superiority of *ᶜilm al-uṣūl* asserts a relative rating of Qur'ānic disclosures. Verses which deal with the foundational theological issues of *tawḥīd, nubuwwah,* and *maᶜād* outrank those whose subject matter is legal.[37] To use some of Fakhr al-Dīn's examples: the excellence (*al-faḍīlah*) of such verses as "Say, He is God, One" (*sūrat al-ikhlāṣ* 112.1) and "The Messenger believed, etc." (*sūrat al-baqarah* 2.285)—this verse is a short Qur'ānic creed citing belief in God, His angels, His books, His messengers—surpasses that of "They will ask you about menstruation" (*sūrat al-baqarah* 2.222).[38] So important does al-Rāzī find this particular argument that he develops it at length. He begins by reflecting upon the Qur'ānic evidence for God's existence to be found in the five kinds of creation mentioned in 2:21–22.[39] From there, Fakhr al-Dīn notes particular Qur'ānic verses which describe the divine attributes (*ṣifāt*) and those which support the complementary aspects of *ᶜilm al-uṣūl,* i.e., *al-nubuwwah* and *al-maᶜād.* He concludes this excursus with a declaration which yet again vindicates his decision to make of the *tafsīr* of this first Qur'ānic mention of God as *al-khāliq* a prolegomenon to the entire enterprise of rational, exegetical theology. Fakhr al-Dīn's assertion merits citation in its entirety for the challenge to gainsaying this *apologia* which it sustains:

> If you were to take a close look at *ʿilm al-kalām* (theology), you would find therein nothing but the repetition of [Qur'ānic] indications/evidence (*al-dalāʾil*) along with their defense (*al-dhabb ʿanhā*) and the refutation of those challenges and specious arguments which seek to repudiate them. Do you think that *ʿilm al-kalām* is blameworthy because of its being concerned with these [Qur'ānic] guiding signs (*al-adillah*), which God has mentioned, or because of its being concerned with refuting the challenges and specious arguments against these? I do not think that any person of sound mind would say that and be satisfied with it.[40]

Not only is reasoning from the fact of creation to the author of that creation a necessary intellectual process for ordinary human beings, the use of *naẓar* and *istidlāl* may be found among the prophets and even the angels. Here al-Rāzī employs a variety of Qur'ānic examples to reinforce the even suprahuman necessity of such ratiocination. (Yet it must be admitted that some of these examples are less successful than others. For instance, the angels' interchange with God over the creation of Adam is less *istidlāl* than *munāẓarah* [disputation].)[41]

The prophetic exempla of this assertion which al-Rāzī offers begin with Adam and end with Muḥammad. The instance of Adam recalls the Qur'ānic competition between Adam and the angels in which the former's powers of intellection prove triumphant.[42] As to Muḥammad, the illustrative range is vast, or, as Fakhr al-Dīn phrases it: "His engagement with the indications/evidence (*dalāʾil*) of *tawḥīd, nubuwwah* and *maʿād* is too apparent to require prolonged attention, for the Qur'ān is replete with it."[43] The specific examples which al-Rāzī uses to highlight this fact are those Qur'ānic occasions in which various heretical opinions are refuted.[44] Concluding this line of argument, the exegete yet again correlates the treatment of 2:21 with his entire exegetical exercise. This selective use of Qur'ānic exempla to underscore the importance of *ʿilm al-uṣūl* and the means to its attainment is justified on the grounds that "its thorough examination is recorded in this entire book," i.e., in the full *al-Tafsīr al-kabīr.*

Having established both the desirability and the superiority of

ʿilm al-kalām, Fakhr al-Dīn raises the stakes in his hypothetical debate with al-Ḥashwiyyah by defining it as *wājib.* This term, commonly translated as "obligatory," has strong legal connotations within Islam. It is traditionally used as one of the designations for the first of the five categories (*al-aḥkām al-khamsah*) by which every human act is often qualified in Islamic law.[45] Al-Rāzī substantiates his use of the designation *al-wājib* with justifications drawn from both reason and authoritative tradition (*al-maʿqūl wa-al-manqūl*), citing among his *auctoritates* such early *mufassirūn* as Abū Hurayrah (d. 58/678) and al-Zuhrī (d. 124/743).

To round out this extended justification of *naẓar* and *istidlāl* as the necessary means to knowing God as *al-khāliq,* al-Rāzī adopts the classical Scholastic device, the *objectio.* He constructs a provocatively escalated five-part argument abjuring the case he has just built. These *objectiones* he then, of course, refutes. Starting with the negation that (1) *naẓar* is not useful for *ʿilm,* Fakhr al-Dīn works through the ascending propositions that (2) even if useful, *naẓar* is not decreed (*maqdūr*), (3) its use is not obligatory, (4) the Messenger did not command it, and (5) it is *bidʿah.* He considers carefully each argument, citing subsidiary lines of disputation and their support. It is, however, for the culminating assertion, the charge of *bidʿah,* that Fakhr al-Ḍīn amasses the broadest range of corroboration. He draws arguments from the Qur'ān, from the Prophetic *ḥadīth,* from the consensus (*al-ijmāʿ*) of the Companions, from the statements of jurisprudents such as Mālik b. Anas (d. 179/795) and al-Shāfiʿī (d. 204/820), and from the corpus of legal prescriptions.

Among these multiple lines of disputation, two are particularly noteworthy. The first is an instance of misrepresentation. As one of the *sed contra* arguments al-Rāzī quotes the Prophetic statement: "Reflect (*tafakkarū*) on creation not on the Creator."[47] In his own rebuttal of this, however, he omits the crucial second clause, the proscription of reflection on the Creator, which is precisely where the potential charge of *bidʿah* would arise. Rather he uses the command to "reflect on creation" as a reaffirmation of his central thesis, i.e., that the God who must be worshipped may only be known by reasoning from the effects of his creative activity.[48] The refutation thus stands as a curious piece of exegetical casuistry, uncharacteristic of the author and disappointing when discovered.

A second line of defense is noteworthy because it represents the tidy reversal of an attempted *argumentum ex silentio.* One possible rebuttal against the permissibility of *ᶜilm al-kalām* is that the Companions of the Prophet said nothing about it: "There has not been transmitted on the authority of a single one of them that he made extensive use of *al-istidlāl* in these matters."[49] That silence is in itself a condemnation. Not so, retorts al-Rāzī, for if the Companions' reticence about the "words of the *mutakallimūn*" (theologians) is an implied condemnation of *kalām,* so too is their reticence about the "words of the *fuqahā'*" (jurisprudents) an implied condemnation of *fiqh* (jurisprudence).[50] Given the clear preeminence of *fiqh* in Islamic life and thought the latter charge is, of course, unthinkable.

Having forcefully argued for the legitimacy of reflective reasoning, Fakhr al-Dīn turns to a more technical discussion of the means to specific knowledge of God's essense (*dhāt*) and attributes (*ṣifāt*). He introduces this *mas'alah* with a succinct summation of the developed argument: "God ordered the worship of Himself yet the order to worship Him is dependent on knowing Him. Since knowledge of His existence is not known by necessity (*al-ᶜilm al-ḍarūrī*) but rather is knowledge based on inferential reason (*al-ᶜilm al-istidlālī*), obviously He here mentioned what shows His existence."[37] So important is this inescapable process of ratiocination from the existence of created being to the existence of the Creator, that God has placed these signs before the minds of the believers at the beginning of the Book.

This contention makes an implicit distinction between the chronology of revelation (as traditionally understood) and the sequence of the Qur'ān as text. Clearly the latter has preeminence in al-Rāzī's thought. The corpus of revelation as presently constituted possesses a theological status and value independent of its historical reception. The synchronic supersedes the diachronic as a hermeneutical element.

Fakhr al-Dīn underlines the importance of early Qur'ānic mention of these creative acts as an exercise in the psychology of conversion. At the very beginning of his full revelatory disclosure God made reference to the grandest elements of His creation—first humanity and then the earth and heavens and their interrelated functions in providing human sustenance.[52] So large do these loom as signs of the divine beneficence that no subtlety of mind, no agility of intellect is needed to understand them. Moreover, that very evidence of God's benefaction to which this early Qur'ānic mention alludes draws the heart to God. This, of course, rather than intellectual stimulation, is their purpose. As al-Rāzī has noted: "The purpose of the Qur'ānic attestations (*al-dalā'il al-qur'āniyyah*) is not disputation (*al-mujādalah*); rather is their purpose the instigation of true beliefs in human hearts."[53]

To support this, Fakhr al-Dīn then proceeds to recount a series of conversion narratives, brief dramatic encounters which successfully pit the likes of Jaᶜfar al-Ṣādiq (d. 148/765), Abū Ḥanīfah (d. 150/767), al-Shāfiᶜī, Aḥmad b. Ḥanbal (d. 241/855), Mālik b. Anas, and Abū Nuwās (d. 198/813) against a variety of agnostic opponents.[54] In each account a natural wonder, a marvel of the divine creativity, serves to enlighten the sceptic, to enkindle the heartfelt fire of faith. Of the dozen which al-Rāzī offers, two must suffice to exemplify this exegetical embellishment. In one story, al-Shāfiᶜī points to the mulberry leaf as evidence of *al-khāliq*. Its one simple form transmutes into manifold materials. Eaten by the silkworm, it becomes silk; by the bee, honey; by the sheep, dung; and by the gazelle, musk.[55] Aḥmad b. Ḥanbal's example may be posed as a riddle. What is like an inaccessible fortress whose walls are seamless, its exterior like molten silver, its interior, purest gold, and from whose two split sides a hearing, seeing creature emerges?[56] Ah yes, another use for the chicken and the egg!

These vignettes are noteworthy not only for their intrinsic charm but for the way in which they skillfully underscore al-Rāzī's essential point. Both the large-scale effects of the divine creative *fiat,* whose mention comes early in the Qur'ān, as well as these small-scale evidences of that same decree are the means by which the mind reaches forth to knowledge of the Creator. Even the coordinate object of *khalaqa* is marshalled to support this thrust. "Who created you and those before you" (*alladhīna min qablikum*) is the full descriptive phrase following the words *rabbakum* (your Lord). In commenting upon this phrase Fakhr al-Dīn yet again balances analytical and reverential concerns. The epistemological process of recognizing one's Creator mirrors that of acknowledging the Creator of one's ancestors, an explanation which would be offered almost a century later by Abū ᶜAbdallāh Muḥammad b. Aḥmad al-Qurṭubī (d. 671/1273) in his *al-Jāmiᶜ li aḥkām al-Qur'ān.*[57] But more important, in al-Rāzī's view, is the testimony thus accorded to God's prevenient benevolence. Al-Rāzī imagines God's paraphrasing Himself by saying: "Do not suppose that I blessed you only at the time when you came into existence. I was blessing you for thousands of years before you were born because I was the Creator of your roots, of your forefathers."[58]

Sūrat al- ᶜalaq 96.1–2

> *iqra' bi-ism rabbika alladhī khalaqa [1] khalaqa al-insān min ᶜalaqin* [2] (Recite in the name of your Lord who created [1] created man from clots [2])

As was noted earlier, the verb *khalaqa* also forms part of the short *sūrah* traditionally held to be the first Qur'ānic revelation.[59] Again, al-Rāzī's treatment of these verses can best be appreciated when viewed against the broader exegetical background. For al-Ṭabarī the phrase *khalaqa al-insān min ᶜalaqin* (who created man from clots) elicits nothing more than the gloss *min al-dam* (from blood) for *min ᶜalaqin.*[60] His twelfth-century counterpart, Ibn al-Jawzī, provides as justification for the phrase *alladhī khalaqa* the divine concern "that the unbelievers would know that He, not their idols (*aṣnāmihim*), is the Creator."[61] Such periphrastic exegesis may reflect a distinction developed by al-Zamakhsharī, a distinction which seeks to explain the sequential repetition of *khalaqa* in these two verses: *alladhī khalaqa khalaqa al-insān min ᶜalaqin* (who created, created man from clots).

Al-Zamakhsharī's distinction is particularly relevant for this study because al-Rāzī repeats it almost verbatim. True to his propensity for grammatical analysis, al-Zamakhsharī ponders whether the first use of *khalaqa* carries an implied object. If not, the sense conveyed by this verb is "the one from whom creation originates, who alone has that ability."[62] On the other hand, perhaps *khalaqa* suggests the objective term *kulla shay'in* (everything), in which case the stress would fall upon the immensity of the divine creative effort.[63] (Although al-Zamakhsharī does not draw the connection, such a proposal would recall the phrase in *sūrat al-anᶜām* 6.102, *khāliq kulli shay'in.*) In either event, according to al-Zamakhsharī's exegesis, the subsequent use of *khalaqa* with an object (*al-insān*) functions as a specification of that part of creation to whom divine revelation was directed and who is "the noblest of that which is on the face of the earth."[64] The Shīʿī commentator, Abū ʿAlī al-Faḍl b. al-Ḥasan al-Ṭabarsī (d. 548/1153), a younger contemporary of al-Zamakhsharī, reiterates this distinction, finding in the repetition of *khalaqa al-insān* a special instance of God's highlighting the created distinctiveness of humankind.[65] Al-Ṭabarsī, however, does not follow al-Zamakhsharī in his second suggestion. Almost as an afterthought the latter offers the alternative explanation that the first use of *khalaqa* is simply obscure or vague (*mubham*).[66] The repetition is therefore needed for emphasis and specification.

As mentioned previously, Fakhr al-Dīn copies—without attribution—this entire section from the *Kashshāf*. Other than indulging his penchant to create numerically tagged subdivisions, al-Rāzī adds nothing substantive. His own contribution to the exegesis of 96:1–2 lies elsewhere. It lies, in fact, in the resumption or reecho of his commentary on 2:21. Yet again, he finds in reference to God's creative activity the pre-eminent proof of divinity. All of creation is a form of instructive nurturing (*al-tarbiyah*) by which God proclaims that "I am your Lord (*rabbuka*) and you are My slaves" (*marbūbī*).[67]

Complementing the exegetical stress in 2:21 on the importance of human effort in coming to a knowledge of God through His creation, al-Rāzī here highlights the Creator as Himself a master teacher. Had God told Muḥammad to say "Recite in the name of your Lord who has no partner," al-Rāzī muses, the *mushrikūn* would never have been persuaded. Thus the divine Pedagogue described Himself as Creator, a descriptive which would compel their attention and acknowledgment. To reinforce the point Fakhr al-Dīn recounts the experience of Abū Ḥanīfah. This famed eighth-century jurist once sent a disciple to Baṣrah to spread his teachings. After a time, the disciple returned, discouraged and unsuccessful. Abū Ḥanīfah then gave him a quick lesson in such techniques of persuasive communication as knowing the opposition and using that knowledge to present an unassailable position.[68] In the same way does God assess His audience and focus attention on the creation of humans, an act which the *mushrikūn* "could not possibly attribute to an idol (*wathan*) because they know that they carved it."[69]

CONCLUSION

In myriad ways, then, has al-Rāzī reinforced his central thesis. We are summoned to worship a God whose existence may be known only through his creation. Therein does he manifest himself, *al-khāliq, al-bāri', al-muṣawwir.* Upon these manifestations must we reflect and reason, must we exercise *naẓar* and *istidlāl,* would we know the Maker (*al-ṣāni*ᶜ). Such an exercise is not, for al-Rāzī, superfluous or—let alone—reprehensible. It is the highest use of human intelligence to which one can aspire, to which, in fact, one is obliged to aspire. Angels and prophets have done so; ordinary humans can seek to do no less.

This is what al-Rāzī draws forth from *rabbakum alladhī khalaqakum* (2:21) and *rabbika alladhī khalaqa khalaqa al-insān* (96: 1–2)—a prolonged and prolific justification for *ᶜilm al-kalām,* a manifesto for the importance of such theological deliberation. Herein does he find warrant for his own exegetical task. From these reflections has he constructed a vindication for the rationalist *mufassir,* a hermeneutical prolegomenon to *al-Tafsīr al-kabīr.* Unlike most of the major classical commentators, al-Rāzī wrote no introduction to his *tafsīr;* one finds there no *muqaddimah* to the Qur'ānic sciences. While his commentary on *sūrat al-fātiḥah* 1 is a book-length disquisition on semantics and theoretical linguistics, it is not until his treatment of 2:21 that one finds deliberate and self-conscious consideration of the principles which were to guide this massive exegetical endeavor.

Throughout the extended commentary on these verses, al-Rāzī skillfully employs those techniques of rational argumentation which the discipline of *ᶜilm al-kalām* had enshrined. His method is both explicative and defensive. Explanation is interlaced with disputation. The anecdotal enlivens the spare outline of rational subtlety, and selective use of traditional material reinforces the base structure of intellection. But at every point is the presence of an *adversarius* sensed. Al-Rāzī as apologist writes to debate, to defend, the shadow of his opponents falling across every page. His text draws energy from the heat of persuasive argumentation. His work comes alive with the swift engagement of thrust and counterthrust.

Yet suffusing the whole is a profound spirituality, an abiding delight in God and His gift of revelation. This is a believer who can compliment his Lord's psychological acuity in directly addressing humankind, His beneficence in the early Qur'ānic mention of major creative acts, and His insightful pedagogy in presenting Himself first as *al-khāliq,* then as *al-waḥīd.* Such pervasive spirituality anchors Fakhr al-Dīn's critical reflection, calling to mind an oft-quoted remark from his final days. This autobiographical fragment, culled from his last testament as dictated to his pupil, Ibrāhīm b. Abī Bakr b. ᶜAlī al-Isfahānī, attests to the comparative relevance of his philosophical and spiritual concerns: "I have diligently explored the paths of *kalām* and the ways of philosophy but have not found what quenches thirst or heals the sick; but now I see that the soundest way is the way of [the] Qur'ān *fī al-tanzīh*" (i.e., read deanthropomorphically).[70] That brief lament adds yet another facet to one's perception of a complex and intriguing personality, complementing the spiritual sensitivity so easily gleaned from his exegetical work. For although al-Rāzī's "great commentary" is a *tafsīr* in which reason reaches beyond the confines of a traditionalist agenda, it never forsakes its primary purpose, that of guiding the believer to an ever deeper understanding and worship of God, *al-khāliq.*

NOTES

1. Drawing chiefly upon the *Kashshāf* of al-Zamakhsharī and the *Tafsīr al-Jalālayn,* Roger Arnaldez has presented an overview of the Qur'ānic vocabulary for creation in his article "Khalḳ," *Encyclopaedia of Islam,* 2nd ed., (Brill, 1960–), 4:980–88. He treats the same material in more summary fashion in the third chapter of his *Le Coran: Guide de Lecture* (Paris, 1983).

2. Muḥammad Fu'ād ᶜAbd al-Bāqī, *al-Muᶜjam al-mufahras li alfāẓ al-Qur'ān al-karīm* (Beirut, n.d.). The Qur'ānic lexicographer al-Rāghib al-Iṣfahānī (d. 502/1108) defines the basic Qur'ānic usage of *al-khalq* as "producing something without an original or without following an example." Thus defined, continues al-Iṣfahānī, the term cannot be applied to human creativity except in a derivative sense. Abū al-Qāsim al-Ḥusayn b. Muḥammad al-Iṣfahānī, *al-Mufradāt fī gharīb al-Qur'ān* (Cairo, 1381/1961), p. 157. The root sense of the term noted by Lane—and by a number of the *mufassirūn*—is that of measuring something (e.g., a sandal, a water-skin, etc.) before cutting (Edward William Lane, *An Arabic-English Lexicon* [1865; reprint ed., Beirut, 1980], 2: 799–800).

3. The danger of selective study of Qur'ānic material has been cogently argued by Fazlur Rahman. In a recent work he remarks that "the Qur'ān must be so studied that its concrete unity will emerge in its fullness, and that to

select certain verses from the Qur'ān to project a partial and subjective point of view may satisfy the subjective observer but it necessarily does violence to the Qur'ān itself and results in extremely dangerous abstractions" (Fazlur Rahman, *Major Themes of the Qur'ān* [Minneapolis, 1980], p. 15).

4. A concise account of those verses which have been suggested as the first revelation may be found in the *muqaddimah* to Ibn al-Jawzī's *tafsīr.* See Abū al-Faraj ʿAbd al-Raḥmān b. ʿAlī b. Muḥammad al-Jawzī, *Zād al-masīr fī ʿilm al-tafsīr* (Beirut, 1404/1984), pp. 5–6. My translation and analysis of this introduction will be published in the forthcoming issue of *Alif: Journal of Comparative Poetics* under the title "Ibn al-Jawzī's Essay on Hermeneutical Principles."

5. Al-Qifṭī gives only the first date of 543. See Jamāl al-Dīn Abū al-Ḥasan ʿAli b. Yusūf al-Qifṭī, *Ta'rīkh al-ḥukamā'* (1903; reprint ed., Baghdad, 1967), p. 291.

6. In his *Taḥṣīl al-ḥaqq,* Fakhr al-Dīn cites his father's intellectual genealogy in both *ʿilm al-uṣūl* and *fiqh,* tracing the former back to the famed theologian Abū al-Ḥasan ʿAlī b. Ismāʿīl al-Ashʿarī (d. 324/935) and the latter to the renowned jurisprudent al-Shāfiʿī (d. 204/820) (Shams al-Dīn Aḥmad b. Muḥammad b. Abī Bakr b. Khallikān, *Wafayāt al-aʿyān wa-abnā' al-zamān* [Beirut, 1388/1968], 4:252).

7. Ibid., 4:260. He went to Marāgha to follow his teacher Majd al-Dīn al-Jīlī. This latter was also the teacher of Fakhr al-Dīn's contemporary, the mystic philosopher Shihāb al-Dīn Yaḥyā al-Suhrawardī (d. 587/1191). See Majid Fakhry, *A History of Islamic Philosophy* (New York, 1970), p. 355.

8. The results of this education were an impressive list of intellectual qualifications. Fakhr al-Dīn's biographer, Khalīl b. Aybak al-Ṣafadī, has summarized these talents: "As distinguished from others like him, he had five qualities which God gathered together for no one else. They were a masterly expressiveness in discourse, a healthy intellect, a limitless store of knowledge, a comprehensive memory (*al-ḥāfiẓah al-mustawʿibah*) and automatic recall of demonstrations and corroborating proofs (*al-dhākirah allatī tuʿayyinuhu ʿalā mā yurīdu fī taqrīr al-adillah wa-al-barāhīn*)" (Khalīl b. Aybak al-Ṣafadī, *al-Wafī bi-al-wafayāt* [Damascus, 1379/1959], 4:248). In the biographical section of a recent study of Fakhr al-Dīn's *Nihāyat al-ījāz fī dirāyat al-iʿjāz,* Māhir Mahdī Hilāl has collected the accolades of al-Rāzī's biographers, both classical and modern (*Fakhr al-Dīn al-Rāzī balāghīyan* [Baghdad, 1397/1977], pp. 57–64).

9. Ibn Khallikān praises his knowledge of *kalām* and logic and refers to him as "the Shāfiʿī *faqīh,* unique in his age and unique of his kind" (Ibn Khallikān, *Wafayāt,* 4:248). Al-Dāwūdī characterizes him as the leading figure of his age in the rational sciences and one of the most eminent in the legal sciences, but most prominently as the *sul-ṭān al-mutakallimīn* (Muḥammad B. ʿAlī b. Aḥmad al-Dāwūdī, *Ṭabaqāt al-mufassirīn* [Cairo, 1392/1972], 2:214).

10. As Ignaz Goldziher has noted, Khwārazm was "the primary home-

stead of the Mu^ctazilī in the twelfth and thirteenth century" ("Aus der Theologie des Fachr al-din al-Razi," *Der Islam* 3 (1912): 222).

11. Ibn Khallikān, *Wafayāt* 4:249.

12. Ibid.

13. Ibid., 4:250. Roger Arnaldez sees al-Rāzī's stance toward such groups as the Mu^ctazilīs and the Karrāmīs to be less that of an opponent than of a conciliator: "La conciliation d'al-Rāzī est peut-être moins une tentative pour accorder des doctrines, en évitant ce qui est excessif et en conservant ce qui est le plus modéré, qu'un effort pour offrir à des esprit différents un champ commun de pensée, où ils puissent tous se retrouver et évoluer à leur aise" (Roger Arnaldez, "L'oeuvre de Fakhr al-Dīn al-Rāzī, commentateur du Coran et philosophie," *Cahiers de civilization médiévale* 3 (1960): 314.

14. Muḥammad b. ^cUmar Fakhr al-Dīn al-Rāzi, *al-Tafsīr al-kabīr,* 32 vols. (Beirut, 1405/1985). For recent work on the manuscript tradition of *al-Tafsīr al-kabīr* see Jacques Jomier, O.P., "Les mafātīh al-ghayb de l'Imām Fakhr al-Dīn al-Rāzī: quelques dates, lieux, manuscrits," *Mélanges de l'Institut Dominicain d'Études Orientales du Caire* 13 (1977): 253–90, and "Qui a commenté l'ensemble des sourates al-^cAnkabūt à Yāsīn (29–36) dans 'le Tafsīr al-kabīr' de l'Imām Fakhr al-Dīn al-Razi," *International Journal of Middle East Studies* 11 (1980), 467–85; and Richard Gramlich, "Fakhr ad-Dīn ar-Rāzīs Kommentar zu Sure 18, 9–12," *Asiatische Studien/Études Asiatiques* 33 (1979): 99–152.

15. Al-Ṣafadī, *Wafī,* 4:254.

16. Ibid.

17. Ibid., 4:249. George Makdisi would undoubtedly question this claim to originality. His own work on Ibn ^cAqīl (d. 573/1119) has highlighted the fact that the sophisticated use of elements of Scholastic methodology is to be found at least a century earlier. See especially "The Scholastic Method in Medieval Education: An Inquiry into its Origins in Law and Theology," *Speculum* 49 (1974): 648ff., and *The Rise of Colleges* (Edinburgh, 1981), pp. 253ff. Makdisi himself draws a connection between Fakhr al-Dīn al-Rāzī and Ibn ^cAqil in the literary genre of *munāẓarāt.* See his introduction in George Makdisi, *The Notebooks of Ibn ^cAqīl: Kitāb al-funūn,* Part 1 (Beirut, 1970), p. xlvii.

18. Abū Ja^cfar Muḥammad b. Jarīr al-Ṭabarī, *Jāmi^c al-bayān ^can ta'wīl āy al-Qur'ān* (Beirut, 1405/1984), 1:160.

19. At the end of his commentary on this verse al-Ṭabarī reaffirms the universal applicability of this command, citing as analogous the divine call to repentance issued even to those whom God knows will not heed it (ibid., 1:161). Two twelfth-century commentators who follow al-Ṭabarī's interpretation here are the Shāfi^cī jurist and traditionist Abū Muḥammad al-Ḥusayn b. Mas^cūd al-Baghawī (d. 516/1122) and the Shī^cī exegete Abū ^cAlī al-Faḍl b. al-Ḥasan al-Ṭabarsī (d. 548/1153). They are, however, careful to note the exemption of "minors" (*al-ṣighār* and *al-aṭfāl,* respectively) and "the insane" (*al-majānīn*). See *Tafsīr al-Baghawī* (also known as *Ma^cālim al-tanzīl*) (Beirut,

1406/1986), 1:55 and al-Ṭabarsī's *Majma*ʿ *al-bayān fī tafsīr al-Qur'ān* (Beirut, 1406/1986), 1:153.

20. Abū Mansūr Muḥammad b. Muḥammad al-Māturīdī, *Ta'wīlāt ahl al-sunnah* (Cairo, 1391/1971), 1:67–69.

21. Ibn al-Jawzi, *Zād al-masīr,* 1:47. The exegetes cited are (1) Ibn ʿAbbās (d. 68/686), al-Ḥasan [al-Baṣrī] (d. 110/728), and Mujāhid [b. Jabr] (d. 104/722); and (3) al-Suddī (d. 128/745).

22. Abū al-Ḥasan ʿAlī b. Aḥmad al-Wāḥidī al-Nīsābūrī, *Asbāb al-nuzūl* (Beirut, 1404/1983), p. 21.

23. Al-Ṭabarī, *Jāmi*ʿ *al-bayān,* 1:160.

24. Ibn al-Jawzī, *Zād al-masīr,* 1:48.

25. While the title of al-Zamakhsharī's commentary is commonly given as *al-Kashshāf ʿan ḥaqā'iq ghawāmiḍ al-tanzīl,* several recent printings, including the one used herein, have appeared under the title *al-Kashshāf* (or *Tafsīr al-kashshāf*) *ʿan ḥaqā'iq al-tanzīl wa-ʿuyūn al-aqāwīl fī wujūh al-ta'wīl.* (The latter would follow Brockelmann, 1:290 and SI, 507.)

26. Imām al-Zamakhsharī, *Tafsīr al-kashshāf ʿan ḥaqā'iq al-tanzīl wa-ʿuyūn al-aqāwīl fī wujūh al-ta'wīl* (Cairo, 1397/1977), 1:47.

27. Ibid.

28. Al-Rāzī, *al-Tafsīr al-kabīr,* 2:90.

29. While Fakhr al-Dīn gives this triadic division a singular hermeneutical prominence, he is not the only exegete to note it. For example, al-Qurṭubī (d. 671/1273) mentions the subsections within *sūrat al-baqarah* 2.1–20, tracing the observation back to Mujāhid (d. 104/722) and Ibn Jurayj (d. 150/767) among others. See Abū ʿAbdallāh Muḥammad b. Aḥmad al-Anṣārī al-Qurṭubī, *al-Jāmi*ʿ *li aḥkām al-Qur'ān* (Beirut, 1405/1985), 1:224.

30. Departing from his usual pattern of simple verse-by-verse commentary, al-Rāzī clusters the discussion of 2:21–25 under the heading *al-qawl fī iqāmat al-dalālah ʿalā al-tawḥīd wa-al-nubuwwah wa-al-maʿād.* See al-Rāzī, *al-Tafsīr al-kabīr,* 2:90.

31. Ibid.

32. Ibid. Perhaps here al-Rāzī is deliberately playing upon one of the ninety-nine names, i.e., *mālik al-mulk.*

33. Ibid., 2:95. In his study of the Muʿtazilī, ʿAbd al-Jabbār (d. 414/1023), Jan Peters discusses al-Qāḍī's analogous use of these two terms: "This activity of the human intellect [moving from the *dalīl/dalālah* to the *madlūl*] is called 'reflection' (*naẓar*); also the verb '*istadall*', tenth form of the root to which also belongs the words '*dalīl*' and '*dalāla*', is used for this act, meaning: to establish an indication and to acquire in this way knowledge, or to infer" (Jan Peters, *God's Created Speech* [Leiden, 1976], p. 68).

34. Al-Rāzī, *al-Tafsīr al-kabīr,* 2:95.

35. Al-Imām Ibn Qutaybah [Abū Muḥammad ʿAbdallāh b. Muslim b. Qutaybah] *Kitāb ta'wīl mukhtalif al-ḥadīth* (Cairo, 1402/1982), p. 92 (French translation by Gérard Lecomte, *Le traité des divergences du ḥadīth d'Ibn Qutayba* [Damascus, 1962]).

36. Al-Rāzī, *al-Tafsīr al-kabīr,* 2:95. Fakhr al-Dīn also includes the cognate religious sciences of *fiqh* and *ḥadīth.* Thus does the *muḥaddith*'s investigation of the *kalām* of the Prophet depend upon the authenticity of Muḥammad's *nubuwwah,* and the *faqīh*'s preoccupation with the divine *aḥkām* derives from the logical priority of the two fundamental categories within *ʿilm al-uṣūl, tawḥīd* and *nubuwwah.*

37. Of the latter, al-Rāzī reckons the total number at less than 600 (*al-Tafsīr al-kabīr,* 2:96.

38. Ibid.

39. The five enumerated are: "The creation of the religiously-obligated (*al-mukallafīn*), the creation of those before them (*min qablihim*), the creation of the heavens, the creation of the earth and the creation of fruits from water which comes down from the heavens to the earth" (*al-Tafsīr al-kabīr,* 2:96).

40. Ibid., 2:97.

41. The Qur'ānic passage from which al-Rāzī draws his example is *sūrat al-baqarah* 2.30.

42. Al-Rāzī, *al-Tafsīr al-kabīr,* 2:97.

43. Ibid., 2:98.

44. Among the heresies thus confronted is that of the Christians, who attribute divinity to the Messiah (*ilāhiyyat al-masīḥ*). This al-Rāzī equates with the views of idol worshipers who believe in the divinity of idols (*ilāhiyyat al-awthān*). *al-Tafsīr al-kabīr,* 2:98.

45. The ranked five are: obligatory (*wājib, farḍ*), recommended (*sunnah, mandūb, mustaḥabb*), indifferent (*mubāḥ*), reprehensible (*makrūh*) and forbidden (*ḥarām*). For a fuller discussion see Joseph Schacht, *An Introduction to Islamic Law* (Oxford, 1964), pp. 121ff.

46. Al-Rāzī, *al-Tafsīr al-kabīr,* 2:100.

47. Ibid., 2:105.

48. Ibid.

49. Ibid.

50. Ibid.

51. Ibid., 2:106. In a discussion of al-Rāzī's exegesis of *sūrat al-baqarah* 2.9 and 12, Roger Arnaldez translates *ḍarūrī* as "intuitive" (Roger Arnaldez, "Trouvailles philosophiques dans le commentaire coranique de Fakhr al-Din al-Razi," *Études philosophiques et littéraires* 3 [1968]: 17).

52. Al-Rāzī, *al-Tafsīr al-kabīr,* 2:107.

53. Ibid., 2:108.

54. Ignaz Goldziher has remarked upon Fakhr al-Dīn's particular regard for Abū Ḥanīfah. See Ignaz Goldziher, *Introduction to Islamic Theology and Law* (*Vorlesungen über den Islam* [Heidelberg, 1910]), trans. Andras and Ruth Hamori (Princeton, 1981), p. 65.

55. Al-Rāzī, *al-Tafsīr al-kabīr,* 2:108.

56. Ibid., 2:109.

57. Al-Qurṭubī, *al-Jāmiʿ li aḥkām al-Qur'ān,* 1:226.

58. Al-Rāzī, *al-Tafsīr al-kabīr,* 2:109.

59. Al-Ṭabarī supports this assertion with fourteen *aḥādīth;* see *Jāmiʿ al-bayān,* 15:251. Al-Wāḥidī, like Ibn al-Jawzī (see note 4 above) devotes a section of the *muqaddimah* to his *tafsīr* to discussing what was the first Qur'ānic revelation; see *Asbāb al-nuzūl,* pp. 11ff. Al-Rāzī opens his treatment of *sūrat al-ʿalaq* with the equivocation: "The *mufassirūn* have claimed that this *sūrah* is the first of the Qur'ān to come down; others say *al-fātiḥah* (1), then *al-qalam* (68)" (*al-Tafsīr al-kabīr,* 32:13). Al-Zamakhsharī, while acknowledging the traditional chronology on the authority of Ibn ʿAbbās and Mujāhid, insists that "most of the *mufassirūn* are of the view that it is *al-fātiḥah,* then *al-qalam*" (*al-Kashshāf,* 6:244). The debate is complicated by the fact that the ninety-sixth *sūrah* is occasionally also entitled *al-qalam;* see Qāḍī ʿAbd al-Jabbār b. Aḥmad al-Hamadhānī, *Mutashābih al-Qur'ān* (Cairo, n.d.), p. 696; and Ibn al-Jawzī, *Zād al-masīr,* 9:175.

60. Al-Ṭabarī, *Jāmiʿ al-bayān,* 15:251. Blood clots are one of a variety of substances mentioned in the Qur'ānic account of human creation. For a chart which classifies the materials mentioned according to the four periods of revelation distinguished by Theodor Nöldeke and Régis Blachère see the recent work by Thomas J. O'Shaughnessy, S.J., *Creation and the Teaching of the Qur'ān* (Rome, 1985), p. 12.

61. Ibn al-Jawzī, *Zād al-masīr,* 9:175.

62. Al-Zamakhsharī, *al-Kashshāf,* 6:244; also al-Rāzī, *al-Tafsīr al-kabīr,* 32:15.

63. Al-Rāzī here adds to his repetition of al-Zamakhsharī by citing the analogous example of *allāhu akhbar,* which carries the implied comparative term *min kulli shay'in. Al-Tafsīr al-kabir,* 32:15.

64. Al-Zamakhsharī, *al-Kashshāf,* 6:244 and al-Rāzī, *al-Tafsīr al-kabīr,* 32:15.

65. Al-Ṭabarsī, *Majmaʿ al-bayān,* 10:781.

66. The term *mubham* is occasionally substituted for the second of that pair of hermeneutical categories drawn from *sūrah āl ʿImrān* 3.7, i.e., *muḥkam/mutashābih.* For further on this see Jane Dammen McAuliffe, "Qur'ānic Hermeneutics: The Views of al-Ṭabarī and Ibn Kathīr," in *Approaches to the History of the Interpretation of the Qur'ān,* ed. A. Rippin (London, 1988).

67. Al-Rāzī, *al-Tafsīr al-kabīr,* 32:14.

68. Ibid., 32:15.

69. Ibid. For a comparison of Qur'ānic and Jāhilī views of creation see Toshihiko Izutsu, *God and Man in the Koran* (1964; reprint ed., New York, 1980), pp. 120–32.

70. Al-Dāwūdī, *Ṭabaqāt,* 2:215. This statement is reminiscent of one that Thomas Aquinas is said to have made in the last year of his life. After a spiritual experience on December 6, 1273, which profoundly affected him, Thomas confessed to his companion, Reginald of Piperno: "All that I have written seems to me like straw compared to what has now been revealed to me." See James A. Weisheipl, O.P., *Friar Thomas D'Aquino: His Life, Thought and Works* (Garden City, N.Y., 1974), p. 322.

Response

Muhsin Mahdi

Does Fakhr al-Dīn al-Rāzī's *Great Commentary on the Koran,* also called *Keys to the Unseen* (*Mafātīḥ al-ghayb,* 32 vols., [Cairo, 1363/1934; reprint ed. Beirut, 1405/1985]) enlighten us on how he sees the relation between philosophy and religion on the question of God and creation? If his commentary on verses 2:21 and 96:1–2 is any indication, then philosophy and philosophical theology (*ilāhiyyāt*) do not seem to play an important role in his understanding or interpretation of creation as a divine act. He quotes and occasionally defends certain *kalām* notions, and *kalām* is sometimes called philosophical theology. But this is an ambiguous use of the term 'philosophical'. Fakhr al-Dīn must have had a clear idea of what philosophy and philosophical theology meant, for, as he says in his last testament and as is clear from many of his works, he had studied philosophy and commented on some of Avicenna's philosophic writings. Yet there is hardly a trace of philosophic reasoning in his commentary on these verses on creation. (See the comical use of the Avicennian terms 'essence' and 'existence' to explain the divine command regarding worship in verse 2:21 [*Commentary* 2:84]; or the use of the kalām-theological statement "It is impossible to know an attribute while being ignorant of the substance [*dhāt*]" out of context [*Commentary* 2:85].)

Here I should perhaps be allowed to defend the use of the expression "kalām-theology." Why *kalām* is not simply called *kalām,* I do not know. It has been called defensive theology, dialectical theology, and rational theology. It is all these things and perhaps more, but to call it philosophical theology and speak of Fakhr al-Dīn's use of technically philosophical discussion can be misleading, especially at a time when philosophizers are planning either to transform philosophy or to bring it to an end. One must be an optimist to go on assuming that such terms as 'philosophy' and 'philosophical' convey limited, i.e., intelligible, meanings as current, nontechnical expressions, independently of their historical designation of particular disciplines and persons and schools. This is perhaps another reason why one ought to stick to the meaning such terms as 'philosophy' and *kalām* had for Muslim thinkers in general and for the author one is trying to understand in particular.

I know that the term 'philosophy' has been used in connection with Fakhr al-Dīn in order to give the impression that he is a great, and even the greatest, Muslim thinker of the Middle Ages, or to suggest that, in order to know what a real Muslim philosopher is (as against those who were called or called themselves philosophers, but were in reality nothing but copies of Greek, i.e., non-Muslim, thinkers), one should study Fakhr al-Dīn. This is not to deny the breadth of his learning or the massive character of his literary production; nor is it to deny that he made a valiant effort to combine the study of philosophy, *kalām,* jurisprudence, Qur'ānic commentary, and a host of other disciplines. The question that needs to be addressed is whether he was able to synthesize or harmonize these disciplines, or merely mix them together, as he was accused to have done by men like Ibn Khaldūn and Ibn Taymiyya. If, as seems to be true, *kalām* was the discipline he was eager to uphold and defend, if his *kalām* was of the type that involved rational argumentation and reflection, and if we need to add the expression 'theology' in order to make the enterprise intelligible to modern Western readers, then perhaps we may call the discipline in question "kalām-theology."

Fakhr al-Dīn was a near contemporary of Averroes. They use the same arguments, which were used by al-Ghazālī already, to defend *kalām* and philosophy, respectively. And if it is true that he attempted to make the Prophet into a kalām-theologian and the Qur'ān into a book of kalām-theology, then this would not have been very different from the attempt by some Muslim philosophers to develop the notion of the philosopher-prophet or to see philosophic arguments in the Qur'ān. Further, the elaborate defence of what he calls "speculation," which has to be understood as a defence of kalām-theology, shows that kalām-theology was not the "queen of the sciences" in Islam, but a discipline that, like philosophy, had to defend its legitimacy and the reason for its existence before a higher court. That higher court alone had the authority to decide whether kalām-theology should or could be practiced at all, or was an innovation to be avoided or condemned—and that higher court was the science of the revealed divine law, *fiqh,* Islamic jurisprudence.

Fakhr al-Dīn perceived that the notion of creation was crucial to the distinction between those who do and those who do not believe in the revealed religions, and that it was closely connected with belief in a certain kind of God, a certain type of prophecy, and a certain manner of resurrection or life in the hereafter. He knew of course that this cluster of beliefs provides the underpinning for the commands and prohibitions contained in the divine law. But he knew also that the science of the divine law did not confine itself to such things as menstruation, as Ayatollah Khomeini was to remind us again in our lifetime. His general argument is that creation proves the existence of God and the creature's obligation to worship Him.

One cannot say that Fakhr al-Dīn's commentary on these verses contains any theory of creation at all. Nor is it systematic in any sense that would be acceptable to philosophy or kalām-theology. For instance, at one point he says that five kinds of creation are mentioned in verses 2:21–22. But he merely enumerates them ("the creation of the religiously-obligated, the creation of those before them, the creation of the heavens, the creation of the earth and the creation of fruits from water which comes down from the heavens to the earth" [*Commentary* 2:96 McAuliffe]). No, there is no argument for creation. Creation is simply accepted as a fact that is easily ascertained by everyone, provided one is not obstinate but is willing to look about and reflect on one's experience. The only argument, if this can be called such, is from reflection on created things, big and small, which reflection is presumed to lead to God as Creator. But is this not a vicious circle? If you start by assuming that all the things you see are created, and not created by human beings or nature, then you are supposed to reach the conclusion that they must have a creator, that is, one views all things, including the heavens and the earth, as one views a silver ring: one must assume the existence of a silversmith who fashioned it.

This is of course the standard argument of kalām-theology. It assumes creation, or rather it assumes that, in order to ascertain that everything other than God is created, all one needs to do is look about and, if need be, reflect upon what one sees and experiences. That is, one rests the case ultimately on common opinion.

If, as seems to be the case, all reasonable women and men seem generally to accept the fact that everything they see about them is created, then the question is how to exploit this generally accepted opinion for human spiritual well-being in this world and in the hereafter. But is this a satisfactory argument? Do the reflections of human beings on what they see and experience lead necessarily to the conviction that all these things are created? Does the conviction that they are created lead to the conclusion that they are the manifestation of a divine act? Does the conviction that they are the manifestation of a divine act lead necessarily to the same conclusions regarding the manner of creation or the nature of the creator or maker? These and similar questions are not raised by Fakhr al-Dīn in his commentary on those verses. And what exactly does Fakhr al-Dīn mean by the exercise of reflection? What did he consider to be the highest use of human intelligence? Finally, why does Fakhr al-Dīn not continue the path from creation to creator by asking what the creation we see about us indicates as to its creator apart from the fact of creation?

The only argument made by Fakhr al-Dīn that makes some sense seems to be a practical one, which can be characterized as pedagogical, using "such techniques of persuasive communication as knowing the opposition and using that knowledge to present an unassailable position" (McAuliffe, p. 289 and n. 68). If this is the character of his argument, then there is no end to the signs of God's power, mercy, compassion, benefaction—and, one must add, anger—to which one can point in the course of natural and human history. And one must agree with him that "The purpose of the Koranic attestations is not disputation; rather is their purpose the instigation of true beliefs in human hearts" (*Commentary* 2:108 McAuliffe). This, rather than any other consideration or principle, is perhaps what guides Fakhr al-Dīn's massive exegetical endeavor, unless of course his commentary on verses 2:21 and 96:1–2 is not indicative of the character of the work as a whole.

But the impression made by Fakhr al-Dīn's commentary on these verses is that this is the work of a successful preacher who sees God and the Prophet in his own image as great preachers (God as the Divine Preacher and the Prophet as a divinely inspired preacher) whose speeches "shake and move the listener" and make effective use of an infinite variety of rhetorical devices to make human beings perform strenuous and difficult actions and yet feel pleasure while performing them (*Commentary* 22:82). According to Fakhr al-Dīn, God engages the listeners in the Qur'ān in a very personal dialogue full of such rhetorical devices as emphasis and exaggeration, meant to make human beings recover from their slumber and not remain in a state of forgetfulness (*Commentary* 2:84).

Creation, especially the creation of humans, is taken to be a proof of the existence of the "maker" or "artificer" (*al-ṣâni*ᶜ); and the use of creation in the Qur'ān is taken to indicate that there is no way to know God's existence except through inquiry into creation as sign and proof for the existence of a creator and his attributes (*Commentary* 2:88–89). This, to repeat, is the standard kalām-theology argument, and Fakhr al-Dīn's commentary argues that kalām-theology does nothing but accept and defend the kind of arguments contained in the Qur'ān, which reports discussions between God and the unbelievers and between the prophets he sends and their opponents. Therefore, a Muslim is under an obligation or is commanded to pursue kalām-theology (*Commentary* 2:88–96).

In his book dealing with rational matters (*al-kutub al-'aqliyya*), Fakhr al-Dīn says, he has proved that God's existence can be explained by the notion of "possibility," or *ḥudūth,* or both, and these with regard to either substances or accidents, making them six ways, for all of which there are examples in the Qur'ān. But the Qur'ān and other divinely revealed books use for the most part the methods easiest for humans to understand, methods that are not particularly complicated, so that everyone, the few as well as the many, can benefit from them. It is in this context that he asserts that the aim of Qur'ānic proofs is not to engage in discussion, but "to implant true dogmas in the hearts," and he quotes numerous examples of people who were persuaded that God exists on the basis of things they understood best, their own past experiences, or things with which they deal in everyday life (*Commentary* 2:97–100). Then he continues to pad his account with extraneous matters about the heavens and the earth, which the learned preacher and his listeners could very well have done without (*Commentary* 2:101ff.).

In commenting on verses 96:1–2 (*Commentary* 32:13ff.) Fakhr al-Dīn poses the question, Why was "who created" mentioned after "your Lord"? His answer is as follows. Because it is as if the servant says, "What is the proof that you are my Lord?" And he answers,

"Because you were in yourself and your attributes nonexistent and then came to exist, but both you and your attributes must have a creator. Thus I am your Lord." The reference to Abū Ḥanīfa's representative in Basra indicates again the importance of rhetorical devices.

The general impression, then, is that Fakhr al-Dīn does not try to prove creation in his commentary on the Qur'ān because the Qur'ān itself does not present a proof of creation but assumes that the listeners believe in creation already. In fact the title placed at the head of the long commentary on verse 2:21 is not "Establishing the proof of creation," but "Establishing the proof of [God's] unity, of prophecy, and of return [in the hereafter]." So what needs proof as far as the listeners are concerned is not creation, but God's unity, prophecy, and life in the world to come. And, by and large, the Qur'ān consists of arguments against those who deny God's unity, who refuse to recognize His prophets, or who deny the existence of a life after this one (*Commentary* 2:88, 90). As far as I recall, there is no argument anywhere in the Qur'ān against those who deny creation, only against those who attribute creation and annihilation to a maker other than God, such as Time.

Finally, it may be useful to ask what is meant by the expression 'creation' (*khalq*) in the Qur'ān and what those who first listened to or read it understood by this expression. Fakhr al-Dīn quotes a number of authorities to the effect that the expression 'creation' means to determine, straighten up, fix, invent—all of which have very strong support in the way 'creation' is used in the Qur'ān itself. God is praised in the Qur'ān as the best of creators, not the only creator. And it is in this connection that Fakhr al-Dīn quotes the opinion of the well known Muᶜtazilite kalām-theologian Abū ᶜAbdallāh al-Baṣrī, the teacher of the Qāḍī ᶜAbd al-Jabbār, to the effect that it is absurd to call God by the name "creator," because determination and straightening up consists of thought, reflection, and consideration, which cannot possibly be attributed to God (*Commentary* 2:97, cf. 32:15).

But what the Qur'ān meant for the original listeners or those around the Prophet, i.e., its original historical sense, does not exhaust its message to believers. For the Qur'ānic message is in a sense ahistorical. It spoke to the first generation of Muslims, it spoke to every generation since then, it speaks to us, and it will speak to the generations that will succeed us. This understanding of the nature of the Qur'ānic message enables Fakhr al-Dīn to accept the historical sense and the way earlier commentators understood the verses he is commenting on, and then proceed to give his own understanding of them. We need to appreciate this way of approaching the Qur'ān if we mean to understand the way commentaries on the Qur'ān tend to reflect partisan views, sects, schools, intellectual movements, social tensions. It enables us also to understand some of the contemporary commentaries on the Qur'ān, especially those that go back to the original historical sense and make use of the transition from pre-Islamic times to the early Islamic community as an illustration of contemporary conditions, urging Muslims to move away from what are considered the heathen conditions of modern life, but also those that read the Qur'ān in terms of modern science and social justice with the aim of reforming a backward Islamic society.

To conclude, then, the way Fakhr al-Dīn proceeds in commenting on the above verses concerning creation must be characterized as purely practical. He was of course aware of the many theoretical accounts of creation or eternity that had existed in kalām-theology and in philosophy. But since he was commenting on the Qur'ān in this work, he needed to understand and reveal to his listeners the primary intention of the Qur'ānic verses dealing with creation. And the primary intention of the Qur'ān in these verses is practical rather than theoretical. (For example, there is nothing in the Qur'ān about creation from nothing or creation in time.) The practical intention is too obvious to miss. Fakhr al-Dīn interprets the Qur'ānic verses on creation from the point of view of the Qur'ān addressing everyone: he looks at them from the point of view of the common believer (not from the point of view of the kalām-theologian or the philosopher) and the way the common believer ought to respond to God's command that he be worshipped. If what Fakhr al-Dīn does in the commentary on the Qur'ān is considered to be part of his work as kalām-theologian, then it must be designated as his practical theology.

Transcendence and Distinction: Metaphoric Process in Ismāʿīlī Muslim Thought

Azim Nanji

> He originates creation; then refashions it—for Him an easy task. His is the most Sublime Symbol in the heavens and the earth. (Qur'ān 30:27)

> Do you not perceive how God coins a metaphor? A Good Word, like a Good Tree, whose roots are deep, and whose branches reach into Heaven. (Qur'ān 14: 24–26)

This essay explores how writers of the Fatimid period of Ismāʿīlī thought during the tenth and eleventh centuries[1] developed an approach that sought to reconcile an understanding of the transcendent and unique nature of God—embodied in the Qur'ānic concept of *tawhid*—with a view of creation as both produced by, and yet distinct from, God. Such an approach, in common with the general discourse among certain other Muslim schools of thought, was concerned with developing rational tools of comprehension that could be applied to scriptural statements. The set of problems they dealt with had dimensions similar to those faced by philosophers and theologians in Islam, as well as their Jewish and Christian counterparts, in developing various syntheses with philosophy, particularly in its Platonic, Aristotelian, and Neoplatonic versions. The access to tools of inquiry afforded by the philosophical heritage of antiquity became for those Muslims committed to rational discourse a resource and an ally that they willingly co-opted in their quest to decipher truths they believed to be embedded in revelation. The reflexive process engendered by the interaction of the two allowed various Muslim groups to articulate distinctive stances towards the relationship of reason and revelation that in turn led to them being identified with various developing theological orientations. Though in time historical and other factors led to the emergence of one or the other orientation as dominant, it is important to note during this period the shared intellectual climate, the commonality of issues, and the existence of a plurality of discourses, which provided the overall context of "exchange" amongst Muslims, and also between them, the "People of the Book," and the classical heritage. The "exchange" also enabled the discussion to take place within a common linguistic framework that had adapted the intellectual tools of discourse and which came to represent, as in the Ismāᶜīlī case, a point of departure for the expression and elaboration of the received monotheistic doctrine of God.[2]

UNDERSTANDING TRANSCENDENCE: THE TOOLS OF INTERPRETATION

Among the tools of interpretation of scripture that are associated particularly with Shiᶜi and Ismāᶜīlī thought is that of *ta'wīl.* This Qur'ānic term, literally "going back to the first or beginning," came to have the connotation of a form of hermeneutical discourse. Jean Pépin, in analyzing the original Greek word *hermeneuein,* concludes that

> as used generally, the word has come to signify interpretation, and that hermeneutics today, commonly has as its synonym 'exegesis'. However, the original meaning of *hermeneuein,* and or related words —or in any case their principal meaning—was not that at all, and was not far from being its exact contrary, if we grant that exegesis is a movement of penetration into the intention of a text or message.[3]

As set forth in Ismāᶜīlī writings, the purpose and goal of *ta'wīl* is to arrive at such an "original" understanding of scriptural texts by going beyond the formal, literal meaning of the text, neither limiting the total significance nor rejecting entirely the validity of such a formal reading, but affirming that the ultimate significance and totality of meaning of any text could only be grasped by the application of *ta'wīl.* Such hermeneutics, in their view, complemented *tafsir,* the mode of formal interpretation in Muslim thought, and did not reflect a dichotomized way of viewing scripture. Rather, it attested to the divine use of language in multiple ways, particularly as exemplified in the Qur'ānic verses cited above, through the use of "symbol" and figurative language. Hermeneutical discourse in Ismāʿīlī thought thus extends the meaning of scripture, like branches reaching into Heaven, to identify the visible which glorifies Him, but it also seeks to penetrate to the roots, to retrieve and disclose that which appears invisible.

In his works, *al-Risālah al Durriyah* and *Rāhat al-ʿAql,* the Fatimid philosopher Hāmid al-Dīn al-Kirmānī (d. 1021) juxtaposes a discussion of speech and language to his exposition of the concept of God and *tawhid.* He argues that languages grow out of words which are composed of letters which allow words to signify specific meanings. But words as well as languages are contingent and relative. Since God is not contingent but absolute, language, by its very nature, cannot appropriately define Him in a noncontingent way and take account of that which makes God different from all that is contingent. Thus language in itself fails to define God as befitting His glory. Language, however, is a beginning, because it is the foremost tool for signifying and representing the possibility of what God is. The fact of being human and possessed of an intellect compels one to speak of and inquire about the agent from whom existentiation (or origination) comes forth. Thus when one speaks of God, one does not necessarily describe Him as He is, but one has affirmed that He is indeed the originator of all that we employ to understand and describe His creation.

The appropriate mode of language which serves us best in this task is, according to al-Kirmānī, figurative language. Such language, which employs analogy, metaphor and symbols, allows one to make distinctions and to establish differences in ways that a literal usage of language does not permit. It can also impel thought to seek new meanings and to develop the necessary tools of discourse to characterize these new meanings. *Ta'wīl,* understood as metaphoric process, has the capacity to relate meaning to its beginnings—for that is not only the root sense of the word *ta'wīl* itself, but also expresses the religious purpose for which such a metaphoric process is to be employed—as a journey to understanding God. This understanding starts as the *ta'wīl* of the words used in the Qur'ān, where God is indeed referred to as the "Sublime Symbol," thus legitimating the use of figurative language. In this sense, metaphoric language employs a special system of signs, the ultimate meaning of which is unveiled by the proper application of *ta'wīl.*[4]

ARTICULATING TRANSCENDENCE: GOD BEYOND BEING AND NONBEING

The articulation of what David Burrell has referred to as the "grammar of divinity,"[5] that is, securing the distinction of God from the world, is also the shared starting point for the Ismāʿīlī formulation of *tawhid,* the Islamic belief in one God alone, who has no partner.

Among al-Kirmānī's predecessors, perhaps the most well-known Ismāʿīlī theologian was Abū Yaqūb al-Sijistānī (d. ca. 971). His works, building on previous Ismāʿīlī writings, enable us to see the formulation of a position in the context of the larger debate in the tenth century among Muslim theologians and philosophers. While discounting those outside the pale of monotheistic faith, whose beliefs, according to him, are polytheistic or anthropomorphic, he classifies others under several broad categories—those who ascribe to God the attributes He ascribes to Himself in the Book, but who do not wish to speculate unduly about these attributes; and those who argue in favor of speculation and wish to negate the attribution of humanlike qualities to God and therefore maintain that God can neither be defined, described, characterized, nor seen, nor be anywhere. He concludes that none of these positions allow one to accord to God the correct worship due to Him, nor do they allow for the articulation of transcendence in an appropriate manner. He states:

> Whoever removes from his Creator descriptions, definitions and characteristics falls into a hidden anthropomorphism, just as one who describes Him and characterizes Him falls into overt anthropomorphism. (Sijistānī, *al-Maqalid,* trans. Hunzai, p. 69)

In particular, he seeks to refute those who follow the Mutazilite position by pushing it to what he regards as its logical conclusion.[6] Like al-Ashari, he points to the problem of separating essential and descriptive attributes and argues that the ascribing of essential attributes, by perpetuating a duality between essence and attribute, would also lead to a plurality of eternal attributes. He argues further that the negation of specific attributes (knowledge, power, life, etc.) cannot be maintained, since human beings also have a share in such attributes. If these were to be denied, the negation would be incomplete, since the denial takes account only of characteristics of material creations (*makhluqāt*) and not of spiritual entities (*mubda'āt*). If one is to adopt the path of negation, he argues, then it must be a complete negation, denying that God has either material attributes or spiritual ones, thereby rendering him beyond existence (*ays*) and nonexistence (*lays*).

In formulating such a sweeping concept of *tawhid,* Sijistānī assumes three possible relations between God and His Creation: God can either resemble His creation entirely, in part, or not at all. In order to affirm the total distinction implied in *tawhid,* the third relation is the most appropriate, involving a total distinction from all forms of creation. Basing himself on a Qur'ānic verse, "To Him belong the *Creation (al-khalq)* and the *Command* (*al-amr*)" (7:54), he divides all originated beings into (1) those that can be located in time and space, i.e., those that are formed (*makhluqāt*), and (2) those that were originated through the act of command, all at once (*daf'atan waḥidah*), and which are beyond time and space and are called (*mubda'āt*). The former possess attributes, while the latter are entirely self-subsistent. The establishing and articulation of true transcendence (*tanzīh*) must therefore deny both:

> There does not exist a *tanzīh* more brilliant and more noble than the one by which we establish the *tanzīh* of our Mubdi' (Originator) by using these words in which two negations, negation and a negation of negation (*nafyun wa-nafyu nafyin*), oppose each other. (Sijistānī, *al-Maqalid,* trans. Hunzai, p. 70)

Thus, the first negation disassociates God from all that can possess attributes, the second, from all who are "attributeless." He is careful to avoid suggesting that even that which is without attributes, defined and nondefined, is God—in his schema God is beyond both, rendering Him absolutely unknowable and without any predicates.

Such a concept of *tawhid* immediately presents two problems for a Muslim: the first concerns how one might worship such a God;

and the second, if He indeed so transcends His Creation, how is it that they came into existence? The "grammar of divinity" affirming distinction now leads in Isma'ili thought to the "ladder of meaning" by which transcendence manifested through creation becomes "knowable."

MANIFESTING TRANSCENDENCE: CREATION AND KNOWLEDGE

Among the most serious charges laid against a doctrine of "creationism"—i.e., the assumption of a Creator as the ultimate cause, through a special act of creation—is that it assumes in the form of a complex deity the very thing that one wishes to explain, organized complexity. It is this relationship between Creator and creation, and the transformation that is implied in the former by the very occurrence of change, that constitutes the greatest intellectual knot that a rational theology must tackle.

It has been argued that Ismā'īlī theology, particularly as expressed in the work of al-Sijistānī, integrates a manifestational cosmology (analogous to some aspects of Stoic thought) within a Neoplatonic framework to create an alternative synthesis. The starting point of such a synthesis is the doctrine of *ibda* (derived from Qur'ān 2:117). In its verbal form it is taken to mean "originating instantaneously," representing, as the late Henry Corbin has it, "l'instauration creatrice primordiale" to explain the notion in the Qur'ān of God's timeless command (*Kūn:* "Be!"). *Ibda* therefore connotes, not a specific act of creation, but the dialogical mode through which a relationship between God and His creation can be affirmed—it articulates the process of beginning and sets the stage for developing a theology of the manifestation of transcendence in creation. By making creation emerge as a result of a process of origination (*ibda*), Sijistānī hopes to maintain his distinction between God and creation by making *Amr,* God's eternal expression of His will, the ultimate point of origin. In this sense, to quote Corbin again: "la philosophie premiere de l'ismaelisme n'est une metaphysique ni de l'*ens,* ni de l'*esse,* mais de *l'esto.*"[7] It can be said to express the distinction between God and creation even more sharply than the schema of emanationism associated with Plotinus.

Al-Kirmānī attempts to distance the Ismā'īlī view from the

emanationist outlook and to resolve what he regards as the ambiguities in Sijistani's formulation by arguing that the process of emanation and its source cannot be differentiated, strictly speaking. He cites as an analogy the light emanating from the sun, which, issuing from the fountain of the sun, partakes of the essence out of which it emanates, since at the point of emanation it is no different from the essence of the sun, its source. They are thus linked, though not identical, by being together in existence; and they could not logically be conceived of, one without the other. Such mutuality cannot be associated with God, for to conceive of existence as emanating from Him necessitates multiplicity in its source, which is its very essence. For al-Kirmānī, then, the only absolute way in which creation and *tawhid* can be distinguished is through a much sharper definition of that which is originated through *ibda,* namely the First Existent or the First Intellect. He states:

> It did not exist, then it came into existence via *ibda* and *ikhtira,* neither from a thing, nor upon a thing, nor in a thing, nor by a thing, nor for a thing and nor with a thing. (Kirmānī, *Rāhat al-ᶜAql,* trans. Hunzai, p. 165)

Like the number one, it contains all other numbers, which depend on it for their existence. Yet it is independent and separate from them, and it is the source and the cause of all plurality. In order to establish the singularity of the First Intellect, he refers to what the ancient sages (*hukama*) have said:

> From the First Existent, which is the First Cause, nothing comes into existence but a single existence . . . or the Prime Mover moves only one, even though by it many are moved. (Kirmānī, trans. Hunzai, p. 166)

Having used the arguments of the ancients for the purpose of validating his point, al-Kirmānī is nevertheless quick to separate himself from the view that all these attributes can then be applied to God, for that would compromise his insistence on absolute transcendence. They can only apply to the First Intellect, which in his scheme now becomes the Source, that which is inherently the synthesis of the One and the many (*Jamiᶜ li-l-waḥdah wa-al-kathrah*). At this stage, anterior to time and space, the two qualities were in the First Intellect, but they comprise the dual dimension that relates the First Intellect to *tawhid,* as well as to the role by which its generative capacity can be manifested. With respect to God, the First Intellect exists to sanctify Him. Such sanctification (*taqdīs*) on the part of the First Intellect reflects the nobler aspect of its dual dimension, where it is an affirmation of its own createdness and distinction from God. On the other hand, the sanctification generates a state of happiness and contentment within it, which produces actual and potential intellects, which in turn become the causes for the creation of the subsequent spiritual and material realms. Al-Kirmānī distinguishes in the First Intellect between multiplicity and diversity. Though the forms within the Intellect can be said to be multiple, they do not yet possess this aspect, since no diversity or differentiation exists within the Intellect. His analogy for the actual intellect is the Qur'ānic symbol of the "pen," and of the potential intellect, the "tablet," which become metaphors for *form* and *matter,* respectively.

Sijistānī, in attempting to resolve the problem of explaining the First Intellect's dual capacity for form and multiplicity, argues for a distinction between the concepts of multiplicity (*kathrah*) and diversity (*tafawūt*). Extending the analogy of the pen, which contains all the subsequent forms of expression in writing—letters, words and names—before they appear in this differentiated form, he tries to argue that they are all one within the pen. Also, this singularity does not resemble any of the expressed forms as they appear subsequently in written form. Thus, each letter, prior to its manifestation, cannot be distinguished from the rest of the letters, "pre-existing" inside the pen.

More interestingly, as Mohamed Alibhai shows in his analysis of Sijistānī's epistemology, he makes the role of the Intellect analogous to that of the *seed* out of which the cosmos, in its spiritual as well as material form, develops. This metaphor, drawn from biology, suggests a process where the Intellect is manifested in the natural domain and participates in time. Such a view of creation seems to imply that the process of generation and development involves the Intellect's participation as a "vital" principle in the cosmos progressively manifesting itself in both material and spiritual forms. The process by which this generation takes place is called *inbiʿāth.* Al-Kirmānī, for example, employs two similes to illustrate this process, one from the natural order, one relating to human relations: the reflection of the sun in a mirror, and the blush on the cheek of the lover at the sight of the beloved. *Inbi^c^āth,* manifestation, thus is contrasted with *fayd,* or emanation. The former, like the image of the sun in a mirror or a pool of water, is mere representation; it is from something and as figure can permit one to retrace it to the original. Such symbolism is particularly suited to evoking the sense of religiosity so central to the Islamic affirmation of distinction between God and creation. The rest of the intellects are manifested, one from the other, leading to the creation of the spheres, stars, and the physical world, including human beings.

In sum, the process of creation can be said to take place at several levels. *Ibda* represents the initial level, *inbi^c^āth,* the secondary level—one transcends history, the other creates it. The spiritual and material realms are not dichotomous, since in the Isma'ili formulation matter and spirit are united under a higher genus. Though they require different linguistic and rational categories for definition, they represent elements of a whole, and a true understanding of God must also take account of His creation. Such a synthesis is crucial to how the human intellect eventually relates to creation and how it ultimately becomes the instrument for penetrating through history the mystery of the unknowable God implied in the formulation of *tawhid.*

When al-Muayyad fi-l-din al-Shirazi (d. 1077) interprets the Qur'ānic verse "God created the heavens and earth in six days" (7:54),[8] he is concerned to show that the "days" stand figuratively for the six major cycles of Prophecy, each of which represents a journey to God. Their existence in time is not a function of priority or primacy; they merely succeed each other, like day and night. The believers in each of these cycles of prophecy are recipients of knowledge which assists in understanding *tawhid.* In Sijistānī, there is a conception of two types of Prophecy, spiritual and material. The first relates to the human intellect, the second to human history embodied in the messages communicated through the various prophets. These messengers come to confirm that which the human intellect already knows, and human beings appropriately, by the acceptance of the message, corroborate the validity of each historical messenger. The actual intellect thus corroborates that which the potential intellect brings to it.

At a more philosophical level, for al-Kirmānī an understanding of *tawhid* requires the believers to recognize that they must in some way "deconstruct" the First Intellect, divesting it of divinity. *Ibda* and then *inbiʿāth* reflect the "descending" arc of a circle, where God's command creates the First Intellect, which is then manifested through successive existents down to the human intellect. The action of the believers can be seen to be the ascending arc, where each unit leading up to the First Intellect is divested of divinity until the process is completed on reaching the One itself. It is in this particular context that he cites a tradition of the Prophet Muhammad: "The believer is the *muwahhid* [literally, maker of the One] and God is *muwahhid*"—the believer, because he or she divests First Intellect of divinity, and God, because he originated the First Intellect as the symbol of the One. It is possible for the human intellect to comprehend this because God provides assistance to the human intellect through his "dual" messengers, making accessible the tools formalized in religious language and ritual, as well as those that reflect an intellectual and spiritual capacity for knowing.

This paper began with an emphasis on the symbolic mode of expression as a crucial means of apprehending God's word and creation. It is perhaps appropriate that it conclude with a narrative from the Qur'ān and its hermeneutic in Ismāʿīlī writings.

The Qur'ānic account of Adam, his creation, fall and retrieval constitute for Ismaili thought what Henry Corbin has called "the drama in heaven." In the Qur'ān, Adam is taught "all the names" (Qur'ān 2:31) by God and subsists in the heavenly state until the act of disobedience which causes him to be expelled to earth. The *ta'wīl* of this story renders Adam as the *homo spiritualis;* the knowledge—"names"—endowed to him is the cognizance of the Primary and Secondary Intellects. His heavenly state is the result of the bliss engendered by his true worship and adoration, a mark of his awareness of the true meaning of *tawhid* mediated through the two Intellects above him. The fall injects the element of rupture into this primordial world, because Adam's mistake is the failure to be constant in his recognition of the eternal, ontological anteriority of the Intellects that precede him. The refusal to recognize their status is also an act of violation of the proper testimony of *tawhid.* The transgression results in a regression. In order for him to retrieve his former status, he must pass back through the stages of his "fall" to recover "paradise." This return becomes the human effort to journey to *tawhid* by learning to divest successively, at each level, elements that might mistakenly be attributed to the principle above. It is by returning to the beginning that Adam, in the sense that he symbolizes all of humankind, recovers his original status. The cosmos becomes the instrument of the purification and the "theatre" in which the struggle must be played out. Corbin points out that the sense of nostalgia and repentance felt by the soul become the energizing elements representing both the return to a paradisiacal past as well as a "conversion *toward* it."[9] Time, the dimension of creation that was engendered in the unfolding of the cosmos, becomes cyclical and is the archetype of its original form in the primordial world into which Adam was first placed.

The almost poetic language of this hermeneutical analysis is somewhat removed from the tone of the earlier writings of Sijistānī and Kirmānī, and it exemplifies the central role of metaphoric process in discovering and opening up new possibilities for reformulating scriptural meanings. Quoting Nasir al din Tusi (d. 1274), who wrote during the Alamut period of Ismāʿīlī history, Corbin suggests

> that to come into this world should not be confused with corporeal presence in the world of existence; it is above all a mode of understanding this existence. To come into this world . . . can have no significance other than to convert its metaphoric reality (*majaz*) into its True Reality (*ḥaqiqah*).[10]

NOTES

1. Many Ismāʿīlī writings of the Fatimid period have yet to be edited, let alone studied in the context of modern scholarship. But recent studies have begun to make more of them available to us. For al-Sijistānī and al-Kirmānī, I have drawn primarily from two recent studies: Mohamed Alibhai, *Abu Yaqub al-Sijistani and "Kitab Sullam Al-Najat": A Study in Islamic Neoplatonism* (Ph.D. diss., Harvard University, 1983); and F. M. Hunzai, *The Concept of Tawhid in the Thought of Hamid al-din al-Kirmani* (Ph.D. diss., McGill University, 1986). Another thesis—Paul Walker, *Abu Yaqub al-Sijistani and the Development of Ismaili Neoplatonism* (Ph.D. diss., University of Chicago, 1974)—as well as several articles by the author, based on the thesis, have also proved helpful. A comprehensive survey of Ismāʾīlī literature will be found in I. K. Poonawala, *Biobibliography of Ismail Literature* (Malibu: Urdena Publishers, 1977). For Ismāʾīlism, see W. Madelung, "Ismailiyyah," *Encyclopaedia*

of Religion, Vol. 7; Azim Nanji, "Ismailism," in *Islamic Spirituality: Foundations,* ed. S. H. Nasr (New York: Crossroads Publishing Co., 1987); and S. H. Nasr, ed. *Ismaili Contributions to Islamic Culture* (Tehran: 1977).

2. I would like to thank Professor Seyyed Hossein Nasr, who responded formally to the paper at the symposium, for his helpful comments and for elaborating the overall Muslim intellectual context in which Ismā'īlī thought can be set, as well as its subsequent influence on Muslim writers and thinkers.

3. Quoted by Eugene Vance, "Pas de trois: Narrative, Hermeneutic and Stricture in Medieval Poetics," in *Interpretation of Narrative,* ed. M. J. Valdes and Owen Miller (Toronto: University of Toronto Press, 1978), p. 122.

4. Professor Nasr, commenting on the notion of *ta'wīl,* suggested a definition that he attributed to the late Henry Corbin—"phenomenology." My own sense of "metaphoric process" as a more comprehensive way of understanding the wider connotation of *ta'wīl* is to see it at one level as suggesting a mode of reading the scriptural text and deciphering its verbal meaning, and also as a tool for disclosing an ultimate meaning which in the view of Ismāʿīlī writers represents "truth" (*ḥaqq*). There is thus one text, but it has two aspects: *zahir* and *baṭin,* a referential aspect and a fundamental one. In this connection, see Northrop Frye, *The Great Code: Bible and Literature* (New York: Harcourt Brace Jovanovich, 1982), particularly chap. 3; and Mary Gerhart and Allan Russell, *Metaphoric Process: The Creation of Scientific and Religious Understanding* (Fort Worth: Texas Christian University Press, 1984), which draws from the work of Paul Ricoeur.

5. David Burrell, *Knowing the Unknowable God: Ibn Sina, Maimonides, Aquinas* (Notre Dame, Ind.: University of Notre Dame Press, 1986) p. 2.

6. For a view of one Mutazilite thinker, see J. R. Peters, *God's Created Speech* (Leiden: E. J. Brill, 1976); and for an overview of the *Mutazilah* as a whole, Josef Van Ess, "Mu'tazilah," *Encyclopaedia of Religion,* 10:220–29.

7. Henry Corbin, *Nasir-e-Khosraw: Kitab-e-Jami' al-Hikmatain* (Paris: Adrien Maisonneuve, 1983), "Etude Preliminaire," p. 45.

8. For a further discussion, see Azim Nanji, "Toward a Hermeneutic of Quranic and other Narratives in Ismaili Thought," in *Approaches to Islam in Religious Studies,* ed. R. C. Martin (Tucson: University of Arizona Press, 1985), pp. 167–68.

9. Henry Corbin, *Cyclical Time and Ismaili Gnosis* (London: Kegan Paul International, 1983), p. 42.

10. Ibid., p. 57.

Response

Seyyed Hossein Nasr

It is fortunate that in this conference on God and creation in Jewish, Christian, and Islamic thought, attention is also paid to Ismāʿīlī philosophy and theology. Only too often has Ismāʿīlī thought been relegated to a separate category removed from the mainstream of Islamic thought and its interaction with the well-known currents of Islamic philosophy and theology, while little is said concerning its influence upon certain schools of Jewish and Christian thought. Actually, the views of such figures as al-Sijistānī and al-Kirmānī, far from belonging simply to a "sectarian" mode of thought, constitute elements of an important philosophical and theological tradition which interacted in numerous ways with Peripatetic and *Ishrāqī* philosophy, Sufism, Sunni *Kalām,* and later Twelve-Imam Shiʿite thought.

In order to bring out the significance of the type of thought with which Professor Nanji deals, it is therefore important to situate it within the matrix of Islamic thought as a whole. As far as the question of the relation between God and creation is concerned, all schools of Islamic theology and philosophy have been concerned with it. They have all sought to preserve the transcendence of God, the One, as His nature has been revealed in the Qur'ān, and to explain the existence of the world. To provide a typology of Islamic thought concerning this question, one can divide the various schools into five main categories—remembering, however, that as in every classification of this type there are certain overlaps and oversimplifications.

There are first of all the various schools of Sunni *Kalām,* as well as Twelve-Imam Shiʿite *Kalām,* which believe firmly in *creatio ex nihilo,* understanding *nihil* or *al-ʿadam* to mean "nothingness" in the ordinary sense of this term. A few of the philosophers such as al-Kindī also hold this position. There are, however, certain later Twelve-Imam Shiʿite theologians such as Ḥaydar Āmulī whose understanding of *al-ᶜadam* is much closer to the view of the later Sufis.

Secondly, there is the *mashshāʾī* or Peripatetic school, beginning not with al-Fārābī in this case but with Ibn Sina who makes the basic distinction between necessity (*wujūb*) and contingency (*imkān*) the basis of his ontology. According to this thesis, the world emanates from the One who is Pure Being, but the One is transcendent vis-à-vis the world and ontologically radically different from the world, for It alone is the Necessary Being (*wājib al-wujūd*). All of creation is only contingent being (*mumkin al-wujūd*), dependent at every moment of its existence upon the Necessary Being, without which the contingent would "be" literally nothing (*al-ᶜadam*). This distinction was so basic and had such a widespread influence upon Islamic thought that its terminology entered even into the language of *Kalām,* although the *mutakallimun* continued to oppose Ibn Sina's ontology and his theory of emanation.

Thirdly, there is the school of *Ishrāq* or Illumination founded by Suhrawardī, according to which God is the Light of Lights (*Nūr al-anwār*); and the whole chain of creatures, both angelic and corporeal, emanate in vast hierarchies of lights from Him. But He remains transcendent vis-à-vis creation because He alone is infinite and absolute while all other lights are finite and relative. Moreover, in all creatures, it is their quiddity or essence (*māhiyyah*) which is real, while in the case of the *Nūr al-anwār,* as in Ibn Sina's Necessary Being, being (*wujūd*) and essence are the same. Suhrawardī's *Nūr al-anwār* in a sense possesses the same ontological status as the Necessary Being.

Fourthly, there is Sufi metaphysics, associated mostly with the gnostic doctrines of Ibn ᶜArabī as developed during later centuries by Ṣadr al-Dīn al-Qunawī, Saᶜd al-Dīn al-Farghānī, ᶜAbd al-Raḥmān Jāmī, and other Sufis, on the one hand, and Ibn Turkah Iṣfahānī, Ṣadr al-Dīn Shīrāzī, and other later philosophers and theosophers, on the other.[1] This perspective bases itself on the doctrine which came to be known as *waḥdat al-wujūd* (the transcendent unity of being), a doctrine which has given rise to many different interpretations over the centuries. In its most esoteric form, which is sometimes called the doctrine of unity of the elite among the elite (*tawḥīd khawāṣṣ al-khawāṣṣ*), it holds that being or reality belong to God alone and nothing else even exists. *Al-ᶜadam* does not mean simply nothingness an usually understood, but denotes the archetypes in Divine Knowledge which are existentiated through the "Breath of the Compassionate."[2] Being and Reality, however, in the ultimate sense pertain only to God, and all creation is nothing but mirrors reflecting various divine names and qualities. Creatures do not possess existence but "appear" to possess existence. As Rūmī says in his famous poem,

> We are non-being (*ᶜadam*), appearing in the guise of
> being (*hastīhānamā*);
> Thou art absolute Being and our being.

A second interpretation of *waḥdat al-wujūd* is provided in its most elaborate form by Ṣadr al-Dīn Shīrāzī. According to him, there is a gradation (*tashkīk*) of being as well as the unity of being. There is only one Being who at the same time through gradation bestows existence upon the quiddities or essences throughout all the different levels of cosmic reality in such a manner that for everything that exists, *wujūd* is principial and *māhiyyah* simply the limitation of that particular existent which without *wujūd* would possess no reality whatsoever.[3]

Finally, there is the school of Ismāᶜīlī thought with which al-Sijistānī and al-Kirmānī are associated and in which God is seen as the metaontological reality who through the act of *ibdāᶜ* creates Being or the Intellect *ex nihilo*. This first creation of God is in turn the source of the coming into being of all lower levels of creation through *inbiᶜāth*. This perspective shares with Sufi metaphysics the doctrine of the supraontological nature of the Principle. In both schools God is above being, even if the Sufis sometimes use the term *al-wujūd al-muṭlaq* (Absolute Being) for God. In this case, what they mean is that the Supreme Principle is absolute and above Being. Yet it encompasses Being, which is Its first determination. Certain Sufis, moreover, make a clear distinction between the Divine Ipseity (*al-Dhāt*), which is above all that can be conceived concerning It, including *wujūd,* and Being which is the most universal of all concepts and the source of reality of all that participates in the realm of existence. The difference between the Sufi and the Ismāᶜīlī teachings comes from the fact that for the Sufis God or *al-Ḥaqq* is above being, yet all being belongs to Him and in the ultimate sense He alone is; while for the Ismāᶜīlī thinkers under consideration here,

He is above being but creates His first creation as the Being which in turn is the source of the hierarchy of existence.

This Ismāʿīlī doctrine was to have followers not only among later Ismāʿīlī thinkers but also among certain later Sufis and gnostics, especially in the Twelve-Imam Shiʿite world. Perhaps the most notable among them is Qāḍī Saʿīd Qummī, a student of the school of Mullā Ṣadrā, who in this question did not follow Mullā Ṣadrā but held a view similar to that of the early Ismāʿīlī figures discussed by Nanji.[4]

As can be seen in this brief survey, Islamic thought chose different paths in coming to terms with the question of the relation between God and His creation. But all of the solutions, whether based on creationism as usually understood or one form or another of what is loosely called emanationism, sought to safeguard the unity and transcendence of God vis-à-vis His creation and the radical hiatus which exists between God and the world whose existence originates with Him and depends upon him.

To turn to some specific points in Nanji's presentation, a word must first be said about the key concept of *ta'wīl.* In order to clear the ground of all possible misunderstanding concerning *ta'wīl,* it should be emphasized that in saying that *ta'wīl* means going back to the origin of something, we do not mean an "origin" posited by the person carrying out the *ta'wīl,* but an origin which is independent of subjective interpretations. The master of *ta'wīl* does not "make up" the inner meaning or the origin but is able, through knowledge, to lift the veil of outwardness, to unveil the inner meaning which is none other than the origin of any manifested being. *Ta'wīl* can therefore be translated as *kashf al-maḥjūb*[5], the unveiling of the hidden or the veiled, as was done by Corbin.

As far as "metaphor" is concerned, it is important to make a distinction between it and "symbol," as we find in most traditional Islamic sources where metaphor or *majāz* is never confused with symbol or *ramz* (also *tamthīl*). If these two have the same meaning in the Ismāʿīlī sources studied by Nanji, then that should be made clear. Nanji has written, "Unlike ordinary language, symbols are more specific and potentially more capable of establishing a link between that which is symbolized and the symbol itself." One cannot logically say that symbols are capable of establishing a link between that which is symbolized and the symbol itself. Rather, symbols alone can establish a relation between the reality symbolized and that which on the external plane embodies the symbol. It is crucial for the understanding of *ta'wīl* as traditionally understood to distinguish between symbolic language and metaphor as this term is currently used in a literary context in the English language.

Nanji takes for granted that the *mubdaʿāt* by their very nature cannot have attributes. Since even God has attributes (*ṣifāt*), according to Islamic theology, it must be made clear what is meant by attributes and why it is that the *mubdaʿāt* have no attributes. Without this clarification, the whole argument becomes nebulous and difficult to follow.

Nanji quotes Corbin's distinction between *ens, esse,* and *esto* without elaborating upon this fundamental distinction. It is important to mention here that for those Muslim philosophers who were Persian, a category which includes most Islamic philosophers and nearly all the well-known Ismāʿīlī thinkers, such as al-Sijistānī, al-Kirmānī, and Nāṣir-i Khusraw, a rich vocabulary concerning ontology was available, drawn from both Arabic and Persian. In Arabic, terms denoting existence or being came to be drawn from the root *wjd* which implies at once being (*wujūd*) and knowledge or consciousness (*wujdān*). In Persian, the term *hastī* (related etymologically to *is, ist, est* in English, German, and French) came to gain a philosophical status, denoting being or existence for those philosophers who wrote in Persian or who, like al-Fārābī and Mullā Ṣadrā, wanted to discuss the semantic differences in the domain of ontology and the difference between *ens, esse,* and *esto.* It is of interest to note that it was not only the Ismāʿīlīs but also nearly the whole later tradition of Islamic ontology which refused to confuse the act of being with the state of being.

As far as al-Sijistānī's epistemology is concerned, it should be mentioned that the use of the image of the seed in connection with the intellect is not biological in the ordinary sense of the term but symbolic, making use of a biological symbol. One cannot but recall the *rationes seminales* of Augustine and ask if there might be any historical connection between them, not through the influence of the writings of Augustine upon Muslims, which seems most unlikely, but through common Greek sources, possibly Stoic ones.

As for the contrast between *inbiʿāth* and Neoplatonism, this needs further clarification. It must be remembered, first of all, that the One of Plotinus is above Being and that in certain forms of Neoplatonism, as in certain schools of Islamic thought, there are levels and a hierarchy of matter and not only a contrast between form and matter.

Ismāʿīlī philosophy and theology are among the richest schools of Islamic thought and have played a much more extensive role in the wider general spectrum of Islamic thought than the so-called "sectarian" situation of Ismāʿīlism vis-à-vis the rest of the Islamic community might indicate. Fortunately, Professor Nanji has brought the contribution of this school of Islamic thought to bear upon the basic theme of the relation between God and creation, a problem which has concerned not only all Muslim, but all religious, thinkers of the Abrahamic world over the centuries.

NOTES

1. See S. H. Nasr, *Three Muslim Sages* (Albany, 1975); *Islamic Life and Thought* (Albany, 1981); and *Ṣadr al-Dīn Shīrāzī and His Transcendent Theosophy* (Tehran, 1978). On Ṣadr al-Dīn Shīrāzī, see also F. Rahman, *The Philosophy of Mulla Sadra* (Albany, 1976).

2. See T. Burckhardt, *Introduction to Sufi Doctrine* (London, 1976), Part 2. Technically speaking, in Sufi metaphysics God as the Truth (*al-Ḥaqq*) is even above the ontological principle.

3. It is not possible to develop this complicated ontology in this brief response. For further elaboration see T. Izutsu, *The Concept and Reality of Existence* (Tokyo, 1971); and S. H. Nasr, "Post-Avicennan Islamic Philosophy and the Study of Being," in *Philosophies of Existence Ancient and Medieval*, ed. P. Morewedge (New York, 1982), pp. 337–44.

4. In discussing both the early Ismāʿīlī thinkers and such figures as Qummī, it should not be forgotten that for Plotinus also the One is not simply continuous with the chain of emanation that issues from it. Concerning Qummī, see H. Corbin, *La Philosophie iranienne islamique aux XVIIe et XVIIIe siècles* (Paris, 1981), pp. 245–85.

5. This is a well-known Arabic expression which is also the title of an important Ismāʿīlī text, as well as the first Persian prose treatise on Sufism.

Name Index

Abahu, R., 133–134
ᶜAbd al-Jabbār, 294n33, 302
Abraham ibn Ezra, 21, 23n5
Abravanel, Don Isaac, 16–22, 23
Abū ᶜAbdallah al-Baṣrī, 302
Abū Ḥanīfah, 287, 289, 302
Abū al-Ḥasan ᶜAli al-Subkī, 278
Abū Hurayrah, 285
Abū al-Husayn al-Basrī, 268
Abū Nuwās, 287
Abū al-Qāsim al-Ḥusayn b. Muḥammad al-Iṣfahānī, 291n2
Abū Ṭālib al-Makkī, 256
Abū Yaqūb al-Sijistānī, 307–308, 309–311, 312, 314, 314n1, 316, 318, 320
Agus, J. B., 109n19
Albalag, Isaac, 11–16, 17, 20, 21
Albertus Magnus, 251
Albinus, 68, 70, 71
Amaury of Bené, 205
Ambrose, 198
al-Āmidī, Sayf al-Dīn, 248
Ammonius, 76
Anawati, M., 263n14
Antiochus, 66
Aristotle, 1, 4, 5, 6, 7, 8, 11, 15, 16, 19, 20, 29, 30, 33, 35, 40, 44, 66, 87, 100, 122, 124, 125–127, 135–142, 147–150, 182
Armstrong, A. H., 78n5, 79n11, 79n12, 80n25, 80n45
Arnaldez, Roger, 291n1, 293n13, 295n51
Atkins, P. W., 107n2
al-Ashᶜarī, Abū al-Ḥasan ᶜAlī b. Ismāᶜīl, 292n6, 307
Atticus, 64, 69–70, 73, 77
Augustine, 81, 198, 200, 222, 229, 230, 235, 242, 244, 320
Austin, J. L., 33
ᶜAyn al-Quḍāh al-Hamadānī, 263n1
Averroes (see Ibn Rushd)
Avicenna (see Ibn Sīnā)

al-Baghawī, Abū Muḥammad al-Ḥusayn b. Masᶜud, 293n19
Baḥya ben Asher, 23n2
Balthasar, H. Urs, v., 76, 84, 193, 195
Barth, K., 193, 229, 233, 244
Barzilay, I., 26n72
al-Baydawi, 263n4
Becker, J., 152, 153n3
Berman, L. V., 152n1
Birchman, R., 80n38
Bleich, D., 170n7, 171n13
Blumenthal, D., 54, 79n12, 121n6, 154–178, 169n1, 169n2, 171n11
Boehme, J., 84
Boethius, 83, 84
Bonaventure, 216n17, 219n80, 221–225
Bondi, H., 107n1
Bonhoeffer, D., 244
Bréhier, E., 23n9
Brody, B. A., 178n2
Buber, M., 154
Bultmann, R., 193

Burckhardt, T., 321n2
Burrell, D., 2, 27–37, 37n3, 37n6, 37n8, 37n11, 37n13, 84n1, 307

Calcidius, 81, 84
Calvin, J., 228, 229, 239
Cherniss, H., 79n13
Chopp, R., 169n1
Clement of Alexandria, 71, 72
Cohen, A., 172n22
Cohen, H., 154
Cohen, R. N., 158
Corbin, H., 309, 313–314, 320, 321n4
Crescas, Hasdai, 18, 19
Crowe, F., 37n12

Damad, Mir, 44
Davidson, H., 2n1, 26n59, 36n1, 143n17
al-Dāwūdī, 292n9, 296n70
Derrida, J., 169n1
Descartes, R., 40, 191
Dillon, J., 79n18, 79n22, 80n26, 80n31, 80n34
Dodd, E. R., 80n31, 82
Donaghan, A., 37n12
Duclow, D., 213, 218n55, 218n59, 219n80
Duméry, H., 76, 84
Duns Scotus, John, 12

Ebreo, L., 23
Eccles, Sir J., 106n1
Eckhart, M., 54, 84, 197–214, 220–225
Edwards, S. A., 37n12
Einstein, A., 106n1
Eliezer, R., 134
Eriugena, John Scott, 54, 81, 197, 205–214, 220
Ess, J. van, 263n13, 263n28, 315n6

Fackenheim, E., 170n9
Fakhr al-Dīn al-Rāzī, 45, 54, 276–303, 292n6
Fakhry, M., 112n36, 143n14, 292n7
al-Fārābī, 1, 29, 38, 45, 88, 148, 317, 320
al-Farghānī, Saʿd al-Dīn, 317
Feldman, S., 2, 3–26, 24n15, 25n59, 25n62, 36n1, 121n8, 142n4, 146n65, 152n2
Festugière, A.-J., 82
Findlay, J. N., 65, 77
Foster, M. B., 93, 98–99
Frank, R. M., 248, 263n23
Frye, N., 315n4

Galen, 109n17
Galileo, 85
Gamow, G., 107n1
Gardet, L., 263n14
Gerhart, Mary, 315n4
Gersh, S., 79n15, 82, 218n55, 219n77
Gersonides, 6–10, 13, 14, 15, 17, 18, 19, 20, 21, 32, 54, 122–153
al-Ghazālī, 2, 11, 31–32, 45, 54, 87–88, 90–96, 118, 246, 248, 250, 251–262, 265–275, 298
Gilkey, L., 54, 226–245
Gilson, E., 207, 219n63
Ginzberg, L., 24n26
Glicker, Y., 152n1
Gold, T., 107n1
Goldstein, J., 24n13
Goldziher, I., 292n10, 295n54
Goodman, L. E., 53, 85–121, 107n2, 108n6, 108n10, 109n14, 111n27, 111n28, 111n30, 113n37
Goodman, M. J., 107n2
Gramlich, R., 293n14
Gregory of Nyssa, 244
Gutas, D., 263n23

Haamkek Davar, 172n21
Halevi, Jehudah, 5, 24n14

Happold, F. C., 225n5
Hardy, P. A., 265–275
Hartshorne, C., 78n2
Harvey, W., 24n9, 128, 142n4, 145n36, 152n1, 153n3
Ḥaydar Āmulī, 316
Hayes, Z., 214, 220–225
Hegel, G. W. F., 241n3
Heidegger, M., 27
Heraclitus, 81, 111n32
Heschel, A. J., 169n1
Hesiod, 83
Hobbs, T., 191
Hoffman, L., 170n8
Honorius III, 205
Hourani, G., 149
Hoyle, F., 86, 107n1
Hume, D., 88, 98, 110n20, 114, 119, 120, 150
Hubble, E., 106n1
Hunzai, F. M., 314n1

Ibn ʿAbbās, 279
Ibn ʿAqīl, 293n17
Ibn Arabi, 265–275, 317
Ibn Ezra, 172n21
Ibn al-Jawzī, Abū al-Faraj, 280, 288, 292n4, 296n59
Ibn Jurayj, 294n29
Ibn Khaldūn, 298
Ibn Khallikān, Shams al-Dīn Aḥmad b. Muḥammad b. Abī Bakr, 292n6, 292n9, 293n11
Ibn Qutaybah, Abū Muḥammad ʿAbd Allāh b. Muslim, 282
Ibn Rushd (Averroes), 11, 12, 16, 148, 298
Ibn Sīnā (Avicenna), 2, 11, 12, 20, 31, 35, 36, 38–51, 87–88, 94, 108n11, 109n20, 116, 148, 198, 250, 256, 265–275, 297, 317
Ibn Taymiyya, 298
Ibn Tibbon, Samuel, 11, 152n1
Ibn Tufayl, 94
Ibn Turkah Iṣfahānī, 317
Ibrāhīm b. Abī Bakr b. ʿAlī al-Isfahānī, 291
al-Ījī, Aḍud al-Dīn, 247
Incandela, J., 37n12
Irenaeus, 238
Ismāʿīl Vāʿiẓ Javādī, 263
Ivry, A., 144n31, 145n62
Izutsu, T., 296n69, 321n3

Jaʿfar al-Ṣādiq, 287
Jāmī, ʿAbd al-Raḥmān, 317
Jami, Abd al-Rahman, 274n8, 275n21
Jastrow, R., 107n2
John XXII, 202
Jomier, J., O.P., 293n14
Jones, R. M., 79n19
Judah ben Simon, 133–134
Justin Martyr, 211

Kahn, C. H., 37n11, 265
Kannengiesser, C., 242–245
Kaplan, L., 144n17
Kapsi, Joseph ibn, 11, 152n1
Kenney, J. P., 53, 57–84
Khomeini, Ayatollah, 299
Kierkegaard, S., 239
al-Kindī, 45, 51, 316
al-Kirmānī, Hāmid al-Dīn, 306–307, 309–311, 312, 314, 314n1, 316, 318, 320
Klein-Braslavy, S., 24n9, 130, 133, 143n13, 145n45, 146n64
Kogan, B., 142n5, 147–153, 153n2
Kook, R. T. Y., 156
Kravitz, L. S., 152n1
Kretzmann, N., 123
Kripke, S., 121n5

Landau, Y., 170n8
Lane, E. W., 291n2
Laurent, M.-H., 217n39
Lee, P., 37n12
Leibniz, G. W., 7

Levi ben Gerson (see Gersonides)
Levine, F. D., 170n5
Lilla, S., 80n38
Loenen, J. H., 80n25
Lonergan, B., 193
Longinus, 69, 73, 77
Luther, Martin, 28, 229

McAuliffe, J. D., 54, 276–303, 296n66
McGinn, B., 54, 84n1, 197–225, 218n51, 218n52, 219n81
Mach, R., 263n2
Machiavelli, N., 191
Macrobius, 84, 217n33
Madelung, W., 314n1
Mahdi, Muhsin, 297–303
Māhir Mahdī Hilāl, 292n8
Maimonides, 4, 5, 7, 10, 11, 12, 13, 16, 19, 23n9, 30, 31, 33, 36, 53, 88, 90–96, 99, 118–119, 122–153, 165, 171n10, 171n13, 171n16, 171n18
Majd al-Dīn al-Jīlī, 292n7
Makdisi, G., 293n17
Mālik b. Anas, 285, 287
Malino, J. W., 121n8, 145n36, 145n48, 169n2, 171n10, 172n24, 173–178
Mamo, P. S., 79n12
Marmura, M., 37n6
Marx, K., 234, 243
al-Māturīdī, Abū Manṣūr, 263n3, 280
Maximus the Confessor, 212
Medigo, Joseph Solomon del, 23
Milton, J., 251
Misner, C. W., 107n2
Mitham ibn ʿAlī ibn Mītham al-Bahrānī, 264n28
Mohamed Alibhai, 311, 314n1
Morewedge, P., 152n2
al-Muayyad fi-l-din al-Shirazi, 312
Muḥammad, 289, 313
Muḥammad Fu'ād ʿAbd al-Bāqī, 291n2
al-Muḥāsibī, 256
Mullā-Ṣadrā, 52n17, 319, 320
Munk, S., 108n10

al-Nabulisī, 275n21
Nanji, A., 54, 304–321, 315n1, 315n8
Narboni, Moses, 11, 152n1
Naṣīr al-Dīn al-Ṭūsī, 247, 248, 314
Nāṣir-i Khowsraw, 251, 252, 320
Nasr, S. H., 273, 315n1, 315n2, 315n4, 316–321, 321n1, 321n3
Neusner, J., 169n2
Nicholas of Cusa, 212
Niẓām al-Mulk, 253
Nozick, R., 152
Numenius, 68, 71, 73
Nuriel, A., 152n1

Oakley, F., 93, 109n13
Ockham, 125, 210
Origen, 72, 76, 244
Ormsby, E. L., 54, 108n10, 246–275, 263n11, 263n15, 263n24, 264n29, 264n30
Owen, H. P., 78n2

Parmenides, 182
Paul the Apostle, 27–28
Pelster, F., 217n43, 217n45, 218n48
Pepin, Jean, 305
Peters, J. R., 294n33, 315n6
Philip the Chancellor, 28
Philo, 1, 3–4, 5, 11, 13, 58, 64, 66–67, 69, 71, 72, 84, 99, 154
Philoponus, 2, 28, 44–45
Pines, S., 152n1
Plato, 1, 4, 5, 64, 65, 66, 77, 81, 87–88, 91, 92, 99, 100, 124, 128, 130, 147, 186, 211, 237
Plotinus, 1, 16, 20, 30, 58, 62, 64, 65, 66, 69, 72–76, 81, 124, 211, 217n33, 321
Plutarch, 64, 66
Poggi, V., 264n31, 264n32
Poonawala, I. K., 314n1

Porphery, 69–70, 75
Proclus, 44
Pseudo-Dionysius, 207

Qāḍī Saᶜīd Qummī, 319, 321n4
al-Qifṭī, 292n5
al-Qurṭubī, Abū ᶜAbdallāh Muḥammad b. Aḥmad, 287, 294n29
al-Qushayrī, 256

al-Rāghib al-Iṣfahānī, 291n2
Rahman, F., 2, 38–52, 51n8, 51n11, 121n3, 291n3, 321n1
Rahner, K., 193, 233
Rashi, 155, 172n21
Ratzinger, J. C., 193
Ravitsky, A., 25n43
al-Rāzī (see Fakhr al-Dīn al-Rāzī)
Reese, W. L., 78n2
Reinert, B., 264n30
Rich, A. N. M., 79n19
Rini, R., 218n54
Rist, J. M., 79n12, 80n45
Ross, W. D., 78n10, 79n13, 79n21
Rudavsky, T., 53, 122–153
Rūmī, 318
Russell, A., 315n4

Saadia Gaon, 8, 22, 24n13, 26n57, 87, 89, 92, 94, 97
Sabellius, 83
Ṣadr al-Dīn al-Qunawī, 317
al-Ṣafadī, Khalīl b. Aybak, 279, 292n8, 292n15
Samuelson, N. M., 37n7, 37n8
Schacht, J., 295n45
Schelling, F. W. J., 84
Schleiermacher, F., 227, 239
al-Shafi i, Ahmad b. Hanbal, 287
al-Shahristani, 263n8
Shapiro, S., 170n9
Shirazi, Sadr al-Din, 317, 318
Siger of Brabant, 202
al-Sijistānī (see Abū Yaqūb al-Sijistānī)
Sirat, C., 25n30
Smith, W. C., 171n10
Sokolowski, R., 37n2, 54, 179–196, 209, 211, 214n1
Soloveitchik, J. B., 171n16
Sorabji, R., 2n1, 26n59, 36n1, 137, 142n1, 153n5
Spinoza, B., 20, 86, 98
Staub, J., 24n15
Stead, G. C., 78n4, 243
Stern, J., 108n10, 108n11, 113n37, 114–121
Stevens, W., 248
al-Suhrawardī, Shihāb al-Dīn Yaḥyā, 292n7, 317

al-Ṭabarī, Abū Jaᶜfar Muḥammad b. Jarīr, 279, 280, 288, 293n19, 296n59
al-Ṭabarsī, Abū ᶜAli al-Faḍl b. al-Ḥasan, 289, 293n19
Taqī al-Dīn b. Taymiyyah, 278
Tertullian, 211, 238
Theophilus of Antioch, 81
Théry, G., 216n24, 218n50
Thierry of Chartres, 84
Thomas Aquinas, St., 2, 12, 30, 34–36, 54, 198, 203, 210, 211, 216n17, 217n31, 217n44, 229, 278, 296n70
Tibawi, A. L., 108n6
Tillich, P., 76, 84, 229, 230
Touati, C., 25n33
Tracy, D., 169n2, 193–196
al-Ṭūsī (see Naṣīr al-Dīn al-Ṭūsī)

Vajda, G., 25n32
Vance, E., 315n3
Vlastos, G., 78n9
Voegelin, E., 87
Voltaire, F.-M. A. de, 98

al-Wāḥidī, Abū al-Ḥasan, 280, 296n59

Walker, P., 314
Weisheipl, J. A., O.P., 296n70
Weiszsäcker, C. F. v., 109n19
Whitehead, A. N., 220, 241n3
Whittaker, J., 80n26, 80n31
Wiesel, E., 170n9
William of Conches, 83, 84
Winston, D., 23n9, 24n14, 111n29
Wolfson, H., 23n3, 23n9, 24n13, 71, 79n17, 79n22, 143n14, 146n62, 146n63, 215n10
Wolterstorff, N., 76

Xenocrates, 66, 68

Zakarīyā' al-Anṣārī, 263n2
al-Zamakhsharī, Abū al-Qāsim Maḥmūd b. ʿUmar, 280–281, 288, 291n1
al-Zuhrī, 285